Supplies and Materials Management

Companion volume by the same author:
Storehouse and Stockyard Management

Other Pitman books of interest:
Effective Warehousing
Purchasing
Stores Management

Supplies and Materials Management

H K COMPTON
AMBIM
Fellow of the Institute of Purchasing and Supply
Associate IEE
Member of the Association of Stores and Materials Controllers

Third Edition

The Institute of Purchasing and Supply

PITMAN PUBLISHING
128 Long Acre, London WC2E 9AN

A Division of Longman Group UK Limited

First published by Business Books Ltd 1968
Reprinted 1972
Second edition published by Macdonald & Evans Ltd 1979
Third edition published in conjunction with
the Institute of Purchasing and Supply 1985
Reprinted by Pitman Publishing 1988, 1989

British Library Cataloguing in Publication Data
Compton, H.K.
  Supplies and Materials Management. – 3rd ed
  1. Materials Management
  I. Title
  658.7   TS161

ISBN 0 273 03036 1

Printed and bound in Great Britain
at The Bath Press, Avon

Preface to the Third Edition

The third edition of this volume represents a marked departure both in layout and content from those which preceded it. The main text has been streamlined to allow for additional diagrams and an expanded treatment of the finance and economics of Supplies and numerous other topics. Definitions have been restricted to those which are fundamental to an understanding of the subjects discussed.

Special attention is called to the fact that, while covering those aspects of physical materials management which relate to purchasing and supply, this volume does *not* include the details of physical materials management. The latter are dealt with in the companion volume, *Storehouse and Stockyard Management* (referred to in the text as *Storehouse*). Readers are also asked to note that *Storehouse* does *not* cover any aspects of stock control except those which affect the actual handling or housing of supplies, upon which it concentrates exclusively. (It should also be pointed out that readers following up references in *Storehouse* to particular Figures and Tables in *Supplies* may find that some numbers have changed between the second and third editions.)

Thanks are due to the Institute of Purchasing and Supply (for whom both this volume and *Storehouse* are textbooks) who have read through the text prior to publication. Material from British and International Standards is reproduced by permission of the British Standards Institution, from whom complete copies of Standards can be obtained.

Finally, I must again express my appreciation to the editorial staff who translate scribbled notes, deletions and sketches into well-ordered printed pages, and to my wife who endures a floor carpeted with papers and who spares the time for checking the text!

1985   HKC

Contents

CONTENTS

CONTENTS

List of Illustrations

List of Tables

LIST OF TABLES

List of Checklists

xv

LIST OF CHECKLISTS

Introduction

Definition

Supplies and Materials Management has been selected as a single collective title to cover what is a very wide area. It is intended to emphasise the need to integrate fully all Supplies activities outside the actual processes of manufacture—and also the need to integrate such activities with production.

The spelling of "supplies" and "supply" with a small "s" is used to include all materials, goods and services used, regardless of whether they are purchased outside, transferred from another branch of the company or manufactured in its own production line.

The spelling of "Supplies", "Supply", "Supplies department" and "Supplies staff" with a capital "S" is intended to cover the functions rather than the individuals who perform them. For example, a purchasing officer may or may not control stock levels and stores. Most firms are too small to have a purchasing officer, but in all cases someone must perform the "Supplies" functions and he or she is therefore covered by this description.

This leads to the first of a number of "axioms". (These are clichés which, although obvious, are fairly fundamental to Supplies. Some, such as the following, may, I hope, stimulate discussion.)

AXIOM: *"How* who does what" is more important than "*who* does what".

Scope of supplies and materials management

The scope of supplies and materials management is outlined below.

Supplies management

(a) Purchasing
(b) Provisioning
(c) Stock control
(d) Supply administration

Materials management

(e) Management of materials
(f) Storage, selection and issue
(g) Handling and distribution
(h) Stores management

xvii

NOTE:
Items *(e)*, *(f)*, *(g)* and *(h)* are dealt with in much greater detail in the companion volume *Storehouse.*[1]* The two books are complementary and should be used together for a thorough study of Supplies.

It would be incorrect to treat "materials management" purely as a Supplies function. Clearly, all who use or manipulate materials must also manage them, particularly those engaged in production processes. Supplies staff should be aware of such involvement and of where their functions meet, overlap or are parallel. Production control involves:

(a) knowledge of in-house manufacturing capacity (parts, processes, sub and final assembly);

(b) agreeing with Sales a manufacturing programme;

(c) matching resulting production load with available resources;

(d) planning materials and parts requirements;

(e) initiating orders (in-house and external through Supplies) to meet programme;

(f) monitoring progress and taking corrective action as required.

The inclusion of areas which affect Supplies emphasises further the need for the closest integration of these activities into the total production and selling organisation of the company.

Techniques
No technique or technical skill can be claimed as unique to Supplies, but Supplies activities do rely upon a greater number of academic and practical skills than most other branches of industrial administration. As many as possible of these skills are covered in this book, while others can only be mentioned. Success in Supplies work depends upon the ability of the staff to apply such skills and also to understand the basic techniques of those for whom they obtain supplies.

Philosophy and aim of the book
The purpose of this book is the objective treatment of the various Supplies tasks. A major aim throughout is the integration of the various operations, and also the integration of Supplies activities into the total operations of the undertaking they serve.

Readership
This book is intended for the following.

(a) All staff engaged full-time in the various branches of supplies

*Numbers in superscript refer to titles in Bibliography, Appendix VII.

and materials management.

(b) Those who manage Supplies tasks part-time in firms that are too small to have specialised staff engaged full-time on this work.

(c) Persons who use supplies in the course of production, processing, design, research and development, prototype manufacture, and so on.

(d) Sales and marketing staffs.

(e) Staff in both "private" and "state-owned" industries, whether working under free enterprise, mixed economy or "controlled economy" systems.

(f) Staff in local authority work who have requirements *from* other sectors of the economy besides providing services *to* them.

(g) Students studying for qualifications for the various institutions concerned with purchasing and supply or who have opted for these subjects in one of the higher education courses in business or management, etc.

Small firms

Although this book is intended for use in firms of all sizes it is hoped that it will be particularly useful for those concerned with supplies and materials management in smaller firms, i.e. up to a total establishment of 200. It can also be valuable for those in smaller companies to know the supplies problems and procedures, the weaknesses and strengths of bigger businesses, whether buying from them or selling to them. (*See* Index for list of areas of special interest to smaller firms.)

Further help and advice for smaller firms is available from Small Firms Information Centres, the British Institute of Management[2] (*see* Appendix II), and the Institute of Purchasing and Supply (*see* Appendix I).

The plan

The preliminary study of Supplies operations and "supplies cycles" is intended to assist those buying from other kinds of industry than their own and also to provide the essential background against which to examine the operations described in later chapters.

Stock control and provisioning are dealt with before purchasing. Some may claim that purchasing should be dealt with first because goods cannot be stored before they are bought. This exemplifies the need to integrate fully the entire Supplies field, even though this may not yet be universal practice. The call for integration becomes more pressing both as firms grow in size and various functions become more decentralised and departmentalised into separate autonomous units, and as a result of the following factors:

    (a) depletion of the earth's natural resources;

    (b) increasing costs of winning such resources from the earth;

    (c) rising living standards demanded by the extractors of the earth's resources, including those in the "developing world";

    (d) need for economies throughout the entire economic cycle.

Cost reduction in Supplies

Special weight is given to cost reduction and streamlining in the Supplies field. Admittedly economies made here do not automatically ensure higher profits. Many Supplies staff have seen their carefully and hard-won gains squandered elsewhere in the organisation.

Bases for comparison

Inter-firm comparisons (*see* Appendix III) can be extremely valuable in checking a firm's own performance or that of its suppliers. The research for this book has been based on:

    (a) total number of persons employed in industrial units;

    (b) "added value";

    (c) sales per employee; and

    (d) value of supplies per unit sale.

These give reasonably consistent results for firms of the same size and industrial classification group as shown by the Census of Production.[37] (*See* Table 5.) They do not, of course, reflect the varying degrees of automation which may be applied to firms in the same industrial classification group. Some may clearly be more or less labour-intensive than others as a result of automation or other factors. (*See* Chapter 13, production costs.)

Terminology

Technical terms and jargon have been avoided as far as possible, and where they are used a definition has usually been given. British Standard Glossaries listed in the *British Standards Yearbook*[79] are also strongly recommended.

    The work of Supplies (particularly purchasing) involves the rapid movement of materials and goods. This in turn depends upon accurate and rapid communications using clear "word-pictures" of the goods themselves and numerical expressions of quantity. Supply work therefore demands correct selection and use of words.[3] Sometimes it even depends upon their spelling and pronunciation. For example, should an invitation to a supplier to quote a price be an "enquiry" or an "inquiry"? What is the difference between "purchasing" and "procurement", "expediting" and "progressing", a "quotation", a "tender" and an "estimate"?

    The selection of words, having regard to their legal, technical and commercial implications, is of particular importance when trading across state boundaries. Here, not only different words but also different shades of meaning for the same word can be involved.

Professional bodies

References appear in the text and appendixes to some professional and technical bodies which are directly or indirectly concerned with Supplies or with those who manage supplies. Some institutions include areas of supplies and materials management in their examination curricula—or may do so in the future when the importance of this subject area becomes more widely appreciated.

CHAPTER 1

The Supplies Cycle

INTRODUCTION

The concept of supplies and materials management has expanded to include wider areas than previously. The entry of the UK into the European Economic Community and the shrinkage of the world and its resources have to be taken into account, as well as the increasing effects of complex international trade.

The overall Supplies concept is illustrated in Fig. 1 and this chapter examines in detail the four supplies cycles: internal, external, economic and global.

Checklist 1 (*see* Appendix VIII) covers many aspects of the

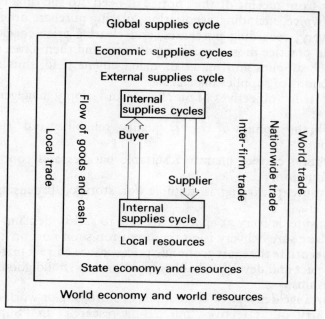

Fig. 1. The overall Supplies concept

Supplies field including the global aspect of world trade (items (15)-(22)). The checklist applies to every size of firm and should be read in conjunction with Figs. 2, 3 and 4.

THE INTERNAL SUPPLIES CYCLE

Every firm has an internal supplies cycle (*see* Fig. 2) for each must consume some materials, goods or services. The actual Supplies function is examined in detail below (paragraph numbers refer to the numbers in circles in Fig. 2).

(1) PROVISIONING involves two main areas of supplies: materials used in the manufacture of the product, and all other supporting goods necessary for carrying on the business. Provisioning must always be a positive, continuing, dynamic activity.

AXIOM: The successful "provisioner" *anticipates* needs.

The provisioning of supplies for manufacture should be carried out in consultation with sales and production departments. In the initial stages, with no past data to go on, provisioning must often be estimated. (*See* Table 10.)

(2) PURCHASING [4] in theory, covers only the acquisition stages of Supplies from receipt of the "notice of need" to the final clearance of the invoice, including negotiation, placing purchase orders, chasing delivery, recording purchases, and clearing price checks on invoices. In practice most purchasing officers find themselves covering the wider supplies and materials management field, thus fulfilling the functions of supplies managers.

The detailed objectives of purchasing and supply management are to ensure:

(*a*) Obtain supplies of *correct* quality: reliability and "suitability for purpose".

(*b*) Obtain correct quantity: suitable batches and containers to suit production.

(*c*) Ensure packaging is suitable for storage, dispensing, work-centres, etc.

(*d*) Ensure delivery at appropriate rate to satisfy demand.

(*e*) Make sure delivery is on time: not too soon nor too late.

(*f*) Negotiate the most economic price; ensure correct price is paid.

(*g*) Select and develop reliable supply sources; build good supplier relationships.

(*h*) Arrange delivery to correct place: store, site or work-centre.

(*i*) Carry out effective "purchasing research" in "Supplies research" context.

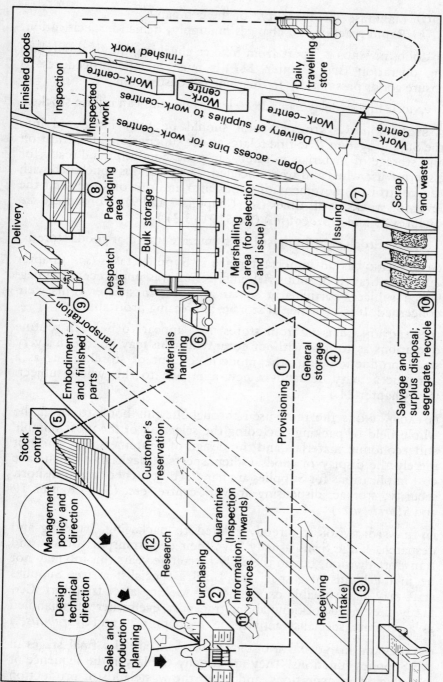

Fig. 2. The internal supplies cycle

(*j*) Maximise "profitability" of the company.

(*k*) Rapid reaction: to changes in supply, demand, specification.

(3) GOODS INWARDS is, apart from invoice checking, the final purchasing operation (*see* Chapter 21). It must include procedures to ensure goods pass rapidly to their correct destination.

AXIOM: Intake delay can add to lead time, and can inflate stocks.

(4) STORAGE *and* (5) STOCK CONTROL should be fully integrated into the Supply system. The first relates to the supervision, identification and storage of materials in safety, in good condition and ready for issue for use when and where needed. The second is concerned with the control of movement of goods into and out of stores and the levels of stocks at all times (*see* Chapters 7 and 9). (For storage *see* Chapter 23 and *Storehouse*.) (BS 5191 (3.3).)

AXIOM: Stock control must be a numerate image of goods stored.

(6) HANDLING has an important place in Supplies tasks (*see* Chapter 20). This branch of industrial engineering was until recently a neglected subject, particularly so far as stores in smaller firms were concerned. It is a partner of storage in creating profitability.

(7) SELECTION AND ISSUE from stores may appear to be such routine operations as to pass without note. While this may be true in a very small production unit, the modern concept of storekeeping as a dynamic activity demands a new approach to this whole subject. (*See* Chapter 24.)

(8) PACKAGING is the term used throughout this book to cover the whole field of packing, including the selection of the most suitable and economic materials and the design of containers, etc. and not merely the display of goods. Other aspects of packaging which have cost implications for Supplies are handleability, checking, transport, security, storage, dispensing at work-centre, etc. (*See* Chapter 19 and *Storehouse*.)

(9) TRANSPORTATION is directly related to packaging, handling and despatch. Large firms usually have their own transport officer and transport division, but in the early formative years this job may not be in the hands of a specialist. Until a specialist arrives Supplies staff may gain valuable experience by looking after transport. Certainly they need to know about transport, even where it is handled as a separate specialist activity. (*See* Chapter 20 and *Storehouse*.)

(10) SALVAGE, RECYCLING AND SURPLUS DISPOSAL are the final stages in the Supplies functions. They are usually the last in the sequence of manufacturing operations, and often the wastelands of production

and the graveyard of profitability! This need not be so. Supplies and materials management should include arrangements for the disposal, further use or salvage of all surplus, redundant, waste and obsolete materials, plant or equipment. If done efficiently this can regain profits which would otherwise have been lost (*see* Chapter 25). (BS 5191 (A).)

(11) INFORMATION SERVICES are very much more difficult to describe as a Supplies function. They depend to a great extent upon the use made of Supplies by management for such tasks (*see also* Chapters 2 and 3 and Fig. 6).

(12) SUPPLIES AND PURCHASING RESEARCH should cover the entire Supplies field. Unfortunately, most purchasing officers are too busy fighting price increases, delivery disasters and other crises to have time to devote to research. However, time spent in this activity could avert or at least minimise the effects of such contingencies. Subjects relevant to Supplies research include:

(*a*) new or alternative sources;
(*b*) new, alternative or better supplies;
(*c*) supply and demand statistics;
(*d*) supplier performance:
   (*i*) price;
   (*ii*) delivery;
   (*iii*) quality;
(*e*) communication, records, reporting;
(*f*) physical aspects of supplies;
(*g*) storage, packaging, dispensing;
(*h*) distribution in factory; and external;
(*i*) integration with other departments;
(*j*) investigation into suppliers' costs.

Since Supplies research involves technical as well as commercial and economic considerations, it is vital that technical colleagues should be involved in, and support, the research. The appointment of a purchasing analyst can greatly assist in providing effective liaison.

The authority to investigate, interrogate and apply diagnostic skills should be given by management to all Supplies staff—there are always savings to be made in supplies and materials management. Diagnostic skill and the ability and authority to apply it are of particular value to purchasing officers and purchasing analysts. It can be defined as: "The ability to look not only at symptoms but also for their causes; not only at end-results but also for side-effects; the ability not only to look at generalities but also to apply the exception principle." Supplies staff must in using their diagnostic skills

5

resist any temptation to encroach in the least degree upon the territory of technical colleagues, or even *appear to do so*! One solution is to avoid making technical statements and use instead the method of asking logical and "leading" questions. The following axiom is a useful guideline.

AXIOM: Technical statements are the prerogative of technical staff.

THE EXTERNAL (INTER-FIRM) SUPPLIES CYCLE

Figure 3 and Table 1 trace a buying and selling transaction between two factories at stage 7 of the total economic supplies cycle (*see* Fig. 4). Stage 7 has been selected for the example because not only is it a common type of business, but it also contains most of the features of the remaining stages. The procedures are given as examples only and it should be remembered that they will vary from firm to firm.

Supply communications are "models" of the materials being purchased, moved, handled and stored. Their flow follows patterns similar to the actual movements of goods they represent.

It must be pointed out that only essential operations are included. Few large firms work on such a streamlined system. It should also be noted that both production and supplies chains are continuous, back towards basic materials and the extractive industries and forwards to the ultimate consumers or end-users.

In the example selected the production factory "P" receives an urgent unpriced order from customer "C", and being an exceptionally good supplier "P" puts work in hand immediately, approaching his supplier "S" for some of the supplies he requires to complete the job. The table starts at this point. (BS 5191 (1).)

TABLE 1. EVENTS IN AN EXTERNAL SUPPLIES CYCLE
(*See also* Fig. 3.)

Event No.:	Action by:	Action taken	Documents, paperwork, references, comments
1	C	Sends urgent, unpriced order[1] to producer "P"	Purchase order BS 5332 (4.8)
2	P	Order received in sales and processed	BS 5191 (4.2)
3	P	Sales immediately acknowledge order[2] and issue instruction to works (production) office	Card/letter/'phone. Works order BS 5191 (4.2)

6

TABLE 1. (contd.) EVENTS IN AN EXTERNAL SUPPLIES CYCLE

Event No.:	Action by:	Action taken	Documents, paperwork, references, comments
4 *[3]	P	Sales confer with purchasing on supplies: availability and price	
5 *	P	Purchasing check availability with stock control and give sales the price paid on the last order ("LIFO")	
6	P	Works office BS 5191 (1.3)	
		(a) plan sequence of operations, etc.;	Works job sheet
		(b) call up jigs, tools, fixtures, gauges, etc.;	Tool requisitions, etc. BS 5191 (4.2)
		(c) obtain drawing from drawing office;	Drawings
		(d) prepare time/piecework sheets;	Work bills
		(e) prepare materials requisition or obtain materials lists/schedules BS 5729 Part 1 (9.5)	Materials requisitions (see Storehouse, parts list)
7 *	P	Works office release above paperwork to work-centre	BS 5191 (3.3)
8	P	When production is about to start, materials requisition handed to stores	Materials requisition
9 *	P	Supplies collected from (or delivered by) stores	(See Storehouse, order picking and issuing)
10 *	P	Completed requisition passed to stock-control office	Materials required
11 *	P	Stock-control office update records, check levels	Stock cards BS 5191 (3.3)
12 *	P	Updating shows that stock-out level (see Fig. 25) is reached	
13 *	P	Stock control call for urgent replenishment by purchasing department	Purchase requisition
14 *	P	Purchasing send enquiry[4] to supplier "S"	Enquiry form (see Fig. 61)
15	S	Sales receive enquiry and *may* acknowledge it. (Had this been a new product or change in specification, sales would proceed as in 16 to 19)	Card/letter, etc.
16	S	Consult drawing/design office on technical details	

TABLE 1. contd. EVENTS IN AN EXTERNAL SUPPLIES CYCLE

Event No.:		Action by:	Action taken	Documents, paperwork, references, comments
17		S	Check with production on capacity BS 5191 (1.3), tooling, lead time, etc.	
18	*	S	Check with stock control on any stock materials	
19	*	S	Check with purchasing on cost and availability of supplies, and if current price and availability are stable or if allowance should be made for escalation of price or extended delivery time	
20		S	If it is highly probable that a firm order will follow, sales may take action as follows:	
	*		(a) authorise Supplies to allocate or reserve materials;	
	*		(b) authorise the purchasing officer to issue a "letter of intent";	
	*		(c) authorise purchasing officer to arrange for supplier to reserve production space in his production programme, and/or put in hand preliminary work such as provisioning	
21		S	Quotation sent to prospective purchase "P"	Quotation form
22		P	Quotation(s) received and collated	(See Fig. 62)
23		P	Purchase order prepared and sent to supplier	(See Chapter 15)
24		S	Sales receive customer's order and check with quotation	
25		S	Sales prepare works order[5]	
26		S	Sales send acknowledgment to purchaser[6]	(See Chapter 17)
27		S	Sales send works order to production who prepare paperwork as at 6 above	
28		S	Instructions released to work-centre and work put in hand	(See Chapter 18)
29		P	Purchaser needs to progress or pre-progress	
30		S	Completed goods inspected (?) packed, and sent to despatch	

TABLE 1. contd. EVENTS IN AN EXTERNAL SUPPLIES CYCLE

Event No.:	Action by:	Action taken	Documents, paperwork, references, comments
31 *	S	Despatch paperwork raised BS 5191 (4.3) (a) invoice; (b) packing note; (c) contents note; (d) advice note; (e) delivery note; (f) transit label;[7] (g) consignment note	BS 5729 (Part 5, Table 1 (1))
32	S	Arrange transport	
33	S	Pack and load on to vehicle, and transit to P	
34	P	Unload goods	
35	P	Check for damage in transit	
36	P	Count/weigh/measure[8]	
37	P	Prepare documents for goods inwards[9]	GRN BS 5191 (4.3)
38 *	P	Arrange for goods inwards inspection if called for	
39 *	P	Move goods promptly to point required —in this case work-centre	
40	P	Manufacture end-product for customer "C" against order at event 1	
41 *	P	End-product inspected (?) and passed to despatch	
42 *	P	Despatch shipping documents, pack, load and ship	
43 *	P/C	Transport to customer "C"	
44	P	Send invoice	
45	C	Settle invoice	

NOTES TO TABLE 1:

(1) For effects of unpriced orders *see* Chapter 22, introduction.

(2) For legal effect of acknowledgments *see* Chapter 17.

(3) Events marked with an asterisk emphasise the need for integration of Supplies activities with those of other departments.

(4) Because the order from "C" was urgent and unpriced, the producer's purchasing officer (at "P") may also send an unpriced order to his supplier "S". This may tend to escalate further the price to "C" (*see* note 1) above what it would have been if all the proper controls had been applied, such as priced orders, multiple source enquiries, etc.

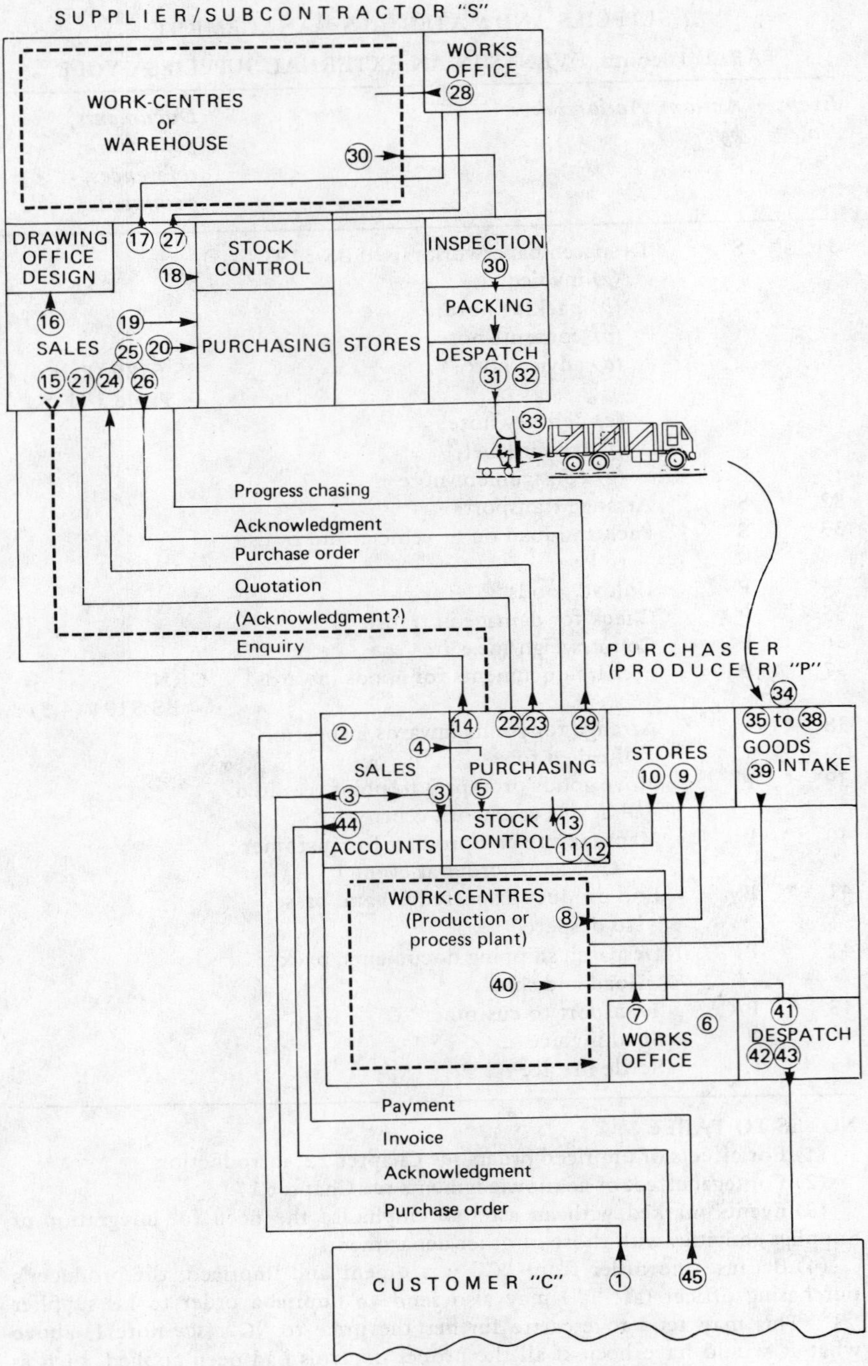

Fig. 3. *The external (inter-firm) supplies cycle*

(5) Small firms may find it possible to use the customer's order documents for this purpose, but in most cases it is necessary to translate the customer's requirements into the terminology at the work-centre which may differ from that used by the customer and may even be incorrect.

(6) (*See* Chapter 15, *Vital components of an order.*) There are very good reasons why acknowledgments of orders should be facsimiles of instructions issued to the works of the supplier. *See* note 5 and Chapter 17.

(7) Transit labels should bear any marks such as the purchase order number in order to identify the package on arrival and speed sorting to the correct bay or store. Preparing the label as part of the sales document set is the practice among the more advanced warehousing, wholesaling and distributive traders. Some purchasing authorities favour the label being prepared as part of the purchase order set. This can have the following advantages.

(*a*) The purchaser can have his label printed in bulk, cheaply.

(*b*) He can ensure that labels bear the relevant purchase order number and any special warnings, transit instructions, etc.

(*c*) Correct consignment instructions are ensured.

(*d*) Mistakes by supplier can be reduced or eliminated.

(*e*) Suppliers are relieved of some clerical work. (Suppliers may claim that administrative work is increased, or they may not use the labels provided by the purchaser.)

(8) In the event of shortage, damage or loss, *see* Chapter 21 and *Storehouse*, goods inwards.

(9) At event 37, after arrival and unloading of the consignment at "goods in" (*see* Fig. 2) at the factory of producer "P", the various consignment documents (listed at event 31) should have been checked and signed where necessary. Rapid completion of goods inwards documents, such as the GRN, and movement of the goods to where they are needed (stores, inspection or end-user) are essential. (*See* Chapter 21 and *Storehouse*, goods inwards for greater detail.)

Event 45 completes the single supplies cycle between industrial units.

The cycle would be very similar between a manufacturing unit and a wholesaler, but with the following variations.

At event 5, a section buyer checks if stock is available. If not, or if the commodity is outside the normal stock range but within the normal field of trading, he may raise enquiries on manufacturers or other main wholesalers.

Advance action as at event 20 may be taken if the probability of an order is very high, if the customer is an important one, or if the customer's purchasing officer so negotiates.

At event 6 the warehouse sales department raise a multi-part document set in the same manner as a factory. The contents of the documents are, of course, different from those of a production unit.

An acknowledgment will not usually be sent (*see* Chapter 17.)

THE TOTAL ECONOMIC (NATIONAL) SUPPLIES CYCLE

The national supplies cycle illustrated in Fig. 4 shows the broad characteristics of supplies throughout the full economic spectrum of industry, commerce and the infrastructure.[138] The reader may care to refer to Checklist 1 and examine his place within the economic cycle *and* that of his main suppliers. This exercise can be very rewarding when negotiating, "trouble-shooting" supplies, checking price increase claims and so on.

Each stage within the economic cycle has its own characteristics and these are briefly summarised in the following pages.

It should be noted that although Fig. 4 refers to the cycle within state boundaries it must be clear that much of the analysis transcends such boundaries.

Public authorities and nationalised industries are shown as stage 10 of the cycle, as the "industrial infrastructure". However, public authorities will participate in each phase, at both the national and local level as will also many private firms in the "service" field.

Suggested areas for Supplies research

Characteristics of organisations throughout the economic supplies cycle are particularly fruitful ground for supplies and purchasing research.

(1) THE RANGE OF SIZES AND NUMBERS OF FIRMS in each product group can indicate potential productive capacity and how much of the market is in the hands of large and powerful units. A year-on-year comparison will show if the numbers of small manufacturing units are falling. If the purchasing officer only buys from the larger firms he will make the extinction of the smaller ones more certain. An increase in the number of units in a product group may mean that profits are high and the purchasing officer should be looking for more competition. On the other hand, it could indicate rapid technological development. In that case purchasing research may be needed.

(2) "SALES HORIZONS" (*see* Fig. 47) of suppliers may assist in ascertaining whether the purchasing officer has achieved the best lead times—and this could save cash on stock investment.

(3) "SUPPLIES HORIZONS" of suppliers may also explain why some are always late on delivery!

(4) THE RATIO OF VALUE OF SUPPLIES TO SALES is a fundamental statistic for both the purchasing officer's and his suppliers' companies (*see* Table 5).

	Stage 1	Stage 2	Stage 3	Stage 4	Stage 5	Stage 6	Stage 7	Stage 8	Stage 9	
Principal purchases	Plant / Spares / Power / Tools / Safety, health, welfare goods	Light/heat / Buildings maintenance / Communications	Vehicles / Spares / Repairs	Fuel/power / Handling / Repairs	Raw materials / Fuel/power / New plant	Packing / Fuel/power / Handling equipment and spares, etc.	Raw materials / Embodiment goods / Tools / Power / Handling equipment / Transport	Packing / Fuel/power / Vehicles / Handling equipment and spares	Domestic expenditure: Housing 14.4; Fuel, light and power 6.1; Food 24.7; Alcoholic drink 3.6; Tobacco 8.0; Clothing and footwear 6.9; Durable household goods 7.4; Other goods 13.5; Transport and vehicles 9.7; Services; Miscellaneous 0.8; Total 100.0	Principal purchases
Proportion of purchases passing to sales	Low (purchases minimised)	Extremely high (maximised with sales)	Nil (purchases minimised)	Extremely high	Very high	Extremely high	High, but often much supporting goods and services	Very high, but often some supporting goods	—	Proportion of purchases passing to sales
Value of supporting goods	Very low	Very low	—	Appreciable	Low	—	Moderate	Some	—	Value of supporting goods
Value of all purchases as % of sales	Low 20–25 %	Very high	Low	Very high	Very high 70–90 %	Very high	Moderate 50–60 %	Very high	—	Value of all purchases as % of sales
Stages in the supplies cycle								(Some passes into further production)		Stages in the supplies cycle
	EXTRACTIVE INDUSTRIES	MARKETS: RAW MATERIAL AND COMMODITY	TRANSPORT (BULK), etc.	RAW MATERIALS WAREHOUSING	PROCESS PLANTS	PROCESSED OR SEMI-FINISHED GOODS WAREHOUSING	MANUFACTURE GENERAL AND FINISHED GOODS	FINISHED GOODS WAREHOUSES AND DISTRIBUTORS	DOMESTIC MARKET	
	Stage 1	Stage 2	Stage 3	Stage 4	Stage 5	Stage 6	Stage 7	Stage 8	Stage 9	

Producers — Consumers / Markets: commodity and futures / Speculators

Stage 10 Industrial infrastructure of supporting industries and services

POWER HEAT LIGHT	TRANSPORT: GOODS	TRANSPORT: PASSENGER	WATER	WASTE-COLLECTION	WASTE-DISPOSAL	WASTE: SALVAGE RECOVERY, RECYCLING	ROADS, BRIDGES, WATERWAYS, PORTS	LOCAL AUTHORITY SERVICES

Fig. 4. The total economic (national) supplies cycle

(5) THE RATIO OF STOCK VALUES (AVERAGE) TO SALES is fundamental to his own company's supply data, and useful if he can get it for his suppliers (see Appendix III). (BS 5191 (3.3).)

(6) THE AMOUNT SPENT ON RESEARCH AND DEVELOPMENT is vital data for his own company and most useful if he can get it for his suppliers.

Stage 1: extractive industries

Extractive industries include many which are capital intensive and others which are labour intensive. They do not necessarily convert their extracted product but sell it through "markets" (see below) to subsequent manufacturing and process stages in the supplies cycle. The ratio of supplies to total sales is very low and tends to be a charge against profitability.

At this stage, as with stage 3 and service industries, there is a pressing need for economy in the whole Supplies field. In mining, for example, the objectives are to win the maximum extraction with the minimum expenditure on labour and materials. In agriculture and fishing the same objectives apply, with the further uncontrolled hazard of weather conditions and the need to husband natural resources—both may incur high and unexpected costs.

Large-scale modern mechanised extractive industries have similar supplies needs to those of manufacturing industries, viz. occurrence of urgent requirements for spares and replacements—but in heavier demand. The shortage of a spare pump can stop a mine from working, but a modern farming operation may also be stopped by the failure of the winnowing fan on a combine harvester, or the failure of a crop-drying plant may ruin the fruits of harvest.

Stage 2: raw material and commodity markets

The marketing of the raw materials produced by the extractive industries is often done through markets known as "exchanges", "terminal markets", "commodity markets" and "futures markets".[5][6][7][8][138] These markets may not physically handle the commodities in which they deal, but seek buyers to consume the output which producers expect to achieve in the future. Advance or "future contracts" are entered into between producers and consumers through the markets. They perform the important service of providing a relatively stable advance price for both producer and consumer by such contracts and "hedging" operations.

Normally the activities of commodity markets are confined to the specialised buying and selling of one or a few groups of commodities. Their only internal supplies activity relates to the need for maintenance of buildings, services, stationery, computers, and communications equipment and materials—unless of course they also stock the raw materials themselves.

(*See also* Chapter 13, markets and market trends.)

Stage 3: transport
As in the first stage, emphasis is upon economies in expenditure on supplies. All items bought or stored to support the operation represent a charge against it.

The scale of operations of such undertakings is often very large and extremely complex. Many include a number of subsidiary and ancillary operations such as warehousing, packaging, transit sheds, vehicle repair shops, ship repairing, pilotage, operation of lighters, stevedore services and many others. It is therefore difficult to discern any uniform pattern in the Supplies operation for a big transport undertaking. Large-scale movements of goods are usually to a close time schedule and there is likely to be an aspect of urgency in most of the provisioning. This is certainly the case in shipping lines and is particularly important on "Liner" services or on "time charter".

Maritime transport undertakings make use of the services of ships' chandlers for their supply provisioning.

Stage 4: warehousing, raw materials
At this stage the profits arising from bulk buying and handling into store are set alongside the economics of distribution—particularly in bulk.

The raw materials warehouse or distributor is closely concerned with the commodity exchange and market conditions, and with the trend of demand in the industries to which the raw materials are distributed.

Supplies and services needed to support the warehousing trade are kept to a minimum, since they will be a significant charge against its operation. This category includes repairs and maintenance of buildings, handling, conveying, control equipment, and transport. Supplies for the last three may involve a high degree of urgency. Delay may mean a loss of sales or demurrage and other charges on idle transport, ships and port installations. Stocks of main selling lines are usually bought and stored in bulk, giving time to avoid the contingencies common to most of the other forms of commerce and industry.

Stage 5: process plants
This is the first positive manufacturing change in the "economic supplies cycle" from raw material to finished product, and introduces the complexity of production and supporting activities.

At this stage, stock levels and intake must be matched accurately with an assured stable production rate and plant utilisation which in nearly all cases must exceed 50 per cent if the plant is to remain profitable.

Control and purchase of raw materials at this stage necessitate strong Supplies policies. Economies made here contribute significantly to profitability. The Supplies operation is made more complex by reason of the "supporting materials" needed to carry on the process. Savings in supplies can be even larger than in other stages. Technical disciplines in process plants tend to result in the rigid control of Supplies. Continuous round-the-clock operation demands close attention to programming, progressing and provisioning. (BS 5476.)

Stage 6: warehousing and distribution, processed and semi-finished materials

This stage specialises in the handling and distribution of goods and materials produced at the previous stages. "Supporting goods" and items may be sold for use in conjunction with the semi-finished material needed by the customer for completion of his finished product. For example, a steel stockholder may carry stocks of bolts, nuts and fasteners used in steelwork assemblies to provide a complete service to the customer.

As in the case of raw material warehousing, at stage 4, the operation will be almost entirely confined to buying, storing and reselling the materials specialised in. However, there is here likely to be a greater diversity and also a higher proportion of supplies for internal use than in stage 4 to cover packing, handling, transport, etc.

The raw materials warehouseman at stage 4 deals mainly with specialist users experienced in the raw materials they buy. The semi-finished goods warehouseman deals as a rule with a much greater variety of clients, many of whom rely upon his skill, advice and service. He must therefore be an expert in the goods handled. The onus is upon him to provide this skill, advice and service, as required by the Sale of Goods Act 1979 (see Chapter 16).

As a result of these considerations the goods and materials handled by a warehouse are often divided among buyers each specialising in one or more groups of commodity so that each will become an expert. (This also follows the practice of most production industries.) A technical service is thus built up and a watch can be kept on the qualitative aspect of each item handled. Each sectional buyer is usually also responsible for the assessment of trends in price, demand and delivery and for the setting and maintaining of stock levels.

Because such warehouses normally carry a much wider range of products than the raw materials warehouse, the Supplies operation is more diverse and usually entails more staff for the same turnover of stock both for buying and for controlling the stock levels.

Semi-finished and wholesale warehousemen are usually distributors and provide their own delivery service. Transport problems tend to be different from those previously met where bulk shipments took place. Movements will be frequent and to a number of delivery points. This is partly due to the fact that the ratio of industrial units (including the construction industry, which is the biggest single user), mostly having a high supplies diversity factor, to process plants taking bulk shipments is very high — probably in the region of 5:1.

Further operations involved in wholesaling are sorting, counting, handling and packaging. These can add considerably to operating costs and the price to the purchaser.

Stage 7: manufacture, general and finished goods

This stage requires not only raw materials but also a much higher proportion of supporting materials for production, research, design and development, factory maintenance, plant extensions, etc.[9][10][11] Where erection and commissioning of plant are included, provisioning will be required for these services also.

Diversity factor of supplies may be very high, varying through "low" and "medium" to "high technologies". "General and finished goods" producers are the most numerous of manufacturing industries. Their Supplies problems are examined in detail in later sections.

Stage 8: warehousing and distribution, finished goods (BS 5191 (2.3).)

Following stage 7, the product may pass into another phase of manufacture or direct to the ultimate consumer at stage 9 or through a wholesale warehouse shown at stage 8.[138] In this case the problems associated with the Supplies function will be very similar to those at stage 6.

With every stage nearer to the final consumer there is usually an increase in the variety of goods handled and in the risk of loss due to changes in design, taste or fashion. (The risk of loss due to fashion and design changes is not confined to distribution of consumer goods, but can have repercussions as far back as stage 1 of the total cycle (extractive) with decreasing intensity. Even in the general engineering field the purchasing officer may find himself confronted with changes in design, of both his own product and that of his supplier, which he could not have predicted.) (BS 5191 (2.6).)

The buyers in such establishments will often be responsible also for sales of the goods they handle in order to keep closely in touch with day-to-day demands and to provide a "Supplies" service to their customers.

Stage 9: domestic consumers — retail outlets
This stage can be regarded normally as the final one of the economic cycle, except when the finished goods pass back into further processes and assembly or are items of capital plant. The volume and types of demand by this important sector to a large extent determine the volume and types of the remainder of the cycle leading up to it. The percentages shown in Fig. 4 for domestic purchases are for 1977. They are typical, but must be checked year by year.

Stage 10: industrial infrastructure
By "industrial infrastructure" is meant those supporting industries and authorities which provide services for the remainder of industry and for the whole community.[138] These include local authorities, nationalised industries, and some private industries providing services of a public nature, e.g. security, cleaning and other services. Each contribute to a greater or lesser degree to all stages in the "total economic cycle". It must not be inferred that because they are placed last they are of less importance than other stages in the cycle — they have a vital role at all stages.

STATE OWNERSHIP (nationalisation) and/or control has in the past been extended to much of the infrastructure as a result of a number of "natural", economic and practical or technical factors (not connected with political dogma) such as the following:

(a) need to co-ordinate operations;
(b) need to standardise services;
(c) high capital investment;
(d) as (c) above with low profits and high financial risk;
(e) technical complexity;
(f) widespread areas of operation, need to avoid overlapping;
(g) need for uniform and stable prices;
(h) public accountability;
(i) duty of safe and continuous service to the community;
(j) government control in the national interest or profit, or help to the economy, or to boost home industries;
(k) duplication of facilities to ensure continuity of service as demanded by statute;
(l) back-up supplies in case of failure, breakdown or exceptional demand;
(m) spares and maintenance — 24-hour availability.

Many of the above factors modify the normal constraints of free random market forces unless rigidly controlled and can also have a distinct effect upon Supplies policies, costs, administration and procedures. For example (*see (j)* above) one Minister stipulated that "more use should be made of public purchasing for the greater benefit of home industries". Although directed to purchasing officers in public services this aim could also be worth examination by those in private industry who—unlike their colleagues in public services— are not obliged by EEC regulations to spread enquiries above a certain value across state boundaries. This principle does not necessarily imply protectionism. It should, however, cause the purchasing officer to bear in mind the well-being of all suppliers including those overseas if he buys from such sources. Healthy industrial bases at home as well as overseas are the surest generators of world trade, antidotes to recession and factors to safeguard the continuance of supplies.

THE SUPPLIES PATTERN OF LOCAL AUTHORITIES and their place in the total economic supplies cycle is less clear than in manufacturing and service industries. In the first place the services they offer vary from place to place. Some provide docks and harbour facilities, others industrial water supply recovered from sewage disposal plants, while a few accept waste for segregation and recovery of materials.

THE ABSENCE OF A PHYSICAL END-PRODUCT in most public authorities makes it difficult to apply the same criteria as for normal industrial production. For example, in many cases, such as hospitals, there are no "sales to customers" and other bases of output must be used such as social cost-benefits. On the other hand, there are a number of aspects where public authorities have similar characteristics to those of commerce and industry. There is, regrettably, a tendency on the part of some of their employees to ignore characteristics which are parallel to those in industry. This tendency should be corrected.

Rates and charges of public authorities of all kinds escalate where such bodies fail to employ good commercial policies and practices. The industrial buyer of services from the "industrial infrastructure" is often confronted with prices which have been fixed nationally (*see* Chapter 12).

THE GLOBAL (INTER-STATE) SUPPLIES CYCLE

After studying overall supplies and materials management problems and the characteristics of industry and commerce, we examine

Supplies in the context of world trade (*see also* Chapter 12, overseas sources).[12][13][14][15][16][17][138]

A continuing flow of supplies is as vital to the survival of those who provide them as it is to those who consume them. Supplies tasks therefore have wider implications than the mere provisioning of the factory or warehouse which uses them.

Factors affecting supplies flow

Figure 5 shows a few of the factors which regulate, stimulate or inhibit the "global" (inter-state) flow of supplies. The diagram has been adapted from a concept by R. M. S. Wilson in an article "The Management of Corporate Intelligence", *Factory Management,*

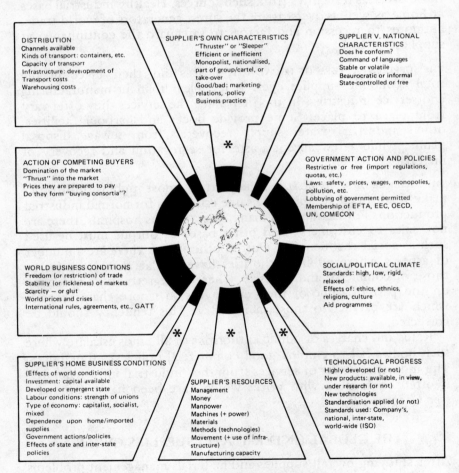

Fig. 5. The global (inter-state) supplies cycle

February 1970. This was intended to apply to marketing but it has been modified and expanded to emphasise its relevance to Supplies. An important application of Supplies integration is exemplified here, namely the fact that marketing and purchasing are, or should be, regarded as complementary—if not always "complimentary"!

Understanding the global supplies cycle

No purchasing officer should consider his education complete without some knowledge of marketing, estimating and selling methods. Similarly, an understanding of the "global situation" is increasingly necessary. All firms of whatever kind and however small have some direct or indirect effect upon the global supplies situation and are themselves affected by it.

Figure 5 is relevant even to those who do not use imports directly. (N.B. Checklist 1, items (15)–(22) also relate to global trade.) The following questions should be asked.

(a) What proportion of the company's supplies come directly from abroad?

(b) What proportion come indirectly from abroad, i.e. through an agent, importer or distributor, etc.?

(c) What proportion of purchased finished supplies are manufactured from imported materials?

(d) Which of the factors in Fig. 5 could influence:

(i) continuity of supply;

(ii) stability of price;

(iii) stability of specification?

(e) What assurance is there that world conditions will not affect any supplies?

NOTE:

Many of the factors shown in Fig. 5 apply not only between independent sovereign states but also between areas within the same national boundaries.

Effects of different economies on Supplies

In Fig. 5, in the box headed "supplier's home business conditions", three types of economy are listed, namely capitalist, planned and mixed. Whatever political arguments may exist concerning these types of economy, it is beyond dispute that all need supplies (and that supplies need management). It is also increasingly clear that global trade is necessary for a healthy world. These two considerations make it essential that not only should everyone study Supplies but also everyone should know how others buy. Such knowledge can assist both buyers and sellers to complete successful negotiations

21

more rapidly. It is, perhaps, not too much to claim that the same outlook will improve world and local relationships.

Trading organisations particularly (but no longer exclusively) of states with centrally planned economies are interested, not only in narrow economic and commercial aspects of transactions, but also in the effects of such transactions upon balance of payments, currency control and so on. These factors may compel the buyer (for example) in an East European State, when buying from the West, to ask for a "counter-trading" transaction,[17] that is to seek to "pay" for his imports, in whole or in part, by the export to the Western selling country of goods from his country. The purchasing officer in the West may then find himself arranging the intake of supplies from the overseas state as "counter-trade" for his own company's exports to that country. This transaction may possibly be negotiated not by him but by the marketing department of his company.

Where the incoming supplies are for resale or other use outside his own firm such matters as "suitability for purpose", Health and Safety at Work Act requirements, etc. should be the responsibility of the marketing department of the importer. Sometimes, however, the incoming supplies will be raw materials or components for use in the production line of the purchasing officer's factory. In such cases the considerations regarding "reciprocal trading" should be noted along with Checklist 24.

Less usually, an importing buyer in a Western state may find himself involved in "counter-trading in reverse", and being asked by his supplier, i.e. the exporter in Eastern Europe from whom he is buying, to "pay" for his imports by supplying goods to the Eastern exporter from his (the buyer's) own state. The goods in that case may, or may not, be of his own company's manufacture.

Counter-trading and other such practices are the subject of conferences run by the Institute of Purchasing and Supply, and for further information reference should be made either to their head of courses or to their Technical Advisory Service (*see* Appendix I). The Department of Trade and The East European Trade Council are primary sources of information and advice on counter-trading.

Regulations and directives of the EEC

The entry of the UK into the European Economic Community has had important implications for international trade and the Supplies field.[18] Supplies staff should be on the alert for new legislation resulting from EEC membership which can affect their work.

CHAPTER 2

Integration and Supplies Policies

INTRODUCTION

World, national and company development all have one require-ment in common without which all policies, however sophisticated, must fail and anarchy result—namely "integration" of their oper-ations. The next chapter examines administration, following it through to "departmentalisation" and the final débâcle of "depart-mentalism". Integration should prevent this. Nowhere in an in-dustrial organisation is the need more evident than in the Supplies functions and their links with the remainder of an enterprise.

INTEGRATION OF SUPPLIES WITH OTHER DEPARTMENTS

The degree of integration, the policies and the scope of Supplies departments, together with their relationships, administration and structure, all depend to a large extent upon the complexity and technology of the process and the product as well as the size and nature of the unit served. It is impossible therefore to do more than set out general principles for guidance in setting up and operating such a department. (BS 5729 Part 1 (7.1) and Chapter 18.)

Figure 6 shows some of the functions common to most industrial manufacturing units. They apply whether the firm is large or small and whether the functions emerge as visible entities in a large unit or remain as "concealed" or occasional functions in a small one. The figure also illustrates some of the relationships between Supplies and the other functions.

Table 2 shows some of the activities of Supplies which require close integration within a Supplies department (where one exists) and with other departments and their policies, along with the stream-lining of administration which is the subject of the next chapter.

The importance of integration is emphasised in the relevant books in the bibliography[19][20][21][22][23] and must be borne in mind when studying the policies examined in the rest of this chapter.

23

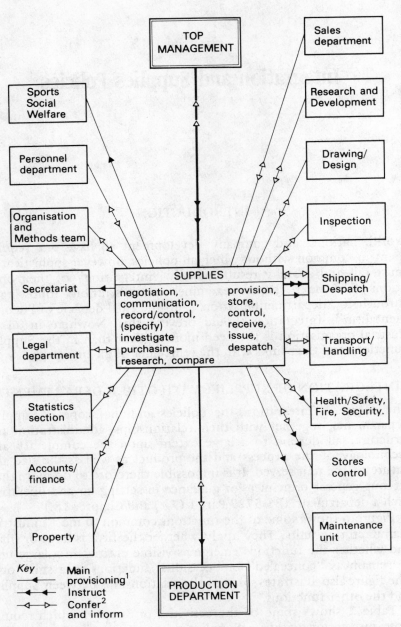

Fig. 6. Relationships between Supplies and other departments within an industrial organisation

(1) Some provisioning of supplies will occur at all points. (2) The degree of conferring needed and volume of information provided will depend upon the complexity and technology of the product. (3) In small companies many of the functions exist only in embryo or combined with others and so are not apparent.

TABLE 2. ASPECTS OF SUPPLIES REQUIRING INTEGRATION OF POLICIES AND ADMINISTRATION

Aspects needing integration	Supplies activities		
	Purchasing	Stores	Transport, and handling
Specification BS 5191 (A)	Fundamental to whole purchasing operation	Size, shape, weight, inspection, hazards, packaging	Size, weight, shape, packaging, provision for, hazards in, handling and transport
Order quantity BS 5191 (3.3)	Economic order size, bulk contracts, etc.	Storage space, unit loads, handling; shelf-life must not be exceeded	Size and weight in relation to transport and handling capacity
Intrinsic value of commodity	Special negotiations plus market studies if value is high	Security, control and insurance	Security and insurance
Urgency BS 5191 (3.2)	Availability and knowledge of reliable sources	Movement, speed through stores	Speed and flexibility of transport and good administration
Packaging and containers	Arrange at order stage to ensure safe arrival and storage (part of costs)	Handling, opening, counting, returning, salvage, recording, i.e. returnables	Handling facilities, return of empties, return loads, etc.
Inspection BS 4891 (9.5)	Test arrangements should be clear at negotiation stage, and on order	Quarantine and release, etc.	—
Shelf-life BS 5191 (3.3)	Order quantity to match shelf-life	Stock levels set to suit shelf-life; special facilities—refrigeration, humidity control, etc.	Special transport where needed

TABLE 2 contd. ASPECTS OF SUPPLIES REQUIRING INTEGRATION
OF POLICIES AND ADMINISTRATION

Aspects needing integration	Supplies activities		
	Purchasing	Stores	Transport, and handling
Dangerous and hazardous goods	May need licences, e.g. explosives	Special segregated stores, special bins, etc.	Special transport and handling facilities
Importation procedures	Import licence; letter of credit; insurance; certified invoice	Special prompt action on ships, international wagons, etc.	Special prompt action on ships, international wagons, etc.
Statutory regulations (home)	Licences and inspection of records, e.g. industrial alcohol	Bonded stores; government inspection; special records	Transport Acts, by-laws etc.
Other legal regulations	Validity of contract, Sale of Goods Act, etc.	Health and Safety at Work Act, Weights and Measures Act 1963, metrication, etc.	Health and Safety at Work Act, international codes, rules and regulations
Methods of charging, weighing, counting, etc.	To be shown on orders	Stores admin. must make provision for exceptions, e.g. dipstick measure, weighbridge tickets	Taring of vehicles, weighbridge tickets, etc.

FINANCIAL SUPPLY CONTROL POLICY

In line with modern management policies there is an increasing
trend towards informing employees of financial, sales and production
data in the hope that productivity and profitability will be improved,
job interest and job satisfaction stimulated and industrial harmony
assured.[24]

The financial controls that are applied to Supplies may in fact be
based on much of the data generated by Supplies itself, viz. costs
of supplies, delivery times, rejection rates and so on. (*See also*
Chapter 13). The disciplines and duties imposed upon Supplies staff

by financial controls and policies may include the following.

(a) Limits above which Supplies must obtain financial sanction before making a financial commitment for their company. (Heads of departments usually have their own financial limits within which they are constrained.)

(b) Ensuring that requisitions bear the signature of the departmental chief concerned where financial constraints are applied. In some firms Supplies staff are also made responsible for seeing that financial limits have not been exceeded.

(c) Providing up-to-date prices of goods, materials and services which are subject to budgetary control. This may also include the assessment of future price trends (see Chapter 13). (BS 5191 (B 1006).)

(d) "Standard costing" which requires cost data for supplies. This is usually followed by the discipline of maintaining purchase prices within the limits set down when the costing figures were first agreed. (See also (f) below.) (BS 5191 (B 1006).)

(e) "Commitment accounting" meets the need to control a firm's outflow of cash at a time of making commitments (placing the orders) instead of waiting for the bills, by which time it may no longer have any cash! Some spectacular disasters which have struck large companies in recent years have highlighted the need for this technique—but it is even more important for smaller firms. (See also Chapter 13, inflation.)

(f) "Cost disciplines" must be expected by every purchasing officer in the course of his operations. Cost office investigations should reveal where he has paid too much for supplies of direct goods. For "standard costing" he will be expected to buy within the limits necessary to maintain profitability based on standard costs. In the case of factory and plant extensions most purchasing officers buy under directions from the board of directors to whom they must account for the orders and contracts placed. Finally, Supplies activities receive the ultimate sanctions of accounts, annual reports, questions at shareholders' meetings, and perhaps in future years questions at workers' councils and other bodies.

STOCK CONTROL AND ITS EFFECTS
UPON STOCK INVESTMENT POLICY

Stock investment policy[25] should be given adequate consideration by top management. It is a major item in the books of almost every company, and ties up much of the wealth of most industrialised states. The various stock levels and their characteristics are examined later (see Chapter 7 and Fig. 25). For present purposes we examine the financial effects of stock control, and to some extent the implications for stock control of financial policies. (For investment policy, *see* Chapter 13.) (BS 5729 Part 1 (9.6) and (10).)

"Policy stock"
This needs special attention, and direction, from management (*see* Chapter 13 and Table 26). However, as indicated above and emphasised in Chapter 13, *all* stock can be regarded in one sense as "policy stock". When setting stock levels conditions apply which are similar to those which determine the optimum size of a purchase order, i.e. the best stock level is that for which the annual costs of storage plus stock investment costs are minimised—usually found at the break-even point. In most cases, however, it is the availability of cash which largely determines the policy for the stock permitted, i.e. the stock levels. Nevertheless, the practical implications of the axiom below are most important.

AXIOM: Stock levels must optimise production.

Stock life (BS 5191 (3.3).)
Policy should be established to determine the length of time goods or materials can remain in store without turning over, as regards both the condition of the goods and cash tied up. Policy may vary for different classifications of stock. It will be chiefly ascertained by shelf-life, rates of obsolescence, speed of technical development and a number of other factors peculiar to the goods concerned.

Action on this point may to some extent be linked with stock control and stock audit. These can give an indication of the rate of stock movement (and lack of movement), thus providing a means for guidance and administrative action particularly in regard to surplus and obsolescent stock. (*See Storehouse, surplus stock.*)

"Safety-stock" (BS 5191 (3.3).)
Sometimes also known as "insurance stock" or, less correctly, as "buffer-stock", this represents capital outlay at full value rather than the average—for reasons which will appear later. The sum invested represents the "insurance premium" against stoppages due to stock-outs of supplies. The costs of safety-stock should not exceed the losses against which they are an "insurance". (*See* Chapter 9, Flow 1.)

Reorder level (BS 5191 (3.3).)
This is the level at which stock control records should trigger off a replenishment of the bin.

NOTE:

Both "safety-stock" and "reorder level" are sometimes referred to as "minimum stock". This can be misleading with disastrous results and it is best to avoid the latter term for that reason.

Maximum stock (BS 5191 (3.3).)

This is a management "policy stock". The average stock, upon which investment is based, depends upon this. Management should therefore lay down maxima at least for classification "A" items of supply for ("A.B.C." classifications *see* below and Chapter 5). Another indirect factor affecting financial policy is the effect of maximum stocks upon the "storage factor" of a stores.

Relationship between financial and Supplies policies

Financial policies can be inimical to stock control and Supplies policies. Companies which take stock control seriously but only act when circumstances force them to do so tend to reduce stocks excessively across the whole range of supplies. Hasty action in reducing stocks based purely upon financial considerations may result in the following:

(*a*) too tightly constrained and reduced stock levels;

(*b*) production starved of supplies—frequent stoppages;

(*c*) increased acquisition costs—frequent orders and intakes, handling, payment, etc.;

(*d*) premium prices for small lot deliveries;

(*e*) inflated costs when finally stocks have to be rebuilt at new prices;

(*f*) may lose tax concessions on stock valuation;

(*g*) increased costs due to rearrangement of existing contracts;

(*h*) delays waiting for new intakes.

Apart from financial policies affecting stock control, the converse may take place. Borrowing money from outside sources such as banks or stockholders depends upon the uncontrollable vagaries of market economics. On the other hand, capital can be generated internally (*interest free*) by merely holding stocks at an economical level through effective stock control, which thus becomes part cause and part effect in financial policy.

Stock targets

The following abridged from BS5729 Part 1 (9.2) should be noted when taking action to achieve stock targets: "Great care should be taken in setting the pace with which to achieve results. It is as important not to go too fast as to go too slowly, and stock often rises before it falls as shortages are cleared by stocks brought in, but moving excess stock is likely to be a longer process. However, the firm will go bankrupt if the move is too slow. If too fast, suppliers may well be upset (e.g. by a 'shut the gate' policy to goods being delivered). By taking greater care, however, suppliers may assist, knowing that a more reliable customer will result."

TECHNICAL POLICIES

Technical policies as approved by management can and should have a big impact upon the policies of Supplies. This should be welcomed as part of their integration into the total structure of the organisation. However, with the increased training of the work-force and as industry becomes more technical, Supplies will find a new discipline in the form of "feedback" from those who actually use the supplies which they provide. The purchasing officer who fails to encourage such feedback deprives himself of a major area for profitability contribution.

In taking account of these facts of life, Supplies strengthen their commercial control, give added edge to their negotiations and improve their relationships with technical colleagues.

Technical change through invention, innovation or technological development may call for changes in policies and provisioning of supplies (see Chapter 5, research and development).

SUPPLY POLICIES FOR VARIOUS CLASSIFICATIONS OF SUPPLIES

Classification of supplies by "A.B.C." analysis (see Fig. 14) results in the classical Pareto curve, described in Chapter 5. Policies in regard to the various classification groups of supplies are outlined below. (BS5191 (3.3).)

Classification "A"
This usually accounts for a high proportion in value of total throughout and controls the profitability of the undertaking. In this field Supplies must adhere closely to company policy, particularly in process industries, with their high material content (see Fig. 4) often confined to a narrow range of materials where error of judgment or lack of control could wreck the whole economy of the firm. It is advisable in the case of all major contracts for classification "A" materials to be agreed by top management.

Classification "B"
There is usually a well-defined break point at "B" in the Pareto

curve consisting of intermediate varieties and values, which make up some of the less important production materials and the more important supporting and "indirect" goods and materials.

Classification "C"

This normally shows a very wide range of variety, but a low total value, mostly comprising supporting goods and materials. In most manufacturing industries, particularly "jobbing", the variety of supplies required is too great for detailed policy and control to be exercised by top management for the full range of requirements and the purchasing department usually has a fairly free hand. Detailed control of *all* items in classification "C" could result in:

(a) costs of control exceeding the value of the supplies controlled;
(b) delays in decisions causing stock-outs and stoppages;
(c) the volume of records, correspondence and filing leading to over-staffing;
(d) controls costing more than possible loss through their absence;
(e) staff inhibited from free and speedy action.

Provided that competent people have been appointed it is cheaper in general engineering to accept a small risk.

The variety of materials handled in the general engineering and jobbing fields may appeal to many as having greater interest than the narrower field, with greater specialisation, in the process and mass-production industries. On the other hand, the scope for spectacular deals is less frequent in general engineering because the materials content is low and more diverse than in most process plants.

For these reasons the supplies manager attains Board status sooner in a process industry than in others. According to a survey by one professional body, 12 per cent of purchasing officers and supplies managers in this field were directors. Obviously these factors influence the ladder of promotion.

SUPPLIER RELATIONSHIP POLICIES AND ETHICS

Management should require its Supplies personnel to act within the ethical codes of good business practice in their relationships with suppliers.[26] *See* Checklist 2, Appendix II, extracts from the BIM *"Code of Best Practice for the Professional Manager in the United Kingdom"*, and Appendix I, the *"Ethical Code"* of the Institute of Purchasing and Supply. (The latter is available free on application to the Institute.)

The application of these objectives has a considerable bearing upon the image of a trading or manufacturing organisation as presented to the outside world in general and to its suppliers in particular, and upon the power of the purchasing officer in his negotiations.

AXIOM: "Accept nothing of money's worth." (Chairman of a large public utility.)

The Corrupt Practices Act and the Prevention of Corruption Acts inflict substantial penalties. The accused must show that by accepting the "gift" or other "favour" he was not influenced in his subsequent course of action, for example in placing a contract. To prove a negative is invariably difficult, often impossible and always costly.

However, there are temptations of a more subtle nature to which Supplies personnel are sometimes subjected.

AXIOM: Good ethics are sound business.

Other aspects can affect both the company's image and its profiability. Firstly, management of supply must be seen to be part of management policy. Secondly, conduct of correspondence can affect relations with suppliers. There is some evidence of a relationship between technical ability and the performance of suppliers and the efficiency of their correspondence. A strong technical department has an influence which can affect the whole of an organisation. Certainly so far as the Supplies function is concerned, the purchasing officer is likely to be judged by his correspondence and the energy and enthusiasm with which his department transacts its business. (*See also* Chapter 12, performance of suppliers.)

EDUCATION, TRAINING AND PROMOTION

Education and training are very important in supplies management. This is particularly so in smaller firms where the competitive aspects are the greatest and where those employed often carry out single-handed a wide range of operations including Supplies tasks, with no Supplies staff to support them.

Where a firm is small but growing the manager must learn to delegate work as the firms grows. He rapidly discovers that he can no longer carry out effectively all the various jobs himself. It is at this point that training in Supplies for at least one member of his staff can pay dividends.

It is sometimes contended by managements of smaller firms that if they train their personnel they may lose them. This may be true but if training were more widespread, such firms could pick up an ambitious and trained "replacement" who is looking for a new environment with prospects of advancement. Here he could apply his newly acquired expertise with energy and skill to the benefit of all concerned.

"Integration" is as important here as in all aspects of Supplies. Training officers and others looking for courses and conferences on Supplies are well advised to select those which will bring the student or delegate into contact with as many as possible of the disciplines shown in Fig. 6.

One of the advantages of the Diploma course of the Institute of Purchasing and Supply (see Appendix I) is that it makes use of the Higher National Certificate and Diploma in Business Studies. Here, classes with mixed backgrounds and jobs give the candidate an appreciation of the other man's point of view and enable him to prepare for an integrated Supplies activity.

"Training for change" is valuable for staffs in small, growing companies. Courses are available at a few management schools for this unusual subject.

Those who aspire to senior positions in Supplies should include environmental areas in their training.[27][28][29][30] For example, purchasing officers should obtain a grounding in marketing and sales while all Supplies staff can benefit from a knowledge of production—not only their own firm's but also of the firms from which they buy, receive, handle or progress supplies.

Promotion in Supplies in most industries is rather slow and the ladder of promotion is unclear. This is because Supplies is a high pressure area and urgency of action tends to blunt the specialisation which takes place in most other functions. There is the further difficulty in that the numbers employed on Supplies are small so that the range of staff levels is also small. A major factor in promotional success is keenness, commercial acumen and interest in supplies, coupled (in most situations) with technical competence.

CHAPTER 3

Planning and Administration of Supplies Departments

INTRODUCTION

The vigorous marketing policy of a "thrusting" company is likely from time to time to involve changes in production, design, costing and supplies. A Supplies department, being a mirror image of selling, must be prepared to reflect such changes in its own administration, structure and development.

Planning and administration should be regarded as the servants of policy and designed and operated accordingly. The planning of industrial operations is always important, but particularly so in Supplies.[31][34] Planning company operations ultimately affects what goes on in Supplies. Sales and production planning determine advance stock levels and forward contracts for main materials, as well as tools and supporting materials if of long delivery.

The administrative function of Supplies includes the detailed assessment of all those activities which enable the work to be carried out; for example, the routeing and number of copies made of each order, the handling of staff, arrangements for meetings and the reporting of them, and the preparation and updating of a departmental manual.

The volume of administrative work therefore depends on many of the policy decisions discussed in the previous chapter and in a complex industry may add considerably to the costs of both stock-holding and acquisition.

It is most important that the "exception principle" is applied here to ensure that 90 per cent of time and effort is not spent upon administration and control of the 1 per cent exception.

CORPORATE PLANNING AND PLANNING OF SUPPLIES

Corporate planning is a management technique which deals in a systematic manner with the long-term objectives of a company and the strategy needed to achieve them.

It entails the treatment of a company as a corporate body rather than a collection of independent departments of which the Supplies department is but one. Supplies department activities will be integrated into the corporate plan. This should result in advanced strategic knowledge and planning for storage capacity, handling and transport facilities. Above all, within the overall scheme, supplies of raw materials, tools and equipment can be provisioned over the appropriate horizons.

Once a company has produced a corporate plan it must be monitored systematically and continuously. One important result of this will be the disciplines laid upon the Supplies department to keep to the plan — along with the other branches of the company.

Within the long-term strategic plan will fall shorter-term objectives and tactical changes. These will require Supplies staff to remain alert and sensitive to different needs of their company as changes occur in sales owing to market forces or innovation, or in supplies owing to price, availability, specification and other factors.

COMMUNICATION

Supplies staff are often involved in arrangement for, as well as participation in, meetings with suppliers, inspectors (visiting and home-based), progress sections, production staff and so on. In connection with the actual supplies themselves there will be arrangements with transport organisations, shipping agents, Customs and Excise officers, bank managers (for letters of credit, supplier status reports, etc.), insurance agents and many more.[138] Above all, this aspect of Supplies work necessitates the ability to communicate well.

Instruction of suppliers is the executive function of Supplies while the control of the supplies and stocks themselves are the essence of the service function of Supplies to production and other users. The following axiom may be a useful reminder of the relationships involved.

AXIOM: Purchasing is *executive* to suppliers but *service* to users.

There are reasons why communication is so important — some of these are more or less unique to Supplies.

(*a*) For a contract to be legally valid there must be communication and agreement. This demands that the communications shall be accurate and clear.

(*b*) If a purchase order is incorrect the wrong goods will certainly arrive (the converse may be open to question!).

(*c*) In other departments of business (the drawing office, accounts department, etc.) some form of independent check is introduced.

However, the only check on a purchase order is the shipment which finally arrives.

(d) Once placed, purchase orders are likely to result in an irrevocable contract as a result of the supplier making the delivery ("performance", *see* Chapter 16). A plea of "mistake" may protect a supplier if he ships incorrect goods, but it is unlikely to legally protect a buyer if he should make a mistake in his order.

Internally, Supplies communications between the three basic areas of manufacturing (selling, making, buying) are sometimes poor, particularly if the purchasing officer reports to and is controlled by his principle "customer"—the production manager. This is likely to inhibit his freedom of movement within the organisation and his free consultation with colleagues outside the production unit itself.

Communication may be improved by the study of human relationships. Not only must communication be clear and accurate, but it is also vital to understand what effect it is likely to have upon the person receiving it—particularly if he speaks a different language (*see* Checklist 24).

AXIOM: "An organisation is a group of roles tied together by a communication network." (Dr B. Muller Thym.)

DOCUMENT PREPARATION

Supplies departments generate large quantities of letters, memoranda, orders, forms, etc. Many of these contain both fixed items, from "Dear Sir" to "for and on behalf of . . .", and variable information. The latter is often amenable to new communication techniques of "word processing". "Word processing" is a newly coined phrase to describe a method used by Supplies officers for many years. In its original form this involved the collection of master documents into a file. The appropriate master document could then be withdrawn as required for copying with the variable data or instructions and messages added. For one example *see* Chapter 15, "model orders".

The frequency and volume of use of each document determines whether it should be run off in quantity and a supply kept by the typist or whether the typist should copy the master document each time it is required. For smaller firms this is a viable "word-processing" system using the old technology but fully compatible with the new, if and when it is introduced. Although small firms are likely to find the new technology too costly for adoption in early years, they may find it of considerable value to discuss it with salesmen who are specialists in this field.

Those who already have a computer will find it is a short step to electronic word processing. The most basic system comprises a visual display unit (referred to as a "VDU") with a keyboard. Such units present the document required upon a screen when the operator depresses the appropriate keys on a keyboard. For example, when preparing a letter or purchase order the typist may either type in the address or call it up on the VDU. Similarly a standard letter or standard paragraphs or phrases may be called up and variable particulars such as date, quantity and specification typed in.

Data produced on a word processor can be fed into the computer system thus recording order details, updating stock records, etc. There are numerous other enhancements and diverse methods of achieving these results by variations in the combination of computer, word processor and printer. The last mentioned reproduces the final documents, purchase orders, enquiries, letters, reports, etc., with any variations required.

A further valuable attribute of the word processor is the facility it gives for corrections or amendments to be made in the text without the need for retyping the whole page of matter (*see also* records, below).

RECORDS AND FILING

Economy and simplification
Economy and simplification of records and filing in Supplies are important. There is so much to remember, control and plan that a mass of records tends to accumulate and be maintained long after the original purpose has been lost and forgotten. The following recommended practices can assist.

"THE EXCEPTION PRINCIPLE" should be applied. A warning is needed, however, to ensure that too high a proportion of time is not spent on exceptional aspects and the normal ones neglected. Among miscellaneous materials (classification "C") there may be some small items which are nevertheless of exceptional importance to the continuity of operations. These need priority attention for control and record. Selective recording, instead of recording all classes in equal detail, proves economic. (*See also* Chapter 12.)

PRIME DOCUMENTS (e.g. order copies) when filed can replace written records and eliminate clerical labour of a most unrewarding kind. In any event it is frequently necessary to refer to the original copies for details. It is thus valuable to spend time devising the best method of filing these and using them thereafter as the record.

"MULTI-PURPOSE" DOCUMENTS (i.e. where each document is made to do many jobs) should be used, thus reducing the volume of paper-flow, accelerating its movement, and advising staff of what is going on. If subsequently filed, these contain at a central point all the relevant information regarding each transaction. Where numerous separate copies of documents are used, "self-preservation" or some other instinct will inevitably lead to each being filed "in case it is ever needed"! (*See also* purchase order records, below.)

RATIONALISATION AND SIMPLIFICATION of records can be made in many purchasing departments. If the basis of each record is examined most can be reduced to two headings: "suppliers" and "commodities". Order copies and other documents can be filed in lever-arch files in "A" to "Z" sequence forming their own records and obviating transcription on to cards, etc.

ELECTRONIC DATA PROCESSING (EDP) can greatly assist in the compilation of records in Supplies by making use of data included in the original supplies documents themselves. As increasing use is made of computers, for example in word processing, the clerical work-load should be reduced. Time thus saved can be employed in making use of statistics obtained to improve stock control, increase purchasing research, make use of variety reduction, and so on.

AXIOM: Records must never cost more than their "value-in-use".

Types of record and filing

Records and filing in Supplies falls into two main groups: records of past action for future reference and day-to-day records for immediate action as in the process of an order being completed. Some departments maintain further records to provide information for departmental reports.

Figure 7 indicates diagrammatically the volume and speed with which documents pass through a Supplies office. It is important to design the recording system so that information is concentrated into the smallest number of locations. The following are some of the more common records with their main function in each case.

PURCHASE ORDER RECORDS (if made) are usually on record cards or visible-edge loose-leaf giving the salient details of purchases of classification "A" and "B" items. Exceptional items in classification "C" may also be included. These records provide information of purchases which pre-date and are out of phase with consumption and should not be relied upon statistically for stock control.

Purchase order copies can be filed in a number of ways, as follows.

(a) Numerical sequence: this is satisfactory where orders are

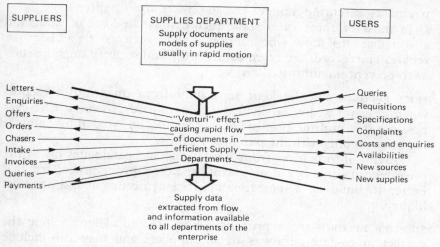

Fig. 7. *Supplies departments as "data traps"*

sequentially numbered or commodity code numbered. A cross-reference to suppliers may be necessary for rapid location.

(*b*) Alphabetical sequence: the name of the supplier is usually known and "pending delivery" or "filed complete" orders can usually be traced easily by this method. (*See* Fig. 69.)

(*c*) Vocabulary/commodity description in alphabetical sequence of commodities purchased is satisfactory provided one type or group only is covered per order. (*See also* commodity/stores catalogue, below.)

(*d*) Product groups of the purchasing officer's own factory.

(*e*) Contract, job or drawing reference.

If order numbers are based on commodity codes, clerical labour is reduced and transcription errors are eliminated. In addition, use can be made of a computer for statistical analyses of purchases, prices, delivery trends, etc.

COMMODITY/STORES CATALOGUES are vital Supplies/technical records needed in practically every size and kind of company (*see Storehouse*). The catalogue must coincide in its terminology with the vocabulary. In the purchasing department the catalogue may also embody the list of potential suppliers in which case the need for a "*where to buy*" record is obviated.

CONTRACTS RECORDS may be kept to monitor the progress of major plant or construction schemes, and contracts for the bulk supply of materials. Other uses of such records may be in the preparation of periodic reports to management, claims for annual rebates, progress payments, retention moneys and so on (*see also* Chapter 15).

In most of these cases some record must be kept of value and also a diary to show when action is due, such as for a claim for rebate. The records are often confidential and security must be such as to prevent unauthorised access.

PRICE RECORDS may be kept separately from quantitative records where it is not wished to divulge the prices paid. However, wherever possible this proliferation of records should be avoided by combining price records with the purchase records.

Copying information from quotations and catalogues on to the price record cards is a time-wasting and error-prone procedure. It is better to build up a separate and efficient catalogue and price-list library.

SUPPLIER RECORDS are a primary supply record. They include the correct up-to-date addresses of all suppliers and may also include the names of executives and representatives with their address and telephone number. (In smaller firms a single supplier record should suffice for whoever does the buying as well as for the typists, who can keep it up-to-date from letters, quotations, business cards and other sources, thus avoiding duplicated records.) (*See also* vendor ratings, below.)

A suppliers' file, with suppliers listed in alphabetical order, can be very useful as a "record in evidence" to contain copies of such communications as terms and conditions of sale, confirmation of discounts, progress and performance reports, capacity register, etc.

APPROVED SUPPLIER AND VENDOR RATINGS (*see* Chapter 12) need to be kept in confidential files available only to authorised staff. Typists may incorporate the code letter (or other symbol) in their address book, but without the translation of the code into actual values of ratings.

RECORDS OF SETTLEMENT TERMS are (next to basic discounts) a "profitable" activity of purchasing (*see* Chapter 22). These records should be available to the pricing clerks and to the invoice checkers.

TECHNICAL RECORDS of specifications and drawings should be kept only in the technical department library unless the rate of consultation and the distances between Supplies and technical departments are very great. It may also be advisable to have a record in sequence of commodities, showing the specifications and drawing numbers which are relevant. It is recommended, however, that this record should be combined with the commodity catalogue.

"WHERE TO BUY" COMMODITY SOURCE RECORDS often cost more in

labour than they earn in time saved. The exception principle should be applied so that information is available only upon what are difficult, strategic, scarce, occasional, or otherwise exceptional and infrequent supply requirements. In any case they can be combined with the commodity/stores catalogue.

SCRAP AND SURPLUS SALES RECORDS (*see also* Chapter 25); some purchasing officers maintain records showing details of each transaction. These include the date, price, payment, name of purchaser and any other information needed for audit and for periodic reports to management (an important record to safeguard the integrity of Supplies staff in this often poorly regulated commercial area).

If, however, normal despatch paperwork is used and suitably coded and numbered, a copy can provide its own built-in record without clerical labour except filing. The records and the documentation should show clearly the origin of the materials or goods disposed of, viz. the work-centre, production unit, etc.

As in the case of the suppliers' list, a list of approved surplus dealers can be very important. Such a list should show:

(*a*) who is reliable;

(*b*) who is creditworthy (note that it is normal practice to impose terms of "cash before collection" for waste and scrap);

(*c*) the range of materials and goods which the firms buy.

PACKAGE RECORDS (*see* Chapter 21, documentation).

PATTERN, DIE AND TOOL RECORDS are important where the purchasing firm issues patterns, dies, tools, jigs and gauges, etc. to its suppliers and subcontractors. Not only is it necessary to know where the various units are situated, but drawings may be revised, in which case the return of the units to the purchaser's works or to an outside toolmaker may be extremely urgent if scrap and waste are to be avoided and production stoppages prevented.

Similar records may be needed for patterns, dies or tools held by the supplier and for which part cost has been paid by the purchaser. In very small firms (25-100 employees) a book showing movement of these items may be adequate, indicating the identity of the item, when it was last shipped and its destination, and finally the date it was returned. However, for reasons explained later (*see* Chapter 15, subcontract orders), this is a vital record and as soon as movements become significant, such a coarse method of recording should be replaced by a card index in commodity sequence with some signalling arrangement to ensure items from completed contracts and subcontracts are returned.

PURCHASE REQUISITIONS can form a natural primary record after processing by merely filing them:

(a) in serial number sequence, if so numbered;

(b) in files for each requisitioning point;

(c) by commodity code, if, of course, only a single or group code appears on each requisition;

(d) with the relevant purchase order, if there is only one order per requisition.

Until the order is placed requisitions should only be found in one of two locations:

(a) in a "live requisition" file with the buyer responsible for processing them; or

(b) with the typist and checkers, etc.

Once received in the purchasing department no requisition should ever leave it unless it is withdrawn for cancellation.

Registers of incoming requisitions are sometimes made "in case they may be mislaid", etc.! This is a wasteful activity which engenders (and may also indicate) a slipshod administration and outlook by staff.

AXIOM: Requisitions are for action today — not to lose or delay!

In very large organisations where requisitions reach Supplies from widely dispersed plants, a "requisition book" may be needed. If requisitions are serially numbered the book need only contain columns bearing serial numbers. As requisitions are received the date of receipt is noted against the serial number. In very large Supplies departments it may be advisable to add the initial of the buyer to whom the requisition has been passed. However, the register should only be kept if requisitioners ring up frequently to query detail, check progress, etc., when rapid location is essential.

SMALL-VALUE AND LOCAL-PURCHASE ORDERS should not need any recording, except as noted in Chapter 15.

ENQUIRY RECORDS should be unnecessary, as their use is purely transitory. (*See*, however, Chapter 14, analysing offers by suppliers). If kept and filed in commodity code sequence they then provide an automatic and valuable record of "where to buy" price, delivery and suppliers.

QUOTATION RECORDS are purely transitory and therefore probably unnecessary. However, it is recommended that quotations themselves be filed in alphabetical sequence of supplier. (Some purchasing officers prefer to file these also in commodity sequence, but this is often not practicable owing to a number of disparate commodities appearing on the same quotation.)

RECORDS OF PRICE MOVEMENTS of classification "A" materials may be logged and possibly charted. These figures can be of value to management through departmental reports.

Some sources of this information are *Procurement Weekly, Purchasing and Supply Management* (monthly), *Trade and Industry,* the *Financial Times,* and reports and research carried out in the company's own Supplies department.

ADVICE NOTES should be filed with the stores inwards copy of the purchase order if the stores certify for goods received. If they do not certify goods received, the advice notes should be filed with the main copy or with the progress copy of the purchase order.

INVOICES: a simple register of receipt of invoices under query may be helpful. Normal invoices should require no record, apart from endorsement of the main copy of the purchase order that the invoice has been passed (or not).

TRADE DIRECTORIES are costly, but it is more costly to retain out-of-date directories. These should be replaced as new ones are available —or dispensed with!

CATALOGUES: classification into commodity groups is difficult and often impossible. A recommended method is alphabetical sequence by name of supplier. Bound volumes should be kept on shelves, and lists and brochures in systems such as lateral filing.

Catalogues should be available to all departments. It may be essential to keep a register of borrowers, but formality should be reduced to a minimum. A simple foolscap sheet on which the borrower from outside the department writes his name and the title, number or identifiable description of what is borrowed should suffice.

A full- or part-time catalogue librarian can continuously audit the library, bringing lists up to date and controlling issues. In smaller firms it is best to delegate one of the buyers or a member of the clerical staff to have general charge of catalogues. Alternatively, where there is a purchasing analyst in post, he may usefully undertake this duty. (*See also* Chapter 4, "size group 3".)

TEST RESULTS AND INSPECTION NOTES are sometimes lodged in the purchasing department but in most cases will be located in the technical departments concerned. A note in the commodity or purchase record may be essential, particularly where failures "blacklist" a commodity or supplier.

REFERENCE BOOKS, JOURNALS, etc., should be numbered, indexed and filed in normal library style of coding for large undertakings. In small firms a member of staff should be designated to look after this work.

CORRESPONDENCE REGISTERS (and records of incoming mail) should be eliminated, or in a very large organisation confined to a central registry. There should be no difficulty in locating "live" mail in a lively, active Supplies office where it is being dealt with, after which it may be filed—or not.

STOCK RECORDS—*see* Chapter 7.

Keeping filing to a minimum (BS 1467; 1749; 3437; 4438.)

The following questions may be helpful. Can documents be:

(a) thrown away when reply is received or job done;

(b) kept for (say) twelve months and then scrapped (unless referred to during that time);

(c) filed with order which may be scrapped after (say) three years, unless important;

(d) filed A to Z by supplier;

(e) filed A to Z by commodity;

(f) filed by commodity code number;

(g) filed under subject, e.g. "VAT", "Customs and Excise", "Planning";

(h) examined for value as records;

(i) filed as records described in previous paragraphs?

To sum up, the most important question is, perhaps, *not* "can the documents be filed" but "can they be scrapped".

SUPPLIES REPORTS TO MANAGEMENT
(BS 5729 Part 4, Table 2 (5).)

Reports and measurements of Supplies performance can often be prepared from the normal records kept in the Supplies office and these should provide management with useful information for future policy.[34][35][36] Reports must be clear, simple to follow and *brief* —not over twenty headings as one authority suggests. The pattern should be similar for each subsequent report so that comparisons can easily be made. The most important guide-line is to ascertain what should interest management and to give this prominence in reports. Reports are likely to cover the following main areas.

(1) ACTIVITIES WITHIN SUPPLIES tend to be overplayed in reporting. The following are the items recommended, which give a clear indication of the work-load with minimum clerical recording.

(a) *Requisitions processed and numbers outstanding.* A useful discipline is a weekly count showing the number of requisitions in "live" files on the last working day of the week, and also the number of those over a week/fortnight/month old. The last-mentioned should be investigated. An accumulation of old requisitions may show a lack of urgency in the department.

(b) *Number of orders placed.* This record can be kept by the individual order typists. It may also be a useful guide to the output and efficiency (i.e. speed, accuracy) of the individual order typists.

(c) *Number of enquiries issued.* The number of requisitions dealt with may not be a true guide to the work-load, because a single requisition may contain many items involving a number of enquiries and orders, or a number of requisitions may be combined in a single order (but *see* earlier note on requisitions). The number of enquiries gives a measure of the problem of locating sources of supply: a large number of enquiries per order placed may denote supply shortages, inefficient recording, or poor knowledge of supply sources and their competitive relationships.

(d) *Number of invoices cleared.* The number of invoices checked by the purchasing department gives a measure of work-load. If only those invoices which vary from the purchase order are checked by the purchasing department, the figure has greater significance. This may reveal inaccurate order pricing, rapid changes in market prices, or careless invoicing by suppliers.

(2) SUPPLIER APPRAISAL (AND VENDOR RATINGS). Other matters such as supplier and inter-departmental relationships are more difficult to report upon. Here the "exception principle" should be applied. Top management will not be interested in knowing that all suppliers were satisfactory. They will, however, wish to learn of any that were not satisfactory and why. In this case "rejects" (5(b) below) may have a bearing also.

(3) EXCEPTIONAL ITEMS OF PARTICULAR INTEREST. Large contracts, price/delivery fluctuations, changes following an organisation and method team investigation, visits to trade fairs and attendance on national, regional or technical committees or conferences may be reported.

(4) STATISTICS: stores throughput, analyses of supplies, financial reports, recovery, recycling, salvage and disposal, past data, etc.

(5) STORES ACTIVITIES (where integrated within Supplies) should form a section of the report including the following aspects.

(a) "Service factor" achieved: comparison with previous periods.

(b) Stock-outs, shortages, rejects, causes, etc.

(c) Number of stock movements: comparison with previous periods, obsolete/slow movers, new items, etc.

(*d*) Health, safety and welfare: accident rate, sickness, etc.
(*e*) Performance of plant: need for new plant, etc.
(For more detailed stores reporting *see Storehouse.*)

SUPPLIES FORMS

Circulation of incoming literature

All companies, large and small, receive from suppliers increasing quantities of printed matter: official, technical, promotional, etc. Much of it is prepared by suppliers with apparently little knowledge of, or interest in, sections within the company which will have to deal with it. One result of these aberrations is the discovery of technical information filed away in an accounts department, or health and safety regulations in a drawing office!

In view of the involvement of the Supplies department with all other departments (*see* Fig. 6) there is much to commend its use as a "filter" and internal communicator with them, by seeing and circulating matter to the various functional departments.

A knowledge of "who does what" in the company will, of course, be essential if the documents are to reach appropriate staff. Where the volume is sufficient, a formal arrangement may be warranted. This can range from a simple circulation slip to a more complicated form incorporating spaces for staff to indicate what action, if any, they require by Supplies. Figure 8 is an example of a circulation slip.

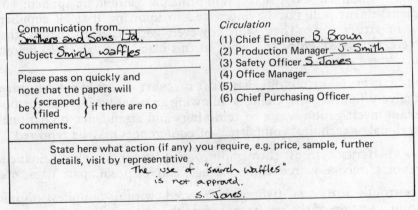

Fig. 8. Circulation form for incoming literature

In addition to the incoming matter it is becoming increasingly important for someone in an organisation to have available some key index to sources of information. If the task falls to Supplies the relevant section of the Bibliography[(37)-(47)] will be helpful as it lists a number of information sources.

Form design for Supplies

Properly balanced and easy-to-read forms are essential for Supplies work and require skill in design and layout. Unfortunately, the work of designing forms is presumed to be unprofitable—or even a "loss-centre" — and as such is neglected. This attitude overlooks the fact that delays and mistakes due to badly designed forms can render other operations unprofitable!" "Flow" and "movement" are essential factors in production, productivity and profitability, and the supplies these entail. Communications of all kinds, particularly forms used for supply, must be carefully designed with these in view, and should model the flow of supplies which they initiate or control.

AXIOM: Faulty forms frustrate flow and plunder profit.

Forms proliferate and tend to become larger and more complicated unless discipline is applied. Staff become accustomed to the "personality" of forms and it is better to expand the use of a particular form than to introduce a new one for every variation which occurs. Any new form introduced should be integrated with any other documents or forms with which it is associated.

Efforts must be made to facilitate completion of forms and above all to make them clearly identifiable and understood by those who use them. It is important to consider what the user will look for first (or should be reminded of) and to give this prominence and so proceed logically through the text. (*See* Fig. 58, for example.)

The cost of placing an order is a major factor in the total costs of acquisition, and the cost of the order set itself along with its preparation is substantial part of this. It is clear that there are savings to be made. However, the comments below are equally relevant to other Supplies forms.

Unlike sales literature, which may need embellishments to impress the customer, the purchase order should be looked upon as a "utility communication". The company's image will be best served by a form which is easy to follow, handle and file. It should not be smothered with conditions in small print of which 90 per cent do not apply and 10 per cent would not be accepted by the supplier.

Two sizes of form should suffice for most situations: A4 for standard order sets and A5 for local-purchase or small-value orders. (BS 1808.)

Supplies manuals or "handbooks"

A Supplies manual can usefully replace the widely dispersed memoranda, angry letters of complaint, etc., which have marked the various crises to which all Supplies departments are subject.[48] However, there may also be disadvantages in a manual (*see* Table 3).

TABLE 3. SUPPLIES MANUALS: ARGUMENTS FOR AND AGAINST

In favour of a manual	*Against a manual*
(a) All will know policy.	(a) Policies change.
(b) Procedures are clarified.	(b) Procedures change.
(c) Consultation on trivial/routine matters is reduced.	(c) May lead to "over-initiative".
(d) Temporary and new staff are guided.	(d) Temporary staff may not have time to read the manual.
(e) Economic and efficient methods are codified.	(e) Codification may inhibit more economic methods being tried.
(f) Disciplines are more easily applied.	(f) Disciplines may destroy initiatives.
(g) Staff working to a system have more time for creative thought and therefore more "job satisfaction".	(g) Working to a system may destroy "job satisfaction".
(h) Preparation may reveal system defects or suggest improvements.	(h) May perpetuate or introduce new defects!

If it is decided to go ahead and produce a manual, the following guide-lines should be helpful.

(a) Top management should sponsor and provide an "introduction".

(b) Divide into sections, e.g. purchasing, stock control, storage, handling, etc.

(c) Build up slowly: avoid initial flood of data sheets.

(d) Layout of pages should be consistent (*see* Fig. 18, for example).

(e) Be selective of subjects: issue first those where guidance is most needed.

(f) Circulate for comments before issuing: staff who participate in preparation of the manual will follow its guidance when issued.

(g) Text must be accurate, simple, clear and concise.

(h) Indicate circulation: it is useful for all to know who has had copies.

(i) For economy restrict circulation to those who need it (*see* note (j)).

SUPPLIES CIRCULAR

NOTES:

1. In case of query please quote Issue No.
Contact the person who signed this circular.
2. All information given is confidential and must
not be divulged outside the Company.
3. The sections are laid out so that they may be
cut and attached into the loose data sheets of
the Supplies Manual, in the appropriate sections.
4. Unless stated to be otherwise dates are with
effect from (wef) the date of this circular.

Issue No.: 145
Sheet No.: 1 of 4
Issue date: 14/10/19-3
Circulation this issue:
1. All stores
2. Production
3. Engineers
4. Accounts
5. Transport/Handling
6. Safety Officer
7.
8.
9.

5. Sections:
   A: Forward supply arrangements (FSAs) and contracts.
   B: Administrative and supply routine matters.
   C: Catalogues, price lists, information sheets.
   D: Surplus items, etc. available for transfer.
   E: Miscellaneous and interdepartmental notes.

145	A	FSA/1111, Smithsons Ltd.: Protective clothing (attached).
145	A	FSA/504, Catson Ltd.: cancelled by 1111 above.
145	A	FSA/313, Binge Ltd.: cancel items b, c, and f.
145	A	FSA/444, Focus Films Ltd.: deliveries now 10 weeks from order.
145	A	Contract C3001, Gunge Consolidated Ltd.: (attached. Please send requisitions.)

145	B	Completed LPO stubs to HQ by 3rd of the month please.
145	B	Specification 3111 replaced by 5002 (attached).
145	B	Please return 5002 to the Purchasing Analyst at HQ.
145	B	(wef) 21/10/19-3 all progress queries to Ms. Quick who takes over from Mr. Urge who retires on that date.

145	C	Tinpot Ltd.: cable fittings, list attached.
145	C	Soaps Ltd.: detergents copy available from HQ on request.
145	C	Popplethwaite Ltd., adhesives: write direct if list required.

| 145 | D | 5,000 goblets 0.5 litre capacity ex Wigton depot. |

145	E	The Assistant Purchasing Officer will next tour stores for inspection and to receive queries w/c 28/10/19-3.
145	E	The Safety Officer asks for the prompt return of all test certificates for lifting tackle which are now due.
145	E	Cav would like to remind all who receive the circular to let him know if they no longer require it in future or if they know of another staff member who should be on the circulation list. In addition, let us know if you have suggestions regarding this circular.

Signed: *Cav Emptor*   Extension: 390   Date: *13/10/19-3*

Fig. 9. Layout and contents of Supplies circular for multi-branch enterprise (*j*) It usually pays to over- rather than under-circulate.

(*k*) No firm is too small to benefit from a manual: especially if growing.

(*l*) Indicate whether the contents are: mandatory, a code of practice, guide-lines, or for information.

(*m*) Indicate clearly the date from which it is effective.

(*n*) State to whom queries should be sent.

(*o*) A separate section on policies (available on restricted circulation) may include:

(*i*) multiple *v.* single sourcing;

(*ii*) policy with small suppliers;

(*iii*) financial policy and technical policy;

(*iv*) free issue materials—policy and procedures;

(*v*) subcontracting and/or "make or buy".

Supplies circulars

Large firms with dispersed plants and varying degrees of decentralisation of Supplies should consider the use of regular circulars as a means of Supplies communication. Figure 9 shows the layout for a supplies circular with examples of some of the many points which may be covered. An important practical point is the indication of the issue number at each entry since these can be cut and pasted into the Supplies manual in many instances.

LOCATION AND LAYOUT OF SUPPLIES DEPARTMENTS

In the sequence of the internal supplies cycle accommodation may be needed for:

(*a*) stock records and control;

(*b*) purchasing office;

(*c*) goods receiving office;

(*d*) stores office;

(*e*) despatch office;

(*f*) interview room;

(*g*) catalogue and record room;

(*h*) typing office.

Offices (*c*), (*d*) and (*e*) (together with any other functional offices such as transport) will usually be best situated near the work-centre, e.g. goods inwards bay, stores, despatch bay, garage. The usual considerations of working space under the Offices, Shops and Railway Premises Act 1963 apply. A further factor to consider is that where offices are the supervisory centre for operations, they should, wherever practicable, be situated to give a clear vision of the functions being performed.

Stock control and stores records may be kept in a stores office or in the stores when the firm is small. When the firm grows the stores office is usually removed to the main administrative block. It then develops within or alongside the purchasing department whose activities depend upon its records. At a later stage the stock control office becomes a decentralised activity within Supplies. Its close relationship to purchasing normally compels it to remain near to that department.

Location of Supplies offices

The selection of the locations of the two main sections of the Supplies offices—stock control and purchasing—is now considered.

In a small to medium-sized plant the administrative offices for Supplies can be placed in the main office block without too great loss of contacts and liaison with production departments.

In manufacturing plants with a total establishment of 750 and above the decision is more difficult. If (as usually) Supplies are within the complex of administrative offices some sacrifice must be made of the close contact with production. On the other hand, it will usually be found that intimate contact with technical, sales and management staffs becomes more important in very large undertakings.

Where the undertaking comprises a number of manufacturing or trading units, satellite offices may be set up at the plants with the main offices at the headquarters of the group. Policy, guidance, direction, and main contracts then flow from the main office. There are risks of duplication of records, loss of local initiative and other factors to be considered in this case.

Layout of offices

Figure 10 shows how an "appraisal procedure" can be used to determine an office layout, in this case for a Supplies office in a general manufacturing firm. The appraisal procedure relies upon "weightings" "marks" and "scores" and has many applications for Supplies tasks such as layouts for stores, transport depots, production lines; comparisons of offers; value analysis; and value engineering.

In many cases weightings must be more or less subjective, as in the example of Supplies office layout. Here, the weightings have been agreed for the various desiderata, and instead of percentages, values from zero to ten have been adopted. Such a range is usually adequate for most operations. Scoring, as its name implies, indicates the success or otherwise by which a feature meets the requirements demanded. Simple scores as in Table 4 below are usually adequate. There can be instances where a more definite bias against accept-

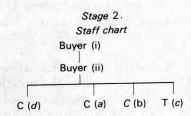

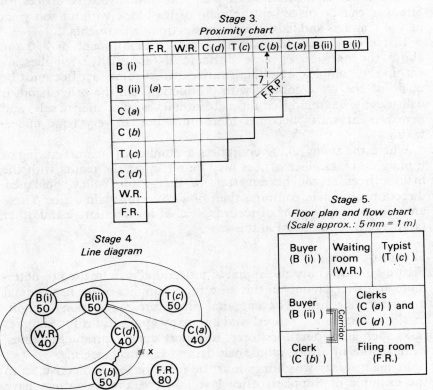

Stage 1.
Activity schedule

Person	Activities
Buyer (i)	Buying, interviews,
Buyer (ii)	supervision
Clerk (a)	Prepare orders, check invoices
Clerk (b)	Catalogues, records, progress
Typist (c)	Typing
Clerk (d)	Stock records

Stage 2.
Staff chart

Buyer (i)

Buyer (ii)

C (d) C (a) C (b) T (c)

Stage 3.
Proximity chart

Stage 4
Line diagram

Stage 5.
Floor plan and flow chart
(Scale approx.: 5 mm = 1 m)

Buyer (B (i))	Waiting room (W.R.)	Typist (T (c))
Buyer (B (ii))	Corridor	Clerks (C (a)) and (C (d))
Clerk (C (b))		Filing room (F.R.)

Fig. 10. Layout procedure applied to a Supplies office
(1) At Stage 3 read from left-hand column to intersection of the appropriate related vertical column, e.g. from B *(ii)* follow dotted line to C(b) (dotted line shown for example only). (2) At Stage 5 the work areas are delineated whether the office is open-plan or partitioned.

ing certain results is needed. This can be done by setting a further control so that if certain features score zero the whole scheme shall be rejected. Alternatively, this can be achieved by allocating heavy negative marking in respect of highly undesirable or unacceptable results. (*See* example at Stage 3 below.)

The task as set out below is divided into six stages, of which five are shown in Fig. 10.

APPRAISAL METHOD:

Stage 1: prepare an activity schedule. This lists the tasks, duties and activities of each member of the team.

Stage 2: layout a staff chart. This should indicate the responsibilities and relationships of the members of the team in line and staff formation.

Stage 3: complete a proximity chart. In the example each functional member of the team who requires accommodation is shown along two sides of a triangle together with any rooms which are not permanently occupied, such as filing rooms, interview or waiting rooms, cloakrooms and so on, which must be taken into account. The sequence is not vital, but it is best to work downwards in seniority or primary activity, and from right to left along the top of the chart. Each square so formed is then divided into triangles by means of a diagonal line. Above each diagonal line is inserted the degree of importance (i.e. "weight") of proximity (or the need to avoid it), according to the following figures.

Weight	Desiderata
10	Essential
7	Important
4	Desirable, but not important
2	Ordinary normal (office) requirements—not important
0	Of no importance at all
− 1	Undesirable—to be avoided if at all possible
−10	Loading of data to ensure rejection where totally unacceptable

NOTE:

Intermediate values have been assigned on the appraisal form in Table 4 below.

The lower triangle beneath the diagonal line is used to show the factors used in making the assessment of the relative importance of proximity. The factors to be considered may include the following.

P = personal contact required
R = reference to files, etc., required
V = very frequent reference/contact, etc.
F = frequent reference/contact, etc.

S = occasional reference/contact, etc.

N = considerations of noise, interruption, etc.

The reasons can be changed or expanded to suit the case. In the layout of a stockyard, for example, proximity might be undesirable because of the risk of fire or other hazard.

The completed square in Fig. 10, Stage 3, can therefore be explained as follows. Buyers may frequently require the services of the clerk (Cb) who deals with catalogues, records and progressing. Proximity of the buyer to this clerk is therefore "important" (=7) and the reasons for this are "frequent" (=F), "reference to files" (=R) and "personal contact required" (=P).

Stage 4: prepare line diagram. The relative positions are not necessarily the final ones. Several attempts may be needed before a clear picture is obtained. The final result resembles "flow" in an electrical circuit—to which, of course, it is analoguous. The small cross-lines at (*x*) on the diagram indicate the importance of proximity and should agree with those on Stage 3. A wavy line indicates an unwanted relationship.

The encircled numerals (e.g. 40) indicate the floor space which is needed, which must comply with statutory requirements while the building layout must satisfy local planning, building regulations, fire, health and safety and other statutory obligations.

Stage 5: floor plan and flow chart. This is now prepared in the light of the preceding stages. Between the various work-centres the same number of lines are drawn as there are cross-line at (*x*) on the diagram at Stage 4. These will show in the manner of a traffic density chart the volume of movement of personnel or paperwork (or, in the case of a storehouse or stockyard, of goods, transport vehicles, or handling equipment, etc.).

Stage 6: appraisal. Before finally putting work in hand an appraisal should be made. (This is similar to the method of analysing offers discussed in Chapter 14.) A form is drawn up in columns as in Table 4. Under column (1) are shown some major factors and considerations of the design and layout of the scheme. There is, of course, no limit to the number which can be added. They must be determined for the process or job concerned. Under column (2) are entered the weightings assigned to each factor in column (1). These weightings must be the result of agreement of all parties concerned as to the relative importance of each factor. (Obviously no factor will be included that is not worthy of any consideration. The lowest weighting in the example is "reception of visitors" = 3.) The weightings are multiplied by marks (*m*) which indicate the estimated success (or otherwise) for each factor as follows:

Marks   *Degree of success*
4   = Completely successful; requirements fully met
3   = An acceptable standard; equal or above average
2   = Average acceptability; reasonably acceptable
1   = Only just acceptable; improvement should be sought if possible
0   = Quite unacceptable (*see also* previous comment on weighting of data to ensure rejection)

Weights multiplied by marks are then entered as scores (s) for each scheme. The results of each score are added at the foot of each column and the total appraisal values are then compared (s = w x m).

It will be seen that scheme "A" shows a higher appraisal value than schemes "B" and "C", although the costs of installation were high and the use of space was poor and movement of equipment was difficult, with two points each.

Centralisation and decentralisation

The economies and other benefits of centralisation are worth consideration. Centralisation and decentralisation should not be studied as competing or conflicting methods. It is the task of management to examine the options objectively and select the one appropriate to the circumstances. (*See* Checklist 3.)

TABLE 4. APPRAISAL FORM APPLIED TO AN OFFICE LAYOUT

Factors and considerations	Weight	Scheme "A"	Scheme "B"	Scheme "C"
(1)	(2)	(3)	(4)	(5)
	(w)	(m) (s)	(m) (s)	(m) (s)
(a) Flexibility of layout	8 X	3 = 24	2 = 16	2 = 16
(b) Work flow and communications	10 X	3 = 30	1 = 10	2 = 20
(c) Interruption/noise	8 X	3 = 24	4 = 32	1 = 8
(d) Costs of installation	7 X	2 = 14	3 = 21	4 = 28
(e) Use of space	5 X	2 = 10	2 = 10	3 = 15
(f) Use of natural light	5 X	3 = 15	3 = 15	4 = 20
(g) Ease of movement of equipment	4 X	2 = 8	1 = 4	1 = 4
(b) Reception of visitors	3 X	4 = 12	2 = 6	2 = 6
Total appraisal values		137	114	117

Figure 11 illustrates the successive stages in the centralisation of a large-scale multi-unit organisation. It is, however, equally applicable to a very large, single unit (as *Storehouse*, Fig. 15). The branches "A", "B" and "C" may be taken to represent main functional

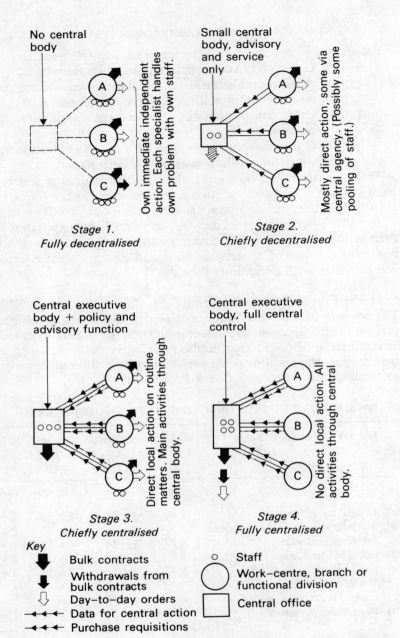

Fig. 11. Stages in development of centralisation of an undertaking
(1) The central body may not grow as rapidly as the branches diminish. (2)
Annual contracts may commence at Stage 2. It is almost certain that annual
contracts will be introduced at Stage 3. (3) An intermediate stage may occur in
which the centre or branch with the greatest usage for a certain material or
equipment acts as the main concentration and ordering point.

divisions, the production work-centres within the plant or stores depots, etc.

The process of decentralisation or centralisation may proceed in either direction. In successful mergers there is often a noticeable tendency to centralise fully at the start and subsequently to decentralise and delegate, often greatly to the profitability of the merger.

There are, of course, many variants of the four examples shown in Fig. 11. The most interesting from the Supplies point of view is where each branch acts as a "concentration point" and makes contracts for the materials of which it is the chief user. It may also act as the central or "concentration storehouse" for that commodity which it supplies to other branches. (*See Storehouse,* concentration stores.)

Service from a centralised Supplies office

In concluding this section an important principle must be established which applies to all centralised agencies, but particularly to Supplies. Demands for goods, materials and services arrive at a central Supplies office from all quarters of the company. Everyone tends to look upon his own needs as being the most vital of any and therefore demands—and expects—priority to be given to them. At this point tact and patience are needed by all Supplies staff to avoid even the hint of favouritism or denigration of any function in comparison with others. The services of Supplies must be seen to be equally available to all. This alone is a cogent reason why Supplies should be under the direct control of top management to ensure an impartial service to all without domination by any functional department such as production.

CHAPTER 4

Staffing and Organisation of
Supplies Operations

INTRODUCTION: NEED FOR A SUPPLIES ORGANISATION

Table 5 shows the general characteristics of the industries listed in the Standard Industrial Classification Orders II-XXI of product groups. The detailed *Censuses of Production* provide valuable information on supplies purchased in relation to sales, and on sales output per employee in firms of different sizes in the same product group. This has implications for Supplies whether one is buying from or buying for such industrial product groups.

Total purchases as a percentage of total sales revenue (column (4) of the table) are useful yardsticks to measure the activity and strength of Supplies activities. However, a warning is needed. Some industries use little, if any, raw materials in the accepted sense of the term. Column (5) has therefore been extracted from the totals in column (4) and gives in nearly all cases some measure of the rate of development in the industry. It includes, for example, new plant and machinery, but in the case of heavy extractive industries it also includes major maintenance supplies.

Column (6) has been included to show the great variation in non-operational staff needed to support different industries. As may be expected, the proportion is highest in firms of high technology, and also in service industries with widely spread administrative territories such as supply and transport networks, etc.

In Fig. 12, curve "B" is based upon a report by the former Purchasing Officers Association (now the Institute of Purchasing and Supply) and subsequent research by the author. Evaluation of the curve should be read from the right-hand scale of the graph, and the values show the probable number of Supplies staff required as a percentage of total establishment for all industries (Orders II-XXI). Unfortunately, data are not available for all individual products, but such as there are show some correlation between the degree of technology of an industry and its Supplies structure. Despite the imprecision resulting from lack of data it is clear that the percentage of staff engaged on Supplies tasks rises to a peak at 100–199 total establishment, afterwards tailing off to about 1 per cent in very large companies. The reason for this is explained later.

TABLE 5: SALES, PURCHASES AND STAFF FOR INDUSTRIAL CLASSIFICATIONS II-XXI

(1) Industrial classification number	(2) Description of industry of product group	(3) Sales in year per employee £	(4) Purchases as % of sales in year	(5) New work as % of total purchases	(6) Staff as % of total employed
II	Mines and quarries	8,674	38	37	11
III-XIX	All manufacturing	14,248	68	6	28
III	Food, drink, tobacco	24,336	69	4	20
IV	Coal and petrol (distr.)	18, 920	97	1	29
V	Chemicals	25,080	75	9	40
VI	Metals, manufacture of	18,038	82	8	25
VII	Mechanical engineering	10,410	60	7	33
VIII	Instruments	7,938	55	15	39
XI	Electrical manufacture	11,200	63	5	35
367	Electronics	9,900	59	5	51
X	Marine	7,680	59	12	23
XI	Vehicles (all types)	12,182	69	5	30
XII	Metal goods (misc.)	11,200	62	5	25
XIII	Textiles	16,836	65	5	19
XIV	Leather goods	11,767	76	3	17
XV	Clothing	5,772	58	3	15
XVI	Bricks, pottery, cement	12,353	52	11	25
XVII	Timber and furniture	8,106	76	5	23
XVIII	Paper and printing	12,209	53	7	34
496	Plastics	10,973	64	8	23
XIX	Other manufacturing industries	10,181	62	7	25
XX	Construction	11,115	31	12	22
XXI	Gas, water, electricity	22,105	60	32	48

Source: Census 1976 (PA1000)

NOTES: (1) Col. 5 includes buildings, plant, machinery and vehicles. (2) Col. 6 represents non-operational (i.e. office) staff.

Random Supplies organisations

The degree of centralisation of Supplies into a single function can vary greatly. Some large companies have no Supplies staff, each functional division being left to buy and carry the stock it requires independently of the rest. Such "random" organisation is, mercifully, rare! Where it is in operation it is almost impossible to ascertain the total man-hours spent on Supplies work or the efficiency

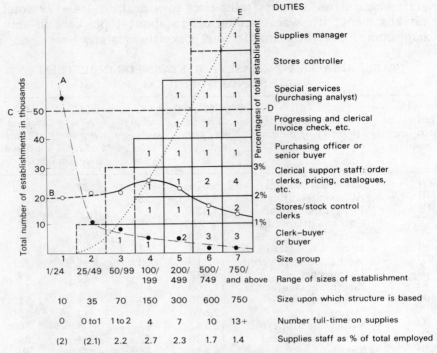

Fig. 12. Supplies organisation for different sizes of industry

Curve A = total number of establishments in each size group. Curve B = Supplies staff as a percentage of total establishment. Line C–D = limit above which a number of specialised services may emerge. Curve E = probable executive content of supplies management function. Broken squares at size groups 2, 3 and 6 indicate additional staff which may be needed. For example even a firm with as few as forty employees may appoint a clerk-buyer.

(or otherwise) of the system, and there may arise the following adverse results.

(a) Suppliers can charge different prices to different departments.

(b) Suppliers may thus gain fortuitous profits.

(c) Stocks may be duplicated in different departments.

(d) Different standards may apply in different departments.

(e) "Variety reduction" is unlikely.

(f) Stocks may be inflated by salesmen hinting at shortages, price increases, etc.

(g) Stocks may be inflated through lack of expertise in stock control.

(h) Specifications may reflect the whim or prejudice of staff.

(i) Errors and irregularities are easier to conceal than in a Supplies department.

(*j*) Departments may vie with one another to increase or over-spend budgets.

(*k*) Negotiators may lack purchasing expertise and commercial knowledge.

AXIOM: Weak supplies organisations profit suppliers.

Development of Supplies organisation

While 100 per cent of firms have personnel problems and supplies problems, only very few have a personnel officer or a supplies manager. Someone must, however, go through the motions (*see* Fig. 6).

In Fig. 12, curve "E" indicates the probable executive content of the supplies management function and its increase with the size of the company—and thus with expenditure upon supplies. This is only a notional indicator, but a Supplies unit should "grow up" into the management structure.

In small industrial units low purchasing power and tight budgets make economical and competitive buying extremely difficult. The setting up of a full Supplies organisation would be too costly to contemplate. Table 5 shows a high ratio of clerical to operational staff in most industries in the UK. From these data it might be supposed that there should be scope for large and thriving Supplies departments in most firms, or at least for a "clerk-buyer" in quite small ones. This is not so because of the extremely large number of administrative tasks that have to be covered in most manufacturing companies, even when quite small (*see,* for example, Fig. 6).

No firm rules can be given for the size of company at which the setting up of a Supplies department will be warranted. However, the short feasibility study which follows may provide a useful guideline and give some hints to the managers of the 60,000 companies with under 100 employees without any formal Supplies organisation.

NOTE:

A report[49] by the British Institute of Management and Institute of Purchasing and Supply, indicated that in 75 per cent of firms investigated, purchasing was a separate function, subservient to no other department. In organisations of over 5,000 employees this figure was increased to over 90 per cent. Similarly, purchasing was found to be an independent function in 53 per cent of cases where turnover was between £1 and £5 million rising to 90 per cent where turnover exceeded £50 million. Complete centralisation of purchasing was reported in 49 per cent of all cases examined. The head of purchasing reported to the managing director or chief executive in 36 per cent of the large undertakings and to the board of directors in 5 per cent. Purchasing departments in 69 per cent of organisations claimed to have the technical expertise to query the validity of items purchased. Discussions with design and production took place in 80 per cent of firms and were conducted on a formal basis in 48 per cent.

Feasibility study for setting up a Supplies organisation in a small company

SECTION (1): general statistics of the firm.[50] The example is hypothetical but is calculated from data which are based on industrial classification order VII, mechanical engineering (*see* Table 5).

Total establishment = 70.
Sales per annum per employee = £10,410.
Total sales = £728,700.
Stockholding costs = 25 per cent of mean stock value.
Supplies = 60 per cent of total sales = £437,220.

Classification of supplies by "A.B.C." analysis (see Chapter 5).
Class "A", raw materials = 70 per cent of all supplies in five main groups = £306,054.
Class "B", secondary supplies = 20 per cent of all supplies in twenty subgroups = £87,444.
Class "C", miscellaneous supporting goods = 10 per cent of all supplies in seventy-five subgroups = £43,722.

(Each subgroup in classification "C" will, of course, include a much greater diversity of items than the subgroups in "B".)

Stock valuation mean at last balance sheet = £145,000.
Rate of stock-turn per annum by conventional notation:

$$\frac{\text{total throughput}}{\text{mean stock}} = \frac{£437,000}{£145,000}$$

giving approximately 3 stock-turns per annum which is about the national average for industry and is of course far too low! However, the accountancy calculation is in any case suspect because it is extremely unlikely that the mean stock will be constant except for a continuous process production plant. For an accurate figure, continuous assessment of data over twelve months, at least, would be essential.

SECTION (2): savings which may result from improved Supplies organisation, procedures, appointments, etc.

Cash savings: prices paid, improved ordering, transport, order size, etc.

	£
2.5 per cent on class "A" supplies (£306,054)	7,651
1.0 per cent on class "B" supplies (£87,444)	874
0.5 per cent on class "C" supplies (£43,722)	219
	8,744

Stock control and storage savings: closer control, better storage, etc.

Classification "A", reduction of 10 per cent on mean stockholding by closer control, more regular deliveries, production-matched quantities, etc.

Mean stock usage = 70 per cent of £145,000 = £101,500.
Stock reduction = 10 per cent of £101,500 = £10,150.
Stockholding costs saved = 25 per cent of £10,150. = £2,538.

Classification "B", reduction of 10 per cent of mean stockholding by the above methods (*see also* below).

Mean stock = 20 per cent of £145,000 = £29,000.
Stock reduction = 10 per cent of £29,000 = £2,900.
Stockholding costs saved = 25 per cent of £2,900 = £725.

Classification "C", reductions may be higher, say 20 per cent (*see* note below).

Mean stock = 10 per cent of £145,000 = £14,500.
Stock reduction = 20 per cent of £14,500 = £2,900.
Stockholding costs saved = 25 per cent of £2,900 = £725.

	£
Total savings on stockholding costs (£2,538 + £725 + £725)	3,988
Savings on purchase prices, etc.	8,744
Total saved per annum	12,732

NOTE:

Savings (particularly on classifications "B" and "C") should be expected from the setting up of even a small Supplies organisation (*see* below, group 3).

COSTS OF SETTING UP A SUPPLIES DEPARTMENT and staffing and running it must be considered and the break-even point re-assessed (*see* Fig. 51) in the light of the other savings which have been estimated. These costs include:

(*a*) salaries and wages;
(*b*) accommodation and furniture, buildings and plant;
(*c*) typing, filing, records (costs may be increased — or reduced!);

(d) equipment: cabinets, computer, VDU, telephones;

(e) consumables—stationery, computer software.

No allowances for these costs have been made in the feasibility study because at size group 3 (50/99 total establishment, *see* Fig. 12), with the possible exception of a clerk-buyer, a redeployment of duties will alone be involved.

Costs of Supplies vary so widely that it would be unwise to attach a definite figure. However, as a guide-line, the results of a report in *Procurement Weekly* (28th May 1981) estimated the average costs of such a department as 1.03 per cent of sales.

AXIOM: "The drop in potential in any organisation is proportional to the length of the circuit." (Dr. B. Muller Thym.)

(*Rider*) "Potential also drops in direct proportion to complexity of circuit." (With apologies to Mr Kirchhoff's Law.)

Expansion

As a firm grows, there arrive an almost infinite range of specialists and their supporting staff. The rate of change of need for all supporting staff tends to increase rapidly when a company reaches a total establishment of 100. At this size management must decide whether to continue to expand or stabilise production and sales at existing levels (*see also* below, size group 3).

It will be noted from curve "B" in Fig. 12 that as a firm grows, the increase in total supporting staff is accompanied by a reduction in Supplies staff expressed as a percentage of total establishment. The following factors account for this.

As the firm expands there will almost certainly be an increase in the number of customers' orders and therefore of works orders. Each works order calls for approximately the same additional production planning and control time. Additional production planning and other supporting staff can then be justified.

However, when examining Supplies staff requirements the situation is different. The increase in production output will not necessarily involve an increase in varieties of supply or in the number of purchase orders. The size rather than the number of purchase orders is likely to increase (unless of course orders are placed job by job). Considerable improvements in productivity by Supplies staff can be expected as the firm grows and production increases. In addition the size of routine purchase orders does not as a rule greatly affect man-hours spent in their preparation. The result is that Supplies staff should not need to increase as rapidly as production staff. (*See also Storehouse.*)

Expansion and integration

The complexity of the total Supplies field provides scope for differences of opinion as to the amount of integration essential to its various operations. Table 2 in Chapter 2 showed a range of activities of interest to all branches of Supplies. If Supplies operations are not integrated in the early formative years, but left to whoever is most interested in the goods concerned, a built-in resistance to integration then develops as the various functional sections grow stronger. These will often be found to pursue decentralised activities without regard to the rest of the organisation or to the evolution of a progressive pattern of change, nor do they become flexible enough to suit an expanding situation.

Unless powerful outside forces intervene, the final patterns of the Supplies organisation when a firm grows large bear the imprint of the original personalities who formed it. It then develops either as an integrated unit or with its various operations decentralised — according to the philosophy of the original founder.

Change

No worker in the Supplies field can expect a job without change unless he or his firm is moribund! Whether the firm expands or not, he must expect changes in the pattern of demand, delivery times, shortages and other "hazards". The introduction of new materials, tools and processes often results in new techniques, controls, suppliers and stores problems. All of these emphasise the need for management to decide at an early stage the pattern to be followed.

JOB SPECIFICATIONS AND STAFF STRUCTURES

Terms of reference

It is essential to give the staff clear terms of reference, and at the same time to ensure that these do not shackle initiative. The pattern of work may change, but once the terms of reference have been set out the volume of work, rather than its content, is likely to vary. When planning operations it must be remembered that final responsibility is not easily delegated. It must, in the last resort, lie with the management to whom the functional departments report. For example, raw materials in a process plant must be under controls which are closely tied to the production and sales policies dictated by top management, who must retain full ultimate responsibility. On the other hand, the responsibility for control of small items in classifications "B" and "C" can be almost entirely accepted by Supplies. Wherever responsibility has passed in this manner, authority must pass too, and both must be clearly set out in the terms of reference.

Foundations for successful Supplies operations

The skill of a purchasing officer and other Supplies staff will be of little avail if management have not provided them with the foundations for their tasks, together with clear job specifications and terms of reference. If management delegate the task of purchasing without having prepared other functional staff to accept the fact that authority to purchase has now moved from them to the new purchasing officer, problems are certain to arise. Below are listed some foundations for Supplies tasks and for setting up satisfactory relationships.

(a) Management should ensure all staff know the terms of reference of Supplies staff and particularly of the purchasing officer.

(b) Management support for Supplies staff must be evident to all, so as to ensure commercial integrity of staff and their impartial service to all (see Chapter 3, final paragraph).

(c) Whoever is in charge of Supplies should report to top management.

(d) Supplies staff have a duty to maximise their contribution to profitability through the supplies they research, obtain and manage (see Table 29).

(e) All must be alert to supplies needs of their company, availability and costs, new developments, and new suppliers.

(f) They should participate in standardisation, variety reduction, value engineering and value analysis without usurping technical functions of other staff.

(g) Staff should have the right and duty to query with users anything regarding supplies which may threaten profitability — and to use their "diagnostic skills" in doing so, with access to top management as final arbiter.

For example, in the event of a request to make an apparently "uneconomic" purchase, the buyer should be entitled to ask the requisitioner if he is fully satisfied with the cost-benefit of the choice he has made. In some firms the Board makes a random (or selective) check of invoices. Where this is done it may be appropriate to ask the requisitioner whether in the event of the purchasing officer being asked to appear before the Board to justify the purchase he would be prepared to accompany him. In short, the greatest strength of purchasing staff is in knowing where the divisions between technical and economic interests lie. (See item (m) below.)

(h) Staff should be capable of acting in close liaison with all other staff, particularly sales, engineers, draughtsmen and designers, (*see also* Chapter 12, visits to suppliers). The attitude of engineers, draughtsmen and designers to Supplies is sometimes rather sceptical or even hostile. The creative tasks of the former tend to isolate them from others — particularly commercial colleagues, who, they fear, may drown their creative instincts in the ice-cold waters of "cash-flow philosophy". (Relate to items (*f*), (*i*), (*k*), (*l*) and (*n*), also *see* "visits".)

(*i*) Staff should observe technical and commercial boundaries given in guide-lines in a Supplies manual. The Supplies manual should formalise and expand the points listed here, and clarify the "techno-commercial boundaries" of Supplies activities by a section on the following lines:

"Technical and commercial disciplines meet and overlap in the Supplies function. Staff in each discipline are expected to understand and respect the discipline of the other. The Company's training officer and training schemes will reflect this."

AXIOM: "Broaden outlook and change opinions." (Motto of a Polytechnic Business School.)

(*j*) The ultimate responsibility for signing purchase orders rests with the purchasing officer under direction from top management (*see also (k), (l)* and *(m)*).

(*k*) If the purchasing officer feels unable to sign an order which he believes to be not in the interests of the profitability of the company he has the right and duty to discuss it with the requisitioner.

(*l*) It must be understood that if the matter cannot be settled by this means it shall be referred to management for a final decision *without incurring* criticism or erosion of responsibility or authority of either party.

(*m*) In any case all staff should be informed that management reserve the right at any time to investigate any particular purchase and/or those over a certain value.

(*n*) Supplies staff should encourage and acknowledge helpful participation of other functional staff in Supply matters (*see* Chapter 12, Introduction).

(*p*) Supplies staff, particularly purchasing officers, should pay as much attention to relationships with their own company's staff as with suppliers.

A purchasing officer may have built up a first-class relationship with suppliers but this will not assist the harmony of the company if his relationships with his own colleagues are poor. It is to be hoped that the purchasing officer will have developed his skill as a negotiator to the point where he is able to handle "internal negotiations" as easily and expertly as those with suppliers.

TABLE 6. JOB SPECIFICATIONS OF SUPPORTING SUPPLIES STAFF

Post	Knowledge of:				Qualities and abilities							
	Prices	Commodities	Sources of supply	Processes and products	Confidential reliability	Neatness of work	Initiative/ foresight	Attention to detail	Sense of urgency	Accuracy	Tact	Orderley mind
Store-keepers	I	I	–/O	D	D	D	–	–	I	V	–	V
Stock-control clerk	–	I	D	D	D	I/V	D	I	I	V	–	–
Progress clerk	–	I	V	D	I	–	V	–	V	I	V	–
Record clerk	–	I	I	O	I	V	–	V	–	V	–	I
Catalogue filing clerks	–	V	V	O	I	–	–	I	–	–	–	I
Buyers	V	V	V	D	V	I	I	I	I	V	I	–
Invoice clerk	I	O	–	–	V	I	–	I	–	V	–	–
Order edit clerk	I	I	–	O/I	V	V	–	V	I	V	–	V
Order checker	–	–	–	–	I	–	–	V	I	V	–	D
Order typist	–	–	D	–	I	I	–	I	I	V	–	D

Key

V = Vital
I = Important
D = Desirable
O = Optional—useful but not essential
– = Unnecessary beyond normal clerical requirements

NOTE:
Many of the points made need review in the light of each particular firm. For example, a knowledge of computers is increasingly necessary for stock control, pricing and records.

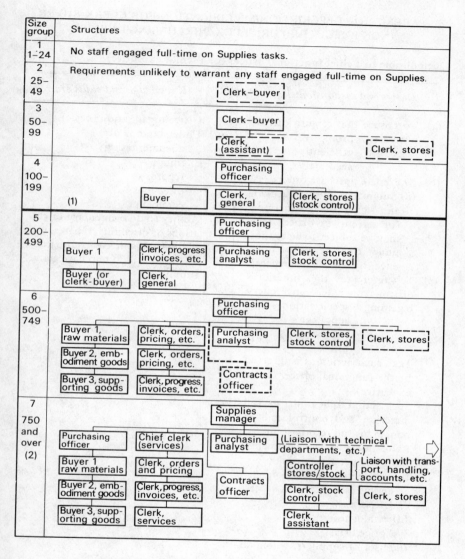

Fig. 13. Suggested staff structure for Supplies organisation
(1) The heavy line denotes the limit of "small firm" status as generally adopted by the Department of Industry's Small Firms Information Centres, the CBI, etc. (2) At 750 employees, the Supplies function should be fully developed.

TABLE 7. JOB DESCRIPTION/SPECIFICATION FOR CLERK-BUYER (NON-EXECUTIVE) OR CLERK/PURCHASING OFFICER

Responsible to a chief functional officer (or a senior executive)

Duties and responsibilities	Knowledge and skills etc.
(a) To ensure that requisitions are processed: promptly; efficiently; accurately. (b) (i) Prepare purchase orders. (ii) Submit order for checking and signature by functional (or executive) officer (this may be subject to delegation under clear terms of reference by the management). (c) To refer to the functional officer concerned any query regarding: specification; supplies; delivery; price. (d) Take such action as is directed by the functional officer (or executive). Such action to be under his full direction and control and to remain his full responsibility. (e) Look after the attachments, filing and proper housing of: (i) documents—requisitioning, enquiries, quotations, orders, GRNs, etc. (ii) catalogues; (iii) price lists; (iv) lists of suppliers, whom to contact, etc. (f) Provide "supplies" information to those authorised to require it. (g) Investigate supplies and help in standardisation and variety reduction.	(a) Office organisation (basic). (b) Understanding of: documentation; filing; records; price lists; catalogues. (c) Ability to do elementary calculations of discounts, rebates, etc. (d) Willing and able to acquire knowledge and skill in purchasing and supply.

AXIOM: *All* Supplies staff should maximise profitability.

Duties, qualities and qualifications

The *supplies manager* or *director* is essentially a leader, organiser, co-ordinator and administrator, and must have had sound management training. He should avoid any natural bias towards a particular aspect of Supplies, but should be versatile enough to switch his attention to points needing action, correction and research.

The *chief purchasing officer* needs a good administrative and management background. He must have technical ability appropriate to the industry without pretensions to technical knowledge. Above all, he must have a high standard of commercial morals and integrity. He must be known and be seen to be fair and honest in his dealings both outside and inside his company. Commercial ability and knowledge are essential. (*See* final paragraph of Chapter 3.)

TABLE 8. JOB DESCRIPTION FOR PURCHASING ANALYST

Responsible to supplies manager or chief purchasing officer.
Purpose: to maximise profitability of Supplies operations.

Duties and responsibilities	*Knowledge and skills*
(a) Prepare and carry out purchasing research.*	Good technical ability, skilled in numeracy.
(b) Monitor work of Supplies in the light of such research.	Possess tact and be able to relate Supplies to technical disciplines.
(c) Ensure the viability of supplies and facilitate the entry of new suppliers.	
(d) Prepare and maintain the stores commodity vocabulary and commodity catalogue.*	Particular responsibilities for cataloguing, etc., of plant spares where this is not done by maintenance staff.
(e) Be responsible for value analysis.*	
(f) Assist in value engineering.	
(g) Advise on standardisation.*	
(h) Maintain the catalogue library.*	
(i) Assist in liaison with engineering, research and development, drawing office and other technical departments.	Also within Supplies act as technical interface.
(j) Monitor specifications (*see* Checklist 13).	

*These items quoted from *A Guide to Industrial Purchasing.* (51)

For reasons which by now are clear, both the chief purchasing officer and the supplies manager should report to top management.

"The function of *Stores and 'Stock controller'* —principally because of the ever-increasing cost of materials and 'space'—must be recognised as a vital part of any organisation which holds significant stock levels. The job calls for a reasonably high level of understanding and ability, should carry support from top management, a measure of executive authority and must not be thought of merely as an experienced storekeeper." (BS 5729 Part 1 (O) abb.). (*See also*, summary of responsibilities in later section "Groups 6 to 9".)

Other qualities and qualification needs of these officials are clear from the text (*see* below, groups 6 to 9 in particular).

Table 6 gives an indication of the requirements for remaining staff.

Staffing structures for Supplies

Figure 13 shows some suggested Supplies structures for different sizes of organisation. At size group 3 is shown the post of "clerk-buyer" for a small company, and Table 7 sets out a suitable job description and specification for this post. Special attention is called to size group 5 based upon the booklet *A Guide to Industrial Purchasing*[51] prepared by the United Nations Development Organisation, and which includes the post of "purchasing analyst" the duties for which are set out in Table 8.

At size groups 6 and 7 a contracts officer (or contracts manager) may be needed under the following conditions:

(*a*) large number of complex high value contracts;

(*b*) many forward supply orders and forward supply arrangements;

(*c*) a lack of adequate legal back-up staff.

The tasks of the contracts officer are to administer contract and subcontract operations, and to scrutinise, administer and advise on contracts including terms and conditions and practical details of administration, etc.

For more detailed specifications for Supplies posts the attention of the reader is directed to the publication, *Training for Purchasing and Supply*.[52] The job descriptions in this were arrived at in collaboration with the Institute of Purchasing and Supply.

SUPPLIES DEPARTMENTS IN VARIOUS SIZES
OF INDUSTRY

General notes

In the following analysis the approach is a general one and the over-riding consideration must always be the *kind* of industry being studied. So far as possible guiding principles have been given and it is hoped these will be adequate for the reader to apply to his own situation and to that of his suppliers.

Group 1

Total establishment: 1 to 24 employees; modal size: approx. 10 ; number of firms in this group: 54,000. (This statistic does not take account of the fact that a number may belong to a group of companies. Where this is the case there are advantages in delegation by group managements of the Supplies function to local levels where initiatives and skills of local staff and suppliers can be made use of.)

There would be no question of setting up a Supplies department in a firm of this size. On the other hand, such small firms meet (on a reduced scale) most of the problems associated with the larger units. They also have to cope with other problems some of which are either not encountered, or are less acute, in larger firms. The need for integrated supply policy, at least, is vital.

Because of its small size the profit margins are very slender and the throughput of materials is low. On a 68 per cent supplies content per unit sold and £14,248 sales per employee per annum, supplies amount to £96,886 per annum for a firm of 10 employees. Unless the range of materials is very narrow and specialised, the normal "A.B.C." stores analysis will divide this sum into very small unit values with the following adverse results.

(*a*) Suppliers are not likely to compete for orders.

(*b*) Prices are likely to be high because quantities are small, and every discount must be fought for.

(*c*) In times of shortage the small firm may find itself starved of materials by suppliers who are looking after their larger customers.

(*d*) In stores the volume of stocks will be low and the margins upon which they operate slender.

(*e*) The risk of stock-out will be much greater than in the larger unit.

Supplies management is of particular importance in smaller firms and should have the close attention of one of the partners or a director. He should watch and control the flow of cash and materials and discern and direct the pattern and development of the supplies situation.

Problems of Small Firms, a CBI report, makes the following comments: "The small firm with a particular interest in research and development is one which has been founded by an entrepreneur in order to turn an invention into a profitable innovation. A small firm which is able to respond quickly to market changes is often better placed than a larger company to introduce and market successfully an innovation." However, this very success contains the seeds of its own destruction. The small firm as it expands may lose its drive and flexibility. This applies with special force to Supplies policies—purchasing, stock control, standardisation, storage and materials management in all its aspects.

Smaller companies should find it advantageous for whoever looks after Supplies to join either the Association of Supervisors of Purchasing and Supply *or* the Institute of Purchasing and Supply and to make use of their Technical Advisory Service (*see* Appendix I).

Group 2
Total establishment: 25 to 49 employees: modal size: 35; number of firms in this group: 10,500.

This group includes a sector of industry which acts as a feeder or subcontractor to larger industrial units.

The average supplies throughput for an industrial unit of modal size in this group will be over three times that of the previous group. Margins are still small, but the amount of business to be placed is such that additional advantages may be won through a prudent purchasing policy by an "embryo" Supplies section.

The main purchasing operation will no doubt continue to be carried on by a partner or director. However, he will find it increasingly difficult and unrewarding to cope with the classification "B" and "C" materials and may well consider delegating some of the more routine purchases to his stores staff or to the principal user of supplies.

Up to this size a storekeeper may be expected to do the physical work, documentation and stock control, the last under the close guidance of the manager. *All* firms should carefully select suitable men for the stores posts as the custodians of their "second most important asset—stocks" (views differ as to a company's most important asset—some consider it to be personnel).

An inefficient storekeeper may allow the stock to deteriorate in quality; fail to have the correct materials available; issue incorrect quantities—either too much resulting in wastage, or too little stopping production; issue incorrect materials; and/or allow workers to draw excess possibly for their private use. In any one of these cases heavy, unseen, and irrecoverable losses may take place. A good storekeeper, on the other hand, will avoid these errors and improve service level (BS 5191 (3.3)) and storage factor.

Group 3

Total establishment: 50-99 employees: modal size: 70: number of firms in this group: 9,000.

Over 80 per cent of manufacturing units remain in the first three size groups of under 100 total establishment, many without growth.

There are a number of reasons for this, the most important being the optimum size of a manufacturing unit for the commodity and demand. Many firms stablise after they have reached this point—the "hundred employee barrier". Further growth demands a disproportionate increase in the number of specialist services needed to support production and also possible expansion or diversification of the product. Small firms have difficulty in meeting additional costs of specialist services. Because of the factors discussed earlier in relation to supplies, the small firm may never reach the position where it can buy sufficiently cheaply to compete effectively with its bigger rivals. Finally, the smaller firm depends as a rule for its development on the leadership of the original management. In many cases lack of supporting middle management and specialist staff inhibits the original manager from making efforts to expand.

The increase in clerical work at group 3 affects not only purchasing but also stock control, intake, storing and issuing and invoice clearance. A corresponding increase occurs in clerical work in sales, production and accounts departments.

It can be expected that orders for the "A" materials will be handled by one of the partners or directors. The small value sections "B" and "C" may be handled as a clerical function, subject to close control and guidance from management. (If values of the various groups are more broadly spread a greater degree of guided delegation can be given.)

CLERK-BUYERS: many firms in this size of group appoint a clerk-buyer so that the placing of orders can be centralised even if negotiation is not. It is very unlikely that the functional staff members will be prepared at this stage to delegate the work of negotiation. The clerk-buyer may act merely as a "rubber stamp" purchasing agent (this latter title is used sometimes to indicate that the function is merely one of an agent without executive authority). Progress beyond this point depends upon the calibre of the man appointed and his knowledge and attitude towards the job. (*See* Table 7.)

Even the operation of "rubber stamping" should not be despised. Accuracy of communications is a first priority in the whole Supplies operation. Inaccuracy causes heavy unseen losses, often "unseen" where functional staff place their own orders (*see also* previous comments on "random" organisation).

Similar considerations apply in regard to the selection of a purchasing man as applied to the storekeeper at group 2—even if he is only at first responsible for clerical aspects of supply.

BENEFITS OF APPOINTING CLERK-BUYER: at this early stage in the company's development a "clerk-buyer" separately appointed or upgraded from the stores should be expected to contribute to the firm's profitability in various ways, especially in the following (*see also* above, feasibility study).

(*a*) Fewer channels of communication.

(*b*) Greater speed of communication.

(*c*) Improved accuracy of communication (particularly orders, etc.).

(*d*) Improvement of all documentation.

(*e*) Correct prices paid for supplies.

(*f*) Other staff released for their specialised duties.

(*g*) Better "company image" with suppliers.

(*h*) Focal point for enquiries.

(*i*) Reduced number of points where undetected errors can occur.

(*j*) Collection of data on supplies.

(*k*) Feedback to/from suppliers/users.

(*l*) Dynamism and diagnostic skill added to Supplies activities.

(*m*) Job enrichment and job satisfaction.

(*n*) Possible savings in stock aspects (particularly classifications "B" and "C") by:

(*i*) variety reduction;

(*ii*) visual stock control;

(*iii*) use of stockists thus eliminating stock;

(*iv*) fewer stock-outs;

(*v*) standardisation.

CATALOGUE LIBRARY: in addition to the placing of orders, it will be found at this stage of development that there is a growing need for catalogues and other information to be collected. This will tend to be done by the various functional people, thus involving considerable wasted effort, correspondence, and duplication of filing space. It is at this time while the firm is compact that a central catalogue library should be started. Duplication should thereafter only be allowed where the physical distances or usage demand.

Group 4
Total establishment: 100 to 199 employees; modal size: 150; num-

ber of firms in this group: 6,500.

Firms of this size usually have a higher productivity than smaller ones owing to the support of a range of specialists to serve the increased number of production operatives. The total of non-operational workers expressed as a percentage of the whole establishment is increased. This means that a higher production efficiency can and must be achieved to ensure continued profitability. One of the most obvious ways to achieve this is through improved supplies management.

Once they are through the "hundred employee barrier", firms in this group tend to grow and change rapidly — unless they become stabilised at the optimum size for the total demand for their product.

At the lower level of about 100 employees, functional and personal influences resisting change may be very strong. A purchasing officer appointed at this stage must be prepared to meet these problems and have the patience and tact to overcome them. His degree of success in this will determine to a large extent whether he is the right man for the job. Ability to develop good personal relations and effective internal negotiation contribute to his success.

It may be possible in this group for one man to cope if given some clerical assistance. Even ignoring Parkinson's law ("work tends to expand to fill the time allotted to its completion") there will be a rapid rise in Supplies activity. Other functional staff are likely to delegate more work to the Supplies staff and call upon them for information and action of many kinds. Soon it may be found necessary to sort out "who does what" even within a small Supplies office, with the result that further specialisation and delegation appear.

Group 5

Total establishment: 200 to 499 employees; modal size: 300; number of firms in this group: 5,000.

The structure of Supplies should by now be firmly established to suit the kind of industry and market. Negotiations for supplies must now be concentrated in a purchasing department and stock control dealt with separately in a stores and stock section.

The effectiveness of negotiations by the purchasing staff at this stage (as at all other stages) depends very much upon the support given by top management. There may still be a residue of the functional pressures mentioned earlier, which can hinder the work of Supplies in general and purchasing in particular.

In addition, the number of functional sections in this size range begins to approach that of the very largest firms. The number of contacts and thus the number of communication linkages will increase in proportion to the possible permutations of staff functions.

Increased committee activity is likely to involve Supplies staff both directly by attending and indirectly by the provision of information.

It will be noted in Fig. 13 that in size group 5 there are two buyers, each of whom can concentrate on sections of the classification curve. The senior man may look after classification "A" materials and his colleague the classifications "B" and "C". The senior buyer may be promoted as the firm grows to chief purchasing officer with wider duties. He may then either combine these with the purchase of classification "A" materials or a further appointment may be made to the buying staff for classifications "B" and "C". At this stage a purchasing analyst may be appointed.

Groups 6 to 9

Size group	6	7	8	9
Range of sizes in each group	500/749	750/999	1,000/1,999	2,000 and above
Modal size in each size group	600	850	1,400	2,500
Number of units in each size group	1,000	450	750	200

Up to 500 employees the organisational plan is fairly clear and could suit most firms engaged in the same sort of industry, but beyond the 500 mark and as a result of diversification of products and other factors, the pattern of organisation can vary considerably.

There may be considerable development in other functions of the firm. This often leads to erosion and even disintegration of the Supplies function. The remedy is to appoint a chief purchasing officer, or better a supplies manager.

When the firm reaches a total establishment of 600 it is likely to hold stocks the investment in which warrants the undivided attention of a stores and stock controller. He will be responsible not only for control of stock levels but also for the entire physical operation of the stores, including such matters as handling, safety in stores, security, stock audit, stores costs, coding, cataloguing and vocabulary. Until the firm is large enough to support such an appointment, the chief purchasing officer may perform this function in addition to his other duties. If he is successful he should be the obvious candidate for the post of supplies manager at the later stage of development.

When the total throughput of purchases approaches £1,000,000, the number of special services in which Supplies is involved increases rapidly (see Fig. 12). These include closer work with technical departments, purchasing research, value analysis, network analysis and planning, attendance at management meetings, and leadership in a number of activities associated with Supplies and its relationship with other functions, such as, for example, standardisation.

Participation in such work will depend upon knowledge and interest by Supplies staff in the undertaking, and acceptance of them by other functional staff.

By this stage the Supplies staff should be integrated into the total fabric of the undertaking, along with such functions as sales, production, planning, technical, administration and accounting.

The management appointment of a stores and stock controller may be made from the purchasing or the stores staff. It matters little provided that a proper balance of technical, administrative, accounting and commercial functions is maintained.

In very large firms the Supplies department may be split into specialist sections such as a catalogue library, standardisation, progress and planning, transport, and packaging and handling. Some of these, for example transport, may become independent divisions in liaison with Supplies.

DEPARTMENTALISATION

"Departmentalisation" of Supplies, as in other areas of administration, is inevitable in larger undertakings. Buying sections become specialised and these in turn attract services appropriate to their specialisms. Allocation of duties needs special care at this stage and the following possibilities should be considered.

(a) Allocate to product groups.

(b) Allocate to suppliers.

(c) Allocate to expenditures on "A.B.C." classification.

(d) Allocate on technological basis.

(e) Allocate to functional departments served.

(f) Make no allocation but share work-load evenly.

(g) Give each group a primary role with secondary relief role of another group or supplies, suppliers, expenditure, etc.

(h) Exchange roles, but not too frequently.

For most industries the third alternative will be found satisfactory. It usually results in senior staff dealing with raw materials, the next section dealing with embodiment goods, etc., and the last section handling supporting goods and services.

Departmentalisation can make it difficult to balance the workload, staff may compare roles and "empire building" can evolve. Even worse, sections may develop "departmentalism" and freeze into isolated units. If this is allowed to occur it will be greatly to the detriment of Supplies services and defeat all attempts to integrate the sections. Some solutions are suggested in (g) and (h) above. These broaden outlooks and experience, share the work-load and enable the relief group to fill in for holdiays, etc. They also inhibit suppliers from "cultivating" particular sections or trying to pursue different policies to their own advantage. It is, however, important to avoid action which could reduce job satisfaction and interest. Both are closely linked with stability of the job. If roles are continually being changed there is no incentive to study any one in depth. More important, the various user departments may lose their direct line of contact with the providers of their supplies.

It may be expected that staff who do not wish to switch jobs or cover for other duties (or receive training) are often those most in need of these disciplines. Ultimately, only those who are "sleepers" will fail to gain job satisfaction from the broadening processes and their fate is probably already sealed!

DELEGATION AND AUTHORITY

Delegation and authority have been mentioned frequently in this chapter and further study of these important aspects of management skill may be helpful.

Delegation takes place when authority is passed to a subordinate person or group from a senior level. Centralisation and decentralisation (see Fig. 11) explain the extent to which authority is concentrated at the centre or diffused throughout an organisation. Modern management schools have encouraged the practice of delegation with the hope of gaining the following results:

(a) giving job satisfaction;

(b) creating commitment to the organisation;

(c) increasing flexibility in performance;

(d) developing initiative, enterprise and innovation;

(e) speeding decisions (but too diffuse delegation can cause conflicting decisions and hence cause delay);

(f) developing closer involvement in implementation of decisions.

When management appoint staff to manage supplies they delegate some of their authority. However, this may be contrary to modern theories of delegation because the Supplies functions will now be centralised whereas previously the task may have been performed by various persons in the organisation as needs arose. It is this very factor which can make it difficult (in the early stages at least) to build up a good relationship and liaison with the user departments served by a Supplies section.

In one example a purchasing officer newly appointed by his

managing director from another post was confronted by an angry production manager who had done the buying. The latter said, "We will get on all right if you leave *my* suppliers alone and don't upset them." The fledgling purchasing officer retorted, "They are *our* suppliers and I will hope to build a good relationship with you and *them* and to give you a good service." When a few years later the same purchasing officer announced he was leaving the firm the first person to visit his office to protest at his going was the same production manager.

The lesson to learn from this is that while management may delegate, for example, the purchasing function, they may at the same time create problems of "centralisation"—or rather, "centralism". The appointed person must try to avoid this, or still worse the "departmentalism" mentioned earlier. With delegation must go authority, i.e. the right to use and exercise power. Authority and power are not, however, synonymous; it is possible—but ineffective —to have one without the other. Both should be clearly defined by management when setting out the terms of reference for the person appointed, particularly in purchasing.

There are further traps for the unwary, especially in Supplies. The inability of the person appointed further to delegate activities may lead to authoritarianism. This tends to generate aspirations for heightened status, arrogance, maintenance of social distance from other workers and colleagues, reduction in feedback, loss of initiative by subordinates, lack of involvement by subordinates in their tasks, loss of job satisfaction and generally poor performance.

AXIOM: Delegate or die!

CHAPTER 5

What Supplies are Needed

INTRODUCTION

What supplies are needed? In what quantities? Where do the needs originate? How may the flow of supplies be efficiently maintained and controlled? It is upon the answers to these questions that much of supplies and materials management depends. The first question is the most important, but to some extent the others are related to it.

Every plant has characteristics which should be understood by those who purchase *from* them as well as those who purchase *for* them.

"A.B.C." CLASSIFICATION

Almost every kind of enterprise has a distinctive pattern of "A.B.C." supplies classification. This is largely governed by its activities and products and reflects its position in the economic supplies cycle.

The "A.B.C." classification is based upon Pareto analysis and is one of the most used of statistical tools for Supplies (*see* Fig. 14 and Table 9; the table is based upon an imaginary "shopping list" for an extractive industry — (*see* Fig. 4).

SUPPLIES REQUIREMENTS OF DIFFERENT INDUSTRIES

Before proceeding further it may be found helpful to study Fig. 15 which indicates the supply needs of the principal industrial product groups, both in volume/value and in kind.

The text on the following pages examines the supply requirements of different industries according to the analysis in Fig. 4, the total economic supplies cycle. The reader must, of course, produce his own "shopping lists" and Pareto curve for his company and that of his suppliers. (These can be abstracted from Census of Production tables.)

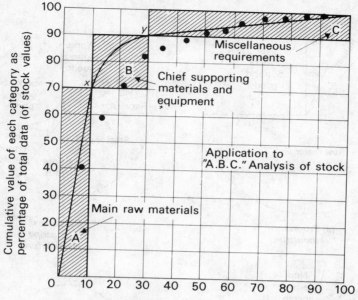

Fig. 14. "A.B.C." analysis: the Pareto curve (BS 5729 Part 3, Fig. 10.)
The heavy line and shaded boxes show the typical shape of the Pareto curve.
The heavy dots plot the cumulative values on Table 9 against cumulative
varieties for that industry: *x* and *y* indicate typical percentage "break" points
between classes "A", "B" and "C".

Extractive industries

(Fig. 4, Stage 1.) Classifications "A.B.C." are less pronounced at
this stage. For one thing there are no raw materials in the accepted
sense. The largest classification "A" comprises fuels in the case of
mines and quarries, and food, fertilizer and seeds in the case of agriculture. New and replacement plant is a further heavy class "A"
commitment in mines and quarries. It may comprise up to 25 per
cent of all purchases.

Classification "B" includes (in the mining industries) a number of
supporting goods and materials, such as rails, steel props, building
materials and steel sections.

Classification "C" includes tools and safety equipment, together
with miscellaneous needs. Many of these are peculiar to pit working
and surface operations such as sidings, graders and coal washeries.

Classifications "B" and "C" in most industries include certain
items known as "strategic spares".

In the case of extractive industries significant investments may be

83

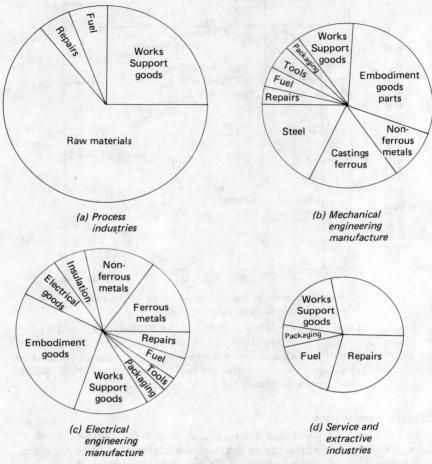

Fig. 15. Analysis of supplies needed in principal industrial product groups
Areas of circles are representative of the total expenditure in relation to sales for each group.

needed in classification "C" spread over a wide variety of spares from coal cutter-heads to electrical equipment.

Service industries
(Fig. 4, Stages 3 and 10.) These show a somewhat clearer definition of classifications "A.B.C.". In most cases fuels are in classification "A". For transport, and particularly the power supply industries, demands for new plant are considerable. These fall largely into classification "A", with the ancillaries falling into classification "B" because of their greater variety.

TABLE 9. SUPPLIES "SHOPPING LIST" FOR A MYTHICAL QUARRY

		Purchases during year			Data for "A.B.C." analysis		
	(1)	(2)	(3)	(4)	(5)	(6)	(7)
	"Shopping list"	Value per annum £000's	Cumulative values per annum £000's	Cumulative % of values per annum	Number of varieties	Cumulative total of all varieties	Cumulative % of all varieties
(a)	Transport and earth-moving equipment	40	40	40	1	1	7
(b)	Fuel and power	18	58	58	1	2	14
(c)	Replacements for plant and equipment	13	71	71	1	3	21
(d)	Plant and machinery (new)	10.8	81.8	82	1	4	29
(e)	Bitumen	4	85.8	86	1	5	36
(f)	Explosives	2.5	88.3	88	1	6	43
(g)	Tar and pitch	2.5	90.8	91	1	7	50
(h)	Vehicles (new)	2.5	93.3	93	1	8	57
(i)	Packing materials (sacks and bags)	2.3	95.6	96	1	9	64
(j)	Buildings (new extensions and repairs)	1.2	96.8	97	1	10	71
(k)	Minerals (for grinding and dressing)	1.0	97.8	98	1	11	78
(l)	Tools (picks, shovels, etc.)	1.0	98.8	99	1	12	86
(m)	Steel (section, etc.)	0.7	99.5	99.5	1	13	93
(n)	Timber (poling boards, props, etc.)	0.5	100	100	1	14	100

NOTES
(1) Figures based on Census of Production tables for extractive industries.
(2) Cumulative values and percentages rounded off to nearest whole number.

Strategic spares in classifications "B" and "C" include, for example, spare engines, gear boxes for transport, and transformers and control equipment for electricity distribution systems.

Service industries are frequently widely dispersed geographically. When using their services it is worth while to check their ability to deal with their own "on site" supply problems promptly. (*See* Table 32.)

Commercial enterprises
(Fig. 4, Stages 4, 6 and 8.) In these, the shape of the curve depends upon the degree of specialisation of the concern. As a rule, classification "A" includes the main selling lines of the business.

The classification "B" goods represent selling lines of intermediate turnover.

Purchasing policy is to cut to the minimum classifications "B" and "C". These add to cost without necessarily increasing revenue or profit. Among classification "C" are supporting goods and materials needed for the operation of the warehouse. These include heat, light and some power. The last-mentioned depends upon the degree of mechanisation and mechanical handling or packing involved.

Process plants

(Fig. 4, Stage 5.) The extremely high ratio of classification "A" materials to total output and to classifications "B" and "C" usually gives special importance to the internal supplies cycle.

This Pareto curve has a very sharp break-even area (*see* Fig. 14 at "B"), indicating that the intermediate section of raw materials and supporting goods is very small, although this depends upon the specialisation or complexity of the process. (BS 5729 Part 3 (6.4).

Classification "A" often includes supplies which are purchased and stored in bulk. The stock-control system and replenishment arrangements must be closely tied to the actual process in the plant. The economic order quantity may be used and a simplified withdrawal system employed.

As suppliers, process plants can have a very strong influence upon the supply and demand system. Sometimes, as in the example below, they may be sole or principal suppliers of rare by-products in addition to their main output in bulk. These characteristics were revealed by events in 1980 in the Middle East affecting supplies to the industrial West.

A leading petrochemical company announced a major reorganisation. This took it out of bulk base chemicals into more profitable speciality products. Bulk-chemicals had been in chronic over-supply and this had enabled buyers to strike dramatic bargains. The closure of the plants resulted in higher prices as capacity was reduced through closures. As supply remained restricted, prices moved still further against the buyer when demands increased for supply from these plants. Finally, an unforeseen effect was the loss of the essential by-products from the bulk-producing plants which had been closed down and which had no significant effect on the market forces of supply and demand but a quite catastrophic effect upon those who relied upon them for their rare by-products.

General manufacturing industries

(Fig. 4, Stage 7.) At this stage the supply characteristics are more diversified. In most mechanical and electrical engineering concerns classification "A" materials include ferrous and non-ferrous metals. The latter are more prominent in the electrical industries together with insulating materials which are often purchased as raw materials or components from process plants.

Electrical industries also buy electrical goods such as motors and relays sometimes from competitiors in the same industry.

In general and electrical engineering classification "B" involves components for embodiment in the end-product. These purchased parts often cover a very wide variety and therefore appear as a large radius in the Pareto curve.

Classification "C" includes fewer strategic spares than in the process plants or extractive industries.

Detailed analysis of requirements for general manufacturing industries

What follows is based upon a review of complex requirements for an industrial unit as envisaged in Fig. 4, Stage 7 and analysed in Fig. 15(b).

(1) RAW MATERIALS (see Checklist 4). It is possible to repeat the "A.B.C." classification in respect of the needs of each department. Variety and value usually reflect the total overall pattern of supply and production and depend upon the complexity of the finished product and of the production processes, jobbing, flow, mass, etc.

A careful analysis and classification should be made of the flow of raw materials vital to production or sales. For demands of sufficient importance and volume multiple sourcing is often essential.

Delivery from suppliers to the actual work-centres (BS 5191(1.3)) can be achieved in a few industries if the programme is accurately scheduled and closely adhered to and if the production-line layout is planned with adequate buffer space. (BS 5191 (2.2).)

For small-scale and jobbing firms separate orders may be placed for main supplies and stockholding avoided as far as practicable.

(2) PROVISIONING FOR NEW PRODUCTS.[54]-[58] This is a very important and "hazardous" aspect of Supplies activities. Figure 16 indicates the areas to consider when obtaining supplies for a new product or new supplies for an "old" or existing one. Table 10 outlines a case history and suggests some of the pitfalls which can arise. (For further comments upon timing see Chapters 11, 14 and 15.) (BS 6470 (1.1).)

(3) SUPPORTING GOODS are generally of classifications "B" or "C" (see Checklist 5). They can be significant loss-centres due to the disproportionate costs of their acquisition, administration, storage and stock control in relation to their total throughput value.

Because supporting goods do not pass into the end-product their costs sometimes escape the job-costing network. The result is that

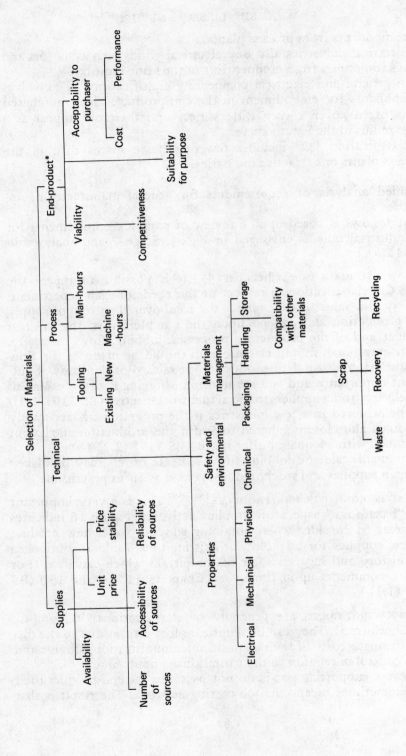

Fig. 16. Supplies for a new product, or new supplies for an old product

TABLE 10. HISTORY OF A NEW PRODUCT

Event number	Date and year no. of event	Event	Comments, references, etc.
1	1.3.—1.	Supplies receive from Sales a schedule of requirements for new product. (No historic data available.)	Target given as 1.6.—1. Quantities based on approximate and over-optimistic forecasts by marketing, technical and production staffs.
2	10.3.—1.	Supplies discover that time is too short to meet target.	
3	30.3.—1.	Supplies inform all concerned that date cannot be met.	Delay in communicating this due to efforts to avoid "loss of face" by having to admit defeat!
4	7.4.—1.	Supplies given new target date of 2.8.—1.	Had the decision been instant the Supplies office could have started work on the project before the Easter shut-down (week commencing 11.4.—1).
5	15.8.—1.	Actual starting date.	Production say they are short of materials, the tool setters could not "find" the tools, etc.
6	29.8.—1.	Production reported to be below target due to tooling problems and inexperience of operatives with the new sorts of materials being used.	NOTE: Supplies department should by now be checking actual performance against forecasts.
7	5.9.—1.	Materials shortages due to scrap materials as a result of event 6.	Extra supplies needed to make good for rejects and scrapped components.
8	8.9.—1.	Stoppage due to stock-out.	Supplies not informed of heavy drain on materials resulting from events 6 and 7. There was no representative of Supplies at the weekly production meeting.

TABLE 10 contd. HISTORY OF A NEW PRODUCT

Event number	Date and year no. of event	Event	Comments, references, etc.
9	9.9.—1.	Supplies place order for further materials and chase suppliers to make good shortages.	
10	13.9.—1.	Drop in usage.	Management decide to re-tool and halt production on a portion of the production line meantime.
11	15.9.—1.	Supplies progress chase suppliers vigorously.	No one told Supplies to stop progressing!
12	22.9.—1.	Enormous build-up of stock due to phenomenal success of the progress staff.	
13	3.10.—1.	On target—at last!	
14	13.10.—1.	Management reduce production target.	Angry customers who had to wait have cancelled and there has been a severe drop in sales.
15	20.10.—1.	Further build-up of stock.	Supplies still not told of slow down.
16	27.10.—1.	Massive fall in production.	All operatives put on rectifications for returns from customers who have been having "teething troubles" with the product.
17	1.11.—1.	Stock building up from new orders placed at event 9.	Due to time lag in adjusting intake, suppliers have held buyer to his original programme, progress statements and contract which inadvertently committed him to the dates he had demanded as a condition of the contract. Suppliers naturally wish to maximise their profits and minimise the effects of the cut back.

TABLE 10 contd. HISTORY OF A NEW PRODUCT

Event number	Date and year no. of event	Event	Comments, references, etc.
18	30.11.—1.	Surge in production and heavy demand on stock.	Factory working night shift to catch up on backlog.
19	8.12.—1.	Supplies discover that 20 per cent of stock is scrap.	It has not been rotated "FIFO" and older stock has now exceeded shelf-life. (*See Storehouse.*)
20	End of seventh year	Sales fall because: new competitors have entered the market; consumer preference has changed; new technical developments have made the product obsolete; economic factors arise— the replacement is half the price; production equipment and methods now out of date.	See *Diversification.* [53]

they can become a serious and undetected drain upon cash and involve loss in profitability—particularly in smaller companies.

NOTE:

A special control system may be needed to ensure that purchase orders call for the correct drawing issue of parts, tools, jigs, patterns, etc.

(4) PIECE PARTS AND PURCHASED PARTS (EMBODIMENT GOODS) (*see* Check-list 6). *Piece parts* is a term usually applied to parts made in the manufacturer's own works as distinct from "purchased parts". They are usually made at the rate required for the manufacturing programme or in economical batch quantities. In the latter case they may be stored and issued in batch-production quantities according to the work-load on the assembly line. In mass-production plants they frequently present special problems to maintain the balanced flow of production. Methods of storage are discussed later.

Purchased parts involve similar considerations to those mentioned above. They fall into the following two main groups.

(*a*) Standard parts and fittings which can be purchased off the shelf. These include fasteners of many kinds.

(*b*) Special purpose-made articles.

However, embodiment goods can comprise both piece parts and purchased parts and usually cover a very wide variety, so they tend to be in classifications "B" or "C". When used in bulk they can be subject to "make or buy" decisions (see Chapter 12). Where the product is highly specialised, however, they may reach classification "A". In this case bulk buying and close stock control have great importance. A trivial, but highly profitable, practice is to ensure that the commodity code is marked on embodiment parts during the course of manufacture. (BS 5191 (1.2).)

Fasteners warrant special consideration, as they are used in practically every manufacturing industry. A stock-out can stop an entire production line, while substandard or substitute fasteners can lead to rejects or failure in use. (*See also* Chapter 10, units of measurement.) A quality assurance scheme is operated by the British Industrial Fasteners Association, also by the B.S.I. (BS 6322, 3643.)

(5) TOOLS (*see* Checklist 7). Production shops and other departments such as pilot plants or research and development departments need tools. When the firm is still quite small, say 50-100 employees (40-80 operatives), tools may be lodged in the main or production store. Above this size, however, the volume of flow and investment in tools soon warrants a specialised tool store.

The tool store is usually associated with a tool room. Returned tools should be examined, then brought into first-class condition before being put back into stock, or replaced if worn out.

If the flow is sufficient the purchasing department can make forward supply arrangements or contracts advantageously. They should have regard to the following.

(a) *Quality*—influences the rate and costs of production, incidence of rejects, setting-up time, intervals between setting-up time, and need for sharpening tools and for replacements.

(b) *Price*—a concealed cost in production.

(c) *Delivery*—potential stoppages in production.

(6) JIGS AND FIXTURES. Jigs are usually associated with specific drawings and thus may be kept for certain jobs. Fixtures may be available for a wide range of applications. They may, in fact, be merely improvements added to a machine or group of machines and their use may not even be specified on drawings. This equipment is difficult to control. The use of fixtures in the smaller shop will often be left to the decision of the operative or his superior, unless their use has been designated on the works planning sheet or drawing.

The stores should see that all jigs and fixtures have their identifying number clearly marked. In the case of the former the number may be related to the parent drawing or part number used in manufacture. Part numbers on fixtures may be related to the plant number or group of machines on which they are to be used. (BS 5078.)

(7) PATTERNS (BS 467) are difficult items to store. They are usually bulky, often irregular in shape, frequently fragile and made of materials which may be subject to deterioration under humid conditions. Their movement and flow are usually erratic and unpredictable. They occupy large volume and accumulate rapidly as jobs are finished. Unless records are kept up to date a muddle soon occurs.

(8) MAINTENANCE (BS 3811) (see Checklist 8, para (13) below, and Chapter 6, terotechnology).[59] Spares are normally classification "C". Purchasing of this equipment may be dealt with by the maintenance department or by the functional department needing them. This is frequently due to the fear that urgency in obtaining supplies may be lost in the commercial efforts of the purchasing department. This is a point at which a dilemma certainly may arise. For example, the repair of handling equipment in an automated store or the replacement of a main valve in the pipeline of a process plant can be of primary importance to the continued operation of the enterprise. Whether the goods are carried in stock as "strategic spares" or are obtained on a panic basis from an outside supplier, availability transcends almost all other considerations.

Such panics obscure the financial losses which could have been avoided by good provisioning through the Supplies departments allied with effective preventive maintenance. Sometimes, moreover, purchasing research may find that a local precision engineer can produce spares of better quality, faster and at lower cost than the original manufacturer of the plant. Some suppliers regard spares as a loss-centre and may even welcome the offer by the purchasing firm to negotiate out of the contract their "exclusive spares clause" from the associated guarantees.

Supplies staff entrusted with maintenance provisioning should streamline procedures to provide rapid methods of communication with suppliers and maintenance staff. The question may well be asked whether Supplies staff who are unable to handle maintenance goods can be trusted to handle raw materials upon the supply of which the whole output depends. (See (13) below.)

Plant numbering and plant registers should be normal practice throughout industry. They assist in provisioning of supplies for maintenance and the plant register number should be introduced into the order number system for spares, etc. This procedure designates the point at which the goods are needed and should alert Supplies and other staff to the special nature and to the probable, or actual, urgency of the orders.

(9) TRANSPORT AND HANDLING SPARES. Profit derives from process and movement. Idle materials and, in particular, idle finished goods consume profits. The mobility of transport and handling equipment is therefore a top priority for maintenance.

A major factor in selecting the transport and handling equipment should be the availability of spares and servicing. Lists of recommended spares and servicing details should be obtained at the same time as the tender, and the two studied in conjunction with each other. (This should be the practice for *all* plant.)

Provision should be made for stocks of items needed for preventive maintenance where these are not available off the shelf. However, purchasing officers must inevitably be prepared for crises from breakdowns or, for example, stoppages as a result of inspections by Department of Transport or Health and Safety Inspectors.

In large undertakings there may be a case for "in-plant" or "consignment stocks" as outlined in Chapter 15. The distributor for the vehicles or handling plant then keeps the repair depot at the factory supplied with the fast-running spares.

(10) CONSUMABLE MATERIALS. Most manufacturing units have requirements for a wide range of indirect materials needed in support of the operation. Apart from those already mentioned, the following are worth noting, all of which are in classification "C". (BS 5191 (2.3).)

Lubricants should be freely available on an open access store basis in the factory. Damage to machinery through lack of proper lubrication usually far exceeds any petty thefts. Damage may result not only in repairs, but also in loss of production. There is also scope here for variety reduction. (BS 5063, 4807, 4412, 6413, PD 6428).

Electric lamps and tubes: correct lighting has an important bearing on productivity. It is therefore essential to have the correct replacements available. Standard lamp bulbs (like lubricants) are subject to pilferage, but fluorescent tubes are less so.

Gases often prove hazardous in storage and this problem is dealt with in *Storehouse.* (BS 4250.)

Solvents and certain cleaning fluids may need segregation in stores and special precautions in handling. These are, moreover, frequently suitable for recovery and recycling after use in the process. (BS 245.)

(11) LABORATORY, RESEARCH AND DEVELOPMENT, OR PILOT PLANT. The work of these departments depends upon the rate of development and the techniques of the industry. The demands on Supplies usually follow the pattern of the industry concerned. Requirements will arise for consumables and tools. However, there can be benefits in the use of standard consumables, production tools and equipment

as used in the main plant. The controlled conditions in research departments and their objective feedback on quality and suitability for purpose can be valuable spin-offs from their main investigations and research. (BS 5191, B 3009-10.)

The activities of these departments can be looked upon as urgent, and they are often geared to the rate of competition with other firms in the same product range and to the rate of technological change.

Much of the equipment bought and used will be specially ordered for delivery direct to site. Normal storage considerations may not therefore apply. If, however, they pass through the stores, then clearance inwards will be an important priority and precautions may be necessary in handling delicate apparatus with special finishes, etc.

Research and development reports may change a whole production policy almost overnight. This in turn may need a complete reappraisal of Supplies policies, as follows.

(a) Purchase orders may need amendments or cancellation.

(b) Stocks may have to be run down or salvaged, etc.

(c) Existing materials in progress may need to be disposed of.

(d) New supplies of different materials may be required.

(e) New requirements may demand exceptional priorities.

(12) PACKING AND DESPATCH (see Chapters 19 and 24). The flow of materials to the despatch bay may fall into several groups (see also Chapter 24).

The demand for packaging is continuous and variable. Many of the materials are unlikely to be needed elsewhere in the works, unless there are a number of packing bays serving separate production lines (see Storehouse).

Supplies may become involved in export as well as import documentation, in which case it may be necessary to set up a shipping office at the despatch area to handle the very considerable volume of documents. Many of these need immediate clearance and long distances between despatch bay and office could be a serious disadvantage.

(13) MAJOR PROJECTS AND PLANT (see Checklist 9 and Appendix VI).(60)-(64) The group of requirements examined here comprise plant and building materials for major extensions or for major repairs and maintenance. Usually these will have been subject to financial estimates submitted to the board of directors before work is started. (See Chapter 13, capital sanctions, and Fig. 58.)

(a) Letters of intent. These may be advantageous in speeding urgently needed factory extensions. Although the use of a letter of intent may facilitate the launching of a project there remain a number of pitfalls for the purchasing officer — particularly on larger projects. The following brief extracts from the National Economic Development Council Report *What's Still Wrong on Site?* mentions a few leading points. (*See* Fig. 65.)

UK constructors seem less able to cope with delays in design and *procurement* (although delays are just as common abroad). Often, insufficient time is allowed for the completion of the earlier stages of projects prior to the start of the construction stage. This results in too little design information and *material* being available to engineers on site and can be a direct cause of delay and low productivity.

A rider could be added here that the low productivity often leads to increased final costs exceeding the capital sanction in many cases.

Most important is arranging the project phases and limiting design changes to make sure that men are never expected to start work on site before the necessary *materials* and drawings are available.

(b) *Responsibilities.* The negotiations for extensions to plant and buildings are sometimes handled by the user departments. Even so, it is recommended that Supplies should have ultimate responsibility for placing and handling the contract as a major and responsible administrative task, including documentation for the actual receipt and handling, arrangements for off-loading, stowage, etc. Checklist 9 highlights many of the problems involved in this category of purchasing and supply.

(c) *Documents to be provided by plant suppliers.* The following list, reproduced by courtesy of the Department of Industry Committee for Terotechnology from their case study No. 1, summarises the documents to be provided by all suppliers of new equipment to facilitate maintenance. (BS 4884.)

" (i) An operator's/setter's instruction manual.

(ii) A maintenance manual for use by mechanical and electrical tradesmen. Such manual to give instruction in the operation of the plant and all instructions necessary for the maintenance of the equipment.

(iii) A routine maintenance schedule for mechanical and electrical trades, itemising tasks and their frequency.

(iv) All necessary circuit diagrams: electric, hydraulic and pneumatic.

(v) On transfer and sequencing special purpose machinery, drawings and diagrams illustrating the state of the work piece at each stage.

(vi) Where the design of the equipment is the supplier's property, a full set of drawings both of assemblies and details.

(vii) Such drawings as will enable maintenance personnel to identify component parts of the subject equipment by manufacturer or supplier and its relevant part or detail number.

(viii) Where proprietary parts are incorporated into the subject equipment, the following are to be supplied.

(1) Manufacturer's catalogues and special instructions.

(2) A schedule itemising each proprietary item by Manufacturer, Manufacturer's Reference Number and the number of such items supplied.

(ix) A 'Recommended Spares' list.

All above information except Item *(viii)*(1) to be supplied on reproduction paper.

(x) A tool list itemising the type of tools required for maintenance purposes, emphasising especially any unusual tools required."

(d) Safety. Enquiries and orders for plant must always be drafted with health and safety regulations in mind (*see also* comment at (8). The Health and Safety at Work etc. Act requires employers to provide plant, a working environment, access to the workplace and systems of work that are, as far as is reasonably practicable, safe and without risks to health. Management must also tell employees "what to do" and "how to do it". This calls for special attention in the areas of "fault location", maintenance, and communications to the operatives carrying out their tasks. The provision by a manufacturer of a highly complex circuit diagram could fail to comply with what was "reasonably practicable" when making such communications with the operatives, and failure to give adequate training could have a similar result. (*See* Health and Safety Executives lists of British Standards.)

(e) Waste. Building and construction works not infrequently generate considerable quantities of waste materials and equipment (and therefore equivalent loss of cash) because of changes to plant specification or programme. Waste also results from bad workmanship, faulty specification, bad storage and handling on site or inadequate site preparation. (*See* Chapter 25.) Major contributions to efficiency can be made at the time of ordering by Supplies paying attention to the foregoing and also to packaging, off-loading, handling, site access, hard-standing areas, drainage of storage areas, and stowage (stacking, sheeting, etc.) on site.

(f) Provisioning by contractor. Where building or construction works are put to outside contract, the contractor usually provisions for the materials himself. Where this is so the case for vigilance by the Supplies department of the purchaser is by no means diminished. The purchasing department of the contractor will be under a discipline to buy at the lowest price so as to maximise his company's

profit within the original tender price. The disciplines of quality or "suitability for purpose" emphasised so frequently throughout this volume are thus likely to take second (or even fourth) place after price, delivery and profit!

(g) *Energy.* When planning extensions or major renovations of plant or buildings primary consideration should also be given to energy conservation. (*See* Fig. 22.)

(h) *Company needs.* On most large projects subcontractors will be employed. In such cases it is particularly important to ensure that the interests of the purchasing client are not lost between the architect, main contractor and subcontractor(s). The purchasing officer should ensure that his company's needs are given full and continuous attention, particularly in respect of the phased programme of the project, of which the purchaser should have full details. Where a network analysis is operated for the programme the purchaser should insist on receiving continuously updated copies.

(i) *Legal protection.* Finally, it should be noted that the Supply of Goods and Services Act 1982 (*see* Chapter 16) gives protection to these contracts which was not available under the Sale of Goods Act 1979.

(14) CONSULTANCY. This is no less a form of "supplies" than actual raw materials. Although the consultancy process is usually invisible the end-product is often only too tangible! Appointment of consultants (such as architects) should therefore be given the same attention as the selection of materials. Negotiations require even greater care than for normal supplies because the consultant is, quite naturally, skilled in selling himself and his commodity, namely his "know-how". Although in most cases the consultant may be appointed by top management, normal purchasing techniques, especially negotiations, should be on sound lines, whether with architects, computer advisers etc.

W. R. Park in *Cost Engineering Analysis* observes that, "Whereas the engineer employed in a factory may have to live with his decisions for many years (no matter how embarassing they may be) the consultant *may* never even find out whether his recommendations were followed or not . . . ." Any contracts for consultancy should be negotiated and the contract drafted with these contingencies in mind and carrying suitable indemnity clauses.

A further important point is that the "purchase" of consultancy itself implies an area of ignorance, or at least insufficient knowledge, by the firm engaging the consultant — otherwise why make such an arrangement? Any contract should include agreement by the consultant to submit to unlimited questioning by his client and to make available all working papers for examination. The terms of the contract and availability of the consultant during, and after, implementation should be agreed at the outset.

Where the consultancy affects supplies some clear lines of communication with Supplies staff must be established and maintained throughout.

On major projects the engagement of specialist consultants such as architects may bring financial control problems. Where the appointment is remunerated in proportion to project cost there is the inevitable risk that, at the best, cost discipline may be lax, or, at the worst, costs may be inflated. There is a further hazard which, although less probable on industrial than on public authority projects, must be guarded against. Architects and plant project specialists have a natural and proper interest in producing an edifice or a plant which may attract their next client. There can therefore be a tendency to add structural or engineering embellishments which add nothing to the productivity of the project but much to its cost and thus to loss of profitability.

(15) SECRETARIAT: OFFICE REQUIREMENTS (*see* Checklist 10). The main categories of need here are stationery, printing and drawing-office supplies. Many firms neglect the economies which can be made in the purchase of these goods. Although they are almost invariably in classification "C", the savings can be significant.

General stationery should be carefully stock-controlled. Shelf-life of paper can be short if the storage conditions are poor. Large stocks of stationery easily become untidy resulting in considerable wastage. Prodigal consumption occurs if the supply appears inexhaustible.

Master control of forms (*see* Chapter 3) can be highly economical, particularly with standard paper sizes and punchings for economic printing and ease of filing.

Closely allied to the master control of forms is the provision of a list of standing type or litho plates at the printers. The savings in setting up for future reprints cuts down delivery time and reduces price.

The needs of a drawing office are often conditioned by the preferences of individual draughtsmen. Their equipment is expensive and savings are difficult to achieve without considerable co-operation. (BS 1340-2-4, 1709, 2457, 2459, 3429, 3460, 3478, 4867, 5459, 5850, 6396.)

It should be noted that office machines are increasingly available under leasing arrangements (*see* Table 32). (BS 3861.)

Computers, their equipment and supplies are a rapidly developing area. Principal points to observe are the need to avoid the pressure of enthusiastic salesmen and learn the terminology and jargon which may become involved in the negotiations. As with any new purchase where one has little experience it is strongly recommended to seek the experience of another user before closing a deal for a new computer or its equipment. (BS 5729 Part 4, Tables 3 and 6: also Checklist 10.)

(16) SERVICES. Hire of plant, security, cleaning, etc.[65] (*see* Table 32) are areas which tend to be neglected by Supplies and left for individual functional staff to deal with, often to the great advantage of the supplier.

The following comments should be helpful when negotiating and administrating contracts for services such as factory/office cleaning, security and so on.

(*a*) Examine supplier's terms and conditions with extra care, particularly for exclusion clauses.

(*b*) All arrangements to be in writing.

(*c*) Reserve the right to cancel in the event of poor performance.

(*d*) Reserve the right to cancel in the event of breach of security.

(*e*) Agree (in writing) arrangements for times of service, keys, passes, etc.

(*f*) Regular meetings for liaison/reports on running contracts.

(*g*) As bailee, arrange secure stowage for contractor's equipment.

(*h*) Names of "authorised persons" to be published and displayed.

(*i*) Establish complaints feedback procedure, from company staff to purchasing.

(*j*) Ensure there is a clear line of communication with contractor for complaints.

(*k*) Arrange for a security bond if this is needed.

(*l*) Safeguard the safety of staff and public, whether or not the latter have access.

(*m*) Insure all parties for all eventualities arising from the service.

(*n*) Obtain and check code of practice of the trade association to which the contractor belongs.

(*o*) Maintain "watching brief" on contractor's relationships with staff. Service contractors rely heavily upon the build-up of personal relationships with actual users. This can be good, or may lead to implanted prejudices and sometimes to expensive commitments—or even fraud.

(17) HEALTH, SAFETY AND WELFARE (*see* Checklist 11). These requirements (as a rule, in classification "C") include such items as cleaning materials, protective clothing and first-aid equipment. Unless the

industry is extractive or very large, few of these requirements warrant bulk purchase. Many are highly specialised and the safety officer usually provides specifications. Several trade associations exist in this area.

Cotton waste and similar cleaning materials are sometimes difficult to control, particularly in regard to quality. For example, where high-grade electrical insulating materials are used in manufacture specifications should include "freedom from metal particles".

Sports and social clubs may use the purchasing department to obtain discounts and service. Where this is so it should be on a formal and regularised basis to prevent abuses.

Canteen needs fall into the following three main categories.

(*a*) Food: normally this will be dealt with on a day-to-day basis by the canteen manager.

(*b*) Fuel: this calls for little comment, except that a separate meter may be of advantage to check consumption costs.

(*c*) Hardware, including canteen plate and cutlery: these represent the classification "B" items of the service. Their costs directly affect profitability and price is important.

(18) FUEL, POWER, WATER, ETC. These supplies are difficult to allocate as fixed or variable costs. They also tend to be heavy loss-centres and difficult to control. These factors are accentuated because many forms of energy are invisible so that wastage such as lost heat, generated noise, etc. go undetected. Whether or not the provisioning of these basic requirements falls within the province of a Supplies department, their costs are critical to the economics of any undertaking. If neglected they can add unseen and unallocated costs to production and the end-product, thus reducing competitiveness or profits or both. (BS 1016–7, 1293, 2074, 2869, 3804.)

The foregoing remarks lead logically to consideration of the economic purchase of fuel and energy. Many forms of energy are under either public ownership or the control of large and powerful corporations. It might be thought therefore that there is no chance for savings to be made by negotiation, but this is not so. Commercial benefit can result merely by seeking which tariff will be most advantageous to the company. It is also useful to investigate how the service is being used. For example, in one small company excessive electricity charges were found to be the result of machines being left running through the tea break. The machines, though running light, plus the tea brewing process, plus the "comfortable" electric fires, took the maximum demand into the next stage on the tariff!

Economical uses of fuel and power are dealt with by, for example, the National Industrial Fuel Efficiency Service which provides advisory and training services.

(*See* Chapter 12, nationalised industries and government agencies, and Fig. 22.)

(19) PURCHASES FOR EMPLOYEES. A firm and consistent policy must be agreed with management regarding purchases for staff and workers. If permitted, the range covered may include:

(*a*) sale of company's own products;
(*b*) purchases outside the company;
(*c*) sales from stores;
(*d*) sales of scrap and waste;
(*e*) staff presents and long-service awards;
(*f*) tool clubs (*see* below).

The policy may, of course, differ for these various groups.

Where operatives provide some or all of their working tools a "tool club" may be set up. Members then purchase from approved local suppliers at special terms for cash on presentation of proof of identity. This is open to abuse and in many towns the local stockists refuse to operate the scheme. Guarantees may be invalidated by such a scheme.

Some firms apply a surcharge, which has the effect of discouraging staff purchases besides helping to cover the cost of such purchasing procedures.

(20) SPARES FOR PRODUCTS SOLD TO CUSTOMERS. In Table 10 no provision was made for spares to service customers! On the other hand this is one of the main features a purchaser should consider in "vendor rating" and value analysis. This is a loss-making area which suppliers and particularly their accountants seek to avoid.

In the early life-cycle of a product, liaison with the sales and marketing department is vital and the method of stock-control should be flexible, frequently reviewed and guided by sales estimates to ensure good customer service. Stock records can provide invaluable data for the sales and technical departments as to the performance of items sold.

However, sooner or later, event number 20 of Table 10 will be reached, and in the last year "z" of the life-cycle decisions may be needed on spares policies for customers. The following procedure is suggested:

1. By year "z", historical data should indicate expected demand "x" per unit sold during its established life-cycle "y" throughout which spares have been made available.

2. From this historical data extrapolate future expected demand for the residual life-cycle of units sold during year "z".

3. Add in during each of the remaining years z+1, z+2, z+3.....z+y

the spares for earlier years.

4. Subject to any other considerations such as shelf-life etc., next compare costs of the following alternatives:

4.1 Take in bulk stock to cover outstanding years at (say) current price.

4.2 If lead-time is short consider buying on a day-by-day basis. No doubt a high setting-up cost will be involved for each order. On the other hand stock-holding and storage costs may be reduced or eliminated.

4.3 Fix and maintain normal stock-holding with re-order level and orders placed as required.

4.4 As 4.3 but using "EOQ" formula subject to the usual constraints in its use.

5. Compare each of the above with the effects upon profitability and future business which the sales and Marketing department expect to result from a good spares policy.

CHAPTER 6

Materials Management in Supplies

INTRODUCTION

The concept of materials management in this book is based upon the definition given in the Introduction and goes beyond the aspects of purchasing and stock control to which the definition is often restricted. Table 11 outlines some aspects of materials management which should be examined throughout the Supplies operations but particularly at the purchasing stages. This chapter looks briefly at the "science of materials" as it affects storage, handling and production.[84] More detailed study is made in *Storehouse* in regard to the effects of applied mechanics and physics upon storage and handling.

Figure 17 illustrates in diagrammatic form the dynamics of supplies and materials management.

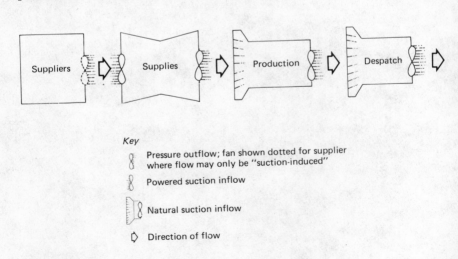

Key

Pressure outflow; fan shown dotted for supplier where flow may only be "suction-induced"

Powered suction inflow

Natural suction inflow

Direction of flow

Fig. 17. The dynamics of supplies and materials management

MATERIALS MANAGEMENT AND ITS EFFECT UPON COSTS OF SUPPLIES

Consideration must be given to costs of supplies, as affected by materials management.[66][67] Those who are inexperienced in the materials management aspects of Supplies may assume that price per unit is the main (or only) criterion. However, as emphasised throughout this book, it is important to consider *total costs* of supplies rather than price alone which is one important factor among many. In high technology industries excellence of product is likely to be regarded as of greater importance than price. Yet it is precisely in such industries that value engineering and value analysis (*see* Chapter 13) can be most rewarding and that Supplies staff can make the greatest contribution. There is also a danger, particularly in larger units with vast capital resources, that expenditure on supplies tends to be overlooked resulting in loss of profitability.

TABLE 11. MATERIALS MANAGEMENT ASPECTS OF SUPPLIES

Storage and materials management aspects	Purchasing and other aspects
(a) *Handling:* off-loading, unpacking, checking, stacking, placing into bins, racks and containers, selection and issue to work-centres, dispensing at work-centres (or by the customers).	Negotiations and orders should lead to selection of the correct methods suited to existing handling equipment; or handling equipment may require modification to suit consignments.
(b) *Preservation:* avoidance of deterioration; also security against contamination, infestation, self-damage of the goods or causing damage to other goods. (BS 5729 Part 5, Fig. 2.)	Packaging should be agreed with supplier with these requirements in view. Storage equipment and locations may need modification, new equipment may be needed, or staff may need to be alerted.
(c) *Flow* of goods and materials is closely related to stores management.	Storage problems should be understood by purchasing staff and work study could affect purchasing indirectly.
(d) *Health and safety* of operatives in the management of materials and goods has general implications. (BS 4891 (7.4).)	The person managing supplies should know the principles, at least, of the Health and Safety at Work Act. The purchasing officer has also to bear in mind that the Act now covers dangers to the public.

TABLE 11 contd. MATERIALS MANAGEMENT ASPECTS OF SUPPLIES

Storage and materials management aspects	Purchasing and other aspects
(e) *Stores control:* the physical or "real life side" of stock control involves materials management in a number of directions. (BS 5729 Part 5, Table 3.)	Stores staff should be trained to: (i) take an interest in all goods stored: (ii) make continuous examination of stock in regard to "housekeeping", idle materials (suggestions for handling, housing and packaging), ordering quantities and so on.
(f) *Properties of materials* should be part of the "interest" taken by Supplies staff (particularly stores) referred to in (e). (See Table 13.)	Application of enlightened interest by staff may lead to amendments in ordering, variety reduction, standardisation and so on.
(g) *Knowledge of basic scientific principles* in handling and storage. (*Storehouse.*)	This area is of increasing importance throughout the whole Supplies field.
(h) *Management of materials* to include design aspects, selection of suitable materials, their packing, transport, handling and storage.	Appreciation of design problems will help Supplies staff to collaborate, with benefits to suppliers, own firm and customers.

Increased costs of supplies through maladministration

There are obviously innumerable factors which can increase the costs of supplies owing to maladministration, and some which can even lead to supplies disasters. Some of the factors have already appeared in the text, and a few are listed below.

(a) Failures in diagnostic skill: no one asked the right questions.

(b) *Or* no one asked any questions!

(c) Communications failed: no one spoke, or no one listened.

(d) Treatment was given to symptoms: first causes were overlooked.

(e) "Feedback" failure: suppliers-to-Supplies-to-users or vice versa.

(f) Basic elementary facts not known or ignored, e.g. electrical machine suffered mechanical failure.

(g) Specialised knowledge was not coupled with realisation of areas of ignorance.

(h) One or more parties suffered from "cognitive dissonance" (a psychological state in which the sufferer persuades himself that his own views are correct and subconsciously (or deliberately) dismisses all alternatives).

(*i*) Sheer prejudice.

(*j*) Incorrect or substandard supplies obtained.

(*k*) Information incomplete or inaccurate.

(*l*) Growth of entrenched, inflexible dogmas—technical, financial or other.

(*m*) Refusal to accept "feedback" of any kind from any source.

(*n*) Communication failures due to terminology (jargon) being incorrect.

(*o*) Inability of Supplies staff to appreciate problems of techincal staff.

(*p*) Lack of tact by Supplies in putting the commercial case to technical colleagues.

(*q*) Excessive red tape: over-recording, under-recording, etc.

(*r*) Too rigid adherence to rules and formulae: over/under-ordering.

(*s*) Lack of urgency or dynamism, not "thrusting" but "sleeping".

Supply disasters and materials management

Table 12 outlines some cost areas and other possible consequences of "supply disasters" of various magnitudes in a supplies chain (such as that at Fig. 3) between a supplier (column 1)), a manufacturer using the supplies (columns (2) and (3)) and the ultimate customer of the manufacturer (column (4)). (*See also* Note (2).)

The reader is invited to consider in sequence the implications to his "company" and the actions he would take as Supplies Manager to correct or mitigate the effects of the situations. For the purpose of the exercise assume that in each case the "ultimate customer" is informed immediately of the prospective delay, "brief", "medium" or "long", and refer to the notes at the end of the table. The customer should be aware of the sorts of costs that may be involved at his supplier's works (the purchaser in the table) as a result of his supplier's disasters and also as a result of his own demands as the customer calling for special action to be taken. He is likely to discover that costs at the works of his suppliers will be passed on to him if the opportunity occurs. Reduction of his supplier's "vendor rating" or the threat of "blacklisting" may prevent him from making the attempt.

There may also be further disasters on the way. For example, if a customer cancels his order, the manufacturer may also have to cancel—or accept materials which are no longer required! Special transport arrangements may be required to ship the finished goods in time for the customer's needs, if "blacklisting" is to be avoided.

TABLE 12. SUPPLY DISASTERS AND THEIR EFFECTS

(1) Duration of delay[1] by producer's supplier	(2) Action taken at the works of the producer as a result of the delay by the supplier (Col. (1))	(3) Consequences of action taken by producer	(4) Action taken by ultimate customer as a result of the delay by the producer
Brief	Next available job is put into work so as to keep production fully occupied until new supplies are received.	Return paperwork to office and materials and part-finished work to stores quarantine, WIP stores, etc. Later, reactivate paperwork, obtain reissue of materials, reset up machines, etc.	Customer does not cancel order, but accepts the delay.[2]
Brief	A stock order[3] is put in hand to keep production fully occupied until new supplies are received.	Return paperwork and materials as above. Costs of activating stock order, but not any additional loss or cost[4] above normal. Normal storage and investment costs will be incurred plus reactivation costs as above.	As above.
Brief	No suitable work to put in hand: production stopped.	Idle man/machine-hours. Materials, etc. left at work-centres with possible wastage, deterioration and/or loss. Some costs when reactivated.	As above.

TABLE 12 contd. SUPPLY DISASTERS AND THEIR EFFECTS

(1) *Duration of delay* [1] *by producer's supplier*	(2) *Action taken at the works of the producer as a result of the delay by the supplier (Col. (1))*	(3) *Consequences of action taken by producer*	(4) *Action taken by ultimate customer as a result of the delay by the producer*
Brief to medium	Supplies action: special transport to collect or deliver special materials; or different materials or specifications may be used. Production action: overtime working initiated when new supplies arrive: or job may be transferred to other machines which may stop other work.	Cost of special transport; special materials may be at premium price; oversize materials may have to be used, resulting in wastage; different specifications may be more costly. Extra production, costs of overtime or of transferring work.	Customer does not accept delay, but insists that purchaser's company takes special action to improve
Long	Other work available for duration of planned time allocated to this job.	Loss of difference in profit between the job cancelled and the substituted work. Possible contingent costs: materials bought specially for the job, wasted or partly machined or assembled, therefore scrap or, if unsalvageable, waste.	Customer cancels order.
Long	No other work available until a replacement order is received.	Costs as above plus idle man/machine-hours until sales department can secure a further order.	Customer cancels order.

TABLE 12 contd. SUPPLY DISASTERS AND THEIR EFFECTS

(1) Duration of delay [1] by producer's supplier	(2) Action taken at the works of the producer as a result of the delay by the supplier (Col. (1))	(3) Consequences of action taken by producer	(4) Action taken by ultimate customer as a result of the delay by the producer
Long	As above.	Costs as above plus potential loss of sales over the normal sales horizon. May also have adverse effect upon the expansion plans of the company and supplies potential.	Customer cancels order and "black lists" the purchaser's company.

NOTES:

(1) "Brief" = 7–10 days approx. "Brief to medium" = 3–4 weeks approx. "Long" = 2–3 months approx. (2) The producer may look upon a brief delay as normal and may not even know of the disasters at his supplier's factory. (However, the producer ought not to be in such a position if he has an efficient Supplies department himself.) (3) Some manufacturers are able to run stock orders to make up lines held in stock for specific orders or for general supply. (4) There may be both unseen gains from activating stock orders, such as improved customer relations, and tangible gains, such as appreciation of stock valuation, etc. (*See also* Chapter 18, forward planning.)

SPECIFICATIONS, QUALITY AND STANDARDS

Specifications and standards should be integrated, but this is not always the case. A specification does not automatically become a standard, but standardisation is impracticable without clear and precise specifications, and the latter are vital to the performance of purchasing and Supplies functions, being the starting point of practically all purchasing. (BS 5532 (4.9).)

AXIOM: Every purchase order *is* a specification.

An engineer *could* produce a new specification for every article made or purchased for use by the firm. In fact, it would seem from observation that many engineers and purchasing officers are "specification conscious" but "standardisation shy".

In public authorities and service industries, both nationalised and private, safety of, and service to, the community are usually of first importance. Not only this, but safety officers in all industries should take an active interest in tools and equipment used by operatives, particularly on sites to which the public may gain access —whether authorised or not the company remains liable.

Technical staff usually produce the necessary specifications for supplies. Those who lack such supporting staff must rely upon national specifications and standards. A purchasing analyst can provide a useful link.

Some firms tend to adopt "standard samples" as their measure of quality for supplies, but this can seriously impede effective purchasing, particularly where the sample alone is acceptable. If samples have derived from a particular supplier he may gain a most unfair and highly profitable advantage over his rivals.

High technology industries have highly specialised needs and their work-forces employ highly individualistic skills. In such cases the Supplies officer tends to be governed by these needs and preferences. Efforts to standardise may also be defeated by the rapid changes made in technological fields. (*See* Appendix IV, British Standards Society.)

Importance of correct specification/quality (BS 4891 (8.1, 8.2).) A specification is as important to Supplies as it is to design and production (*see also* Checklist 12). Unless a correct specification is furnished, the purchasing officer cannot be sure of procuring the correct goods nor the inspection department of checking quality. Factors which may tend to prevent the purchasing officer from receiving an adequate or correct specification can be ignorance, laziness or carelessness of the requisitioner. Sometimes the latter does not remember or is unsure of the specification and relies on the purchasing officer to fill in the details and order correctly. Unfortunately this situation is most likely to occur where the purchasing officer works closely with functional colleagues. The more he "nurses" them the more they will tend to rely upon him. There is a potential danger here, as an error of judgment on his part could lead to inevitable recriminations and loss of harmony. Chief among the careless mistakes are: misquoting of makers' catalogue numbers, incorrect quantities, and faulty, inadequate or misleading descriptions (such as "best quality" when "normal quality" is adequate and "best quality" might be unmachineable on the company's production plant).

It is not normally the job of the purchasing officer to produce specifications but to see that he obtains them. If, however, the purchasing officer finds it necessary to draft a specification he should ensure that it is agreed with the department which gave rise to it

Name of company	Title of standard	Standard No. . . . Page No. . . . . . . Issue No. . . . . . . Date . . . . Circulation . . . .
	Illustration	

1. Scope and object — A brief expansion of the title to indicate the range of interest covered by the standard.

2. Field of application — e.g. The standard may be limited for use on a particular class of goods or by a particular manufacturing unit.

3. Method of reference — The standard form of words and sequence of information to be used on documents which call up the standard or items in the standard.

4. Related specifications — e.g. The standard may be one of a series of company standards, or it may be in accordance with all or part of a national standard.

5. Technical data — Range of sizes and code identity.
Dimensions and tolerances.
Material specification.
Colour or finish.
Limitations, e.g. loading, working temperature or mounting position.
Performance data.

6. Packaging — e.g. Marking—quantity per package—protection against damage.

7. Inspection data — e.g. Minimum tests or sampling information.

8. Approved suppliers* — Suppliers whose product has been tested and found to meet the specification at a satisfactory price.

Courtesy British Standards Institution

Fig. 18. Layout and headings of a typical company standard
(1) Taken from BS PD3542.[69] (2) This example is suitable for covering a component or a range of similar components but with suitable modifications the general style can be adapted to other types of standard such as process specification. (3) *Most organisations regard this information as confidential and prefer it to be available only in the purchasing department. (4) *See also* BS PD6489, "Guide to the Preparation of a company standards manual".

or with the technical standards officer of his company.

Supplies staff are unlikely to undertake technical monitoring of specifications. However, there are good reasons why they should monitor the commercial and economic implications. (*See* Checklist 13 and Chapter 4, terms of reference.)

Where staff have been disciplined and trained in standardisation and variety reduction, the designer making a new drawing or the purchasing officer receiving a requisition for new material will automatically ask himself whether this is near or identical with something made or purchased previously and then act appropriately.

(*See also* Chapter 14, ethics and policies in negotiations.)

Layout for standards and specifications

The layout and headings of a company standard are suggested in Fig. 18. This example shows many of the features which a supplies manager would wish to include in his purchasing or material specifications.

It must be emphasised that no standard should be regarded as unchangeable for all time. Efforts to impose rigid conditions upon any technical or practical operation end in frustration and final evasion or neglect.

All working drawings should refer to standards so that in the event of alterations to drawings standards will also be automatically revised. If a purchase is involved, this will again have the effect of notifying Supplies of any change through the commodity catalogue.

In addition to the standard number (shown at the top right-hand corner in Fig. 18) the standard should show the commodity code number of the article or material where this exists, or alternatively the drawing or part number.[68][69][70][79]

Changes to specifications or standards

No change should be permitted without authorisation, a check on costs and suitable documentation. However, it sometimes occurs that a supplier changes his specification without consulting his customers. The excuse is usually made that the change embodies an "improved design" or "will give better or more economical performance". In all such cases three lines of action by the purchasing officer are essential:

(*a*) check with the appropriate authority that the new specification is acceptable;

(*b*) examine the change with the assumption that the supplier is reaping some financial benefit from the change in specification;

(*c*) negotiate a fair share of the savings for his company.

Vocabulary: commodities (BS 2474, 1000.)

Specifications and standards are essentially technical documents. Their preparation will inevitably be carried out by the technical department of the firm, which should also produce the classified index of commodities or vocabulary on which all supplies and preferably other codes should be based. A copy of this index must be kept by Supplies for ready reference to the specifications and standards as

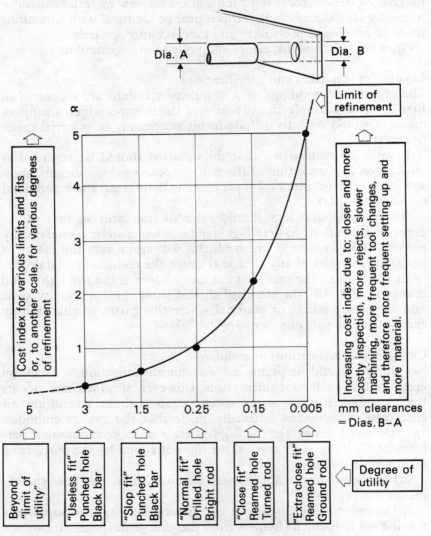

Fig. 19. "Over-specification" or "building cost into product"
Based on article by Arthur Garratt in *Value Engineering*, April 1968.

requests for materials, prices and other data are received.

Commodity codes are directly related to "vocabulary". Their development is examined in detail in *Storehouse*. It must suffice here to mention the following main points.

(*a*) The commodity code must (like the vocabulary name from which it stems) be unique to the article described.

(*b*) Both the name and code should be used throughout the firm.

(*c*) The commodity code should be specified in every purchase order. (BS 5729 Part 5, Table 2 (2(6)).)

(*d*) Suppliers also should be told to quote it in all documentation and, where appropriate, upon the actual goods themselves.

The stores catalogue (or commodity catalogue)

Every firm, particularly smaller ones, should consider the production of its own stores (or commodity) catalogue (*see Storehouse*). This combines vocabulary with references to codes, drawing numbers, specifications and standards, and may include instructions for ordering, storage, etc.

Approved materials lists

Arising from the activities of specification and standardisation the need may well arise for a list to be prepared of those items which are approved. As with the "vendor list" (*see* Chapter 12), there may also be a section for materials which are unacceptable and banned.

Over-specification

Over-specification can arise from a number of causes and should be avoided (*see* Fig. 19).

Results of standardisation

If the purchasing officer knows the advantages of standardisation which accrue to the supplier as well as to his own firm (*see* Checklist 14), he should seek to secure for his company at least a share of the supplier's financial gain. It has been earned by himself and his technical colleagues as a result of establishing the standard and for this work his company should not go unrewarded. (*See also* Chapter 14, enquiries and BS PD6495 (IFAN Guide 1), "Calculation of the profitability of (company) standardisation projects".)

Simplification and variety reduction

To gain the full benefits of the technical disciplines of specification and standardisation these must be coupled with simplification and "variety reduction" (*see also* Checklist 14). (BS PD6470 (2.7).)

"Simplification" is the technique of eliminating complexities of design by streamlining, omitting non-essential details, combining functions of different details and so on.

"Variety reduction" is a similar technique to simplification. In this case the process involves reductions in the numbers of types, sizes, grades, and so on, of products manufactured, purchased, stocked and sold.

Simplification, variety reduction and value analysis all belong to the same stable and should run together. Like many modern technical disciplines it is impossible to establish clear-cut boundaries. It is also difficult to establish a demarcation between purchasing and production in this context. All these techniques demand that the investigations be made objectively without bias and preconceived ideas, as are normal for those working close to any particular operation—even for Supplies staffs.

A specialist (such as a purchasing analyst) trained in the techniques can often spread his enthusiasm for them among the rest of the organisation. Where, however, the firm is too small to employ such a specialist, it should make use of the leadership of its purchasing officer. (He should already be using investigation, interrogation and introspection; if he is not, they will soon be forced upon him by the colleagues for whom he obtains supplies.)

The fact that purchases have usually passed through at least one stage of production (viz. at the supplier's works) and will pass through another in his own factory leads the purchasing man to have a foot in both camps. While not being directly involved in design or production, he can maintain a watching brief, but must apply within his company the same tact and leadership he is called upon to devote to his negotiations with suppliers. It will also bring him closer to his colleagues and make him more sensitive to their problems. (*See* Chapter 4, terms of reference.)

Preferred numbers

"Preferred numbers" are closely allied to standardisation, value analysis and, in particular, to variety reduction. They have important implications for design and Supplies.

Draughtsmen and supplies managers with knowledge of preferred numbers may reduce supply costs. For example, Fig. 20 shows that a $\frac{7}{8}$ in. (22 mm) length of screw was more costly than the 1 in. (25.4 mm) length in every case. Similarly, the number 9 screw was dearer than its larger neighbour of same lengths. Knowledge of preferred numbers by Supplies staff should enable them to avoid obvious pitfalls and understand the apparent inconsistency of some quoted prices. (Similar comments apply to metrication; *see also* Chapter 10, units of measurement.) The catalogue from which Fig.

20 is taken was still in use when discovered—despite being undecimalised and unmetricated!

STEEL RAISED COUNTERSUNK HEAD WOOD SCREWS

ARTICLE 601–17

Nickel plated

. *Price per gross*

Subject to current rates

Length	SCREW GAUGE									
	2	3	4	5	6	7	8	9	10	12
$\frac{3}{8}$ in.	2/2	2/1	2/4							
$\frac{1}{2}$ in.	2/2	2/1	2/1	2/9	3/1		3/9			
$\frac{5}{8}$ in.		2/2	2/3	2/6	3/—	2/11	2/11			
$\frac{3}{4}$ in.			2/6	2/9	3/2	4/2	3/9		5/6	
$\frac{7}{8}$ in.					3/10		4/8			
1 in.			2/11	3/4	3/6	4/8	4/3	5/7	5/9	
1$\frac{1}{4}$ in.					4/1	5/3	4/9	6/2	6/5	9/3
1$\frac{1}{2}$ in.	N.B. BS1210:1963				5/7		6/2	7/5	7/4	10/4
1$\frac{3}{4}$ in.	preferred sizes are printed						6/11		9/4	
2 in.	in **bold type**						8/—		10/10	12/11

Wrapped in grosses

Fig. 20. Extract from ancient catalogue: undecimalised and unmetricated, but still in use when discovered

When planning production to meet the demands of customers for a wider than normal range of choice this must be balanced against increased costs of production, stocking and distribution. Experience has shown that requirements are often adequately met when the sizes follow a geometric progression derived from preferred number series.

The adoption of the series by designers, supplies managers and others avoids the selection of a much wider range of disconnected series which prove increasingly difficult to rationalise as time proceeds.

Correlating preferred sizes for quite different products can sometimes prove advantageous. For example, the designer of power-driven pumps may be able to plan capacities which suit the powers of standard motors. Such correlations should be applied with advantage to newly developing industries. Many standards, such as those for wire gauges, bolts, nuts and electric lamps, already embody preferred sizes. Figure 21 shows the development of 5—10—20 series of sizes. (It is taken from the now withdrawn BS 1638, which is

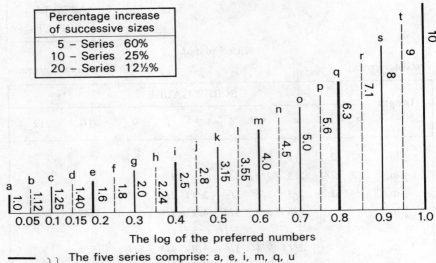

Percentage increase of successive sizes	
5 – Series	60%
10 – Series	25%
20 – Series	12½%

The log of the preferred numbers

———— }
———— } The five series comprise: a, e, i, m, q, u
———— } The ten series comprise: a, c, e, g, i, k, m, o, q, s, u
----   } The twenty series comprise: a, b, c, d, e, f, g, h, i, j, k, l, m, n, o, p, q, r, s, t, u,

Fig. 21. Preferred numbers series

(1) See BS PD6481. (2) The figures on the vertical bars indicate the length at each step. These are drawn to scale. It would have been equally valid to draw areas or volumes increasing in the same proportions.

superseded by PD6481: "Recommendations for the use of preferred numbers and preferred sizes". PD6481 also supersedes BS 4318 and DD29. *See also* ISO standard R3.)

In conclusion, it must be emphasised that the procedure is for guidance only and is not infallible. Too wide steps may involve wastage and increased manufacturing costs. Too narrow steps (i.e. too many sizes) are likely to involve higher tooling costs and increased stocks.

Pitfalls in standardisation

Standardisation incurs risks. There may be a tendency to rely on standards as if they had innate virtue instead of bringing objective thought to the problem concerned. They can then be a hindrance to new thought and those able to develop new ideas may become frustrated.

So far as the Supplies function is concerned, there are two further hazards. First, standards may be applied to conditions where the quantities are such that for little or no extra price a more suitable purpose-made article could be purchased or made in the factory. Secondly, manufacturers may collaborate to rig their prices so that the benefits are nullified.

Use of brand names for industrial buying

Purchase by brand name places the buyer in entire dependence upon the supplier with minor exceptions. For example, the old repealed Sale of Goods Act 1893 (Section 14(1)) established the principle that the "sale of a specific article under its patent or trade-name does not imply its fitness for *any* particular purpose unless the brand name so claims". Later enactments and cases support this.

Trade names or brands may derive from registered or unregistered trade marks and are devised to improve a company's image and enhance selling prospects. They may conceal or abbreviate long and unpronounceable chemical names or reveal the tie-up of the product with another company which was party to its development or to its sales policy and programme. To add to the confusion, distributors of the goods may re-christen the material with their own brand names.

The brand or trade name does not (unless it says so) represent specific compositions of materials. Substantial savings can often be made if it is discovered what composition the name stands for. Cleaning compounds of comparatively simple chemical formulae often command premium prices solely by virtue of their prestige packaging and sale under brand designations.

The purchase by brand name, however, may be justified:

(a) where a brand has been found superior to all others and its formula is secret and cannot be discovered or matched elsewhere;

(b) for unimportant applications where the effort of devising a technical specification would not be worth while;

(c) where the usage is too small to warrant the preparation of a specification.

Use of market grades

Specification by "market grades" is chiefly confined to natural commodities such as cereals, timber, textiles and the like. (The method does not meet the needs of most engineering industries which usually require inorganic and synthetic materials.)

In market grades, well-established grade or quality designations are clearly understood by both buyer and seller in the trade. Timbers, for example, are subject to gradings conforming to the customs of the trade. These grades are well defined according to freedom from defects, straightness and length of grain and appearance, etc.

Specification by sample

Most purchases by market grades involve the use of a sample. The method can also be appropriate where the goods are already in existence as distinct from the crop which has yet to be grown and harvested. (BS 5532 (3).)

The use of a sample may avoid a lengthy specification and for natural products it may be the only satisfactory method of description. When used for industrial products it usually reveals a lazy buyer or incompetent technical support for the purchasing operation.

It is most important to establish at the time of making a contract for purchase by sample which sample is the governing one—that of the supplier or that of the buyer.

Where a contract is a "contract for purchase by sample", Section 15 of the Sale of Goods Act 1979 lays down the following conditions.

"(*a*) There is an implied condition that the bulk shall correspond with the sample in quality.

(*b*) There is an implied condition that the buyer shall have a reasonable opportunity of comparing the bulk with the sample.

(*c*) There is an implied condition that the goods shall be free from any defect rendering them unmerchantable which would not be apparent on reasonable examination of the sample."

Purchase "subject to assay"

Purchase "subject to assay" is employed for the products of mining where, for example, the final content of the ore cannot be known prior to its extraction. In such cases a price is agreed "subject to assay" after mining when the assayer or analyst presents his report. Since the bulk may vary in content a number of random samples are taken to get a fair average from testing.

Prototypes

Prototypes are as a rule exceptional requirements and as such need exceptional treatment. Technical considerations are paramount. However, these must not be allowed to obscure the commercial and economic factors. Further aspects are examined in Chapters 11 and 15.

THE SCIENCE AND PROPERTIES OF MATERIALS

Up to this point we have looked at the fairly conventional areas of supplies and materials management. However, the advance of technology will not permit those who buy, store and use materials to ignore their mechanical, chemical and other properties. Nevertheless, it must be made clear that this book is not a textbook on technical matters. It can only provide guide-lines for those engaged in supplies

TABLE 13. PROPERTIES OF MATERIALS AND POSSIBLE EFFECTS UPON SUPPLIES AND MATERIALS MANAGEMENT

Properties	Effects and points to note in storage etc.
Inert:	Outdoor unprotected storage
Active:	Protective wrappings, segregation from other materials
Toxic:	Protective clothing, segregation from foodstuffs, special stores, double doorways, "air-traps", etc.
Pollutants:	As above but note that some substances are harmless in isolation but become pollutants, toxic or noxious in combination with other materials
Noxious:	May be harmless in themselves but give rise to industrial disputes regarding working conditions.
Corrosives:	Special containers, tanks, bins, ambient conditions, segregation
Explosives:	Special isolated stores, explosion vents, blast walls, earth mounds, special doors, anti-static equipment (wheels v. floors, etc.)
Flammables:	Catchment sumps, bund walls, fireproof buildings, sprinklers, training, drills, alarms
Low flash point:	Temperature-controlled store and equipment
Radioactive:	International/national regulations, safety equipment, training, drills, alarms, etc.
Hygroscopic:	Humidity and temperature control
Magnetic:	Segregation from delicate instruments, etc.
Abrasives:	Wear due to dust in handling equipment, etc.
Friable/fragile:	Cushion mountings, cradles and anti-vibration mountings required
Low melting point:	Special in-store precautions, e.g. avoid under-floor heating
Moisture content sensitive:	Control humidity, etc. (e.g. timber), moisture content
Perishable:	Ensure FIFO stock rotation plus special storage conditions and equipment (BS 5191 (B2001))
"Freezable":	Does material freeze at near normal temperature? (Some liquids and liquefied gases)
Vermin/pest attractive:	Special bins, hoppers, containers, etc.
Mating surfaces: (e.g. valve flanges):	Special protection in transit, handling and storage
Corrodible:	As above, and ensure FIFO stock rotation

TABLE 13 contd. PROPERTIES OF MATERIALS AND POSSIBLE
EFFECTS UPON SUPPLIES AND MATERIALS MANAGEMENT

Properties	Effects and points to note in storage etc.
High relative density:	Check loadings on transit, handling and storage equipment
Low relative density:	Check volumetric demand on storage space, which is likely to be high
Fine gauged, or "miniaturised":	Special lighting, unit containers, weighing counters
Liquids:	Tanks, drums, etc., precautions for spillage, evaporation, dispensing into smaller lots. Measuring: dipstick, "water gauge", electronic eye
Semi-rigids (e.g. rubber):	Protection to support upper loads
Rigids:	May require support when lifting, handling, transporting, storing
Low viscosity:	Precautions against spillage and spreading—particularly if flammable, etc.

and materials management who must rely upon their technical colleagues for technical advice and decisions. (BS PD6470 Section 1 (1.1).)

Basic mechanics and properties of materials

Mechanical failures in the broadest sense, including physical failures due to ambient conditions, are a frequent cause of supply disasters. For example, many electrical plant failures are first triggered off by a mechanical failure. A dielectric may be of the correct type and thickness but conditions in store may have permitted contamination and deterioration. Alternatively, the same dielectric may fail due to excessive mechanical stress and strain in a rotating machine or moving parts. (*See Storehouse*, science in stores.)

Table 13 outlines the well-known properties of materials and their possible effects upon the way in which they must be managed.[70][71][72]

With the increasing developments in technology more effort should be expended on the training of Supplies staff in the basics of mechanics, properties of materials and other technologies appropriate to the product group of the industry in which they are engaged. Even where the product group is in a low technology area the need for knowledge of basic principles remains for applications in storage and handling of supplies.

122

Corrosion technology and similar operating conditions

Corrosion technology influences the economic selection of materials, and protection for machinery, plant and products. Corrosion protection will increase in importance as longer life-cycles are demanded due to rising costs of plant replacement and the exhaustion of the earth's natural resources. (BS 5493.)

All too often enquiries, specifications and orders for materials, plant and equipment fail to give adequate details of operating conditions. The supplier then escapes from any indemnity in respect of breakdown which may, for example, be due to operation of the plant in damp conditions which have caused corrosion. For reasons given in Chapter 16 it is most unwise to rely upon recent legislation in this matter since much of this is designed for consumer protection and does not always cover a business sale.

As a result of the foregoing considerations the purchaser should take the following precautions.

(a) State fully the operating conditions.

(b) Communicate the fact that the materials, goods or plant must be suitable for operation in these conditions.

(c) Repeat the facts on the purchase order or other contract.

(d) Check any contract documents from the supplier—particularly the acknowledgment—to make sure there is no "escape clause" concealed in the small type. (See Chapter 17, checking acknowledgments.)

Cybernetics

(See Checklist 15.) Cybernetics[73] covers a wide field of communication and control. Controls require accurate communication and feedback to the point from which control action is taken. The following are some examples of communication feedback or cybernetics.

(a) Mechanical handling equipment when fully or partially automated requires accurate location to be fed back into the control system so that when working automatically, forks, etc. are adjusted into the correct position for pallet entry.

(b) Progressing of supplies needs feedback of information on current performance against a contract so that correct and adequate action is taken to ensure supplies are delivered when required. (This can be automated by computer.) (Figs. 33, 68, 70, 71, 72.)

(c) A decision whether to check all invoices or only those over a certain value could save costs (see Chapter 22). Incidence of errors, their frequency and magnitude must be fed back to the decision point.

(d) Setting and maintaining stock levels by feedback from a stock control system are a good example of cybernetics applied to produce a stable situation.

(e) The design of communication systems so as to avoid errors is part of the cybernetic concept; for example, a digital clock or meter where only a single value is displayed, a form designed in such a manner that the user is led to read and complete the data in correct sequence, levers controlling handling plant marked and interlocked to avoid malfunctioning. (BS 3693.)

Conservation of resources

Conservation of resources[74] is dealt with in Chapter 25 from the standpoints of recycling and recovery. "Resources" are to be understood as covering a much wider range than materials and include money, manpower, machine utilisation, fuels and services. However, this section is confined to materials management with particular reference to the design and procurement stages and leading into the production phase.

Checklist 16 gives some guide-lines on the topic and the reader's attention is drawn to the work of the British National Committee on Materials. This body exists to devote attention to "all aspects of materials science and technology". It may be useful to check whether the trade association for the reader's own firm (or that of his suppliers) works in association with this national committee.

Conservation of materials at design and development stages is still not universally practised. Management should ensure that it is included along with the disciplines of standardisation and variety reduction.

Areas where conservation can be applied are also examined in *Storehouse* as regards both conservation in stores and conservation in the selection and issue of materials from stores.

SOME EXAMPLES OF CONSERVATION are given below together with possible benefits and losses (indicated by plus and minus signs).

(a) *Use of hollow bar instead of machining from the solid:* (−) costs more per tonne; (+) but there is a net saving on raw material despite the higher cost per tonne; (+) less material actually used; (+) less tool wear because of less material removed; (−) a further item to stock (because usually some solid must continue to be carried in stock); (−) may need a larger range of sizes to cover all requirements; (+) no "metallic flow" of metal disturbed (which may occur when machining from the solid); (+) fewer tool changes; (+) therefore less down time; (+) lighter for transport, handling and storage; (+) therefore lower freight and handling costs; (+) faster cycle times in production; (+) therefore better delivery times to customer; (+) lower maintenance costs because machining operations are less onerous; (+) may be possible to manipulate and machine at a different work-centre thus making for a more flexible production layout.

(b) Use of "free-cutting" materials: (−) may be more costly per tonne; (+) but should improve machinability; (+) thus higher speeds and feeds; (+) may give a better surface finish; (+) therefore closer approach to limits given on the drawings; (+) therefore lower inspection costs; (+) fewer rejects, and better delivery to customer.

(c) Fabrication instead of casting or machining from the solid: (+) lighter assembly; (+) therefore lower costs of transport, handling and storage; (+) avoidance of delays waiting for patterns to be produced, curing time, etc.; (+) fewer patterns to store, preserve and modify; (−) slower in production unless jigs, fixtures and automation are applied; (++) possible better use of natural strengths of materials because no cutting of "flow lines" or grain structure, thus gaining strength and providing a higher weight strength ratio.

(d) Rebuilding of plant (see also Note below): (−) may render void the original maker's guarantees: (−) can never be "as good as new"—any such claims should be suspected, challenged and checked; (+) can assist the cash situation of the company (it may be a temporary expedient with cash flow in mind); (+) considerable saving in price *vis-à-vis* new equipment; (+) operatives may give better output on a rebuilt machine with which they are familiar than a new unit on which they may have learning problems; (+) delivery may be much quicker than waiting for new machines; (+) teething troubles of new machines may be avoided; (+) new types of machine, if introduced, may need additional spares to be carried, new service-men arriving at the factory, etc.

NOTE:

The distinction between "rebuilding" and "reconditioning" is important and must be clearly understood. Every enquiry and negotiation should establish which is on offer and the purchase order must make it clear which has been accepted. The only true safeguards are for the purchaser to spell out exactly what he has in mind, to check his supplier's acknowledgment and other documents to ensure there is concensus and to ensure that some written guarantee is obtained from the supplier.

DESIGN FOR RECYCLING is a fundamental but generally ignored aspect of design. The following points should be noted.

(a) Use materials which can be salvaged from production offcuts or process waste.

(b) Design in such a manner that process waste or production offcuts become a useful or saleable by-product.

(c) Design or use materials which at the end of the useful life of the product can be recycled, refurbished, used for a secondary purpose, cannibalised for spares and so on.

(d) Avoid materials (or design features) which prevent salvage, recycling, etc. as above.

PURCHASE OF FUEL AND POWER is included in Chapter 5. Savings in the use of these vital items of supply are as important as the savings to be gained from effective materials management of raw materials.

Figure 22 outlines areas of savings in fuel and power consumption. Many of the areas will not fall within the direct purview of Supplies. However, practically all of them have some implications for purchasing, negotiation, storage, etc.

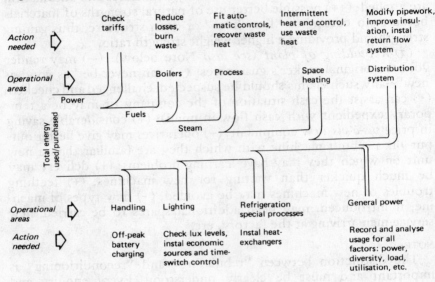

Fig. 22. Energy flow and conservation

Ergonomics

"Ergonomics" is a new term adopted to describe an old, but often neglected, technique.[75][76] Supplies staff are not expected to study the topic in depth, but whoever initiates requirements for supplies—especially for plant—should have some regard to ergonomics where this is relevant.

Checklist 17 gives a few guide-lines to apply when purchasing plant and equipment which involves ergonomics.

Quality assurance and quality control

(1) DEFINITIONS. The British Standards Institution defines "quality" as: "the totality of features and characteristics of a product or a

126

service that bear upon its ability to satisfy a given need". The phrase "given need" (or "end use") has important legal implications for contracts. (BS 5191 (A), 5532 (4.2), 6143.)

Another definition of "quality" given by J.B. Supper (*Electronics and Power*, 28th November 1974) is that: "quality is conformance to an agreed specification". Supper explains this as follows.

> The value of this definition lies partly in its emphasis upon the agreement between the purchaser and the supplier as to what is to be supplied. Nothing can be defined absolutely and all specifications must have some areas of ambiguity and uncertainty. It is of the utmost importance that the ambiguous areas and other specification weaknesses are identified as early as possible in the purchasing process. The art of producing a good specification lies not in the elimination of all ambiguity—since this may be impossible— but in reaching a satisfactory balance between residual ambiguity on the one hand and cost and time on the other.

It must be pointed out that in the event of an appeal to the law upon these and related matters the courts will seek to find the "intentions of the parties to the contract at the time it was made". It is therefore a good discipline when drafting specifications to keep in mind the ultimate intentions as to use and objectives of the equipment specified. (*See also* Chapter 16.)[77]-[82]

(2) INTEGRATION. The following quotation (also from Supper, *see* above) calls attention to the need for integration: "A good quality product cannot be produced in a poor manufacturing organisation. A good organisation must have good capabilities in design, development, production and purchasing. However, *none of these can be placed in a watertight compartment.*"

(3) ANALYSIS OF SUPPLIES REJECTS. Supplies staff have a direct interest in quality assurance and quality control as regards the actual safe arrival of undamaged supplies, and an indirect but none-the-less vital interest in the quality ("suitability for purpose") of *all* goods used in their factory.

The graphical presentation of data can greatly assist in the analysis of causes of problems such as transit damage. The following examples and discussion are based on the curves in Fig. 38 (Chapter 8).

The curves are taken here as referring to goods of types "A" and "B" arriving regularly in bulk shipments during 25 two-weekly periods. The ordinates represent (to a different scale) the number of goods arriving damaged as a percentage of the total arriving in each intake. Examination of the curves may prompt a number of questions regarding causes of rejects, including the following.

Goods "A".

(a) What action was taken with the supplier and haulier following the rise in rejects for intakes from 11 to 15?

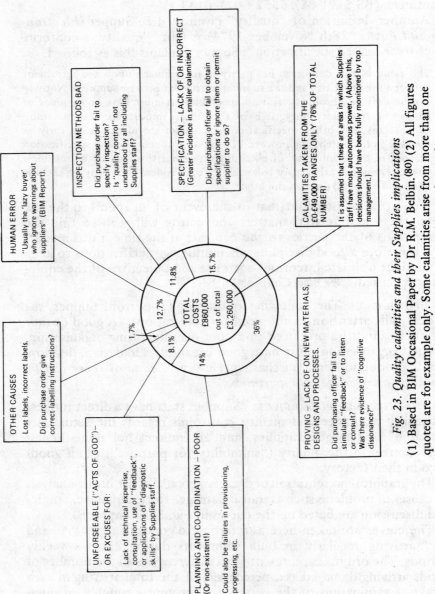

HUMAN ERROR

"Usually the 'lazy buyer' who ignore warnings about suppliers". (BIM Report).

INSPECTION METHODS BAD

Did purchase order fail to specify inspection?
Is "quality control" not understood by all including Supplies staff?

SPECIFICATION – LACK OF OR INCORRECT

(Greater incidence in smaller calamities)

Did purchasing officer fail to obtain specifications or ignore them or permit supplier to do so?

CALAMITIES TAKEN FROM THE £0-£49,000 RANGES ONLY (76% OF TOTAL NUMBER)

It is assumed that these are areas in which Supplies staff have most autonomous power. (Above this, decisions should have been fully monitored by top management.)

OTHER CAUSES

Lost labels, incorrect labels.

Did purchase order give correct labelling instructions?

TOTAL COSTS £860,000 out of total £3,260,000

11.8%
15.7%
12.7%
1.7%
8.1%
14%
36%

UNFORSEEABLE ("ACTS OF GOD") – OR EXCUSES FOR:

Lack of technical expertise, consultation, use of "feedback", or applications of "diagnostic skills" by Supplies staff.

PLANNING AND CO-ORDINATION – POOR

(Or non-existent!)

Could also be failures in provisioning, progressing, etc.

PROVING – LACK OF ON NEW MATERIALS, DESIGNS AND PROCESSES.

Did purchasing officer fail to stimulate "feedback" or to listen or consult?
Was there evidence of "cognitive dissonance?"

Fig. 23. Quality calamities and their Supplies implications

(1) Based in BIM Occasional Paper by Dr R.M. Belbin.(80) (2) All figures quoted are for example only. Some calamities arise from more than one cause and no correction has been made for this nor for total costs.

(*b*) Does comparison with previous years show any seasonal pattern?

(*c*) If so, is there lack of all-weather protection during bad weather?

(*d*) What caused the exceptional disaster shown dotted at intake number 15?

(*e*) Why was the improving trend (intakes 1-9) suddenly reversed at intakes 10-15?

(*f*) Did the supplier change his haulier, for example, at shipment 10?

Goods "B".

(*a*) Why is the trend rising?

(*b*) Why are there regular cyclical oscillations?

(*c*) Are there two suppliers, one more careless in loading than the other?

(*d*) Alternatively, are there two hauliers to which the same strictures apply?

In both instances it would be useful to investigate the points at which damage may occur, i.e. during loading, transit, trans-shipment or even at intake.

Figure 23 should also be studied here as it illustrates a number of possible causes of "supply calamities"; also refer again to Chapter 12.

(4) ANALYSIS OF PRODUCTION REJECTS. The quality assurance and quality control of the goods themselves is a complex and sensitive area which directly affects production, processing and, of course, the end-users. However, no purchasing officer need wait long to receive complaints resulting from supplies which are substandard.

For this analysis the curves in Fig. 38 can again be used. This time it is assumed that the ordinates represent percentage rejects per batch manufactured and the abscissa the batch numbers (which may or may not coincide with production periods). The curves now represent production output of commodities (say, finished parts) "A" and "B". (NOTE: Letters "A" and "B" do *not* here relate to classification.)

It would seem that rejects of "A" were purely random. Before making this assumption, however, comparison should be made with samples over previous periods or batches to see if there is any pattern.

Curve "B" reveals what may be a more serious situation (depending, of course, upon actual quantities). This curve displays a number of characteristics (some of which apply also to curve "A").

(*a*) The percentage of rejects appears to be increasing at a steady rate.

(*b*) Can a trend be deduced or calculated?

(*c*) Would the deviations from the calculated trend line within the band a-a, a_1-a_1 produce a "normal distribution"?

(d) Why are the fluctuations so regular? Could it be due to alternating suppliers providing different qualities of materials?

(e) What caused the "disaster" at batch 15?

(f) Can the trend be reversed as appears to be the case with commodity "B"?

(5) IMPLICATIONS FOR PURCHASING. Quality assurance and control requirements should always be specified where applicable on purchase orders or their accompanying documents. In the latter case the relevant documents must be mentioned upon the face of the purchase order to which they refer.

Tolerances, limits and degree of control specified must be appropriate to the needs of the supplies being purchased.

(6) EFFECTS OF INEFFICIENT QUALITY CONTROL. Too rigid limits and too tight control can add to costs (see Fig. 19). On the other hand, too wide limits and slack control can have the same effect. Other adverse effects, however, can result from either or both extremes, as follows:

(a) misleading data and/or statistics:

(b) incorrect deductions from data and statistics;

(c) excessive volumes of data from detailed inspection reports so that vital statistics are "drowned" in a mass of detail and important errors missed;

(d) unfair treatment of some suppliers, perhaps because of fluctuating effectiveness of inspection;

(e) unbalanced inspection or fluctuating effectiveness;

(f) overlooking general requirements when checking detail.

(7) SUPPLIER PERFORMANCE. When attending production, inspection meetings or other similar occasions Supplies staff should be in a position to compare and present suppliers' past quality performance as well as present performance. This is particularly important where Supplies have introduced new supplies or new suppliers. Prejudiced assertions may be heard that the new supply or the new source is inferior to previous ones.

(8) RELEVANT AUTHORITIES include the following.

(a) The Institute of Quality Assurance.

(b) The National Council for Quality and Reliability, now administered from the British Standards Institution.

(c) NATO Basic Inspection Requirements for Industry. It should be noted that it is advisable to write NATO conditions into any contracts which are subject to "NATO conditions in regard to inspection of materiel".

(d) The British Standards Institution, which offers an approach to quality assurance by its registration of firms of assessed quality capability. This scheme is operated as a complement to BSI's third party certification, i.e. the Kitemark and the Safety Mark. It is based on a Scheme of Assessment and Supervision (SAS), which lays down quality-control requirements applicable to all manufacturing industries.

British standards which are relevant are included in British Standard Handbook No. 22, "Quality Assurance".

Feedback and quality control

Feedback links are essential in quality control and in terotechnology (*see* below, and *see also* Chapter 8, feedback loops). Figure 24 indicates the flow of feedback essential to quality control from *all* who have to do with supplies. As drawn, the diagram only indicates the feedback links. To complete the "loop" (*see* Fig. 35) action would be needed by, say, Supplies to replace the faulty items or, say, production or the supplier to rectify them.

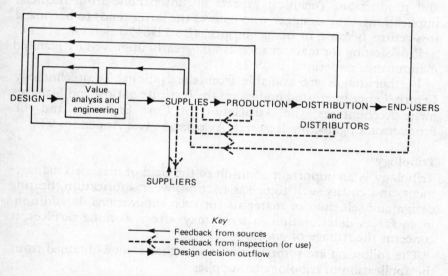

Fig. 24. Feedback links for terotechnology and quality control

Terotechnology and supplies

Terotechnology should interest all who study supplies management, for its application may well determine the use (or non-use) of equipment and materials.[83] The implications are wide as may be seen from the following definition provided by the Department of Trade and Industry's technical section.

Terotechnology is a combination of management, financial, engineering and other practices applied to physical assets in pursuit of economical life-cycle costs. It is concerned with specification and design for reliability and maintainability of plant, buildings, machinery, structures, etc. It is also concerned with installation, commissioning, maintenance, modifications and replacement, and with design, performance and costs. The subject is seen to fall into two main heads, separate but clearly interrelated. These are financial and technical.

The financial aspects are closely associated with value analysis, and in particular with value engineering because terotechnology should be introduced at the design stages of a product. It should also be introduced during standardisation, variety reduction and general assessment of tenders and quotations. If a designer is to optimise "life-cycle costs" he must realise that one of his basic raw materials in design is the information feedback he receives and upon which he can act. A Supplies department can be an invaluable source of such feedback since it is in continuous touch with suppliers and production. Technical aspects are inseparable from financial implications. Any designer who ignores the latter tends to become a loss-centre because of his negligence. (BS PD6470 Section 1(1.1).)

Provisioning for maintenance can be greatly improved by planned maintenance as defined in BS 3811.

Further details are available from the National Terotechnology Centre. Other interested bodies are the Institute of Cost and Management Accountants, the Association of Cost Engineers and the Production Engineering Research Association (*see* Appendix V).

Tribology

Tribology is an important addition to the field of materials management, and covers such topics as friction, wear, lubrication, bearing design and selection of materials for such applications. In addition, in so far as deterioration in store may affect working surfaces, it concerns the storage of goods.

The following are some of the results that can be obtained from the application of tribology to supplies.

(*a*) Fewer failures of prototypes and finished products.

(*b*) Avoidance of design corrections.

(*c*) Avoidance of failures early in machine-life (often due to friction, etc.).

(*d*) Life-cycle extended through reduction of inbuilt wear factors.

(*e*) Increased reliability through fewer wear failures.

(*f*) Better design through use of tribological design data.

(*g*) Reduced costs of power, maintenance, components, downtimes.

(h) Climatic effects upon wearing surfaces reduced or eliminated.

(i) Environmental effects upon wearing surfaces reduced or eliminated.

(j) More suitable rubbing surfaces (e.g. bearings).

(k) Selection of suitable lubricants.

(l) Use of rubbing or joining materials which are compatible with one another.

(m) Use of corrosion resistant materials.

Information is available from the Department of Industry and the National Centre of Tribology.

CHAPTER 7

The Stores Cycle:
Methods of Stock Control

AXIOM: It usually costs more to stock too little than too much. (Heinritz.)

INTRODUCTION

British Standard BS 5729 Part 1 (1) introduces the "concepts and objectives of stock control as part of management strategy", whilst modern stores management rejects outworn concepts of a store as "a place where goods are kept until they are needed, or dumped in case they may be needed some day". Stores should be considered as a profit-earning service to production or, in the case of a warehouse, to distribution. Storekeeping should contribute directly to profitability and be concerned with flow, lead times, storage costs, acquisition costs, materials handling, work study, preservation, preparation, packaging, pre-selection and issue, packing and despatch and other physical aspects (*see Storehouse*). (BS 5191 (2.3).)

The aim of this chapter is to indicate some methods for controlling stock which are applied to the succeeding sections which examine the characteristics of "flow" and demand for supplies.[85][86]

In the same way that specification is related to technical and physical needs, so the general levels of stocks should be related to the sales and production needs. Policy and control should be directed and exercised by Supplies and management. (*See* Chapter 2, stock investment policy.)

The quantities to be purchased, controlled and stored must be closely studied by Supplies in the light of overall company policy, the needs of the various departments served, and the "A.B.C." stores classification (*see* Chapter 5). At the same time Supplies may generate "feedback" to management which may further influence policy.

In the case of classification "A" materials, management must maintain control, or invite serious losses. Speed and volume of turn-over are usually the main considerations in classification "A" materials. Good availability, often at the expense of poor rate of turnover, is a frequent characteristic of classifications "B" and "C" materials.

Objectives of stock control

The primary objectives of stock control are (a) to maintain a reliable flow (b) of the correct materials (c) in good condition (d) to the work-centres—or despatch points (e) with the minimum inventory and (f) at lowest overall cost. (BS 5729 Part 1 (3.1).)

Classification "A" materials will be the major activity in propor-tion to the value, variety and frequency of movement of materials. However, it will be found that classifications "B" and "C" materials tend to attract a disproportionately large share of activity because of their much greater variety despite smaller usage.

Variations in demands on stores are related to production and sales, and are likely to be greatest in the classification "A" materials, which are direct production items, and least in classification "C", supporting and indirect materials. Demand for supporting materials is dependent upon the rate of production, the general maintenance of the factory and the support of production. The demand for direct materials will clearly be subject to the results of the following con-siderations and supply checks.

(a) *Sales policy.* Whatever may be forecast by statistics based on past demand must obviously be looked at and checked in the light of future estimated sales.

(b) *Budgetary control estimates.* These will be based upon the financial strength and policy of the company, and should take account of all sales and production trends, targets and price trends. Supplies fall within the control of budgetary estimates.

(c) *Production capacity* to absorb the materials, etc.

STOCK LEVELS

Setting stock levels

Once the pattern of external supply and internal demand has been ascertained it is necessary to set stock levels. These depend upon the following further considerations.

(a) Probabilities of a stock-out based on different stock levels and taking account of variations in the supply position and in production demand.

(b) Costs to the enterprise of production stoppage owing to stock-out.

(c) Variations in internal and external lead times.

135

NOTE:

When discussing stores policy it is useful to express demand in terms of consumption per production period and multiples of the lead time, e.g. if 200 units per week are used and the lead time is four weeks, calculations should be based on blocks of 800 units. (*See also* week numbering.)

Controlling stock levels

Most stock control systems rely upon replenishment of stock on the following bases. (BS 5729 Part 1 (8).)

(*a*) Reordering when stock falls to a predetermined reorder level. Flow is then in cycles on a quantitative basis.

(*b*) Reordering on a fixed time interval basis. Flow is then cyclical on a time basis only. (*See* (*e*) below and BS 5729 Part 3 (4.3).)

(*c*) A combination of (*a*) and (*b*), i.e. stock checks at regular times for the approach of stock to reorder level.

(*d*) Frequent/continuous monitoring if demands or intakes fluctuate.

(*e*) Review classes: "A", monthly, "B", quarterly, "C" half-yearly. (BS 5729 Part 3(4.3).)

(*f*) Record inputs (computer or manual) direct from store. (BS 5729 Part 5 (0.4a).)

(*g*) The closer the control the higher its cost. (BS 5729 Part 1 (3.3) abb.)

(*h*) The more complex the control the greater the risk of error. (BS 5729 Part 1 (3.3) abb.)

NOTE: The few instances where supplies do not pass through stock records should only be allowed with great reservation and be considered most abnormal. (*See* Note 10 Fig. 31 and "exceptional transactions" and Chapter 9 "recording of special data".)

Statistics from stock records

In discussing the methods of setting stock levels it must be made clear that, however sophisticated the methods of obtaining and keeping them, stock control records are largely "historic", the only important exception being the "pre-allocation record" (*see* Fig. 31).

As in most other fields, historic records cannot be used reliably to forecast the future without the application of statistical methods, observation, investigation, intuition and above all "diagnostic skills".

AXIOM: "Backsight" minus foresight = disaster!

EFFECT OF EXTERNAL CONDITIONS. Even where the most advanced statistical methods are employed in conjunction with accurate records there is need for intelligence and insight in their application. For example, stock records for a particular standard stock item may show a steady demand over a long period and the statistician may predict a further steady demand over a subsequent period ahead. However, the forecast may be upset by one or more of an almost infinite number of factors as the example which follows:

AXIOM: Foresight minus "backsight" = disaster!

Five factors are listed below, all of which could occur in any sequence or singly or in combination. There could be $5 \times 4 \times 3 \times 2 \times 1 = 120$ different possible basic variations (the multiplicand of the series is known as the "factorial"). If secondary variations environmental to each factor were also considered, the possible conditions would be almost infinite and only a computer *might* calculate them. The five factors are as follows, secondary factors shown in parentheses.

(a) Faulty materials may have been shipped from the supplier or have just arrived. (Deteriorated during transit.)

(b) The supplier may be about to suffer his first stoppage (owing to an unforseen industrial problem).

(c) The machine shop may be just about to scrap a considerable quantity of material through inaccurate machining. (The tools may have been set up incorrectly for the job—or it may be due to one of 9,999 other production hazards.)

(d) The sales department could have just booked an important export order (the terms of which may contain a clause stipulating a delivery entailing the immediate acceleration of production).

(e) There may have been a failure on the part of *the supplier* to obtain sufficient materials (possibly due to a failure of his own Supplies department).

NOTE:

Production stoppage (also known as "down-time") is not caused only by stock deficiency. Supplies departments may also be involved directly or indirectly in the following (BS 5191 (2.6)):

(a) time taken for tool change, including procurement from tool store;

(b) materials shortage or delay in intake or internal distribution;

(c) difficulties in use, manipulation or processing of materials;

(d) setting-up time for tools;

(e) maintenance.

It is in the face of changing conditions that stock levels must be controlled and records kept for this purpose. Because the records will be models of the levels controlled and of the material flow, it will help if a clear picture is obtained of the levels involved.

Different stock levels (BS 5191 (3.3))

Various levels are shown diagrammatically in Fig. 25, some or all of which may be present according to the stock streams being discussed. They are examined starting at the lowest, "deficiency", level, progressing through to the highest level, "maximum", and beyond this to excess.

(1) "DEFICIENCY" is not a fixed level but a measure of the amount by which stock fails to meet the needs of the users. It suggests an

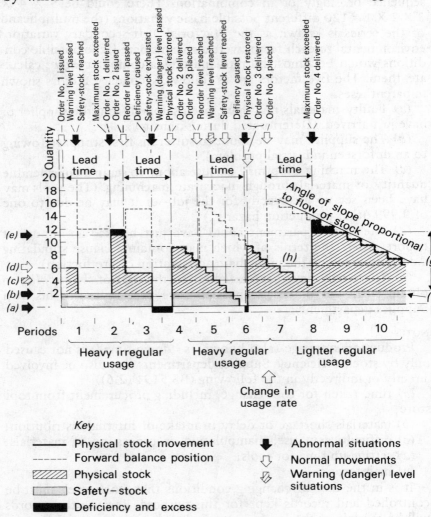

Fig. 25 Basic stock levels

actual or prospective production stoppage and may reveal that there has been a failure in stock control, purchasing or suppliers—or all three.

(2) EXHAUST BIN LEVEL is the point known as "stock-out". The implications to all concerned (particularly the progress chasers) are too obvious to need elaboration. (*See* Chapter 18.)

(3) SAFETY-STOCK LEVEL is set to provide for exceptions of supply or demand (*see also* Chapter 2). There are, of course, instances where the safety-stock level and reorder level are identical, e.g. where replenishment is immediate. (BS 5729 Part 1 (3.6f).)

(4) A WARNING (DANGER) LEVEL exists in practically every stores situation, but is seldom presented in formal terms. For the purpose of progressing it is the "point of no return" after which a stock-out is inevitable if delay occurs. A computer program can readily include "warning levels" set at such a value that if there has been some delay at the supplier's works the action of progressing will reveal this in time for the purchasing department to take one of the following steps.

(*a*) Find an alternative source of supply.

(*b*) Enable the sales department in turn to warn their own customer of possible delay.

(*c*) Inform production who may be able to revise the shop-floor programme and transfer work.

(*d*) Put extra pressure on the supplier to force him to keep his original delivery. (*See* Chapter 18, pre-urging.)

(5) REORDER LEVEL (OR PROVISIONING LEVEL). Where throughput is sufficient to warrant the use of stock control based upon demand, a formula can be used (*see* policies "B" and "C" in Fig. 34 and Table 15). With reasonably steady demand, stable lead times and reliable sources of supply, the reorder level (Rol) is found by multiplying the total units of expected lead time (Lt), in, say "weeks", "production" or other periods, by expected demand (usage) per unit of lead time (Ult), then adding an allowance for safety-stock (Ss) (Fig. 32 (22), BS 5729 Part 1 (6.2e)):

$$Rol = (Lt \times Ult) + Ss.$$

For example, in Table 15, policy "B", the total demand in 12 weeks is 12 units, i.e. one unit per week of lead time, with Lt = 4 weeks,

$$Rol = (4 \times 1) + Ss.$$

This very simplified example reveals the importance of safety-stock, because without it there would be a stock-out and deficiency so that production would cease at week five.

(6) MAXIMUM STOCK LEVEL is, as its name implies, the level above which the stock should not be permitted to rise. For classifications "B" and "C" materials this level is normally set by the stock controller (*see also* Chapter 2). If large intakes are normal it is important to check the possibilities of simultaneous intakes exceeding maximum storage capacity.

(7) FORWARD BALANCE LEVEL, like "deficiency" level, is a non-physical level showing the forward position of stock under certain conditions. In Fig. 25 the dotted "forward balance line" shows what stock would be on hand if all outstanding purchase orders were instantaneously delivered. (*See also* Fig. 31, item 20, and notes.)

(8) EXCESS LEVEL has no limit but calls for immediate attention in every case. Not only may investment costs be excessive but more serious may the holding of materials long past their shelf-life (in one case in the author's experience, twenty-one years' stock!) (*See* Chapter 26 *Storehouse*, Checklist 42 and BS 5729 Part 1 (9.3).)

Rates of stock-turn (BS 5191 (3.3))

(*See also Storehouse.*) When examined in the traditional manner the rate of stock-turn can be used to give a general indication of success (or failure) in control of inventory. (Rate of stock-turn = total usage ÷ mean stock.)

The lower the rate of stock-turn the longer will be the stock-life, producing a number of adverse effects upon each company's financial performance and cumulatively upon the national economy. A United Nations Report ("Inventory management performance", David L. Ray, *Purchasing and Supply Management,* February 1981) gives some idea of the problem in six major industrial countries (*see* Table 14).

EFFECTS OF SLOW RATES OF STOCK-TURN. If the mean rate of stock-turn for a company is, say, one stock-turn per annum, the effects will include some or all of the following.

(*a*) High probability that some stock will be held for considerably longer periods than 12 months.

(*b*) Serious risk of stock-life exceeding shelf-life.

(*c*) Cash tied up for equivalent period, therefore . . .

(*d*) . . . opportunity costs deprive firm of plant, tools, sales promotion, supplies, etc.

(*e*) Interest charged if stock financed on outside borrowing, and . . .

(*f*) . . . interest charges fluctuate, and . . .

TABLE 14. MEDIAN STOCK-TURN PERFORMANCES, 1969-75
(Using added value outputs)

Country	Stock-turns per annum
Australia	2.3
Denmark	2.3
Japan	3.1
UK	1.8
USA	3.0
West Germany	3.0

(g) . . . if borrower runs into trouble this is the very time the loan may be called in.

(h) Stock-outs can still occur (*see* Fig. 26 and Fig. 42, Flow 5).

(i) Costs build up during stock-life and reduce profits (*see* Fig. 49).

(j) Sluggish stock-turns and sluggish supplies flow often indicate sluggish management.

(k) High stock may inhibit firm taking advantage of seasonal glut or price fall.

(l) May prevent or inhibit trial of new materials or sources of supply.

(m) May invite pilferage: "no one will miss" slow moving stock.

(n) Large stocks encourage profligate use.

METHODS OF STOCK CONTROL (BS 5729 Part 1 (8))

Some popular methods of stock control are outlined here, and a summary with comparisons of four stock-control policies is given at the close of this chapter.

Basically most stock-control methods depend upon the establishment of a reorder level (*see* above). Controls fall into two main groups, (a) visual and (b) clerical, the latter including not only manual card records but also control by computer, etc.

Physically each method entails the holding of a stock sufficient to maintain production until the replenishment arrives. It is the setting and adjustment of this important level to suit demand that will determine if the operation is successful or not.

As usually exemplified, the stock level is shown as falling at a steady rate, shown by a smoothly sloping curve (as at A in Fig. 26). The angle of slope ϕ indicates the rate of depletion of the bin. The steeper the slope the faster the rate of depletion and the shorter the lead time which must be obtained to achieve replenishment before stock-out occurs.

In practice the demand curve is seldom a smooth line, but a series of discrete steps, each step representing an issue of stock from the store. Moreover the steps are seldom equal!

The shaded portion below each curve in Fig. 26 represents the actual volume of stock carried at any instant. The total shaded area is therefore the volume of stock over the whole period. The average height of the curve is the average value of stock held throughout the period.

The curve of demand at A is a straight line only where stock flow is uniform. This usually occurs only in highly specialised classes of industry such as process, mass and continuous-production plants.

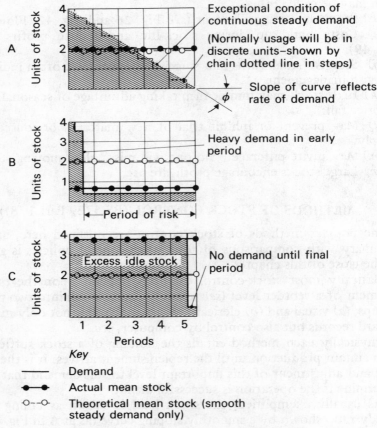

Fig. 26. Mean stock levels related to flow of supplies

The curves at B and C show extreme examples of other curves of demand. Most requirements lie somewhere between these two. It will be seen that the same reorder level must still be maintained because otherwise stock may not be available at the final period. It will also be noted that the shaded portion under the curve at C shows a very high average stock level and therefore high investment in stock. The demand for this high average stock did not occur in this example until the last week. This is the cause of the high idle stock figure.

Most formulae for economic order quantity (*see* Chapter 10) assume the theoretical rate of smooth average usage as the basis for calculation. It must be explained that this is only true where the actual usage results in the coinciding of the lines which represent "actual mean stock" and "theoretical mean stock" as at A. This does not occur at B or C where the shaded portion of the figure clearly upsets the balance assumed in the formula, which assumes constant rate of usage. If the pattern were regularly of these shapes (i.e. if the major demands were always early or late in lead time) it would be essential to modify the calculations and to recalculate the economic order quantity (EOQ) or re-programme intakes.

Visual control: imprest method

This method involves setting a maximum level for the bin and making periodical inspections. The bin is then topped up as required immediately to the maximum level.

A too-frequent occurrence of stock-out conditions could indicate either that the maximum level needs adjustment or that the demand should be looked into, as with open-access bins (*see* below). In setting the stock level it must be borne in mind that each replenishment costs money, but that a stock-out with no reserve will hold up production.

Visual control: open-access bins using bin tags (Fig. 29)

Open-access bins for materials or parts (such as fasteners) may be used singly or in multiples situated around the factory adjacent to the production lines, or in a special open stores area. Operatives help themselves to the stocks without having to make records, leave their work-centre or queue at stores serveries. (BS 5191 (3.3).)

The imprest system is satisfactory with replenishment direct from the main stock. In the case of a number of such bins, a mobile stores may top up the bins at fixed times, or when signalled as explained below.

Stock control is not applied at the point of issue and detailed control and recording of each transaction is neither possible nor necessary, thus eliminating booking errors, costs, delay, etc. Overall control can be maintained at the store from which replenishment is made. The stock control records of quantities issued in topping up the open-access bins by imprest will reveal if the quantities drawn off appear excessive. Enquiries can then by made at the production meeting, which a member of Supplies should attend. The production manager can examine if an irregularity has occurred. ("Irregularities" could include the scrapping of parts and materials and their replacement from the bin without divulging the fact that rejections had occurred, or pilferage or profligate use.) If the production department had failed to keep Supplies informed of changes in demand, the examination may have the effect of reminding them to do so in the future. Since replenishment is immediate no great hardship should result from stock-out at the bin. However, where this cannot be tolerated, the "two-bin system" (*see* below) can be introduced at the open-access bins.

Obviously there are limits to the classes of goods which can be dealt with by this means. It would be unethical to include "attractive" items. Even though the staff using the materials might be honest, they would be put in an invidious position if someone from another department helped himself. In any case they could not be expected to exercise the custodial duty of a storekeeper.

Visual control: two-bin system

The term "two-bin system" should be restricted to the visual method of stock control using two bins, or one bin divided at two levels. One section only is used at one time, and on its exhaustion the second is broken into and steps are taken to replenish the exhausted bin as follows.

A "travelling" bin tag (*see* Fig. 27) may be hung on to the first bin front. When the first bin is exhausted the tag (2) is removed and placed above the bin in a slot or on a hook (1). The storeman from the central stores on his rounds collects the tag and takes the necessary steps to replenish the bin. The removal of the bin tag may leave a brightly coloured signal exposed which was previously concealed by it (3). This arrangement calls attention to the state of the bin until the replenishment arrives and the bin tag is replaced over the coloured signal.

If the bin tag is not collected and taken to the stores it should remain in the "alert" position until the bin has been refilled.

The bin tag shown in Fig. 27 acts as a travelling requisition. As in the case of the issues from open-access bins, no clerical work is involved by operatives who use it. This obviates the possibility of clerical errors, particularly those of booking, transcription of bin numbers and similar details.

The provision of the second bin for reserve stock usually involves a certain wastage in stores space, but when used for open-access bins at the work-centres the wastage in space may be offset by the avoidance of unauthorised stores being set up at the work-centres.

Instead of two bins, a divider can be placed horizontally at a fixed reserve level. When removed it is hung up as previously described or passed to the stores office. A third bin may be allocated for "safety stock". (BS 5729 Part 3, Fig. 7, BS 5191 (3.3).)

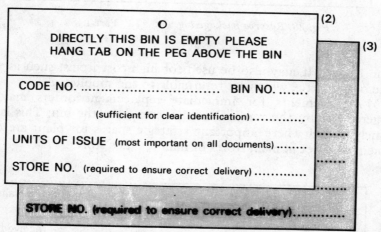

Fig. 27. Loose or travelling bin tag for visual bin control
See Fig. 29 for normal fixed bin tag. Other uses for bin tags suggested by BS 5279 Part 1 (8) are for (a) items on "special issue" only, (b) obsolescent items (i.e. those to be used first), (c) new items, (d) customer's "free issue", (e) "preferred", and so on.

Visual control: reserve package
An important variation of the two-bin method, often used for such items as stationery, involves the parcelling up of a reserve quantity, the last parcel bearing a tag or label as in Fig. 28. The action to be taken is obvious.

Visual control: "one-for-one" basis
This method has the following two variants.

(a) Issues are only made against the return of an equivalent unit. Examples are issues of tools, protective clothing or items involving

```
┌─────────────────────────────────────────────────────┐
│                                                       │
│               USE THIS PACKAGE LAST                   │
│          On breaking into this package please         │
│                                                       │
│  DETACH THIS TAG AND PASS AT ONCE TO STOCK-CONTROL    │
│                       OFFICE                          │
│                                                       │
│       FIRST CHECK THAT NO LOOSE STOCK REMAINS         │
│                                                       │
│  CONTENTS (description sufficient for clear identification) ...... │
│                                                       │
│  CODE NO.  (required to ensure correct reorder, and for stock-  │
│               control purposes)                       │
│                                                       │
│  STORE (OR OFFICE) (required for delivery)............ │
│                                                       │
└─────────────────────────────────────────────────────┘
```

Fig. 28. Reserve package tag. (BS 5729 Part 1 (8))

some hazard. It may also be used for high-cost items, such as propane bottles, etc., which are returnable to the supplier.

(b) Arrangements for immediate replacement orders may be triggered off by the removal of the item from the bin. This is extremely useful where important strategic spares for plant are concerned, whether in main stores or maintenance stores.

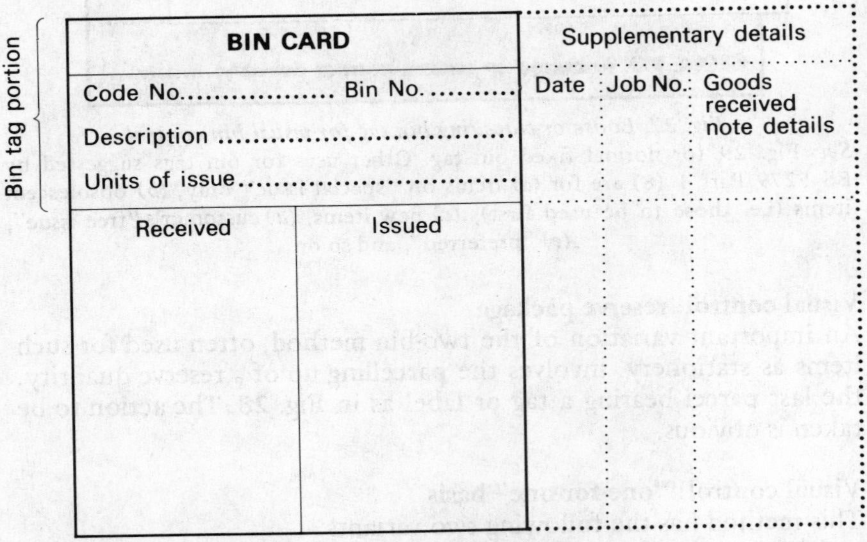

Fig. 29. Bin card and bin tag (fixed)
See Figs. 30 and 31 for stock record card.

Visual/clerical control: bin cards (BS 5191 (3.3))
(*See* Fig. 29.) Formerly this was one of the chief methods of stock control. However, it has fallen increasingly into disfavour for the following main reasons.

(*a*) It can involve delay in the actual movement of materials at the bin while the storeman or other operative writes up the record.

(*b*) The clerical operation may be done under pressure of urgency, so that errors are likely to occur in recording.

(*c*) The writing of the people using the bin may not be clear.

(*d*) The records may get soiled, writing facilities may be bad.

(*e*) Lighting may be inadequate for clerical work at the bin face.

(*f*) Bin cards may be replaced at the wrong bin.

(*g*) Bin cards may be lost.

The bin card system has the advantage that the record is up to date at each transaction. It may be used in situations where the goods are of high intrinsic value and can then be checked visually against the records at frequent intervals.

If data entered become more complicated, such as balance, date, order number, the bin card should be removed to a central point and "promoted" to the status of a stock control record. It should be replaced by a bin tag at the bin (*see* Fig. 27) showing only the basic data.

Clerical stock control: cards
However sophisticated the methods employed, whether by computer punched cards or manual cards, the basic operations of clerical stock control will be similar. These involve the establishment of a reorder level and the recording of at least two main stock movements—receipts and issues—and their resultant: the physical stock balance.

Clerical methods of stock control depend for their success on the proper preparation of the basic data and in particular on:

(*a*) the coding system;

(*b*) the vocabulary or stores catalogue;

(*c*) units of issue and measurements;

(*d*) the design of the documents and the speed of their transmission to the control point;

(*e*) accuracy of documentation.

As the largest proportion of stock control records are still in manual form, a few guiding principles are given below.

It is important to select the type of record appropriate to the class of supplies. A very simplified record card such as that illustrated in Fig. 30 may be used for classification "C" supplies. A re-order level has been shown but this is unnecessary if replenishment is

Reorder level: 100 litres							Group code No. 2444		
Description: CUTTING OIL									
200	150	125	40	100	50	250	200		

Fig. 30. Simplified stock card with running totals only

available immediately at all times.

A fully developed record card as in Fig. 31, is needed for most stock of all classifications. The numbered paragraphs below relate to the sections in Fig. 31 and it will be readily noted that a number of features are progressively added according to the needs of the stock control section.

(1) DESCRIPTION (primary information). *See Storehouse.*

(2) COMMODITY CODE NUMBER.[87][88] Coding, the most important element in setting up stock control, is dealt with in considerable detail in *Storehouse*. (BS 5729 Part 5, Table 2.) *See* Fig. 33 and "scrap" detail on Fig. 32 for examples of code developments, also Chapter 6.

(3) CHECKING COLUMN. Initials of those handling extremely valuable goods, stock checkers, etc. Can also be used for cross-references where a number of items from different cards are issued off one requisition.

(4) ALL RECORDS REFERENCES. Purchase or production orders, GRNs, requisition numbers, etc.—all dates entered at 4a.

(5) UNITS OF ISSUE. This is frequently omitted from stock-record cards, but should be included, particularly where supplies are in process of metrication. (BS 5191 (3.3).)

(6) WARNING LEVEL. *See also* Chapter 18.

(7) CONSUMPTION RECORD. This may be needed as either a short-term or long-term record. In the latter case it is best kept on a separate card with a year to a view. Subsequent years can be shown one below the other. This makes comparison between similar months easier. (*See also* Fig. 36.)

(8) QUANTITY ORDERED is actually a purchase record and may thus

148

Consumption record (7)
Period | 1 2 3 4 5 6 7 8 9 10 11 12
Quantity
Units of purchase .... (19).
Units of storage ...... (20).
Suppliers (1). (16)

Class .(14).......... Units of issue .(5).........
Order quantity ....
Location (15)........ Card number ....
Max.....ROL ..... Warning.(6).Safety– ......
level stock
(17) User department(s) ....
(2)...............(3)..............

Pre-allocation record (10)		Order record		All records (3)		Check	Stock record			Forward stock balance (11)	Stock ledger	
Quantity allocated	Free balance	Quant. ord.(8)	O/S (9) dues in	Date	Ref. (4)	Check	In	Out	Balance (physical)	Forward stock balance	Unit price (12)	Total value (13)
(1)	(2)	(3)	(4)	(5)	(6)	(7)	(8)	(9)	(10)	(11)	(12)	(13)
	100	100	200	2/5	241507/..				140	340		
20	80			3/5	Job 7701			10	130	330		
10	70			3/5	Job 7731			30	100	300		
50	20			–	--			–	100	300		
30	-10/90	100	300	3/5	241507/8			–	100	400		
40	50			4/5	241507/1		100	–	200	400		

Vocabulary description (1) Channel Mild Steel

Review date (18) ●●○

Commodity code (2) 241507

First digit, 2 = storehouse number 2(= steel store)
Second digit, 4 = channel section
Third/fourth digits, 15 = 15 cm deep sections(S)
Fifth/sixth digits, 7 = 7 cm wide flanges(F)

4   15(S)   7(F)

Fig. 31. Stock-record/control card

be a duplication. It is needed where the "dues in" column is used so that the latter can be correctly updated.

(9) ORDERS OUTSTANDING, "DUES IN". This column is used if it is required to know the commitments against purchase orders outstanding. This may be necessary both as regards financial commitments and for the purposes of progressing supplies.

(10) PRE-ALLOCATION (FORWARD ALLOCATION) RECORD: QUANTITY ALLOCATED. This is used where it is intended to relate stock levels to future demands for jobs planned and notified in advance to Supplies by production or sales. The system merely requires the entry in "allocated" column of the future demands as these are received. In next column is entered the "free balance". Each time zero is

149

reached a fresh order is placed. The new order quantity is entered in "free balance" column and subsequent future demands are offset against it until zero is again reached and a fresh order placed. Columns (8), (9), date and (4) are then entered.

The system is not successful if there are significant movements of stock which have escaped passing through the allocation record. Such may be, for example, small-value orders, replacements to customers, issues to meet rejections or jobs scrapped in production. A further difficulty arises if bookings are made on a long-term basis in advance of issue. Where this occurs separate cards must be used for each period ahead and it is then essential that orders are placed, phased and progressed accordingly. (BS 5191 (2.3).)

(11) FORWARD STOCK BALANCE. This column is required where usage in normal lead time exceeds the quantity covered by each order of normal (or EOQ) value. As each replenishment order is placed the column is credited with the amount. As physical withdrawals take place it is lowered until reorder level is reached and a further replenishment demand is then made. The ordering is thus always ahead of the intake; this corrects the stock position before physical exhaustion of the bin takes place. (*See also* Fig. 25.)

The values in the forward balance column are found by adding the physical balance (column (25)) to the "dues in" (column (9)). An example of forward stock balance is given in Table 14, policy "D".

(12) UNIT PRICE. A price column may be used to show the value of the articles for inventory. The use made of this will vary according to whether the costing methods for stock are based on "first in first out", "market price", "last in first out", "average price", or "standard price", etc. (*see Storehouse*).

(13) TOTAL VALUE. Where used as a stock ledger or inventory, the total value will be shown in this column.

(14) CLASS. Where the coding does not designate the class of material it may be necessary to show this. This is also used where "class" or "group" codes are employed.

(15) LOCATION. This information will be necessary where the card is used at a central point and the coding does not indicate the location of stock.

(16) SUPPLIERS. A list of suppliers is essentially a purchase record, but it can be of assistance to the stores to know who are the approved suppliers.

(17) USER DEPARTMENTS. For some applications it may be of advantage to show the work-centres or user departments served from the bin.

(18) VISIBLE EDGE, top or bottom as required to suit filing, etc. This may bear a simple box for review dates or signals such as the following:

Single red dot = review stock each "quarter day"
Two red dots = review on first working day each month
Three red dots = review at commencement of each week

More elaborate signalling devices should be avoided.

(19), (20) UNITS OF PURCHASE, UNITS OF STORAGE *See Storehouse.*

(21) MAXIMUM STOCK LEVEL.

(22) RE-ORDER LEVEL.

(23) IN—receipts into store.

(24) OUT—issues from store.

(25) BALANCE—physical quantity in stock.

Vertical-card trays for stock control

Cards with columns for the same basic data as in Fig. 31, but housed vertically in mobile or fixed trays, provide a visible edge for rapid retrieval, location, filing and action. Such a card is illustrated in Fig. 32.

This recording method is particularly useful in medium-sized offices where purchase and stock control records can be combined and made mobile by the use of a trolley if stock control and purchasing are not located in the same place.

In front of each stock card a travelling purchase requisition can be inserted. This is removed from in front of its stock control card immediately reorder level is reached and sent at once to the purchasing department. Whether or not it is necessary to make any entries on this card depends upon the procedure adopted: such entries should be avoided unless some essential use is made of the information, and particularly if the information is already recorded on purchase records. When the purchase requisition card is removed it exposes the coloured (or other distinctive) marking on the edge of the stock control card. This then acts as a daily visible reminder of items "at risk". The purchasing department (or the progress section) can retain the requisition card until delivery as a "trigger" for progress chasing and only release it back to stores when a goods received note is received to clear it.

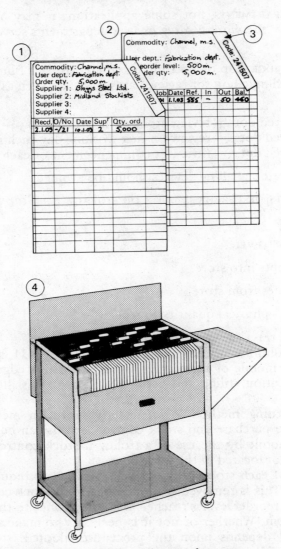

Fig. 32. Vertical-card stock control system
(1) Travelling requisition. (2) Stock-control card. (3) Coloured flash on edge of stock-control card. (4) Mobile stock record trolley with sorting tray.

Computer control (*See* BS 5729 Part 4, Table 1 for checklist.)
Where computer control is not yet used it is beneficial to design the stock control system to allow for its later introduction.[88][89][90][117]

Success in manual and particularly computer stock control depends upon the accuracy of preparation, assembly and presentation of data. For this, coding is of first importance. Computers cannot correct faulty data, but they can reject faulty data if "check digits" or other devices are introduced into their program.

Computer control is usually associated with visual display units (VDUs) upon which the tabulated data of stock levels (for example) are immediately available upon keying in the commodity code and other symbols required to activate the computer. Where, as in a process plant, stock records are continuously updated direct from the process the VDU will indicate instant states of stock, rate of material flow, approach of stock-out, trend of demand, and many other factors and data depending upon the program. In such a case the computer is said to be working "on line" and in "real time". Where the computer is fed with data on an historical basis such as from punched cards it is said to be "off-line" and the data displayed on the VDU along with statistical information will have a time-lag from the actual event or state of stock levels, etc. due to lead time in preparing the data for display.

An example of computer operation of stock control and purchasing is shown in Fig. 33. Although the tabulation relates to a public authority, it would be equally suitable for a production factory or commercial enterprise.

In practice the purchasing officer of the authority receives each week a tabulation of the full stock inventory. He also receives each fortnight a "request to purchase" tabulation, and also a tabulation showing which purchase orders need to be progressed. The fortnightly "request to purchase" tabulation need show only those items which require ordering action. A complete tabulation of all items may also be available on request. For the sake of example the last three have been combined in Fig. 33. The additional column (14) shows the progressing action needed which would normally be the subject of a separate tabulation. Since the illustration is taken from a full tabulation, columns (13) and (14) are in many cases blank because no immediate action is needed.

The following notes relate to the columns in Fig. 33. Where comments are the same as for Fig. 31, the note reference for that figure is given.

(1) MULTIPLE FIGURE CODE (e.g. five figure). (*See* Fig. 31, note (2).)

(2) DESCRIPTION. (*See* Fig. 31, note (1).) Twenty-four spaces are allowed for in the print-out. Full descriptions are as follows.

(g) = Chamber cast iron 900 mm × 1,200 mm.

(1) Line	(2) Code No. / Stores vocabulary (Description)	(3) Store No.	(4) Stock in hand	(5) Qty O/s	(6) Order number	(7) Date of order	(8) Qty allt.	(9) Reorder level	(10) Lead time (wks)	1	2	3	4	5	6	This month	(12) Unit Price	(13) Purch.	(14) Prog.
(a)	21062 Box surf hyd road	25	12	30	11810	44/9	0	48	12	8	8	8	8	18	4	0	4.12	A	D
(b)	21066 Box surf sgl stn ft	12	7	24	11817	44/9	0	18	10	2	2	2	2	6	1	1	3.06	A	E
(c)		21	1	3	10002	10/9	0	13	40	2	2	2	2	8	3	0			O
(d)				6	11170	40/9	0												
(e)				4	13648	50/9	0											B	
(f)	22231 Chmbr Cl 900 1200	34	11		11131	40/9	3	3	60	1	3	2	3	4	5	5	31.10		
(g)		25	3	50	11719	42/9	44	2	10	1	0	1	0	0	0	0			C
(h)	28281 Fltr plt 1000 1000	6	80					30		30	10	12	10	11	7	3	3.03		
(i)		18	5				0	4	10	2	1	3	2	2	0	1			
(j)		21	5				0	4	10	1	0	1	1	1	0	0	2.15		
(k)	29431 Gully Rd Opn Cl 300 300	5	20	10	11131	40/9	8	8	30	4	3	4	2	4	4	4		B	
(l)		12	3				2	2		1	1	0	0	1	1	0			
(m)		16	10				8	8	40	0	0	0	0	0	0	0	10.00	B	
(n)	29555 Vlu gt 75	16	10	12	12649	50/9	20	20		8	7	9	6	8	8	8			
(o)		26	6				2	2	5	10	40	30	30	20	50	10	5.11		O
(p)	31111 Cbl 0.75 twn blk pvc	12	500	100	11799	43/9	50	50	12	2	1	0	1	2	0	0	4.12	A	
(q)	32119 Strtr P B 3	12	2				3	3	16	1	0	0	1	0	0	0	15.00	B	
(r)	22134 Strtr Y D 30	12	2	4	12001	44/9	1	16		1	0	0	1	0	0	0			E

Fig. 33. Computer print-out for Supplies tabulation

(b) = Filter plate 1,000 mm × 1,000 mm.

(n) = Valve gate 75 mm.

(p) = Cable 0.75 mm twin black PVC

(3) STORES NUMBER. Each store point is given an identity number. The computer arranges the tabulation within each part number in sequence of store numbers, e.g. for code 21066, stores numbers 12, 21 and 34 are the only ones with these goods in stock.

(4) STOCK IN HAND. This is the figure according to the computer records for the week being tabulated. It is shown separately for each store point.

(5) QUANTITIES OUTSTANDING–ON ORDER. (*See* Fig. 31, note (9).)

(6) ORDER NUMBER. Purchase order number.

(7) DATE OF ORDER. The date on which the purchase order was placed is shown in code by the week number and the last digit of the year, e.g. (line *(a)*) Order 11810 was placed in week 44 of year 1979.

(8) QUANTITY ALLOCATED. This shows the quantity still in stores—or in reservation stores—which has been allocated to jobs. For purposes of inventory valuation this quantity may be included in column (4). The computer will, however, take this into account when calculating for column (13).

(9) REORDER LEVEL. This is the level set by the purchasing department in the normal way. If the computer prints out a letter "B" in column (1), however, the purchasing officer will review his reorder level.

(10) LEAD TIME (WEEKS). This is the delivery time estimated or actual and given by the purchasing officer to the computer section for incorporation in the computer records.

(11) USAGE EACH MONTH. This is printed out showing the usages in the last six months and also the current month up to the date of tabulation being worked upon. (*See also* Fig. 31, note (7).)

(12) UNIT PRICE. In many installations the unit price differs from the purchase price and makes allowance for costing, overheads, etc. There is no reason why the basis should not be made to suit any individual case. However, it will often be found that the needs of inventory accounting do not permit the use of the straight purchase price. (*See also* Fig. 31, note (12).)

(13) ACTION–PURCHASING. This column, together with (14), is the most important in the tabulation. If letter "A" appears, it indicates that a new order may be required since the existing stock and out-

standing orders may not bring the bin into credit at the current rate of consumption.

If letter "B" is printed, this indicates that at the present rate of consumption the reorder level may need adjustment.

In both these cases there may have been exceptional circumstances which gave rise to the printing out of the letter. The purchasing officer must therefore examine each case on its merits.

Letter "A" is based upon a computer program which takes account of stock in hand—column (4); quantity on order—column (5); quantity allocated—column (8); reorder level—column (9); lead time—column (10).

Letter "B" is based on the following: stock in hand—column (4); quantity on order—column (5); quantity allocated—column (8); reorder level—column (9); lead time—column (10); monthly usage—column (11).

(14) PROGRESS. In this column are printed letters indicating the due date of outstanding orders.

"E" = Due in eight weeks from date of tabulation.
"D" = Due in four weeks from date of tabulation.
"C" = Due in two weeks from date of tabulation.
"O" = Overdue.

The data in this column result from the date of the purchase order and the lead (or delivery) time.

GENERAL COMMENTS. (Refer line by line to extreme right-hand columns (13) and (14) of Fig. 33.)

Line (a). Stock in hand at column (4) plus orders outstanding at column (5) is below reorder level of 48 at column (9). Letter "A" is therefore printed out at column (13).

There is an order numbered 11810, delivery of which is due in four weeks' time. (Order date week 44) + (lead time 12 weeks)—(week of tabulation 52) = 4. The purchasing department note that letter "D" is printed out at column (14) to call attention to this.

The exceptionally heavy withdrawal from stock in month 5 needs investigation and it may be necessary to accelerate delivery of outstanding order 11810 to correct the stock levels as quickly as possible.

Line (b). This stock item is in almost the same condition as code 21062 at line *(a)*, but delivery is not due for eight weeks, as indicated by letter "E", column (14).

Line (c). Letter "O" has been printed out at column (14) indicating that order 10002 is now overdue. It should have been delivered at week 10 + 40 = 50.

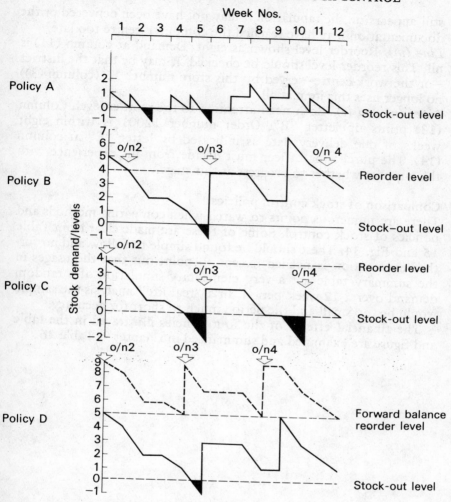

Fig. 34. *Some methods and policies for stock control and their effects*
Shaded areas = deficiency.

Lines (c), (d) and (e). All refer to the same stores point no. 21,
column (3). (The computer can arrange the entries in sequence of
order numbers as shown in column (3).)

Line (f). The print-out of letter "B" at column (13) indicates that
the reorder level may need adjusting. Examination of column (11)
shows that there is a definite trend of increased demand. Moreover,
the lead time column (10) shows a serious deterioration in delivery
on orders subsequent to number 11817.

Line (b). Delivery was due in the week of tabulation ("52"). As it still appears on the tabulation it may not have been delivered or the documentation may have reached the computer centre too late.

Line (m). Reorder level shown as eight. Demand at column (11) is nil. This reorder level should be checked. It may be that the district —or the work-centre—served by this store number 16 (column (3)) no longer uses this item at all.

Lines (n) and (r). Both need attention to the reorder level. Column (13) prints up letter "B". Order number 12001 is within eight weeks of due delivery date as indicated by letter "E" at column (14). The purchasing officer must decide from his experience with this supplier whether to progress at this stage.

Comparison of stock control policies

There are numerous points to watch when comparing methods and policies of stock control. Some of these are made clear from Table 15 and Fig. 34. These should be found simple to follow and no further explanation is needed except to point out that the usages in the summary table are a very elementary simulation of a random demand over a 12-week period. In a "real life" analysis the sample would be too small and the period much to short for accuracy.

The financial effects of the four policies illustrated in the table and figure are examined and summarised in Chapter 9, Table 26.

TABLE 15. COMPARISON OF STOCK CONTROL POLICIES
DEMAND SUMMARY TABLE
(same for all four policies, "A" to "D" inclusive)

Week	1	2	3	4	5	6	7	8	9	10	11	12
Usage	1	2	0	1	2	0	0	2	0	2	1	1
Usage per 4-week period			4				4				4	

(Demands are random but total usage is the same for each 4-week period, and there is no trend.)

TABLE 15: POLICY "A"

Fixed regular intake quantity of 1 unit per week.
Intake to be made at commencement of each week.
No stock control needed as intakes are predetermined and fixed.
Quantity per order may be "EOQ", "average demand" or upon some other basis.
Reorder level not required for the reasons above.

Week No.	Action	In	Out (usage)	Physical balance	Comments
1	Initial order received	1	1	1	
1			1	0	Stock-out
2		1	2	−1	Deficiency: stoppage for ½ week
3		1	0	0	Stock-out
4		1	1	0	Stock-out
5	Regular	1	2	−1	Deficiency: stoppage for ½ week
6	equal	1	0	0	Stock-out
7	weekly	1	0	1	
8	intakes	1	2	0	Stock-out
9		1	0	1	
10		1	2	0	Stock-out
11		1	1	0	Stock-out
12		1	1	0	Stock-out

TABLE 15: POLICY "B"

Fixed intake quantity of 5 units per order/intake.
Day/date of intake depends upon day/date of reorder.
Lead time 4 weeks from date of order.
Reorder level fixed at mean demand in lead time: 4 units.

Week No.	Action	In	Out (usage)	Physical balance	Comments
1	Initial order received	5		5	
1			1	4	Reorder level
1	Order No. 2 issued				For delivery end of week 5
2			2	2	
3			0	2	
4			1	1	
5			2	−1	Deficiency: stoppage for ½ week
5	Order No. 2 received	5		4	Reorder level
5	Order No. 3 issued			4	For delivery end of week 9
6			0	4	
7			0	4	
8			2	2	
9			0	2	
9	Order No. 3 received	5		7	
10			2	5	
11			1	4	Reorder level
11	Order No. 4 issued			4	For delivery end of week 16
12			1	3	

NOTE:
It is assumed that replenishment orders are placed on the same day that reorder level is reached and notified to the purchasing department — if not, why not?

TABLE 15: POLICY "C"

Fixed intake quantity of 4 units per order/intake.
Day/date of intake depends upon day/date of reorder.
Lead time 5 weeks from date of order.
Reorder level fixed at 4 units (i.e. less than lead time × demand per week).

Week No.	Action	In	Out (usage)	Physical balance	Comments
1	Initial order received	4		4	
1	Order No. 2 issued				For delivery start of week 6
1			1	3	
2			2	1	
3			0	1	
4			1	0	Stock-out
5			2	−2	Deficiency: stoppage of whole of week 5
6	Order No. 2 received	4		2	Reorder level −2
6	Order No. 3 issued			2	For delivery start of week 11
6			0	2	
7			0	2	
8			2	0	Stock-out
9			0	0	
10			2	−2	Deficiency: stoppage whole of week
11	Order No. 3 received	4		2	Reorder level −2
11	Order No. 4 issued				For delivery start of week 16
11			1	1	
12			1	0	Stock-out

NOTE:
See note at policy "B".

TABLE 15: POLICY "D"

Fixed intake quantity of 4 units per order/intake.
Day/date of intake depends upon day/date of reorder.[1]
Lead time 5 weeks.
Reorder level fixed at 5 units on the forward balance column.

Week No.	Action	Dues in	In	Out (usage)	Physical balance	Forward balance	Comments
1	Order No. 1 received		5		5	5	Initial intake
1	Order No. 2[2] issued	4			5	9	Due start of week 6
1		4		1	4	8	
2		4		2	2	6	
3		4		0	2	6	
4		4		1	1	5	Reorder level
4	Order No. 3 issued	4 + 4			1	9	Due end week 9
5		4 + 4		2	−1	7	Deficiency: 1 unit of production lost in second half of week
6	Order No. 2 received	4	4		3	7	
6		4		0	3	7	
7		4		0	3	7	
8		4		2	1	5	Reorder level
8	Order No. 4 issued	4 + 4			1	9	Due end week 13
9		4 + 4		0	1	9	
9	Order No. 3 received	4	4		5	9	
10		4		2	3	7	
11		4		1	2	6	
12		4		1	1	5	Reorder level
12	Order No. 5 issued	4 + 4			1	9	Due end week 17

NOTES:
   (1) See note at policy "B". (2) Special order for extra quantity.

162

CHAPTER 8

Statistics and Mathematics for Suppliers

INTRODUCTION

Supply statistics cover a very wide field and reflect the production and sales patterns of the company for which they are prepared. This is a further reason for the close integration of the three primary functions of industry: buying, making and selling. The chief statistical analyses required include stock movements, price and delivery trends, characteristics of demand by users such as production, and incidence of rejects and late deliveries. This chapter describes some of the statistical tools used in supplies and materials management.

For statistical and other techniques referred to in other chapters *see* index under *statistics. See also Storehouse,* under queueing, scheduling, centre of gravity, etc. Other techniques are fully covered in the relevant books in the Bibliography.[91]-[94][138] Reference may be made in particular to Harper's *Statistics.*

Throughout this chapter the examples are based upon the data in Table 16 and the associated curves in Figs. 37 and 38. These are treated as applying to stock movements and control, but could equally apply to many other Supply phenomena. The examples are over-simplified so as to demonstrate the methods employed rather than to provide actual data and statistics—both of which the reader must compile from his own environment.

RELIABILITY OF STATISTICS AND THEIR EFFECTIVE USE

Criteria for reliable Supply statistics and their effective use
To be reliable and effective, the following criteria should be met:
   (a) Period reviewed must be long enough to include all typical seasonal variations and trends.
   (b) Range must be wide enough to embrace all significant exceptions and variations. (BS 5532 (2.7).)

(c) *Documentation* must be accurate—"go back to originals" (Reichmann[111]).

(d) Data must be *appropriate* to the research.

(e) Data must include or take account of *environmental* factors.

(f) Data which could lead to *false conclusions* must be excluded.

(g) *Objectivity* must be applied throughout.

(h) *Subjective factors* must not be ignored, e.g. cost-benefits.

(i) *Review* monitor and re-appraise data continuously over the entire field involved.

(j) Check *"reasonability"*, e.g. do percentages add up to 100?

(k) *"Population"* (number of "events" in sample) must be sufficient to represent the whole. (BS 5532 (2.2).)

(l) Keep formulae and calculations as *simple* as possible.

(m) Watch for any *trend* and reasonableness of *variances.*

(n) *Look back* and check each new result with preceding step(s).

(o) *Watch periods* reviewed, e.g. weeks or production periods?

(p) *Compare results* with expectations and check variances.

(q) *Ensure bases* are compatible, e.g. metric or imperial?

(r) *Results* of one analysis may not compare with others, e.g. highest-priced goods may occupy least volume (*see* Fig. 46).

(s) *Units* may not be comparable—*see* "collation of data" in later section.

(t) *Emphasis* on high-value low-variety data may lead to important exceptions in the low-value high-variety range being ignored, e.g. vital spares for plant.

(u) The *pattern* of data or its basis may change.

(v) *"Think forward"* use authority to *"act forward"*.

(w) *Co-ordinate data* from suppliers, users, production, sales, etc.

(x) *Review* demand frequently or continuously (to suit circumstances).

(y) *Adjust* stock levels and policy promptly in changing circumstances.

(z) *Revise* orders promptly in changing circumstances.

AXIOM: False data are worse than no data.

Risks in using statistics.

Wide experience and considerable diagnostic skill is needed in Supplies analysis as substitutes for mathematical dogma and statistical arrogance. Electronic data processing has nil "IQ", moves with the speed of light and can thus make mistakes with the same rapidity. The human brain also utilises electrical impulses but although slow it has the necessary inbuilt selective intelligence to avoid mistakes.

AXIOM: Computers are fast but foolish, humans are slow but sure.

There are so many disconnected variables in Supplies that a practical, pragmatic, agnostic and even cynical approach should be made to Supply statistics and statistical methods. For example, many theories for control of stock and economic ordering, etc. claim to be infallible.

The immediate problem for most supplies managers is to know what to do about the apparently unpredictable situation where things seem to persist in going wrong—and where Murphy's Law ("if things can go wrong, they will") seems always to prevail. Note that the probability of their doing so is in proportion to the factorial of the things which can go wrong.

Collection, collation, calculation and checking of data

Collection of data for Supply statistics requires special care if subsequent analysis and presentation are to meet the criteria listed above. Skill is needed to ensure that the correct questions are asked and that the degree of accuracy required (time-scale) etc., are clearly stated.

Collation of data by tabulation (or other presentation of this kind) must ensure that the basis is common and that data can be truly compared. In Pareto analysis, for example, attention is called to the difficulty in selecting compatible and common bases for comparison, viz. variety v. weight, size v. value, etc.

If the statistics are the result of simulation or a random sample the significance of any variances must be considered. The difference between expected and actual results could be due to the expectation being incorrect, or to a combination of other errors, mathematical, statistical, subjective and so on. Mathematical tests are beyond our scope here (although some are merely listed below). However, the statistician should look for logical, practical explanations and above all avoid "cognitive dissonance".

Tests of validity involve, broadly speaking, comparison between actual and expected or practical and theoretical results and forecasts. They include the following (*see* relevant books in Bibliography).

(*a*) "Null hypothesis": an assumption that the variations are due to chance alone. The variations are then compared on this basis.

(*b*) Mathematical test of the null hypothesis, e.g. whether the sample mean(s) falls close to the expected figure.

(*c*) Calculation of "confidence levels".

(*d*) The χ^2 ("chi-squared") test, or method of least squares.

(*e*) Line of best fit.

FEEDBACK (STATISTICAL) AND FEEDBACK LOOPS

Figure 35 illustrates a simple feedback system which applies in theory whether clerical or automated by mechanical or electronic means. The system (S) may, for instance, simulate a process, or an electric circuit, or the flow of materials, or other data based upon change. (PD 6470 (1.1).)

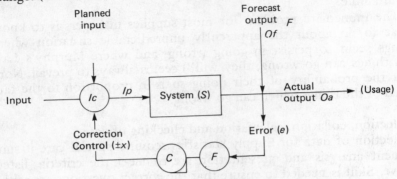

Fig. 35. Simple feedback system
Applies with or without computer "C".

In the example in Fig. 35 the system typifies flow of supplies. Input Ip has, we shall assume, been planned and passes through stores to output Of which has been forecast by sales and production departments. The probability of freedom from error between planned input Ip and actual output Oa is extremely low. Any error generates feedback at the output end of the system. The computer C (or clerical records) contains the planned input Ip which it compares with the error $(Of - Oa) = (e)$ according to its program. It then notifies the controller of input. The latter may be a human agent who will decide the degree of correction ($\pm x$) to apply. On the other hand, it may be a fully automated system in which the correction is imposed upon the input so that it is regulated automatically.

There are few limits to the feedback system which can be applied wherever planned input and output vary. Some Supply examples of feedback of planned supply versus actual results are:

(a) flow (usage) through stores;
(b) expenditure;
(c) lead times;
(d) stores activity (order picking, etc.);
(e) service factor;
(f) estimates of future prices;
(g) total usage.

It is essential to exercise intelligent judgments when using feedback to control supplies, particularly if corrections ($\pm x$) are embodied in a computer program. Instability of the system can result if feed-back is applied without any intelligent restraint. For example, in Fig. 38 the exceptional demand at period 15 could suggest an error of 100 per cent and lead the computer to call for a highly inflated increase for the next input (i.e. the next purchase order). (*See* Fig. 33 line (*a*).)

GRAPHICAL REPRESENTATION OF SUPPLIES (BS DD52)

The highly numerate are sometimes scornful of the graphical presen-tation of statistics. However, for most of us they make intelligible the mysteries concealed in towering forests of figures. Their use is particularly apt in Supplies since the data usually represent actual physical goods and supplies.

There are, of course, pitfalls. For example, curves ("A") and ("B") in Fig. 38 have been set out to show a number of characteris-tics of statistical data of which demand for supplies is one. Curve ("A") is entitled "random demand" and was produced by a suitable method to ensure it was random—but is it? Could it be that if the 25 periods represent a year's working the troughs and peaks were seasonal? To find out graphically, a "3-D" chart may be needed. Curves of previous years are mounted on thick card and cut to the

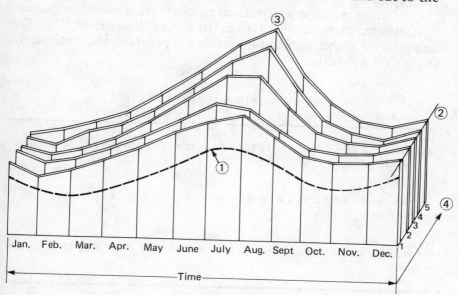

Fig. 36. "3-D" charts

(1) General seasonal trend. (2) Secular trend. (3) Seasonal peaks.
(4) Year 1 to now.

contours of the curves. If mounted behind one another any long-term characteristics (trends, peaks, troughs, exceptions) will be clearly revealed as in Fig. 36.

"A.B.C." ANALYSIS, THE "PARETO PRINCIPLE"

The Pareto "principle" (it is not a "law") states: "In any series of elements to be controlled, a selected small fraction of the number of elements [usually (Auth.)] accounts for a large fraction of the total effect." (BS 5729 Part 3 (6.1).)

This technique[95][96] (*see* Chapter 5, Fig. 14) is applicable to many supplies problems. It may be used to display in tabulated or charted form the following analyses.

(*a*) Frequency of movement of each variety of supplies in relation to total movement of all supplies.

(*b*) Volume of stores occupied by each variety as a percentage of total storage volume available—or utilised.

(*c*) Weights of stock (or consignments) stacked, shelved, handled or transported as a percentage of total weights, or maxima.

(*d*) Numbers of each value-range of purchase orders as a percentage of total number of orders placed.

(*e*) Value spent on each variety of supply as a percentage of the total spending.

(*f*) Delays in delivery, rejections against total delivered, inspected.

However, there are limitations to the application of "A.B.C." analysis (*see* above, criteria for reliable Supply statistics, particularly (*r*), (*s*), (*t*) and (*u*)).

TABLE 16. SUPPLIES FLOW DATA

(a) Period number	1 2 3 4 5 6 7 8 9 10 11 12 13 14 15 16 17 18 19 20 21 22 23 24 25	Total
(b) Flow (A) (random)	(0) (14) 9 7 8 7 5 7 7 6 4 6 9 8 6 6 10 8 9 7 5 8 8 5 5 7 7	
(c) Flow (B) (with trend)	(0) (14) 4 5 5 6 5 6 5 7 6 6 8 7 7 7 8 7 8 7 7 9 8 9 8 10 9	174

NOTES:
(1) Random flow (A) *see* curve (A), Fig. 38. (2) Trend flow (B) *see* curve (B), Fig. 38.

FREQUENCY CHARTS (OR HISTOGRAMS)

Frequency charts are a simple device used to present, in visual form the pattern of a statistical sample. It enables predictions to be made regarding the future tendencies—such as stock demands—of the sample analysed. (BS 5532 (1.1, 1.2, 2.9).)

Characteristics of frequency charts

The various characteristics of frequency charts are outlined below. The numbered paragraphs refer to numbers in circles in Fig. 37.

(1) DISTRIBUTION CURVES. The shape of distribution curves ("normal" and otherwise) is important. Where the resulting curve is bell-shaped,

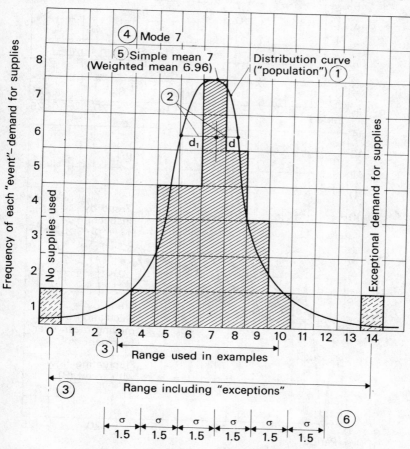

Fig. 37. Histogram applied to supplies
Numbers in circles refer to paragraphs in text.

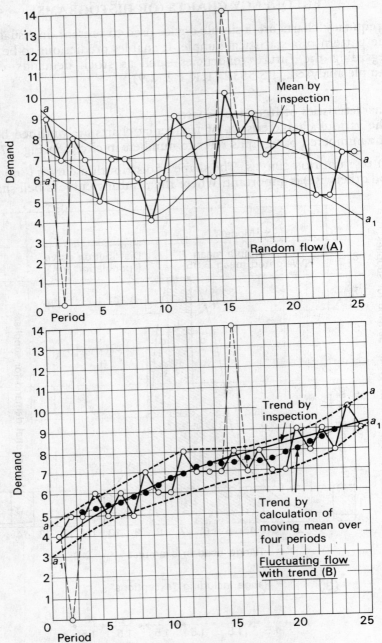

Fig. 38. Examples of supplies flow, based on Table 16
Lines *a-a*, a_1-a_1 enclose "confidence belt". *See* text, regression analysis.

as in Fig. 37, a fairly high degree of predictability may be discerned. The taller the peak in relation to its width at the base, the higher the degree of confidence with which a result can be deduced. If the curve consisted of one single vertical bar this would indicate that there was a steady demand (or other constant data). In that unlikely event further analysis would be unnecessary, deductions could be "certain". If the curve degenerated into a flat horizontal line, it would indicate that all values were equally likely to occur and that no deduction could be made with hope of success—a more familiar condition in supplies management. Other characteristics are discussed in Chapter 6.

It is important that the following provisos are kept in mind when using frequency charts in Supplies.

(a) The frequency chart gives no prediction in regard to time. It is, as a rule, a collection of "slices" of data assembled in order of demands (or other values) and not in relation to the sequence or date on which they occurred.

(b) Except when the frequency chart is based on variations in a trend it gives no information about trends. In fact, in Fig. 38, graphs (A) and (B), which are based on the same stock demands but in different sequence, produce identical frequency charts, although curve (B) has a rising trend and curve (A) a random indefinite one.

(c) Exceptions must be looked for and "exceptional" action taken. (*See* Chapter 9, intermittent exceptional demands.)

(2) "ASYMMETRY" (i.e. "skewness") of curves does not greatly affect the accuracy of prediction unless it is excessive. The lack of symmetry is a natural consequence of many situations which occur when supply data vary more in one direction than in the other (*see* Fig. 66, involving variable lead times). "Skewness" is measured by the variations in deviations of the curve from the mean, shown in Fig. 37 by the example where d_1 exceeds d.

(3) RANGE OF DATA taken by itself is a poor guide for future action. It tells nothing of the relative values between the upper and lower limits, nor what goes on in between.

"MODES", "MEANS" AND "MEDIANS" all have relevance to statistics for Supplies. They are a common source of elementary, but often serious, error in statistical analysis. The details which follow may help to avoid these pitfalls. (BS 5532 (2.28–31).)

(4) MODE is not necessarily a good guide unless the range is very narrow and the curve has a very high peak. (*See* Figs. 37 and 66.)

(5) SIMPLE MEAN (unweighted) is the total of the values (*v*) divided by the number (*n*) of different values recorded. In Fig. 37, ignoring

the exceptions of zero and fourteen, the mean is

$$\frac{\Sigma v}{n} = \frac{4 + 5 + 6 + 7 + 8 + 9 + 10}{7} = 7$$

This mean happens to coincide with the mode, but had the chart been more skewed this would not have been the case and the mean could have been even more unreliable than the mode for considering future action (*see also* Fig. 66.)

THE PROGRESSIVE MEAN is obtained by adding each weekly or other figure to the previous total and dividing by the number of weeks up to and including that one. A few steps of the progressive mean have been calculated as shown in Table 17. It would be seen from a graph that a progressive mean curve tends to flatten out with time. Even fluctuations such as shown dotted at week 15 in Fig. 38 have little effect. This is referred to as the "smoothing effect". The result is a "die-away" curve as shown in Fig. 39 (*see* "exponential smoothing" below.)

Because of the gradual smoothing out of exceptions, trends and other characteristics the application of the progressive mean can lead to false deductions in supplies calculations such as forecasts, etc. In Table 17, columns (6) and (10) show the errors which arise when using each entry at columns (5) and (9) to forecast the next line below, e.g. for curve (A) if the progressive mean of 8.00 at period 3 under column (5) is used as a forecast for period 4 an error of +1.00 will occur. Line (g) shows the total errors in periods 1 to 6 regardless of sign. (*See also* statistical forecasting, below.)

"EXPONENTIAL SMOOTHING." The "smoothing" effect of the progressive mean results in the "die-away" curve in Fig. 39. If one unit is added to or deducted from a particular series, what difference will it make to the progressive mean? Take the first 20 weeks (or other periods) and calculate the difference, as shown in Table 18.

When studying data such as usage/flow of supplies it will be readily seen that when the period is short (viz. one week) one additional unit has an appreciable effect. At week 2 it adds (or subtracts) 0.50, i.e. 50 per cent of the added unit. As time passes the effect becomes less and less apparent. For example, in the twentieth week it only affects the average by 0.05 or one-tenth of what it did at week 2, when it added or deducted 0.50—it now adds only 5 per cent of the additional unit. Equally important is the fact that the smoothing between each stage grows progressively less. See line (d): 0.017 for five weeks 16-20 over week 15 compared with 0.17 for week 3 over week 2, i.e. 10 times the difference for one week at weeks 2-3 (line (a)) than for the five weeks 16-20.

TABLE 17. CALCULATION OF PROGRESSIVE MEAN
(Based on curves (A) and (B), Fig. 38, and Table 16)

| | | Curve (A): Random demand (usage) | | | | Curve B: Trend demand (usage) | | | |
(1)	(2)	(3)	(4)	(5)	(6)	(7)	(8)	(9)	(10)
Line	Period	Usage in period	Calculation	Progressive mean	Error using col. (5) to forecast	Usage in period	Calculation	Progressive mean	Error using col. (9) to forecast
(a)	1	9		9.00	–	4	–	4.00	–
(b)	2	7	(9+7) ÷ 2	8.00	+2.00	5	(4+5) ÷ 2	4.56	–1.00
(c)	3	8	(9+7+8) ÷ 3	8.00	0.00	5	(4+5+5) ÷ 3	4.67	–0.50
(d)	4	7	(9+7+8+7) ÷ 4	7.75	+1.00	6	(4+5+5+6) ÷ 4	5.00	–1.33
(e)	5	5	(9+7+8+7+5) ÷ 5	7.20	+2.75	5	(4+5+5+6+5) ÷ 5	5.00	0.00
(f)	6	7	(9+7+8+7+5+7) ÷ 6	7.17	+0.20	6	(4+5+5+6+5+6) ÷ 6	5.17	–1.00
(g)			Total errors (regardless of sign)		5.95		Total errors (regardless of sign)		3.83

TABLE 18. CALCULATION OF CURVE OF EXPONENTIAL SMOOTHING
(see Fig. 38)

Line (a)	Period Nos.	1	2	3	4	5	6	7	8	9	10	15	20
Line (b)	Units added		1	1	1	1	1	1	1	1	1	1	1
Line (c)	Line (b) ÷ Line (a)		.50	.33	.25	.20	.16	.14	.12	.11	.10	.067	.05
Line (d)	Difference		.50	.17	.08	.05	.04	.02	.02	.01	.01	.03	.017

MOVING MEAN. The exponential smoothing of the progressive mean curve explains the importance of the moving mean. In this the calculations are a little more complicated than for the progressive mean. The earliest entry of the previous calculations is omitted for each new total. Using the sample example as in Table 17, proceed as in Table 19, taking a three-week moving mean ($n = 3$). Columns (6) and (10) again show the errors which arise when using columns (5) and (9) to forecast the next period. (BS 5729 Part 2 (4.2.2.).)

The curve based on a three-week moving mean is very responsive to individual weekly changes. As a trend it would be useless, because on reaching week 15, allowing for the exceptional demand (see Fig. 38) could give the impression that a continuing rapid rise in demand was in view. If a ten-week moving mean is used, the latest movement is reduced to 10 per cent of its value and inclusion of

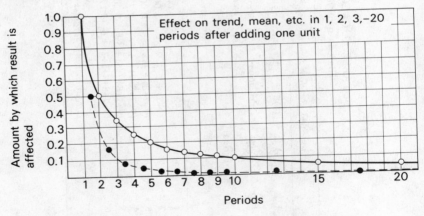

Key
—○— Effect of each additional unit (Table 18, line (c))
- -●- - Rate of change in the effect of adding one unit
as time progresses, (Table 18, line (d))

Fig. 39. Smoothing effect of time on the progressive mean

TABLE 19. CALCULATION OF MOVING MEAN (3 PERIODS)
(Based on curves (A) and (B), Fig. 38)

		Curve (A): Random demand (usage)				Curve B: Trend demand (usage)			
(1)	(2)	(3)	(4)	(5)	(6)	(7)	(8)	(9)	(10)
Line	Period	Usage in period	Calculation	Moving mean	Error using col. (5) to forecast	Usage in period	Calculation	Moving mean	Error using col. (9) to forecast
(a)	1	9	—	—	—	4	—	—	—
(b)	2	7	—	—	—	5	—	—	—
(c)	3	8	$(9+7+8) \div 3$	8.0	—	5	$(4+5+5) \div 3$	4.7	—
(d)	4	7	$(7+8+7) \div 3$	7.3	+1.00	6	$(5+5+6) \div 3$	5.3	−1.3
(e)	5	5	$(8+7+5) \div 3$	6.7	+2.3	5	$(5+6+5) \div 3$	5.3	+0.3
(f)	6	7	$(7+5+7) \div 3$	6.3	−0.3	6	$(6+5+6) \div 3$	5.7	−0.7
(g)			Total errors (regardless of sign)		3.6		Total errors (regardless of sign)		2.3

exceptional peaks such as shown dotted at week 15 would be less likely to lead to a false conclusion. It is often advisable to examine curves in relation to both the long-term trend curve and the progressive and moving means to determine whether a sudden change is likely to be transitory or permanent.

THE WEIGHTED MEAN is an important statistical device which takes account of the "weight"—in this case the number of occasions upon which an event occurs (see also Chapter 2, Table 4). The calculation for this example, based on Table 16, is as follows:

$$\frac{1 \times 4 + 4 \times 5 + 4 \times 6 + 7 \times 7 + 5 \times 8 + 3 \times 9 + 1 \times 10}{25 \text{ (the number of weeks)}} = \frac{174}{25} = 6.96.$$

This mean is more reliable than the others so far considered because it takes account of all the data. (See Chapter 9, probabilities and exceptions.)

THE MEDIAN can be useful when examining the symmetry of data about its mid-point, for example the incidence of oversize and undersize rejects on a large intake.

FREQUENCY, as its name implies, merely records the number of times each event occurs. The total must be the number of observations— in Table 16 it was 25. (The exceptional demands were ignored in the example, but should normally be taken into account.)

(6) "DEVIATION" OF DATA, LEADING TO THE "STANDARD DEVIATION". Deviations of the various values from the mean ("d_1", "d" in Fig. 37) give a rough indication of the use which can be made of the data in forecasting, etc. However, these data cannot be used directly without further refinement by calculation, such as that for obtaining the "standard deviation" which is more reliable than others such as, for example, the simple mean.

The greater the variability of the data being compared the greater will be the deviations from the mean and consequently the greater the standard deviation. It follows that the greatest confidence can be placed in data where the standard deviation has the lowest value.

Standard deviation tables are available for "normal" and other distributions. The formula for calculating the standard deviation is as follows.

Standard deviation = the square root of the sum of the squares of
(BS 5532 (2.34))   the deviations from the mean, after dividing
                     by the number of "events" in the sample.

This formula will be familiar to electrical and other engineers as the "root-mean-square" or "effective" value of a curve.

Table 20 shows the calculation of the standard deviation for the example in Table 16. It will be seen that the range lies between 3 and 11, i.e. range = 8. However, six times the deviation of 1.5 is 9 which is outside the range. Deductions based upon this example should not therefore be regarded as very reliable, although probably near enough for rough practical purposes here.

TABLE 20. CALCULATION OF STANDARD DEVIATION

Value	Deviation from mean	Square of deviation	Frequency	Frequency × deviation squared
4	−3	9	1	9
5	−2	4	4	16
6	−1	1	4	4
7	0	0	7	0
8	+1	1	5	5
9	+2	4	3	12
10	+3	9	1	9
(Totals)			25	55

Standard deviation $= \sqrt{\dfrac{55}{25}} = \sqrt{2.20} = 1.5$ approximately

Trends in Supplies

Trends in usage, deliveries, prices, rejections, etc. are vital statistics for successful Supplies operations. Methods for ascertaining a trend vary from the highly sophisticated to the simple examination of data or the visual inspection of a graph, e.g. the trend drawn in by inspection of curve (B) in Fig. 38. Trends may also be calculated by tabulation as in Table 21, based on the moving mean (see dotted trend line in curve (B) in Fig. 38). The differences in column (6) are the basis for Table 22 and the frequency curve in Fig. 40. The curve is very skewed and because it is dealing with a trend it may be assumed that it indicates a tendency for the trend to increase.

Forecasting a trend in most stock control situations is more easily done by the "EWMA" method described later. In this case the word "trend" is inserted into the formula. (BS 5729 Part 2 (4.3.2.).)

TABLE 21. CALCULATION OF TREND

(1) Period	(2) Usage (Table 16)	(3) Total for each moving 4 periods	(4) Add in pairs	(5) Trend (column (4) ÷ 8)	(6) Differences between successive trends in column (5)
1	4	—	—	—	—
2	5	—	—	—	—
—	—	20	—	—	—
3	5	—	41	5.125	—
—	—	21	—	—	0.250
4	6	—	43	5.375	—
—	—	22	—	—	0.125
5	5	—	44	5.5	—
—	—	22	—	—	0.125
6	6	—	45	5.625	—
—	—	23	—	—	0.250
7	5	—	47	5.875	—
—	—	24	—	—	0.125
8	7	—	48	6.000	—
—	—	24	—	—	0.375
9	6	—	51	6.375	—
—	—	27	—	—	0.375
10	6	—	54	6.750	—
—	—	27	—	—	0.125
11	8	—	55	6.875	—
—	—	28	—	—	0.250
12	7	—	57	7.125	—
—	—	29	—	—	0.125
13	7	—	58	7.250	—
—	—	29	—	—	0.000
14	7	—	58	7.250	—
—	—	29	—	—	0.125
15	8	—	59	7.375	—
—	—	30	—	—	0.125
16	7	—	60	7.500	—

(continued)

178

TABLE 21 contd.   CALCULATION OF TREND

(1) Period	(2) Usage (Table 16)	(3) Total for each moving 4 periods	(4) Add in pairs	(5) Trend (column (4) ÷ 8)	(6) Differences between successive trends in column (5)
—	—	30	—	—	
17	8	—	59	7.375	0.125
—	—	29	—	—	
18	7	—	60	7.500	0.125
—	—	31	—	—	
19	7	—	62	7.750	0.250
—	—	31	—	—	
20	9	—	64	8.000	0.250
—	—	33	—	—	
21	8	—	67	8.375	0.375
—	—	34	—	—	
22	9	—	69	8.625	0.250
—	—	35	—	—	
23	8	—	—	—	
—	—		—	—	
24	10		—	—	

TABLE 22. FREQUENCY OF DIFFERENCES IN TABLE 21.

Difference (column (6))	Frequency
−0.125	1
0	1
+0.125	8
+0.25	7
+0.375	3

THE UNKNOWABLE, THE UNPREDICTABLE AND THE EXCEPTIONAL

"Real minimum stock can be achieved only if the future can be foretold exactly, an impossibility" (BS 5729 Part 1 (3.3)).

The unknowable and the unpredictable are usually at least as important in Supplies as what can be known or confidently predicted. The "tails" of the frequency chart in Fig. 37 do not reach the base

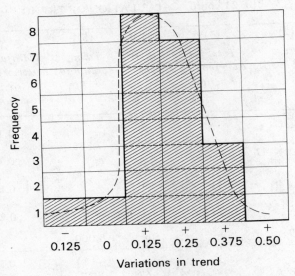

Fig. 40. Frequency chart of trend

line in either direction. This is a warning that demand might some day exceed 14 or "returns to store" might reverse the nil demand to a positive inflow of surplus stock from cancelled production or another outside source (*see also* Chapter 9, intermittent exceptional demands).

Exceptions in statistical data must be expected throughout Supplies activities. Exceptionally high prices, long deliveries (or no deliveries), excessive consumption (or none!) are all contingencies which are "certain" to arise. However, the word "certain" is used here hypothetically. There is no certainty in most predictions, only "probability". (BS 5532 (1).)

The questions to be asked about the "exceptions" are as follows:

(*a*) Can they be eradicated?

(*b*) Will they affect the mean? (In Table 16 it had been assumed "not"—a most unwise assumption in practice—and the modal value has been substituted. It would have been more accurate to take the mean around the exceptions, e.g. of periods, 1, 2 and 3, and 14, 15 and 16.)

(*c*) Do they always occur at the same period in time?

(*d*) Are they seasonal?

(*e*) May they affect other data?

(*f*) Are they random and unpredictable?

AXIOM: There are few "absolutes" in statistics but many "probabilities".

STATISTICAL FORECASTING

Statistical forecasting is often needed for estimating future demands and usage, probable deliveries by suppliers, price trends and so on. Some methods of forecasting are outlined below. (BS 5191 (2.1).)

(a) Current level (BS 5729 Part 2 (0.3c) abb) "Current level of demand can be an adequate forecast for the immediate future where the horizon of interest is short."

(b) Progressive mean (Table 17) may be used, taking the last result for the next forecast. This like method *(a)* can conceal numerous errors leading to incorrect action.

THE MOVING MEAN is better than the progressive mean as it is capable of being made extremely sensitive to change. (BS 5729 Part 2 (4.2.2).)

EXPONENTIALLY WEIGHTED MOVING AVERAGE ("EMWA") is, despite its name, a simple yet accurate alternative to other methods. It takes account of the passage of time in the estimate of each forecast. The formula used is as follows (BS 5729 Part 2 (4.2.4)):

$$\text{Forecast for Next period} = \text{forecast for this period} + \alpha \left\{ \text{actual result for this period} - \text{forecast for this period} \right\}$$

Factor "α" is known as the "smoothing constant" and the portion in brackets is the forecast error. Any value can be given to "α" from a very low figure (such as 0.001) to a maximum of 1.0. Varying "α" has the same weighting effect as changing the number of periods for calculation of the moving mean. Thus, if "α" is given the highest value of 1.0, the forecast for the next period will be precisely the same as the current or latest actual result with no adjustment for errors in forecasting. If "α" is given the low value of 0.01 the new forecast will be adjusted by only 1 per cent of any error in the last forecast. For most purposes a value of 0.1 or 0.2 is taken. In Fig. 39 this corresponds to the sharp change in direction of the "rate of change" curve where the effects of change are more radically smoothed out of the final result. When applied to Table 16, periods 1 to 6 the total error for the random data line "A" (in Fig. 38) is 1.8 and for data line "B" it is 1.4. This is therefore better than any results in Tables 17 or 19.

NOTES:

1. When applying the formula it is important to make sure that due note is taken of the plus and minus signs.

2. BS 5729 Part 2 (4.2.6 abb) points out that: "A number of systems exist which relate the smoothing constant to the level of recent values of the forecast errors and these are frequently built

into stock control packages. Such modifications generally lead to poorer forecasts and unless frequent shifts in the underlying levels are expected they should be treated with care."

Regression analysis

The drawing in of boundaries, known statistically as "regression analysis", is a useful device to ascertain characteristics which may not otherwise be apparent from the data. "Scatter diagrams" are a similar device (see Fig. 55): in this case the centre or mean of the dots forming the data and especially their boundaries can be useful in preparing and comparing statistics. (BS 5532 (2.44).)

In Fig. 38, lines a-a and a_1-a_1 have been drawn approximately through the maxima and minima, omitting the exceptions which should be dealt with separately. These lines enclose what may be termed the "confidence belt" and within this "belt" fall major changes and values of data in the sample.

Seasonal characteristics (BS 5729 Part 2 (4.4))

First it must be established whether the "wave-form" shape of, for example, curve (A) in Fig. 38 is a regular annual pattern. If the twenty-five periods were of two weeks each the curve could show annual seasonal characteristics, and this has been assumed in the example of seasonal forecasting which follows (see Fig. 41).

FORECASTING TRENDS (BS 5729 Part 2 (4.3.1. and 4.3.2.) [abb.]
'Trend' is a change in the underlying level of data such as "issues per period".
Measure of "trend" is the change in average of data per period from one period to the next, as measured by the equation:

| Trend (this period) | = | mean of data per period calculated at end of this period | − | mean of data per period calculated at end of last previous period. |

Forecast of trend can be done by the EWMA method using the formula:

$$\text{Forecast of trend for next period} = (1 - a) \left\{ \text{forecast for this period} \right\} + a \times \left\{ \text{actual data this period} \right\}$$

Seasonal forecasting with seasonal adjustments (BS 5729 Part 2 (4.4.1))

This is frequently needed for such statistics as stock demands, price, and availability changes, etc. The simple example in Fig. 42 is based on the following assumptions.

(a) Last year's demand was typical of past years.

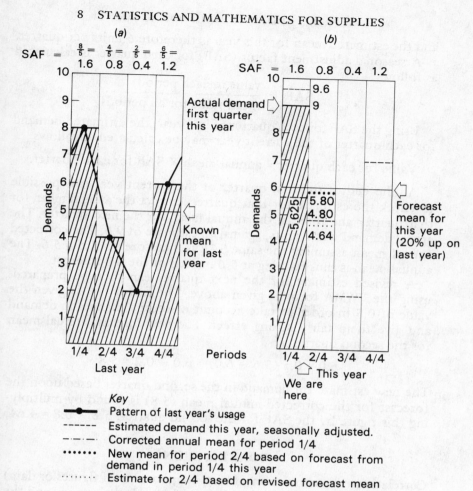

Fig. 41. *Forecasting demand with seasonal corrections*

(*b*) As in the past the demand has seasonal characteristics (*a-a*, a_1-a_1, curve (A) in Fig. 38).

(*c*) A provisional forecast has been made for the current year.

(*d*) The first quarter of the current year has just ended.

(*e*) The forecast for that quarter can now be corrected to the actual demand.

(*f*) It is now desired to forecast a firm requirement for the second quarter of the current year.

(*g*) This forecast must take account of the normal seasonal characteristics already noted.

(*b*) The year-on-year trend shows a regular increase of 20 per cent per annum. The mean demand last year was 5 units per quarter, and the estimated mean for this year is therefore 6 units per quarter.

A seasonal adjustment factor (SAF) for each quarter is calculated as follows:

$$SAF = \frac{\text{value in each period}}{\text{mean value for all periods}}$$

Using the SAF for each quarter of last year, the estimated demand for each quarter of the current year may be calculated as follows:

Value for each quarter = annual mean × SAF for each quarter.

At the end of the first quarter of the current year it is possible to check the estimate for that quarter, correct the annual mean for that quarter and forecast the annual mean for the next quarter. The actual demand was 9 units, against an estimate of 9.6. The corrected annual mean assuming the same SAF is therefore $9 \div 1.6 = 5.6$. The annual mean is thus running at 5.6 instead of the 6.0 forecast.

A revised estimate for the next quarter can then be prepared, using the EWMA formula given above. The factor "α" is given the value of 0.5 in order to take account of recent changes in demand and give them fairly strong effect. The new forecast annual mean for the second quarter is:

$$6.0 + 0.5 \ (5.6 - 6.0) = 6.0 - 0.2 = \underline{5.8}$$

The new estimate for demand in the second quarter based upon the forecast for the corrected annual mean (5.8) is found by multiplying this figure by the SAF for the second quarter: $5.8 \times 0.8 = 4.64$.

CORRELATION

Correlation (the association of two or more sets of figures or data) is an area of statistics filled with traps for both the unwary and the wary. (BS 5532 (2.43).)

For example, production output and materials input are closely related and when a curve is plotted parallel lines may be expected. Such a relationship is given the highest statistical coefficient of correlation, viz. "1" (the highest value used in statistical analysis). On the other hand, if the times of day at which vehicles arrrived with supplies could be plotted against each day of every week, it might produce a display known as a "scatter diagram" because dots representing each arrival would be scattered more randomly indicating that there was little correlation. The statistician would give this a low coefficient (*see* Fig. 55).

There is much more to statistical correlation technique than can be mentioned here, e.g. the need for ranking of various factors into some kind of order before comparing them. However, in Supply problems it is important to look for unexpected and environmental factors outside the actual numeracy involved in producing the correlation. These factors are frequently subjective and therefore difficult, or even impossible, to convert to numerical data. (*See* Chapter 6, preferred numbers.)

CONCLUSIONS

Limitations of supply statistics

The fallibility of statistics is clear but seldom admitted, especially in the field of Supplies. Nevertheless, a study of statistics in Supplies can give a very good idea of "why things go wrong" even though the prediction may be less than 100 per cent reliable. The statistics may merely prove the situation random and unpredictable and recognition of this can lead to practical solutions.

Always suspect Supplies data or statistics which are given to several places of decimals—these probably conceal hidden errors.

As a rough check always see if percentages add up to 100! Note the suggestion in BS 5729 Part 2 (0.2) which reads ". . . an estimate of future demand should be expected to be wrong".

CHAPTER 9

Supply Flow Patterns: Characteristics, Policies and Controls

INTRODUCTION

Having studied the methods of control available and the statistical devices for guiding policy, we now examine some of the most common types of "supply flow patterns.", the security given to continuity of production (and/or sales) by the correct provisioning and control of supplies and the "uncoupling effect" of stocks.

EXAMPLES OF SUPPLY FLOW PATTERNS

Figure 42 is designed to show a few examples of such supply flow patterns including the buffer and uncoupling effect of stock. (In the figure, costs and stocks are proportional to shaded portions.)

The examples assume that the stock replenishments arrive at the commencement of each period (but *see* Chapter 18). A further assumption is that the issues occur evenly throughout each period concerned (but *see* Fig. 26).

Characteristics

The main characteristics of supply flow patterns are as follows.

(1) FREQUENCY CHANGE (between intakes and withdrawals): flows 2, 3, 5, 6, 7, and 8. As a rule the greatest frequency changes occur in classification "B" and "C" materials where the stock withdrawals are usually at a much greater frequency than the intakes into stores.

(2) PHASE CHANGE: flows 3, 4, 5, 6, 7 and 8. Wherever a frequency change takes place there must also be a phase change, but the converse does not always apply. In this condition the deliveries into stores may be at the same frequency as the withdrawals, but out of phase with input (*see* flow 4).

(3) "OUT-OF-PHASE" occurs wherever a frequency change takes place.

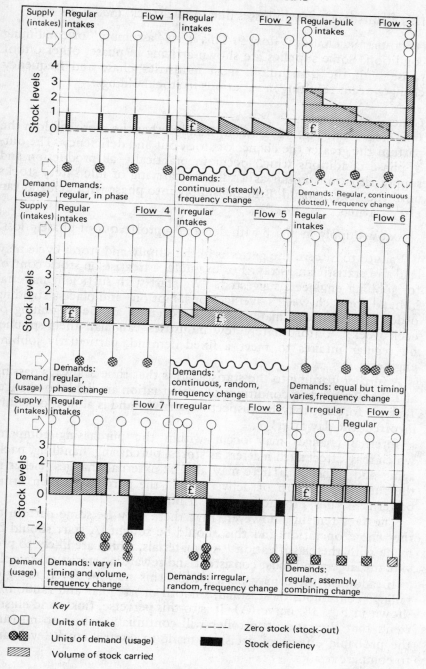

Fig. 42. Supply flow patterns

This results inevitably in losses due to idle stock. (*See* Flow 4.)

(4) COMBINING CHANGES: flow 9. This is an "assembly" or combining condition. Some supplies are shown arriving in phase, other out of phase with the demand. In most industries phase and frequency changes occur resulting in variations in stockholdings.

General comments

It is clear from Fig. 42, flows 6, 7 and 8, that the more random the pattern the greater the chance of stock-out and deficiency. The out-of-phase conditions which occur in practically all production and supply situations entail as a rule the carrying of idle safety-stocks until the next demand. Bringing supply into phase with demand can effect savings.

AXIOM: Supply in-phase with demand = profit; out-of-phase = loss.

Failure to discern the patterns in the supply and stores cycle may lead the statistician astray. For example, a treatise on stock control for jobbing engineers suggested: "We start with sufficient material in hand for each week's average consumption—and place a standing order for sufficient material to be received at the beginning of each week." Unfortunately few industries can plan their supplies by regular intakes to meet a fixed demand, particularly jobbing engineers.

A further warning to the statistician is that time is always passing and the surrounding conditions of any situation are liable to change. Today's forecast may be suspect tomorrow—and is almost certainly incorrect the day after!

Internal changes may occur within the purchasing company which may affect such matters as stores, purchasing, handling, packaging and transport. There may also be external changes, either in the supplier's pattern of delivery or in the purchaser's own firm's patterns of sales, production or distribution.

The fact remains, however, that there *may* be some pattern to the whole operation and this should be sought. A start should be made with the classification "A" materials, which are likely to provide the largest and most consistent and rewarding statistical sample.

In addition there may be a trend. This may be level, rising or falling, continuous or seasonal, smooth or irregular and random as shown in Fig. 38, curve (A). It is to this perverse, fickle and elusive trend that the stock controller will continually return to measure the probable effects of decisions made to control stock levels and to compare results.

Flows in Supplies

Flow 1: regular equal intakes in phase with regular equal demand
The demand in flow 1 absorbs the total delivery directly it is received
and available. Examples are the immediate issue to the shop floor
in the case of batch production or where a process plant, working
on the same system, takes full input direct into the process flow for
treatment during the succeeding days of the week.

Smoothness of demand for main materials may be reflected in
smoothing of demand for the supporting materials (classifications
"B" and "C"), but these seldom achieve the same degree of regul-
arity and smoothness as classification "A" materials.

In theory the provisioning of this type of production should be
straightforward. The margins, however, are usually so fine that great
skill is needed in setting and maintaining the intake schedules to
ensure continuity of production. Profitability is maximised by elimination of stockholding. There is therefore no uncoupling effect so
rendering the very profitability itself highly vulnerable to changes in
supply or demand through the effects which produced it. Moreover,
the profitability of process plants relies upon continuity of production and a high plant utilisation factor. (*See* Chapter 1, process
plants.)

This is one of the instances where all major supply decisions must
be subject to confirmation by top management. The only stocks
held are the supplies in transit from the suppliers' works to the
actual work-centres or process plant. Any hold-up here may stop
the whole factory in a matter of hours.

This can also have a "doubling effect". For example, suppose
the deliveries are made regularly to the plant and there is a breakdown in the purchaser's process causing a complete stoppage. The
supplier may then have his own production problems and may not
be able to halt production at once so stocks build up. If his storage
space is limited because he does not normally reckon to carry stock,
he may insist on making delivery. The "doubling effect" is then
transferred to the plant of the purchaser who must make storage
provision for housing addition stock. Moreover, the materials may
be "active" chemicals and hazardous to store, or possess a short
shelf-life. These factors add greatly to the complexity of the problem.

Because there is no "uncoupling" effect provided by flow 1, and
if there is lack of confidence in the continued stability of demand,
due to breakdowns, etc., or in the reliability of suppliers, uncoupling
must be provided by means of safety-stock (not shown in the diagram).

Safety-stock would be a continuing charge against the operating costs of the plant. Management must therefore assess the risks they are prepared to accept. For example, the complete stoppage of a small single-product process plant (e.g. in industrial classification V) of, say, 60 total establishment could involve a loss of £30,000 sales value a week (*see* Table 5). If the material content of the product is 75 per cent of sales value and it is decided to lay in a safety-stock to cover a single week's production, this will entail a safety-stock level of £30,000 × 75 per cent = £22,000.

Assuming the emergency which called for this safety-stock occurred once in each production year of 50 production weeks, the total average safety-stock carried (assuming that the whole of the safety-stock is issued at the commencement of the week in which it is used) could be:

$$\frac{49}{50} \times £22,500 = £22,050$$

(*see* condition C, Fig. 26).

Assuming total storage costs at 20 per cent per annum, the cost of carrying this safety stock would be:

$$£22,050 \times \frac{20}{100} = £4,410$$

per annum. This is the insurance premium to avoid one week's loss of production per annum. It provides a net saving of £30,000—£4,410 = £25,590 on what would otherwise have been a week's stoppage, with sales at £30,000 a week for a premium of £4,410.

(This example presumes that a single material only is used in the end-product—a most improbable situation.)

By negotiation the supplier's performance may be made more reliable, so that each emergency only lasts half a week. A saving of 50 per cent can then be made by halving the safety-stock, thus reducing the charges from £4,410 to £2,205 per annum and increasing company profit—or reducing losses—by this amount.

It must be clearly understood that the frequency of the emergency can affect this calculation, particularly if the first stock-out is not corrected nor the safety-stock replaced before the next emergency arises. (Where these conditions occur, the flow is no longer 1, but is 5, 6 or 8.)

Flow 2: regular and equal intakes, smooth continuous demand

In flow 2 material is delivered into store at regular intervals in equal quantities at the start of each production cycle, and issued at a steady rate during each cycle. This flow is exceptional and applies to continuous production or process. However, in flow 2 the material cannot all be passed direct to the work-centre or process, but must be held in store and issued as required. This volume (50 per cent of weekly usage) of stock carried in store will therefore incur storage costs at, say, 0.5 per cent per week.

It should be pointed out that although the material in flow 1 passed immediately into production (or process) instead of into stores, it still remained a charge against the overall operation as "work-in-progress". Further differences between flows 1 and 2 are the conditions of frequency change and uncoupling. The latter in flow 2 gives some cover against emergency but only during the earlier part of each period.

Flow 3: regular bulk intakes, equal or smooth continuous demand
The purchasing department may, for economic and practical reasons, arrange for planned bulk intakes to match a long-term demand. There are other reasons apart from price for bulk intakes, such as the following.

(a) Crops only available on a seasonal basis, e.g. timber, grain, etc.

(b) Transport only available seasonally: ports frozen, weather inhospitable.

(c) Balance of freightage against extraction, handling, storage, e.g. ores (bulk ore carriers).

(d) Restrictions on exports by supplying states.

(e) Supplier's process: e.g. bulk, batch production.

For this flow considerable volumes of stock will be likely, resulting in corresponding increases in costs of inventory and storage. In addition, handling equipment and storage facilities will have to be such as to cope with seasonal peak intakes.

As in flows 1 and 2, provisioning must ensure that the rate of intake is correct. Flow 3 can also illustrate continuous smooth demand as shown by the dotted line.

There is a frequency change and uncoupling. The latter is particularly evident in the earlier stages of each manufacturing period, owing to the large stockholding from bulk shipments. Towards the end of the period, however, the value of the uncoupling effect is lost. The final result gives no more security than the previous examples. However, the risk does not occur with such frequency as in flow 2.

Flow 4: regular and equal intakes and demands but out of phase
Flow 4 is included merely to demonstrate the costs of poor phasing. An almost precise analogy occurs here between the waste power due to out-of-phase conditions in electric power systems where

191

costs are incurred to feed in power which does no useful work.

The uncoupling effect in flow 4 is of little value, since once a batch withdrawal has taken place a potential stock-out situation results for the remainder of the period, with the prospect of a stoppage.

There may be situations in which a phase change is unavoidable. The processes of the supplier may prevent shipment being in phase with demand, or an inability to arrange transport may prevent correct phasing. Savings can be made if the purchasing department, in co-operation with the supplier, eliminates the out-of-phase condition and thus contributes to profitability.

Flow 5: intake lead time variable, demand regular and steady

This (more usual) flow is a good starting-point for studying the effects of variable total lead times and deciding what action to take. Variable lead time is a threat in every flow and is one of the most significant factors in determination of stock levels. (BS 5191 (2.5).)

It is important to recognise that total lead time has two disconnected components, namely, "internal" and "external". It should be noted that for practically every production operation, and particularly in the case of process plants and continuous production, it is better to have a lengthy lead time which is regular rather than a short one subject to unpredictable and uncontrollable fluctuations.

Normally those plants which have regular steady demand (flows 1, 2 and 3) are large consumers of materials. This alone tends to have a smoothing effect on suppliers who can in their turn keep production at a steady level. Moreover, because of the heavy consumption of materials the purchasing department should be in a sufficiently powerful position (in all but the very worst conditions) to achieve a supply pattern in which the variations in lead time are restricted within a narrow range. The assessment of risk is then relatively simple, employing elementary statistical analysis (*see also* Table 35).

The diagram for this flow reminds us that despite heavy stock investment a stock-out can occur and safety-stock is essential unless the flow can be improved.

Flow 6: regular equal intakes but intervals between equal demands variable

Assume here that six equal intakes have been planned to anticipate the total usage in the period under review, by using, for example, the EOQ formula or simply by dividing the number of intakes into suitable intervals and quantities.

192

Variations in the times of occurrence of demands are almost universal throughout industry, with particularly adverse effects upon smaller firms where demand is low, fluctuating (*see* flow 7) or intermittent. For example, a jobbing engineer who manufactures steel tanks, hoppers, chutes, etc. may be able to estimate fairly closely his total annual quantities of joists, angles, channels and steel sheet. It is unlikely, however, that he will be able to know *when* orders can be expected to arrive at his sales office. If he opts for regular intakes without further control or back-up he may well lose profit in the early periods through excess or idle stock and later may find himself confronted none-the-less with possible shortages or stock-outs as indicated on the diagram. He must therefore either inflate his stock to provide safety cover or consider the use of a stockholder or other back-up supply.

Flow 7: regular equal intakes but both timing and volume of demands variable

As with flow 5, this is a contingency found in most manufacturing industries. The diagram shows the futility of trying to match regular intakes to such a demand. If total long-term estimates are correct, by the end of the final period the situation will be in balance. However, on the way idle stock, stock-out and shortages have occurred. EOQ and similar formulae are not applicable.

Flow 8: intakes irregular and out of control coupled with unpredictable demands which vary in frequency and volume

Here the diagram (like the other flows) can only point to the problems involved. Whereas variations in timing and volume of demand, as in flows 6 and 7, may be beyond the control of the purchasing officer, he will receive no sympathy from his "customers" if he permits intakes to get out of control. Almost every conceivable disaster has occurred according to the diagram at flow 8.

Flow 9: combining or assembly demand, random intakes of some items (BS 5191 (1.2))

In what are frequently highly complex supply situations, many industries produce their manufactured goods by the assembly of components bought from outside sources or made and stocked within the factory. In either case the whole operation depends upon regular intakes in phase with assembly demand.

In such a condition the success of the production operation is as good as the poorest incoming delivery—except where high stocks have been built up to safeguard the position.

Aspects of control which should be specially considered here are coding and classification. Wherever practicable these should be co-ordinated in relation to each main assembly. For example, the works planning office may supplement the stock-control records with a master assembly record to ensure that material flow is maintained, or network analysis applied (*see* Fig. 71).

In flow 9 the assembly requirement is regular. However, it may not be regular, since many situations arise where assemblies are made according to customers' requirements. In such situations stocks must be increased to provide uncoupling.

Another important aspect clearly shown in flow 9 is the situation where deliveries vary for different parts of the assembly. Either stocks may build up because of this, or it may be necessary to build them up to keep the whole operation in phase.

Production assembly systems fall into the general patterns outlined below (with many variations).

(*a*) Sequential assembly with initial stock for the complete job and paced assembly for each assembly stage. The Supplies department may need to provide accommodation for part-finished assemblies if the line goes out of balance or provide balancing stock to restore balance. (*See* BS 5191 (3.3)—"buffer stock".)

(*b*) As (*a*) but supplies injected into the production line at each stage. In this case balancing stock may be needed to cope with contingencies such as scrap, rejects, tool failure and so on.

(*c*) Combining assembly where a number of materials or components are supplied for immediate single operation assembly. In this case the supplies manager must be prepared for special action if there is lack of balance between the various assembly rates because these are all running in parallel but some at a different rate from others. (*See Storehouse*, Fig. 16.)

ANALYSIS OF INDIVIDUAL FLOWS AND REMEDIAL ACTION

Following the general surveys it is essential to analyse the flow patterns individually. Reference should be made to Fig. 38 for greater detail when studying the notes below.

Periods of demand

Each period in Fig. 38 could represent two weeks. If the periods were shorter, say one day, no confident prediction could be made. If the periods were in years, prediction would be more reliable. The time-scale is therefore vital. Where the periods are short a greater number of samples of earlier periods must be taken to gain accuracy for prediction (*see* Fig. 36).

Trends and cycles

No well-defined trends or regular cycles are revealed from curve (A) in Fig. 38 although there is some indication of a cyclical drop in demand every four and a half periods or so. It would be wise to study a reasonable number of other 25–period samples. If the pattern were repeated or if the shape of the curve were seasonal, draw in the short-term mean (say month by month) and the boundaries of maxima and minima shown at a-a and a_1-a_1 in Fig. 38 and compare these visually with previous similar periods.

Cyclical demands

Curve (B) in Fig. 38 shows almost regular cyclical fluctuations in demand. These stand out even more clearly when the long-term trend is drawn in, shown chain dotted.

The fluctuations can be due to a number of causes such as:

(a) surges in production, possibly due to bad planning;

(b) variations in sales, possibly seasonal, if the time-scale is long (say annual);

(c) inadequate transport arrangements, causing delays in supplies or deliveries;

(d) cyclical shortages of materials, due to bad stock control, poor buying, etc.

Each fluctuation represents by its area a financial value. If this is large Supplies should investigate whether it is possible to smooth out the peaks and fill in the troughs. If it is possible, a direct saving in stock carried per unit of output may then be achieved, up to the mean of the peak above the long-term trend.

Intermittent exceptional demands

Intermittent and exceptional demands often occur superimposed upon a continuous demand, as shown dotted at period 15. In this case additional stock may be needed to cover the exception, or a purchase order may be placed as a "special requirement". It will depend upon how "intermittent" the requirement is and whether or not its frequency is increasing.

When making such an assessment of supply requirements it is important to decide what shall be regarded as "intermittent". There is no clear gradation from intermittent to continuous demand. The latter can be merely the integration of a number of smaller intermittent demands. It could be that the exceptional intermittent demand does not occur at more than six- to eight-month intervals — or is seasonal.

Only after records have been kept for a number of years may it be possible to construct both a curve or demand and a frequency chart of exceptional demands. These can indicate if and (possibly) when the demand is likely to repeat and if stock should be established or pre-allocated to meet it. All forecasts should be carefully checked with sales, production and in some cases maintenance, giving special and objective attention to exceptions. (*See* Fig. 36.)

THE ZERO DEMAND IN WEEK 2 may be due to the annual works holiday or regular planned maintenance shutdown. Both are fully predictable and no advanced statistics should be needed for provisioning. On the other hand, where stocks have a short self-life or there are other hazards it may be necessary to make special arrangements.

THE EXCEPTIONAL HIGH DEMAND IN WEEK 15 may be due to semi-predictable factors such as seasonal trading or a sales drive, or unpredictable factors such as rejections on the shop floor. A number of courses are possible to meet this situation depending upon its characteristics and causes.

For example, a high sales demand may occur at very irregular and infrequent intervals, much longer than the statistical samples available, thus preventing accurate prediction of anything except a "warning signal". To ignore such a signal will almost certainly involve delays on orders to customers whose demands may have caused the peak. However, before finally abandoning the statistical approach, it may be worth extending the size of the statistical sample, for example, comparison with a number of years. This may show that an exceptional order always arrives but at different instants of time each year, or that it varies in magnitude but always arrives about the same time.

Where this is so the frequency chart (*see* Fig. 37) can be extended to include the exceptions, thus making its range broader. The standard deviation after re-calculation, however, will be larger and prediction therefore less confident. In fact, prediction may so lack confidence that the stock controller is forced back upon his original solution, namely the continuous carrying of extra safety-stock to meet the special demand.

Finally, it may be possible to "negotiate" the peak. The customer may have his own problems of seasonal or unpredictable production demands, and co-operation between the sales, production and Supplies departments of supplier and customer may produce effective results.

REPLACEMENTS are all too frequent causes of peak demands arising from the intake of faulty materials, rejects due to faulty machining or process plant failure. The major consideration is the speed which replacement materials will be forthcoming.

Most suppliers (particularly "secondary" suppliers) give priority to such replacements so as to gain customers or protect their reputation. The purchasing officer may influence the situation by putting suitable pressure on the supplier. The production manager of the supplier may in his turn make demands on his own Supplies department for extra raw materials. (He may also need some persuasion to introduce replacements into an already full and profitable production run.)

PRODUCTION PEAKS. Mention was made earlier of the need for management to smooth out cyclical fluctuations wherever possible. An equally important point of production policy is involved with peak demands. A management that habitually allows heavy production peaks to occur is certain to suffer. The machine-shop capacity is likely to be inefficiently loaded. Machines may be idle for long periods and at other times heavily overloaded, and stock levels inflated to cover the cyclical demands, wasting stock investment at each trough in the cycle. It is always important to decide whether the peaks can be controlled, eliminated or ignored. (See Fig. 38(B).)

LARGE UNPREDICTABLE DEMANDS. Intermittent demands of considerable magnitude (such as plant or ship construction) may arrive from customers at unpredictable intervals. The total lead time for obtaining materials may be shorter than the time between the receipt of the customer's order and the commencement of production. Where this occurs the problem is easily solved by interdepartmental co-operation between sales and Supplies departments. The receipt of the customer's order can trigger off advance provisioning, letters of intent, base stock control, pre-allocation, etc.

RECORDING OF SPECIAL DATA. Whether exceptional transactions are passed through the stores records is a matter of stock control policy. If they do, they can distort statistical results and lead to incorrect provisioning. On the other hand, if retained in special records they can provide data for future research into the demand and supply patterns. Similarly, the materials themselves may or may not pass physically through the stores. This must be a part of the general storehouse policy in co-operation with production. If the materials go direct to the work-centre, then the purchase order number should embody the production job number, thus earmarking the goods. If they are to be under stock control, then the commodity code must appear to ensure correct recording. (See Chapter 7.)

SHORTAGES. Unfortunately unpredictable conditions are particularly likely in times of shortage. Because there is a shortage, buying firms may receive additional orders from customers. Supplies departments must then find additional supplies to meet this demand. In such circumstances they often meet shortages stimulated by the demands of firms engaged in similar production to their own and competing in their market, resulting in a "knock-on" effect.

Many sources of supply depend for their stability upon the diversity of demand. Random conditions may develop in a situation which has hitherto been regular and stable. Excessive buying from either one or a group of customers can produce a random and unpredictable state of supply which is unstable and subject to "knock-on effect" once the shortages become widely known.

This situation can also occur where a number of branch stores or depots are served from a main central store. Due to a shortage or other cause one or more stores may make excessive demands to correct their deficiency, which may produce a cycle of shortages throughout the organisation.

In the first case the foresight of the purchasing department must be developed. In the second case discipline on stores and stock control may be the solution. A further possibility remains. The sales department may be able to regularise the pattern with customers.

Random intakes should be avoided where possible, but in periods of shortage they are most likely to occur. Shortage may be due to an increase in production in a certain commodity group, accentuated by a long delivery occuring at the same time as increased production is demanded.

Conditions such as those in flow 8 prevent the application of the economic order quantity formula as the formula depends for its accuracy upon knowledge in advance of the the average value of stock. Obviously the future average value of stock cannot be known where the future is unpredictable as regards mean stock levels and prices of supplies (*see* Fig. 26).

DATA AND STATISTICS FOR
SUPPLIES MANAGEMENT POLICIES

Data and statistics of supply

SPEED OF REPLENISHMENT AND LEAD TIME. Accurate and rapid replenishment of stock is always important. The rate of replenishment is a governing factor of stock levels. It may be:

(*a*) faster than the rate of demand;
(*b*) equal to demand by planned scheduled deliveries;
(*c*) slower than demand due to shortage of supply, inefficient purchasing, poor stock control, or accelerated usage rate.

Replenishment may be instantaneous at the turn of a valve or the push of a button. If this is so, the problems of stock control are greatly reduced, because lead time is virtually nil. The condition may exist together with an unlimited supply, in which case there is little need for more than work-in-progress stocks at the work-centre or alongside it. Such a condition of immediate supply is unusual in classification "A" production materials. It is fairly common for general stores and certain classifications "B" and "C" goods such as small tools, fasteners, lubricants and other consumables.

Supply may be immediate, but not unlimited, in which case safety-stock may be needed, depending upon the degree of importance of the goods, continuity of production and risks involved.

Lead times may be regular but lengthy. If so the main stock levels—reorder and safety-stock—depend entirely upon the demand pattern and risks which are acceptable. (*See* Chapter 7, reorder level.)

AVAILABILITY OF SUPPLIES. The delivery rate and available capacity of suppliers are no less important than the speed of replenishment. Several conditions may arise which affect stock control policy. For instance, there may be only one acceptable supplier, whose total capacity must at least equal the total demands taken over a suitable production period, otherwise a stock-out ultimately results. The maximum demand from the production line may exceed availability, or lower demand may cause accumulation of stock at the supplier's works.

In the last case, what does the supplier do with such surplus? Does he sell the material elsewhere, possibly to a competitor? Does he turn over his surplus capacity to other products? Can the purchaser negotiate with him to store such surplus for later use? If this is agreed, he may be able to make extra-rapid delivery to customers from this immediately available stock. An alternative may be for the purchaser to accept additional materials from the "lean" weeks, storing these as safety-stock. In such a case maximum stock levels must be very carefully watched.

With regular intakes, therefore, the supplier can be given a weekly delivery rate, based on the expected demand for the whole period as well as the supplier's capacity, but surpluses must be dealt with, as already explained, within the maximum limits.

NUMBER OF ACCEPTABLE SUPPLY SOURCES. Multiple sourcing can provide not only an additional source of supply but also competition and service. This is of particular importance when the demand is rising, especially where the main supplier is likely to gain a monopoly position with his customer or to be approaching his maximum capacity.

Data and statistics of demand

PROBABLE TOTAL USAGE IN TOTAL PERIOD. This can be regarded as the framework upon which the overall stock control and purchasing policy will hang. If the total quantity can be known, it should be possible to reduce the evils of overstocking. This figure should also enable stock scheduling to be carried out.

Within the framework of total demand, however, there can be a number of disconnected variables. The pattern may be expected to reflect all the characteristics of the other periods and flows.

The first essential is to obtain data on the production and/or sales plan. Often the plan will only be available within widely varying limits, and the purchasing department should seek to negotiate supplies to cover such variations. Enough has already been said to emphasise the importance of this work by Supplies.

RISK OF STOPPAGE ACCEPTABLE TO MANAGEMENT. It is seldom within the terms of reference of Supplies to decide what risks should be regarded as acceptable to management. The more diversified the production, the more difficult it is to make any firm policy decision. Machine hourly rates are likely to vary and the variety of materials and the fluctuating demands on stock pose problems. Where the company employs standard costing and/or budgetary control, it is easier to determine policy on stoppage costs.

Enough has already been said to give guidance in assessing the probable risks in various situations. The costs of the stocks to cover these risks should be estimated by Supplies, leaving management to calculate the costs of stoppage and to make their decision.

STOCK INVESTMENT POLICY. This must be a top management decision. Conditions similar to those which determine the size of purchase orders may apply viz. the optimum value of total stock may be that for which the annual costs of storage and stock investment costs are equal while their sum must be minimized. In most cases, however, it is availability of capital which largely determines the amount of stock permitted. Management of investment in stock can be effected by establishing financial limits, targets, budgetary control, etc. However, the simplest and most direct method is well-planned and regulated stock control (*see also* Chapter 2 and BS 5729 Part 1(8)).

AXIOM: Stocks must optimise production.

POLICY FOR SAFETY-STOCK. For practical purposes and assuming that the frequency curve of demand approximates to a "normal" distribution, the following guide-lines can be adopted to achieve the desired service factor (or "service level"). (BS 5191.)

Deduct mean demand/usage from maximum expected demand/usage and divide by three, then proceed thus:

For a service factor (BS 5729 Part 1 (7.7)) of 84 per cent add one-third to the mean.
For 96 per cent add two-thirds to the mean.
For 99 per cent add the total difference.

AXIOM: Costs of safety-stock must not exceed costs of risks avoided.

For greater precision it is necessary to calculate the standard deviation σ for each actual stock situation being assessed. Curve (a), Fig. 43 shows the familiar presentation of probability for a "normal" curve as applied to quality control where limits L to size (for example) are set at either side of a mean (μ) or target

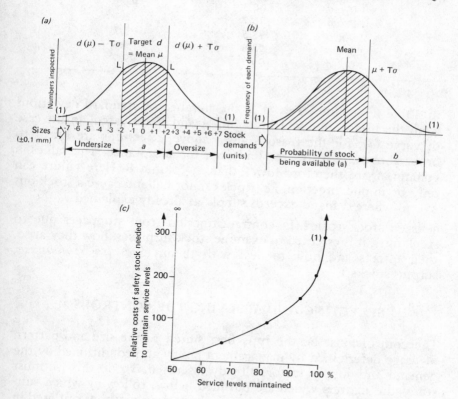

Fig. 43. "Normal" probability curves and curve of "service levels"

201

dimension d. (BS 5532 (4).) In stock control, however, only one tail to the curve is important because all lesser events (i.e. demands) are covered: the appropriate diagram is shown at (b), with the probability of stock-out at b and probability of stock being available at a.

TABLE 23. SOME PROBABILITIES FOR CURVES OF "NORMAL DISTRIBUTION"
(See also Fig. 43)

| $T \times \sigma$ | *Percentages (approx.)* | |
	Curve A units accepted	*Curve B stock adequate*
$0.5 \times \sigma$	38.0	69.1
$1.0 \times \sigma$	68.3	84.1
$1.5 \times \sigma$	86.7	93.3
$2.0 \times \sigma$	95.5	97.7
$2.5 \times \sigma$	98.8	99.4
$3.0 \times \sigma$	99.7	99.9

In Table 23 column $T \times \sigma$ is the number of standard deviations from the mean upon which colums A and B are based. In the case of curve (a), for the reasons given above, rejections are likely to occur above and below the limits set for acceptance. The values in column A are therefore lower than in column B. Here failure can only be in one direction, i.e. stock cannot fail and cause a stock-out except where demand exceeds supply as already explained.

SURPLUS STOCK POLICY. In contradistinction from stoppages due to stock-outs, it is essential to examine stock surpluses, how they arise, their effects and how to deal with them. (*See also Storehouse*, surplus stocks.)

SELECTING AND APPLYING THE CONTROLS

The control must be the type best suited to the size and pattern of usage determined by management policy and conditioned by the demand and supply factors already discussed. To do this we must study the matters which are outlined below, following which suitable controls may be selected from the various methods outlined in Chapter 7. (BS 5729 Part 1 (8–9).)

(a) Is there a predetermined ordering quantity based on:

(i) economic ordering quantity or other fixed quantity;
(ii) commitments limited by financial policy or restriction;
(iii) customs of the supplier(s) trade?
(b) What is the cost of a production stoppage?
(c) What risk of stoppage is management prepared to accept?
(d) How much can be invested in stock?

Size of orders is dealt with in Chapter 10. A small order quantity entails frequent intakes and handling into stores. It may also result in frequent stock-outs. Money restriction, due to shortage of capital or financial policy, may also affect the size of order. The custom of the trade of the supplier may limit the size of order or incur surcharges on consignments which are non-standard or below a certain size.

AXIOM: "Stock buys time" (A. Battersby) "but costs cash" (Auth.).

Controls for supplies on medium to long horizons

The methods of ordering described in Chapter 15 can be selected to provide some measure of control and must be chosen to suit the system of stock control which is employed. The latter may include:
(a) the "self-regulating stock scheduling and planning system" as illustrated in Fig. 72 or "MRP" (Chapter 18);
(b) the use of the pre-allocation columns shown in Fig. 31;
(c) process control programmes linked directly as "supply controls" by direct telephone or on-line computer.

Controls for supplies with steady demand only

This condition (flows 1, 2, 3 and 5) can be dealt with by the control of supply through fixed delivery contracts of various kinds discussed in Chapter 15 and by the application of the economic order quantity or similar methods.

Controls for varying demands for supplies

As the most common conditions (flows 6, 7 and 8) with an almost infinite number of variants, this situation calls for selection from a number of methods of control as appropriate. It must not be overlooked that safety-stock may certainly be needed to cover both varying demands *and* varying lead times. Care is also needed in selecting the control if the lead time is such that the normal order quantity is less than consumption during the lead time—at normal rate of usage.

Controls include:
(a) reorder levels (*see* Fig. 31) (formula Chapter 7);

(b) forward allocation (Fig. 31. Notes 10 and 11);
(c) self-regulating stock scheduling and planning (see Fig. 72);
(d) materials requirements planning (Chapter 18).

Controls for "in-production" supplies. ("W.I.P.") (BS 5729 Part 1 (7.8))

"In-production supplies" comprise chiefly "work in progress" (BS 5191 (2.3)), or, in the case of process plants "materials in process".

They are generally in the charge of production or process control unless they are held in a work in progress store in the main stores complex. Wherever "W.I.P." is held—e.g. at the production (or process) line or in stores it can be a heavy drain upon profitability and company resources (see Fig. 34) and should be rigorously controlled to match production (process) needs. This can be achieved by production/process control in liaison with production/process planning or, if in stores, by specially kept stock records linked to production planning or to "materials requirements planning" (q.v.) where this is practicable. BS 5729 observes that: "W.I.P. controls usually concentrate upon the class 'A' items at far greater speed through production in smaller batches dictated by reorder quantity, leaving the class 'C' items to follow the speed of production."

An unseen cost of W.I.P. is often incurred by the poor facilities for handling output from machines and its stacking, palletising, and conveying to stores or subsequent stages of production.

CONTROL FOR TOTAL THROUHGPUT AND ADJUSTMENTS. Whatever means are employed to control and adjust the ordering quantities the total throughput must equal the sum of the individual demands. Adjustment of quantity from week to week should not therefore in any way alter the annual total from the supplier. A fluctuating demand may involve hidden costs to the supplier, who may therefore seek to revise his price. Any such price change must be set off against any savings in stock charges resulting from closer control of ordering. There may also be increased costs of administering the ordering arrangements, such as, for instance, weekly instead of monthly or quarterly.

A fixed quantity such as the EOQ should in theory give the lowest overall costs, and based on a constant usage this would be true. In Table 16 (Chapter 8) demand varies from 4 to 10 and the stock control system has to carry this variation, the result being that the average stock may be inflated unless steps are taken to avoid this.

TABLE 24. RISKS OF STOCK-OUT AND COSTS OF THEIR AVOIDANCE

	(1) Demand in each period[1]	(2) Frequency of each demand	(3) Maintained stock levels[2]	(4) Percentage frequency of each demand and of cover given by each stock level[3]	(5) Cumulative percentage cover by each maintained stock level[5]	(6) Percentage risk of stock-out for each maintained stock level[6]	(7) Reduction in risk of stock-out for each unit of maintained stock added[7]	(8) Cost of each unit of extra stock added[8] £	(9) Cost of each 1 per cent reduction in risk of stock-out per unit stock added[8] £
(a)	4	1	4	4	4	96	—	—	
(b)	5	4	5	16	20	80	16	50[9]	3.13
(c)	6	4	6	16	36	64	16	50	3.13
(d)[10]	7	7	7	28	64	36	28	50	1.79
(e)	8	5	8	20	84	16	20	50	2.50
(f)	9	3	9	12	96	4	12	50	4.17
(g)	10	1	10	4	100(?)[4]	0(?)[4]	4	50	12.5
(h) Totals		25		100					
(i)[11]	(14)	(1)	(14)	(4)	—	—	(4)	(200)	(50)

COST CONSIDERATIONS

Probabilities and exceptions: risks of stock-outs and costs of their avoidance

Where events are random (as in line *(b)* in Table 16, Chapter 8) a simple statistical rule gives the probability of their occurrence. This states that the probability of an event happening is equal to the number of times the event occurs in the sample divided by the total number of events observed in the sample. (BS 5532 (1).)

NOTE:

A frequently made statistical error is to assume that an exceptionally high result will be followed by an exceptionally low one. This (in the absence of other data such as a trend, seasonal conditions, "habits", etc.) is unlikely. The probability is that the next result will be closer to the mean rather than exceptional.

Table 24 is based upon the example in Table 16, line *(b)*. It exemplifies a number of points arising from a statistical analysis of the data, and shows some of the economic implications.

NOTES TO TABLE 24:

(1) The actual demands for supply (column (1)) and physical movement must always have prime consideration before "economic order quantity", supplier's batch quantities or other constraints are applied.

(2) Column (3) shows the maintained stock level and presumes that this level of stock (but no more) will always be available.

(3) Column (4) shows the approximate frequency of each demand as a percentage of all demands, i.e. in 25 weeks; thus in lines *(b)* and *(c)*, $4 \times 100 \div 25 = 16$ per cent. This also indicates the cover given by each maintained stock level.

(4) It will be noted that in line *(g)*, the final figures in columns (5) and (6) are queried. This is a reminder that there is no such certainty in this kind of statistic as will produce either a 100 per cover or a zero per cent absence of risk!

(5) Column (5) shows the percentage cover given by maintaining stocks at the levels shown in column (3). Each increase in stock must cover all the previous sizes of demand so that each line must cover all the frequencies which preceded it. Thus, in line *(c)* the total is (from column (4)) $4 + 16 + 16 = 36$. (Fig. 43(b).)

(6) However, "good news is no news" and we are interested less in the weeks which are covered than in the risks of being out of stock and this is the purpose of column (6), "risks of stock-out".

(7) Column (7) shows the reduction in risk for each unit of stock added, e.g. from column (6): line *(a)* minus line *(b)* = 96 − 80 = 16.

(8) Columns (8) and (9) indicate the financial costs of the seven stock-level policies discussed. In column (9), line *(b)*, the first additional $50 of stock buys an extra 16 per cent reduction in risk of stock-out at line *(b)* over line *(a)* using column (7). The cost per 1 per cent reduction is therefore £50 ÷ 16 = £3.13.

At line *(g)* the additional £50 buys 4 per cent extra security and the cost per 1 per cent has thus increased to £12.50.

(9) Capital invested in stock has been assumed to be valued at a constant level of £50 per additional unit. The figure is important to management as indicating the amount of money they must lay out for stock to meet production and sales targets, and also to see how this will affect their cash flow.

However, the figure may be far from constant: additional storage accommodation and equipment may be needed, high interest may be charged on additional borrowing, and handling costs may be increased.

More than this, the costs of safety-stock may attract further additional costs such as deterioration due to exceeded shelf-life, small-lot and high freight charges for urgent replacements when drawn upon in a emergency, higher prices paid to secondary suppliers than on the main contract and so on.

(10) Line *(d)* had been taken as the normal maintained or target level and this it is seen covers about 64 per cent of all demands. Had the histogram (Fig. 37) been a "normal curve" it would have covered 66.6 per cent. Lines *(a)* to *(d)* are "working-stock" and lines *(e)* to *(g)* are "safety-stock".

(11) Line *(i)* has been added to show the effect of covering the exception at week 15 for 14 units demand. It will be seen at column (9) that the costs of additional insurance against stock-out escalate rapidly if the exceptions are added. (*See* note (9) above.)

Costs of stoppages (BS 5729 Part 1 (5.2))

The costs of being out of stock may far exceed any savings effected by cutting back on safety-stock. Table 25 introduces these costs into the equation, and the example has been contrived to find a "break-even point". This should of course be sought in any real-life exercise which the reader attempts in his own situation. (BS 5191 (B 5005).)

In the table, costs of stoppages are assessed at £1 for each unit lost from one week's production. (This, like the remaining data, is for example only. Losses would be much greater in practice! *See* Table 12.) Moreover, actual costs vary widely between industries.

TABLE 25. COSTS OF STOPPAGES PLUS COSTS OF IDLE STOCK
FOR VARIOUS MAINTAINED STOCK LEVELS

Line	Risk % as column (6) Table 22	Number of weeks stopped		Cost per week of stoppage (idle time, etc.) (£)	Per annum			Main-tained stock levels	Fre-quency of each demand
		(½ year)	p.a.		Cost of stop-page— idle time, etc.	Cost of carrying idle stock (£)	Total costs idle time plus idle stock (£)		
(1)	(2)	(3)	(4)	(5)	(6)	(7)	(8)	(9)	(10)
(a)	96	(24)	48	1	48	nil	48.0	4	1
(b)	80	(20)	40	1	40	0.5	40.5	5	4
(c)	64	(16)	32	1	32	3.0	35.0	6	4
(d)	36	(9)	18	1	18	7.5	25.5	7	7
(e)	16	(4)	8	1	8	15.5	23.5	8	5
(f)	4	(1)	2	1	2	26.0	28.0	9	3
(g)	0	(0)	0	—	0	38.0	38.0	10	1
(i)	—	—	0	—	0	88.0	88.0	14	

Costs of idle stock

Costs of idle stock must be set off against stoppages which have been
avoided through holding idle stock. The incidence of idle stock, its
duration and costs are often overlooked or ignored despite the seriously adverse effect they can have upon the cash flow of a company,
particularly a smaller one. The calculations can be extremely complex, but what follows is based upon the data of the simple model
used throughout this chapter.

Basically, costs per annum of idle stock = idle stock unit/weeks ×
value per stock unit × holding costs per week. An example of assessment of idle stock unit/weeks is shown below for line (c) of Table 25
for which the maintained stock level is 6 units of stock.

Subtract from maintained stock level the next lower maintained
level and multiply this by the frequency f with which each lower
demand occurs.

Thus at column (9):

(line (c) − line (b) × f (i.e. column (10)
(6 − 5) × 4 = 4 unit/weeks

then:

(line (c) − line (a) × f
(6 − 4) × 1 = 2 unit/weeks.

Total at line *(c)* is thus (4 + 2) stock unit/weeks. Substituting in the formula above, taking holding costs as 25 per cent for a year of 50 working weeks, i.e. 0.5 per cent per week idle:

Costs per annum (of 50 weeks) of idle stock =
        (4 + 2) × £50 × 0.5% × 2 = £3 (£1.50 in 25 weeks).

The break-even point in the "total costs" column of Table 25 shows that stock is warranted up to 8 units but that the costs would escalate so rapidly if the exception at week 15 were covered that it would be unlikely to prove economic to provide for this contingency.

It is misleading merely to assess the savings on the economics of average stocks. For example, a reduction in maximum stocks may not only save "total holding costs" but also avoid the need for costly stores extensions and release capital for other purposes, or building space for production, etc.

NOTE:

It must be re-emphasised that the calculations above are based on the assumption that replenishment of stock is made up to the "maintained stock level" in time for the commencement of each stock period. For a more realistic assessment with varying lead times, take the curve of random usage in Table 16, Chapter 8, set reorder level and order quantity both at 7 units and safety-stock at 10 − 7 = 3 units, and recalculate. The costs of idle stock will be found to be significantly higher than with "instant replenishment" and the value of on line computer control will be appreciated.

Comparative costs of stock control and provisioning policies

In addition to a statistical analysis of supplies flows, a study should be made of costs resulting from the various methods of controlling stock, viz. setting reorder levels, using pre-allocation, etc. Examples are given in Table 26 based upon four common methods of control and their effect upon costs resulting from the actual stock carried. (This leads logically to considerations of ordering quantity in the next chapter.)

The reader should substitute his own data which when analysed by these methods will provide meaningful statistics.

The table falls into two sections. "Subtotals" include only the direct costs of supplies (i.e. acquisition and holding costs). A comparison of these alone would lead to the selection of method and policy (C) as the best option.

When costs due to actual production stoppages are taken into account a very different conclusion is arrived at. The "total costs"

TABLE 26. COMPARATIVE COSTS OF FOUR STOCK-CONTROL METHODS AND POLICIES
(See Table 15 and Fig. 34)

	A	B	C	D	Notes
Mean stock carried	0.54	3.21	1.17	2.62	
Costs of mean stock	£27	£160	£58.5	£131.0	At £50 per stock unit
Storage costs per 12 periods (weeks)	£1.62	£9.63	£3.51	£7.86	At 24% p.a. say 6% per 12-week period
Costs of acquisition					
Number of orders issued each 12 periods (weeks)	12	3	3	3	
Number of intakes	12	3	3	3	
Costs of orders *total*	£12	£3	£3	£3	At (say) £1 per order
Costs of intakes *total*	£36	£9	£9	£9	At (say) £3 per intake
Subtotals	£49.62	£21.63	£15.51	£19.86	Supplies costs only
Number of stoppages	2	1	2	1	
Duration of stoppages in periods (weeks)	1	½	2	½	
Costs of stoppages	£100	£50	£200	£50	At £100 lost for each week stopped
Total costs	£149.62	£71.63	£215.51	£69.86	

line assumes that production is completely held up with no substitute orders to replace the suspended jobs. It does not take account of the periods of stock-out when supplies would not be available had a higher or sudden demand arisen.

Other costs
Costs of inefficient stock control have been examined in relation to stoppages of production due to stock-outs and loss of sales. There are, however, other costs. Not only may production be stopped and customers let down, but suppliers also may suffer from "stop-go" imposed by demands from purchasing. "Stop" may involve the supplier in heavy storage and rescheduling costs, while "go" may involve him in overtime and many other costs. Finally the purchasing firm's credibility as a customer may suffer and sooner or later costs will be recovered by suppliers and prices will rise.

CHAPTER 10

Order Quantity

INTRODUCTION

Different types of quantity

It is necessary to differentiate clearly between the various "quantities" referred to in Supplies terminology.

Order quantity may be fixed for delivery in a specified time open in regard to total ultimate needs, rate of delivery or timing. For example, a smaller firm may improve its bargaining position by offering its supplier an extended time for its commitment while leaving the final quantity open for future adjustment.

Intake quantity is not, as often supposed, identical with order quantity but it must (as a rule) be related to usage. Errors may occur in the application of the economic ordering quantity, which in its usual form assumes that each intake involves a separate purchase order and therefore full Supplies costs.

Many theorists of the economic order quantity (EOQ) formula overlook the following fundamental Supplies rules.

(*a*) Total usage equals sum of individual demands.

(*b*) Total ordered must equal total usage.

(*c*) Formulae must never inhibit flow of supplies. (*see also* Checklist 19.)

Intake quantity may significantly affect intake costs (*see* Chapter 21).

Usage rate quantity is usually outside the control of Supplies and depends upon production and sales. Whether intakes are planned to match the usage rate or as bulk deliveries is, however, a matter of Supplies financial policy, since cash must be invested if bulk intakes are made and stock inflated.

Batch quantities may refer to those of the production line of the purchaser or that of his supplier or both. Reconciliation of both supplier's and purchaser's production batch quantities can be profitable.

Economic order quantity is examined later in this chapter. It is based on the proposition that the economic quantity to order is that which minimises totals of acquisition and holding costs. The minimum total costs usually—but *not* invariably—occur where the holding and acquisition costs equalise.

Implications for safety-stock

The Supplies department is mainly concerned with efforts to purchase and stock the most economic quantity. In theory the best size of order is *usually* that for which the cost of acquisition breaks even with the cost of carrying the active (i.e. moving) portion of stocks held. It is important to note that it is only the active portion ("cycle stock" (BS 5191 (3.3)) taken into account, safety-stock is excluded.

Safety-stock is idle stock. As a continuing charge it does not directly affect the economic order quantity. When it is withdrawn from the stores to meet an emergency, it leaves the stock control without its "insurance" cover. Replenishment is then a matter of greater urgency than the maintenance of the economic order quantity. The production manager is unlikely to be supportive if told that supplies are held up because of the application of the EOQ (or any other) formula.

Safety-stock may, however, be seriously affected by the order quantity selected, i.e. EOQ or other quantity taken as standard. If the latter results in small orders being placed, the safety-stock level will be reached more frequently—and may be drawn on more frequently for this reason (*see* Fig. 34, policy A). If this occurs often enough, it becomes part of "live" (moving) stock and the stock levels must be adjusted and the economic order quantity recalculated. If the order quantity throws out a figure giving one week's supply then the chance of passing safety-stock level will occur 50 times more often than if the calculation provides 50 weeks' supply per acquisition. This condition must be carefully studied before deciding the order quantity.

ECONOMIC ORDER QUANTITY (EOQ)

The EOQ formula (simplified form) (BS 5729 Part 3 (3.2))

The following simplified formula is easily derived from first principles on the assumption that the most economic lot is that for which the acquisition and holding costs are equalised (BS 5191 (3.3)):

$$EOQ = \sqrt{\frac{2 \times A \times S}{C \times I}}$$

Where: EOQ = economic order or batch quantity[1]

A = total annual usage[2]

C = value per item or unit purchased

S = acquisition cost per order, per batch or per intake.[3]

I = storage and carrying (holding) costs, expressed as a per cent— on mean stock values throughout the operative period—usually twelve months or 50 working weeks.

2 = a constant derived from the denominator and the division of "I" by two, so as to produce theoretical mean stock value.[1]

Substituting as an example from Table 27, Class "A", Column (1):

$$EOQ = \frac{2 \times 80 \times £5}{£50 \times 20\%} = 9 \text{ (approx) units per order.}$$

With annual usage 80 units per annum, the number of orders is (A ÷ EOQ) 80 ÷ 9 = approximately 9 orders per annum, and with 50 production weeks per annum the coverage of each order would be about 6 weeks. This will be seen to agree with the dip in total costs on curve A of Fig. 44.

It will also be observed that in Fig. 44 what may be termed "an indifference margin" x occurs around the optimum order size in each case, and that the margin x increases as the item value and total usage value per annum fall. This margin provides a negotiating area for the purchasing officer similar to that indicated in Fig. 55.

NOTES:

(1) The formula is only mathematically valid if acquisition costs and holding costs are rectilinear, and if intake and usage (or demand) are regular and constant. (BS 5729 Part 3 Appendix C2(b).)

(2) BS 5729 points out that other than annual quantities may be used in the formula but that values must be expressed in the same units of time.

(3) It will be noted that the BS 5729 formula adopts the symbol "S" for acquisition costs which it defines as "the processing or set-up costs per order". This use of production terminology is a reminder that the supplier (or manufacturer) may incur "setting up costs" for each acquisition/intake in addition to the purchaser's own processing costs for each order placed.

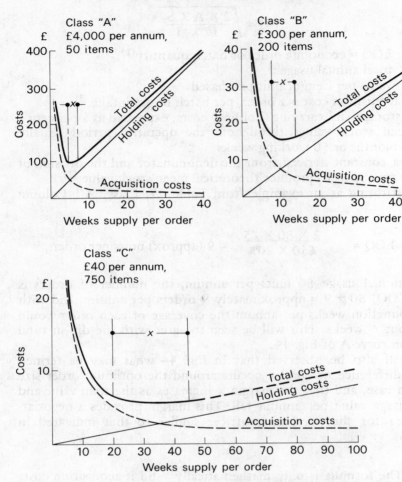

Fig. 44. Charts of economic order quantity

Application of the EOQ formula

The EOQ formula can be used where the demand is reasonably large and continuing provided that supply and demand (usage) do not fluctuate too widely. It can also be used as a guideline for low value, low usage items which are nonetheless carried as regular stock. (Used correctly it may avoid the holding of twenty years' stock of a small item—as was discovered in the stores of a small company with cash-flow problems—used incorrectly it may lead to them!)

Before proceeding to apply the EOQ formula there are further points to consider, as follows.

TABLE 27. CALCULATION OF ECONOMIC ORDER QUANTITY

(1) Classification of supply. Annual usage. Cost per acquisition	(2) Acquisitions (orders) per annum	(3) Acquisition costs per annum (£Ac)	(4) Holding costs per annum (20% × Col. (6))/2	(5) Total costs per annum Cols. ((3) + (4))	(6) Value per order (annual usage ÷ Col. (2))	(7) Weeks supply per order (50 ÷ Col. (2))
		£	£	£	£	
"A"	1	5	400	405	4,000	50
£4,000	2	10	200	210	2,000	25
£Ac = £5	4	20	100	120	1,000	12.5
EOQ →	9	45	44	89	444	5.5
	16	80	25	125	250	3
	50	250	8	258	80	1
"B"	1	2	30	32	300	50
£300	2	4	15	19	150	25
£Ac = £2	3	6	10	16	100	17
EOQ →	4	8	7	15	75	12.5
	5	10	6	16	60	10
	6	12	5	17	50	8
	10	20	3	23	30	5
"C"	1	2	4	6	40	50
£40 EOQ →	1½	3	2.5	5.5	26	34
£Ac = £2	2	4	2	6	20	25
	4	8	1	9	10	12.5
	6	12	0.7	12.7	7	8
	8	16	0.5	16.5	5	6
	10	20	0.4	20.4	4	5

(a) If the rate of usage is large enough and sufficiently stable to apply the formula, some form of forward supply contract or other arrangement (see Table 31) should be explored. One aim (among a number of others) should be to reduce total Supplies costs (see Checklists 4, 18, 19, 20 and 35).

(b) If full purchasing (sourcing, enquiring and ordering) procedures are used for each intake on large quantities of supply, the streamlining of procedures may be more profitable than the application of the formula.

(c) The EOQ is often associated with operational research techniques for supplies and materials management problems. These techniques involve the preparation of mathematical models of systems such as stock control, market forecasts and so on. Such models are usually based upon historical data. Where this is the case with the EOQ, the result can be highly misleading, unless care is taken to examine trends and other environmental conditions. For example, an estimate of stock required would be totally erroneous if, unknown to the investigator, the company had decided to discontinue or reduce production!

Limitations of the EOQ formula

The reader may already have gathered that EOQ formulae have their limitations. In particular, the theory assumes the following conditions to be true—but this may be far from the case.

(a) Opening and closing stocks will be the same.

(b) Stock flow is smooth and continuous.

(c) EOQ is that for which aquisition costs equal holding costs. (See Note 1 above.)

(d) There are no delivery delays.

(e) Prices and costs remain constant throughout the period to which the EOQ applies.

(f) The EOQ does not exceed shelf-life at normal usage rate.

(g) There are no financial restrictions, such as budgetary control.

(h) Costs of goods and holding costs are accurate.

(i) Total costs are relatively insensitive to size of order or intake.

(j) Aquisition costs are as low as practicable and stable.

(k) There is no danger of unbalanced stocks or obsolescence if usage falls.

(l) There is no conflict between stock levels and production schedules.

Other methods of order quantity control

Three further methods of determining order quantities are nomographs, tabulation of costs and planning schedules. The first two are examined below, while the last is dealt with in Chapter 18, self-regulating stock schedules and forward planning systems.

NOMOGRAPHS. A nomograph can be used as a form of ready-reckoner by means of a cursor placed across vertical scales graduated logarithmically, from which can be read, for example, order quantities, etc.[97]

TABULATION OF COSTS. Calculations of EOQ by tabulation, as in Table 27, are laborious and may merely confirm what would have been shown by the EOQ formula. This is evident from the example already given for Class "A". Similar results could be obtained for Classes "B" and "C".

However, the step-by-step tabulation may be justified for major Class "A" requirements, where for example, changes in holding or acquisition costs may vary at different intake or holding quantities. Optimum size of intake, after allowing for the overriding needs of

216

(1)		(2)	(3)	(4)	(5)	(6)	(7)
		Intakes during the twelve months commencing 1st January 19–4					
(a)	Tonnes per intake	1,000	500	250	125	100	83
(b)	Value per intake	£10,000	£5,000	£2,500	£1,250	£1,000	£833
(c)	Transport costs (per annum)	£1,000[1]	£1,200[1]	£640[2]	£640[2]	£800[2]	£720[2]
(d)	Containerisation[3]	£500	£500	–	–	–	–
(e)	Palletisation[4]	–	–	£32	£65	£80	£100
(f)	Handling at intake	£200[5]	£300[5]	£480	£960	£1,200	£1,500
(g)	Documentation[6]	£5	£10	20	40	50	60
(h)	Acquisition costs (c) to (g)	£1,705	£2,010	£1,172	£1,705	£2,130	£2,380
(i)	Mean value of stock	£5,000	£2,500	£1,200	£625	£500	£416
(j)	Holding/investment costs at 30 per cent per annum on mean value at (i)	£1,500	£750	£360	£186	£150	£123
(k)	Total costs (b) + (j)	£3,205 (1,505)[7]	£2,760 (£1,300)[7]	£1,532	£1,851	£2,280	£2,503

Fig. 45. Assessment of optimum intake quantities by tabulation

EXAMPLE: 1,000 tonnes of "gunge" per annum at £10 per tonne contract price.

NOTES:

(1) Rail freight to purchaser's sidings. (2) 32-tonne palletised lorry loads to raw "gunge" store direct (approximately £10 per load). (3) Disposable intermediate bulk containers in special rail wagons (*see also note* (7)). (4) Pallets, returnable. Each stacked with bagged "gunge" and shrink-wrapped. (5) includes extra handling equipment hired for off-loading of large intakes. (6) Documentation £5 per intake: IBC containers sealed and computer controlled. (7) Figures in parentheses allow for integrated handling direct to process (*see Storehouse* Fig. 66 "integrated supplies") giving savings in depalletising, debagging, rehandling to process.

production, can vary considerably as a result of negotiations (*see* Chapter 14, and Fig. 60).

The tabulation for analysing and selecting the optimum quantity should be set out as in the example in Fig. 45 incorporating a number of variables not included in the formula.

COSTS OF ACQUISITION, STORAGE AND HOLDING

Acquisition costs (BS 5729 Part 1 (5.2.1.a), BS 5191 (B 5006))
These are chiefly under the control of the purchasing department (*see* Checklist 20). As normally understood they include the costs of the full ordering and intake routine for each order, as follows.

TOTAL ACQUISITION COSTS

Administrative costs
Requisition from stores
Enquiry and negotiation
Summary of quotations
Order processing
Delivery chasing if necessary
Goods intake
Invoice checking payment, etc.

Physical costs
Packaging and preserving
Handling and transport
Intake costs
Checking and counting
Unpacking
Return of empties
Documentation

Fixed costs
Buildings and plant. (*See also* Chapter 4, "feasibility study".)

Acquisition costs have a greater effect upon liquidity and profitability in a small enterprise than in a large firm where the costs are swamped by the demand.

AXIOM: Savings in acquisition costs often exceed those of EOQ.

The factors which determine acquisition costs can be divided into the following categories: internal conditions, external conditions and adjustable or negotiable conditions. These are discussed in turn below.

(1) INTERNAL CONDITIONS. The chief of these is the cost of placing orders. There are several methods of calculating this cost and the reader must decide which of the following is most suitable for his situation.

(*a*) Divide the number of orders per annum into the total cost per annum of the purchasing department only, assuming the department's role is confined to order placing.

(*b*) As above but include intake costs, documentation and physical handling.

(c) As (a) or (b) but first deduct salaries of senior staff if these provide services to other departments besides the administration of actual purchasing.

(d) As (c) but also deduct all costs of departmental activity not directly associated with order-placing, e.g. stock control, value analysis, storehouse management, catalogue library, supplies circulars, etc.

(e) As (d) but apply weightings to take account of differences in acquisition costs between simple "ex catalogue" buying and orders and major contracts involving enquiries and more complex and costly procedures.

(f) Any of the foregoing but taking account of streamlining by the use of small-value orders, local-purchase orders, etc.

(2) EXTERNAL CONDITIONS (i.e. outside the Supplies department). These include the forecast rates of usage, company sales policy, trade prospects, production plan and capacity.

In addition to the forecast, the actual rate of usage must be considered to take account of variations from the production plan due to increased or reduced output, and of scrap and rejects in manufacture.

Other external conditions over which the purchasing department has little or no control include trends in market price. Within the limits of demand set by production and sales, the market may have a determining effect on purchasing and on the stock levels set—regardless of the economic order quantity (see also Fig. 57).

A further factor is the "prospective supply pattern", particularly where this is a world condition, as in the case of certain metals and other sensitive commodities.

Rate of change of the company's designs, although not directly influencing the acquisition costs of specific orders, can have an important bearing on the cost of the Supplies operation in general, and of purchasing in particular. Frequent changes in technical policy and design can add greatly to the work and thus to the cost of staffing and running a purchasing department.

In the narrower field of general supporting materials, i.e. classifications "B" and "C", the supply situation can have a distinct effect on the acquisition costs, as well as on storage charges. In the first place, long and unpredictable deliveries may lead to inflated stocks to avoid stock-outs. The need to progress and chase unsatisfactory suppliers will add greatly to the true overall acquisition costs.

(3) ADJUSTABLE OR NEGOTIABLE CONDITIONS. In addition to external conditions which the purchasing department cannot control, there is a wide field in which adjustment and negotiation are possible.

(a) *Price* is the first and most obvious condition and is usually related to the size of orders. It also depends upon whether price is firm for the duration of the contract or if it will be subject to adjustment based on labour and materials (*see* Chapter 13).

(b) *Size of orders* will be controlled by the demands of sales and production and by the company's money management policy. There may be some latitude governed by the degree of "uncoupling effect" (*see* Chapter 9) provided by the stockholdings. Certainly the production department is not interested in the size of order placed so long as there are adequate supplies. On the other hand, it is interested in the size of actual intakes into the works. The purchasing officer can help by seeing that the quantity in each consignment is suited to the production batch.

(c) *Packing and transport* arrangements also affect acquisition costs (*see* Chapters 19 and 20). For example, the purchasing officer may be able to negotiate a change in batch size at the supplier's works to the economic advantage of both the supplier and his own factory. This can affect the number, sizes and types of containers used, which must be kept to the minimum. It can also assist in standardisation of handling equipment.

(d) *Consignment stocks* may be negotiated by the purchasing department. Acquisition costs in this case are virtually transferred to the supplier, who may seek to recover them in his price, either openly or concealed within the price and discount structure.

(e) *Batch size:* the formula for the economic order quantity may also apply to the optimum batch size for the supplier's manufacturing programme. When negotiating, a slight adjustment to the size of batch per intake can enable the supplier to reduce his price. If the reduction in price exceeds the increase in costs of storage and interest for the increased quantity, then the new batch size should be accepted—provided that the storage space is available and that the quantity does not exceed total expected needs or shelf-life. (Other factors which may affect quantity are listed in Checklist 19.)

Where powered handling is introduced it enables greater flexibility per tonne handled than older methods. The purchasing officer may need to "sell" ideas to his supplier for their mutual benefit. (*See* examples at Fig. 45.)

Storage and holding costs

Storage and holding costs are vital components of total supplies costs and have important implications for quantities stocked and sizes of intake batches into stores (*see* Checklist 35). General storage costs are analysed in some detail in *Storehouse*, storage costs as regards equipment used in stores are examined in chapter 23 of this volume. (BS 5191 (B 5003/4).)

"Holding" or "investment costs" of stock depend upon the financial conditions prevailing at the time of review, i.e. costs of money, interest rates, availability of overdraft and so on. Important factors which the normal EOQ formula does not take into account are the cubic volume of storage equipment so used. Figure 46 shows the wide divergence in costs of storage volume occupied by three common commodities, while Fig. 75 indicates the relative costs of some common storage equipment (this is discussed further in *Storehouse*).

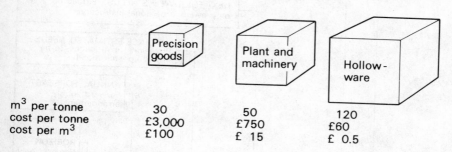

	Precision goods	Plant and machinery	Hollow-ware
m³ per tonne	30	50	120
cost per tonne	£3,000	£750	£60
cost per m³	£100	£ 15	£ 0.5

Fig. 46. Variations in value/volume costs for some classes of supplies

In general, lower stock levels on Class "A" stocks show savings in storage costs which far outweigh savings in acquisition costs. At the same time continual ordering and review of bin levels, price and consumption trends are likely to prove very rewarding.

GENERAL GUIDE-LINES ON ORDER QUANTITIES

In the light of the preceding discussion on the EOQ formula and acquisition and storage costs, it is possible to suggest the following general guide-lines for order quantity policies.

(*a*) Class "A", bulk requirements: place contracts with regular intakes, say, every 5-10 weeks, or as needed by production.

(*b*) Class "B", intermediate value goods: 10–16 weeks' supply.

(*c*) Class "C", small value items: buy and stock from 20–50 weeks' supply.

(But *see also* the points listed in Checklist 19.)

OVER- AND UNDER-ORDERING

At the commencement of this chapter it was stated that as a rule the quantity ordered must equal the demand—equated of course with production needs. It is, however, also necessary to examine the reasons for and effects of over-ordering, that is, purchasing in excess of normal demand over normal production policies or horizons (*see* Fig. 47).

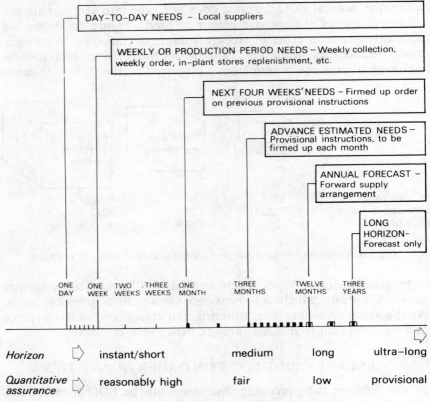

Fig. 47. Supplies horizons

Causes of over-ordering

These include the following.

    (*a*) Increases planned exceed actual production.

    (*b*) Increased sales forecasts exceed actual sales.

    (*c*) Speculation on market prices, or to hedge against inflation.

    (*d*) Speculation in the face of actual or expected shortages.

    (*e*) Supplier pressure: threats of shortages or long delivery times.

    (*f*) Supplier inducements: bulk/quantity discounts.

    (*g*) Sharp practice or fraudulent action by suppliers.

    (*h*) Shortages by some suppliers in a multiple sourcing arrangement leading to over-ordering or duplication elsewhere because of over-reaction.

(i) Shortages due to demand outstripping supply with result as in *(h)*.

(j) Spurious demands by functional user department.

(k) Inadvertently large demand due to error in the system or feedback error.

(l) Incompetence, of requisitioner or Supplies staff, because of lack of control.

When examining the problem of over-ordering it is useful to establish the duration of the over-supply and the length of the future commitment which has been entered into. The volume of storage capacity must be assessed and the costs estimated for an additional storage capacity to be hired or built to house the extra stock.

If extra production (*see (a)*) or increased sales (*see (b)*) give rise to the over-ordering, close collaboration is called for on the financial aspects of profitability. It is probable that the marketing side of the company will have secured the business for increased production and sales at a unit (or margin) price which demands savings in costs of supplies. It will not assist the company's profits if 10,000 units are sold at a unit price reduction of 1p as a result of production unit costs being reduced by 0.5p and a purchasing discount for extra quantity of a further 0.5p, if financing costs for extra stock plus storage costs for (say) hired or other additional storage capacity needed amount to an additional cost of 1.01p per unit.

Speculation on market prices (*see (c)*) is less likely to be met in an industrial undertaking and must always remain top financial management policy. (*See also* Chapter 13 and Fig. 57.)

Speculation in the face of actual or expected shortages (*see (d)*) is a more frequent characteristic of the industrial scene. An efficient and alert purchasing officer should have achieved a position from which he can get prior indications, or receive reliable information, of probable shortages. Having satisfied himself and his board of the need to speculate in order to safeguard production needs he must decide how to arrive at the level of over-ordering needed. Multiple sourcing may be possible, or an existing supplier may accept increased order quantities. However, as shortages develop and a seller's market emerges this solution becomes more difficult to achieve—an argument for prompt action before the chronic stage is reached.

Supplier pressure and threat of shortage (*see (e)*) is a familiar ruse among some suppliers. The purchasing officer should suspect the "kindly and confidential" hint from a supplier—the more confidentially it is given the greater the need to check it and investigate the situation.

Bulk quantity discounts (*see (f)*) must always be examined against the positive financial gains versus increased costs.

AXIOM: Quantity discount must exceed costs of extra quantity.

Causes *(g)*, *(h)* and *(i)* require little comment since they should be considered subject to the disciplines and skills for which the purchasing officer was trained.

Spurious demands by functional user departments (*see (j)*) are examined in Chapter 14, ethics in negotiations.

Inadvertence (*see (k)*) and incompetence (*see (l)*) should lead to urgent investigation of the Supplies organisation even if they arise outside its immediate purview because this organisation is looked upon by many managements as the "long-stop". Inadvertence can be the result of:

> *(i)* lack of order checking;
> *(ii)* lack of scrutiny of requisitions;
> *(iii)* stock-control errors;
> *(iv)* poor liaison with sales, production or other departments.

Legal implications

The law is likely to give the supplier maximum protection unless he has knowingly and fraudulently misled the purchaser so that he over-ordered. The possibilities for cancellation of over-orders are thus very remote unless the purchasing officer has persuaded his supplier to accept a "break clause" in his contract. Such an arrangement is unlikely to have any legal weight unless it is negotiated at the time the contract is first entered into. These considerations lead to the conclusion that any deliberate over-ordering must be accompanied by close and continuous monitoring and control of the contract from start to finish.

UNITS OF MEASUREMENT

Units of measurement should be a primary concern of all who buy, handle or use supplies.[98] The slow move towards metrication may be partly due to the failure of central authorities to bring to the attention of Supplies staff, particularly purchasing officers, the benefits which can accrue from its adoption. An example of savings through the adoption of metric standards was given by an official of the British Steel Corporation as far back as 1975. He explained that simply by changing dimensions as specified on a purchase order into standard metric units, a customer saved over £1,000 on a single order for steel plate. Even older workers find, once they get used to the change, that measurement calculations are greatly simplified.

There are dangers in metrication, of course. Workers may add or take away too many noughts in their calculations! Another is possible substitution; this occurred on a bridge structure when Whitworth bolts were used in place of the slightly larger (but unavailable locally) metric equivalent shown on the drawing. The Whitworth bolts failed in service and fatalities resulted.

Harmonisation of measurements is as equally important within a firm as it is between the firm and its suppliers. Larger firms may find it of advantage to set up a "metrication committee" on which a member of Supplies should sit. Smaller firms should at least ensure closest liaison between the draughtsman, production staff and whoever does the buying and selling. (BS 350, 5233, PD 6461, PD 6470 (2.4).)

CHAPTER 11

Timing, Frequency and Duration of Orders

INTRODUCTION

The timing, frequency and duration of orders can be important to the negotiation of the most profitable arrangement for supply contracts.

TIMING of the placing of orders is a Supplies matter, but is frequently confused with the timing of intake. Clearly, the timing must be such that intake shall be in phase with requirements. If timing also involves an earlier intake than necessary, storage/holding costs will be inflated (*see* Fig. 49). However, timing is also important in relation to market conditions. Although the purchasing officer is not expected to speculate he must not ignore the market and must negotiate accordingly (*see* Fig. 57).

Other factors which may affect timing and frequency, or both are:

(*a*) methods of stock control—periodic or continuous review, etc.;

(*b*) prospective world shortage, or glut;

(*c*) seasonal availability;

(*d*) seasonal demand;

(*e*) seasonal transport facilities.

(*See also* Chapter 18, *targets*.)

ORDER FREQUENCY may be at fixed intervals or controlled by stock levels (*see* Fig. 25). If a separate order is placed for each intake it may have a significant effect upon the acquisition costs. Costs should be greatly reduced by streamlined order methods. Frequency may also be affected by the EOQ. The purchasing officer should adjust the frequency of intakes to the economic frequency without issuing orders for each intake, thus reducing the purchase order costs.

DURATION OF ORDERS varies inversely with frequency, but it is again emphasised that there is no reason why every intake should incur the expense of a full order procedure.

SUPPLIES HORIZONS

Supplies horizons are important in determining the timing, frequency and duration of orders. By "horizon" is meant the length of time over which it is reasonable and prudent to make arrangements for provisioning. Figure 47 indicates various "supplies horizons" upon which Supplies policies must be based, and also suggests some policies for adoption.

In commerce and industry a number of considerations must be taken into account. It will help if these are studied in relation to the "A.B.C." analysis of supplies (*see* Fig. 14) and supply flow patterns (*see* Chapter 9). Classification "A", basic raw materials in, for example, a process industry must be secured by placing contracts for considerable periods ahead—sometimes up to three years or even longer. The types of contract to secure such long-term arrangements are discussed in Chapter 15.

Overcoming lead time (BS 5191 (2.5))
Since lead time is a contributor to overall duration (and also the timing) of orders, means of reducing it should be considered as an aid to profitability. Figure 48 suggests some areas for savings.

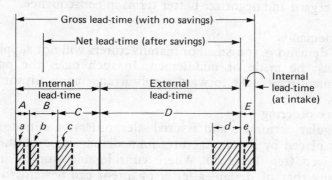

Fig. 48. Areas for savings in lead times

DURATION AND TIMING OF CONTRACTS

Period contracts
Period contracts are usually let with the starting dates and periods

to suit those of the process or production planning of the purchaser or supplier, or both. They usually coincide with the financial year of the enterprise, governed by the forward planning or physical conditions. On long-term contracts the first year's supply may be covered by a firm delivery programme, the second year by a provisional one, and the third merely by a reservation on the output of the supplier. Obviously such long-term thinking is the prerogative of larger units. However, the same thinking could be applied by smaller industries more often than is realised (*see also* Chapter 18, forward planning systems.)

"Futures contracts"

The timing of these can be made to suit the buying firm and the practice of the market concerned. Normally such contracts are made as soon as the purchaser can estimate his forward commitments.

Continuing contracts (running contracts)

If demand is continuous and large, purchases may be direct from a factory and not through an intermediary (merchant, wholesaler or distributor). In these circumstances it is unnecessary to place contracts with starting dates strictly in phase with the production programme. The purchasing department is then able to spread its contract and negotiation work over the year instead of being overloaded at financial or production periods. It may also assist suppliers in this regard and negotiate better terms in consequence.

Small demands

Where demand is too small or manufacturers will not supply direct, use must be made of middlemen. In such cases the purchasing department may make forward supply arrangements advantageously.

Advance ordering

For regular customers and assured sales, orders on outside suppliers can be placed by a manufacturer immediately his customer's order is received (*see* Table 1). Where considerable work is involved—including that of design—a letter of intent can be sent to the supplier as soon as the customer's order is reasonably assured. Such pre-ordering when boldly and skilfully employed can reduce costs and, by improved service, win new customers and retain old ones.

"Immediate" (hand-to-mouth) ordering.

Class "C" materials usually include items for maintenance. These may be on a "one-for-one" basis—or on a "no stock at all" basis!

The time to place the order in these cases will then be governed by the breakdowns which have occurred. However, the introduction of planned preventative maintenance can make radical improvements here.

Supply and intake in advance of usage — costs during stock-life
Supply in advance of need can be costly in terms of cash tied up in stock, possible deterioration or damage in store, congestion in store and so on. However, it may be justified where shortages exist or are expected, or a price rise is forecast, and where seasoning or other pre-treatment of the goods is needed. The benefits must be measured against the costs throughout stock-life. (BS 5191 (3.3).)

Figure 49 demonstrates the effects of holding stock longer than necessary before production, the costs of holding finished stock (or of delaying despatch and/or invoicing) after finishing production, and finally, further losses if payment is delayed after receipt of the goods by the customer.

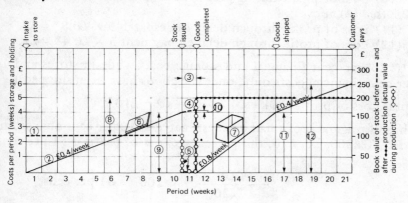

Fig. 49. Costs of holding stock

In the example, stock of £100 purchase value is taken into stores ten weeks before production commences, despatch is delayed for five weeks afterwards in a finished state, and final payment is not made until five weeks later. Storage and holding costs (2) are calculated at 20 per cent per annum (of fifty working weeks) on the *full* stock value. This assumes that the *whole* stock does not move at all until week 10 and that the storage costs are the same for all stock, ignoring "value/volume ratio" (*see* notes (6) and (7) below).

The following notes refer to the numbers in circles in Fig. 49 and trace the costs and other effects during "stock-life".

(1) Stock bought for £100. The market price (replacement cost) could increase or decrease during stock-life.

229

(2) Storage and holding costs given as £0.4 per week, but could vary, i.e. stock may deteriorate, interest rates may change.

(3) Production period could be much longer than a week, e.g. building a ship or a power station.

(4) Once stock is transferred from stores to work-centre the storage costs cease, but holding costs (interest) charges continue. In the example these are taken as 10 per cent of stock valuation.

(5) Directly production starts the realisable value of the stock is likely to fall to zero but remains on the books at full vlaue.

(6) Value/volume ratio (*see* Fig. 46) varies from item to item of stock; 20 per cent may be inadequate or excessive.

(7) Volume after manufacture may increase, e.g. sheets (6) into tanks (7), or may decrease, e.g. timber in the round into planks.

(8) "Added value" shown as 100 per cent; could be much higher, e.g. in precision engineering.

(9) Loss of profit in weeks 1 to 10 = £4.

(10) Loss of profit during production: interest of raw stock, say, £0.2 (*see* (4) above).

(11) Loss of profit through delay in despatch 5 × £0.8* = £4.

(12) Loss of profit through delayed payment 5 × £0.4* = £2.

(*20 per cent financial and storage costs while in stores and 10 per cent financial costs only, once the goods have been shipped.)

Total Loss of profit = £4 + £0.2 + £4 + £2 = £10.2.

Thus, if original profit had been estimated as 10 per cent on a selling price of £200, i.e. £20, the percentage loss of profit is 51 per cent, i.e.

$$\frac{£10.2}{£20} \times 100 = 51 \text{ per cent}$$

while the loss chargeable directly to Supplies would be 41 per cent, i.e.

$$\frac{£8.2}{£20} \times 100 = 41 \text{ per cent}$$

"Job-by-job" ordering
Ordering on a "job-by-job" basis for non-stocked and often non-standard supplies is common in jobbing industries and is seldom entirely absent in any industry. This is an instance where good liaison is essential between Supplies, sales and production. Sometimes Supplies can assist sales colleagues to obtain valuable orders by making supplies available with "letters of intent", advance ordering and other procedures.

Fixed reorder interval system (periodic review) (BS 5729 Part 3 (4.3) abb.)

[This may be subject to adjustment to meet contingencies. Auth.] If usage varies the reorder quantity must change. In the reorder level system the reorder quantity can be fixed. Regularly used items can be ordered to EOQ formula, sporadically used items should be ordered as far as possible in quantities to match expected actual usage. BS 5729 suggests this be done by "ordering up to maximum" where this allows for EOQ (or similar rule) plus safety margin to take account of usage during the fixed interval period which may not be covered by the ordinary supply and lead-time considerations of safety stock. (*See also* Chapters 7 "Controlling stock levels" and 18 "Materials requirements planning".)

Repeat ordering

It must never be assumed that a supplier's delivery times on repeat orders will be those of previous orders. An enquiry should be sent prior to the placing of any important repeat order. The purchaser should himself allow a delivery margin, giving his supplier adequate time for preparation and planning. This also leaves less room for excuses later (*see also* new lines and prototypes, below).

New lines and prototypes

As suggested in Chapter 5 and Table 10, the time allowed for supplies to be obtained is seldom adequate for new products. Over-enthusiasm, excessive optimism, euphoria and refusal to accept other people's opinions often blind those concerned to the true "horizons" caused by such time-consumers as:

(a) the actual design time;

(b) design changes;

(c) provisioning;

(d) production;

(e) production modifications at shop floor, retooling, etc.;

(f) proving—test bed and in the field, etc.;

(g) "calamities" necessitating reworking, new design, etc.;

(h) other delays—communication failures, and the sheer weight of communication needed for the operation.

Except where the firm to whom such a purchase order is given is a specialist in prototypes and development work, the purchaser is well advised to allow up to twice the lead time estimated by the supplier. This of course varies with the nature of the job and the experience of the supplying firm, and the experience the purchasing officer has had with them in the past.

Development contracts

Development contracts always repay careful "nursing". Delays frequently occur quite needlessly through lack of day-to-day care and interest by a purchasing department. For example, design changes may be initiated by technical staff, but no one checks for resulting changes in delivery or price.

Sometimes the trouble stems from poor relationships between Supplies and technical staff. (*See also* Chapter 4, terms of reference.)

Development contracts are often on a "long horizon". In this case it may appear that no urgency exists to get the order placed. However, the time lost is added to the far end of the time-scale and delay is inevitable.

AXIOM: Initial delays = terminal disasters.

Seasonal buying

A further aspect in the timing of purchase orders relates to situations where the demand and/or supply are seasonal and the commodity is not dealt with in the futures market. It will often be found that both the buyer and the seller suffer from seasonal fluctuations—which may not be in phase. A buyer's market often exists immediately the season has ended—unless there has been a shortage. A seller's market often exists immediately before a season starts. The timing of orders can be critical in either of these circumstances.

The too early placing of a firm order may catch a falling market (*see* Fig. 57). Placing the order too late may result in loss of availability or a sharp rise in prices. Here is needed the skill of the buyer with his knowledge of statistics and markets to help him. It is usual for specialist buyers to be employed for such commodities.

Lead time is a major consideration in all cases which determines when the order shall be placed.

CHAPTER 12

Selecting Supply Sources

INTRODUCTION

Subject always to management policies, the selection of suppliers is the prerogative of Supplies, who should be fully charged with the task of selecting satisfactory suppliers to ensure the continuity of adequate supplies of suitable quality at stable economic prices and in time for use. These are basic to the future success of any company.

For classification "A" materials company policy may dictate the choice of suppliers, the splitting of orders between a number of suppliers, reciprocal trading, group trading, and technical policy.

Directives from management governing sources of supply can greatly inhibit commercial outlook and activities. A careful watch must be maintained to see that commercial benefits from reciprocal trading are not outweighed by losses due to increased prices, substandard quality, or delays in delivery.

While ostensibly helping to foster business, reciprocal agreements can harm relationships and damage trading if disputes arise, particularly in the areas of service and supply. The fortunate supplier of a committed customer is unlikely to use his best efforts to solve the customer's problems. He may even be tempted to concentrate spare sales effort thus gained in finding and servicing new customers—possibly to the great disadvantage of the committed ones.

Where management directives are vital to a firm, it should be clearly laid down who shall negotiate and who shall maintain the lines of supplies communications. Failure to do this has been known to result in duplication of orders, incorrect instructions and costly misunderstandings.

Collaboration and participation of other staff in Supplies activities
A Supplies department should encourage all other departments to collaborate in suggesting new and improved supplies and sources of

supply. This deliberate policy of integration of Supplies activities and of open-mindedness pays off—particularly if the suggestions are acknowledged to those who made them. This attitude has the effect of improving communications in the reverse direction, i.e. suggestions from the purchasing department to the other functional divisions. (*See* Fig. 6.) Every "service" department strengthens its position by feeding on ideas from outside. Its position is weakened by an "iron curtain" of departmentalism and an effort to assert an authority it may not possess.

FACTORS TO BE CONSIDERED IN SELECTING SUPPLIERS

When selecting suppliers a host of considerations fall within the province of Supplies staff, who must be free to discuss them at management level. A few are noted below. The order in which these are considered will vary according to the situation.

Performance of suppliers

Scarcely any other aspect is as vital as this. It falls into three main sections: technical, delivery and financial. (*See also* Checklist 21.)

Most supplying companies believe that their internal disorders cannot be seen by outsiders. However, these defects, or their effects, may be all too obvious to the firms they supply. The purchasing officers of their customers are (or should be) in a unique position to see through their suppliers' "corporate cloak" and make an appraisal of the corporate body within, indeed it should be the duty of purchasing officers to do this. (*See* Fig. 50 and Checklists 21 and 25). (BS 4778 (31).)

TECHNICAL AND QUALITY PERFORMANCE of suppliers must be specified, appraised and monitored by the technical staff of the company. (Technical appraisal is part of "value analysis" and is discussed in Chapter 13.) Technical performance in relation to efficiency in handling technical problems tends to be subjective and difficult to analyse and quantify. Quality performance is less difficult to measure and may be crudely stated as the percentage of satisfactory goods received in relation to total intake. However, the task of assessing quality performance can be made more difficult for the purchasing officer in many cases owing to time-lag between intake and inspection—or worse still the emergence of rejects much later at the work-centre. Supplies administration should progress goods through to early inspection at the goods inwards stage (*see* Chapter 21).

DELIVERY PERFORMANCE falls directly within the province of the purchasing officer. It has the same relationship to him as specification does to his technical colleagues. If he bears this in mind he will gain a better appreciation of the outlook of the latter when they complain about the quality of a particular consignment.

It is often impossible to rectify supplies which have proved defective, but there is always hope that a supplier's bad delivery performance may be improved by energetic progressing. Late deliveries may bring disaster, but the activity of progressing also is costly. A supplier who offers a low price may in the end turn out to be the most expensive because of this. (*See* Chapter 18 "progress records and reports".)

An unwelcome and unacceptable feature of supplier performance may sometimes be encountered, particularly in a seller's market when suppliers may deliberately extend lead time in the hope of committing customers to larger orders or the extension of the term of contract. If (as is usual) reorder level is based on lead time, the purchaser is likely automatically to increase his reorder level to compensate for the extended lead time, thus resulting in larger order quantities and over-ordering.

FINANCIAL PERFORMANCE of suppliers is a major commercial consideration of Supplies. This includes the ability of the supplier to hold the prices he has given, to establish a satisfactory price structure and to build up and maintain a sound financial base for his operations. Trading experience alone can answer the first point. For the second, however, a careful analysis of prices offered with a breakdown of setting-up costs (if available) and a check of consistency of quantity discounts may show if the price structure is by calculation or by guesswork. A sound financial base is vital for all major supplies sources. (*See* Figs. 50, 51, 55, 59, 60 and "learning curve".)

Prices offered may decide whether or not there shall be more than one supplier for a particular material. Where the business is split there is often some sacrifice in the matter of price paid. Unless the volume of business is exceptionally large (*see also* below), it is unlikely that two suppliers will give such keen prices as a single supplier for the total quantity.

"Break-even" analysis can also be used here (*see* Fig. 51).

AXIOM: Suppliers' performance reflects their own supplies performance.

Volume of business and "multiple sourcing"

If the volume of business is very large, so also will be that of supplies within classification "A". They are sure to be vital to continuity of production, and the purchasing department may arrange for additional supplier(s) to "buffer" the main supplier. From a purchasing point of view this provides the following benefits.

(a) Provides second flow of supplies if first dries up or demand exceeds supply.

(b) Creates and stimulates a competitive situation.

(c) Is a spur to the long-established supplier.

(d) Is a potential threat to the near monopolistic supplier.

(e) Gives opportunity to compare qualities, specifications and performance.

(f) Increases possibilities of new developments.

(g) Secondary supplier makes special efforts in emergencies hoping to increase his share of the business.

Possible disbenefits are that:

(a) extra tooling may be needed;

(b) free-issue materials may have to go to the extra suppliers;

(c) the secondary supplier probably charges a higher price than the main one.

Approved lists and "black lists"

Applications by suppliers to be included in an approved list may result in the purchasing officer being put in a dominant position to negotiate, except where there has been prior publication (see also vendor rating, below).

Inclusion in a list may rest with functional departments as well as Supplies. The management should, however, insist that the notice of election to the approved list be made only by the purchasing officer. If this precaution is not taken the authority and power of the purchasing officer as an agent of the company is greatly reduced (whereas it should have been strengthened) and the sales policy of the supplier may harden and commercial negotiations prove barren.

There may, of course, be a "black list" as well as an approved list. The implications of a "black list" are clear and the supplier is unlikely to receive orders. More difficult is the decision whether or not to inform him he is "blacklisted". If, however, "vendor ratings" (see below) are indicated upon enquiries and orders, very useful discipline can be applied. Suppliers will take note of their rating and seek to gain improvements in it.

Vendor rating

Vendor rating should be a regular task of every purchasing officer. It involves an objective analysis of supplier performance and its evaluation by a rating scheme. An example is shown in Fig. 50.

It must be emphasised that the scheme should be simple and so far as possible capable of completion from data available within the

VENDOR RATING AND VISIT REPORT SHEET			
Supplier and address: Wm Wiffin Ltd. Wigan			
Date: 1.10.78 Evaluated by: Bill Smith.			

	Features evaluated	marks	weightings	Total
1	Specifications, compliance with (quality performance in use)	2		
2	Technical services	1		
3	Communications — accuracy, adequacy, speed	2		
4	" — advice of trouble (in good time)	3		
5	" — replies (writes) as promised (phones)	0		
6	" — representatives, efficiency, briefing of	1		
7	" — quotations, acknowledgments, etc. (see 3)	2		
8	Finance: adequacy, prices — stability, competitive, honoured	3		
9	Delivery: veracity of promises, at convenient times, etc.	2		
10	" : physical, packaging — units, loads, handling, etc.	4		
11	Plant: capacity, condition, age, maintenance *	2		
12	Plant: layout *	1		
13	Materials management: handling (see 10)*	2		
14	" " : storage equipment (see 10)*	3		
15	" " : "housekeeping" in stores and works*	2		
16	" " : quality control in manufacture*	3		
17	Working conditions: factory "housekeeping"*	2		
18	Industrial relations: staff and work-force*	2		
19	Attitude to customers: by staff and management	2		
20	(Other matters briefed for visit)*Check spares availability, etc.	2		
	Total	41		
	Vendor rating index (divide total by number of features evaluated).	2$^+$		

Suggested marking	Vendor rating index	Code	Comments.
4 = Exceptional 3 = Good 2 = Fair 1 = Lowest acceptable 0 = unsatisfactory, negotiate an improvement 20 = totally unsatisfactory candidate for "black list")	4 to 3 Fully acceptable 2.9 to 2 Acceptable (subject to low scores) 1.9 to 1 Very suspect 0.9 to 1 "Black list"?	B to F G to K L to P Q to Z	Rating H given subject to improvement at item 5 by purchasing officer.
	NOTES: 1. If weightings are used, appropriate adjustments must be made to vendor rating index. 2. Items marked * are by visits only.		

Fig. 50. Combined twenty-point vendor rating scheme and visit report sheet

home base of the purchaser. This may be done from delivery and inspection reports, comments from engineers and users, etc.

The example in Fig. 50 should be self-explanatory and will suffice for most situations. "Weightings" (*see also* Table 4, Chapter 2) can of course be added in the extra column if special significance is to be given to certain features, such as items 2 and 15.

There are serious risks in applying mathematical processes to decision-making procedures in Supplies—even to stock control but particularly to vendor rating. The risks are so great as to lead some supplies managers to dismiss mathematical vendor rating as: "a load of nonsense . . . . The real secret of using scientific business solutions is knowing where you cannot use them" (Mark Barratt, *Purchasing and Supply Management*, July 1981). The warning is salutory if somewhat over-dogmatic and should be qualified by the words: "without the sanction of intelligent and deliberate judgment of the total problem and its environmental or associated aspects".

Security of supply

This follows logically as a deciding factor in number and choice of suppliers. The cost of a stoppage and its probabilities should be estimated (*see* Table 12). If this is greater than the loss in price-advantage through employing two or more suppliers, then adopt multiple sources. This may be done by sharing the business equally or by employing one supplier as a "back-up" source. It would be a mistake to assume that this condition can only apply to classification "A" materials. There are often supporting materials which are essential to continuity of production.

For an example of security consider a year of fifty working weeks and two suppliers who each give a "service factor" of 98 per cent, that is, either may fail one week in fifty. Both can provide 100 per cent of requirements which are shared 50/50 between them on contract. If supplier "A" fails one week in fifty, the chance that the second supplier "B" will do so is one in forty-nine. The chance that both may fail simultaneously is found by what is known statistically as "conditional probability", calculated by multiplying the reciprocals of probabilities:

$$\frac{1}{50} \times \frac{1}{49} = \frac{1}{2,450}$$

(i.e. simultaneous failure can be expected once in 2,450 weeks!) There is thus a substantial gain in security by the use of a second supplier. If, of course, the second supplier is not so good as the first and fails, say, five times in fifty, security is then:

238

$$\frac{1}{50} \times \frac{5}{49} = \frac{1}{490}$$

which is still a good security.

In many cases the second supplier may only have, say, 20 per cent of the contract and this will greatly reduce his value as a back-up source. He may, however, be "able, ready and willing" to provide 100 per cent supply on an emergency basis hoping for more business!

Patents, copyrights, processes and royalties

Purchase from a particular source may involve additional costs on one or more of these counts. Their very existence may enforce a decision to purchase exclusively from a particular source.

Inter-state trading requires extra vigilance in this matter. In October 1973 a convention on the grant of European patents was signed by members of the EEC and other countries. Points claimed in favour of the European Patent System are economy, speed of grant, and ability to assess with greater ease and certainty than at present.[99]

Service

A supplier may be found who over a number of years gives outstandingly good service in quality, delivery, and after-sales service. If so, he may get orders at a slightly higher price than his competitiors. This premium must be set off against technical merit, continuity of supply, service, etc. Such suppliers should be warned that the longer they hold a contract the shorter the time must be before they lose it to another supplier!

Capacity

The manufacturing capacity of suppliers must inevitably sway the decision in placing any orders. This is not the same consideration as reliability mentioned earlier. A firm may be quite reliable within its rated capacity, but unable to produce the additional volume required. Not only must suppliers have sufficient capacity for normal demands, but there is also a need for flexibility. It may be necessary to consider their ability to handle increased output or to reduce it. Even when the supplier has the necessary capacity, he may favour other purchasers with delivery, or price, etc.

Location

The location of suppliers can be a determining factor in their selection. Speed of delivery, accessibility, short lines of communication and low freight charges all have to be taken into consideration.

A further factor which may influence purchasing policy is whether the supplier is located in one of those areas which may from time to time be selected for government or EEC aid, such as the following.

(a) Grants for new machinery and plant.

(b) Grants for new buildings and adaptations.

(c) Additional employment grants.

(d) Removal grants (i.e. bringing the source of supply closer to the purchaser if the latter is himself in an assisted area).

(e) Training services for workers within industry or moving to an assisted area.

The possibility of using such governmental assistance should be considered in the context of supplier development (*see* next section).

SUPPLIER DEVELOPMENT

Supplier development is a very valuable aspect of supplies management. A firm which has a dynamic sales policy seeks to nurture and develop its customers so that healthy trading may expand between them. Similarly a dynamic Supplies organisation should endeavour to develop its company's suppliers to ensure a continuance of economic sources. Purchasing officers are in fact in a stronger position with their suppliers for supplier development than are their sales colleagues with customers for customer development.

Clearly, supplier development is less likely to prove rewarding when dealing with larger suppliers who, it may be supposed, are already fully developed. On the other hand, however large the supplier or small the potential of the buyer, a "thrusting" company will welcome opportunities to develop and improve its productivity and service, if only to consolidate its position with customers.

Supplier development may also include the acquisition of the source of supply. When considering this alternative it must not be overlooked that the converse also may occur. An example is that of major supplier (Delta Metals) which in the late 1950s embarked upon a programme of vertical integration by buying up its own customers, thus ensuring its market. Clearly, such major strategy is part of top management policy and its negotiations will not fall to the lot of many purchasing officers! On the other hand, an understanding of this strategy may help in appreciating the risks and options available and how they may arise and affect the supply situation.

A small manufacturer may develop a purchasing relationship with a major supplier who can achieve a virtual monopoly of supply to him. This small company is now in a highly vulnerable position.

This is especially so if the large supplier is seeking to diversify his product range, or if he feels the need to control and stimulate the outlets for his goods and materials.

Apart from development of suppliers the question must also be asked whether the purchaser has any ethical duty to support his suppliers. Here the test should be one of "reasonableness". How far is it reasonable to sacrifice price or delays in delivery to ensure a supplier remains in business? Is he a "sleeper" to be laid quietly to rest or a "thruster" with a temporary cash-flow problem who should be encouraged and sustained as a future profitable source of supply?

Setting up a supplies consortium

Supplier development may involve the setting up of a consortium of members from a group of companies of which the individual Supplies departments are more, or less, decentralised (*see also* Fig. 11). This strategy improves price bargaining, but other benefits may include better quality, delivery and transport (which may be pooled, for example) and the possibilities of containerisation, powered handling, computerisation and so on.

However, care must be taken, particularly in regard to price bargaining, that the arrangements do not conflict with the Directives of the EEC or the General Agreement on Tariffs and Trade (GATT). It is also a prerequisite that standardisation between groups is completed *before* the consortium commences to negotiate. Instances are known where—on complex plant—engineers have disagreed on specification after negotiations have commenced. This can react greatly to the advantage of suppliers who may exploit and even foster the differences.

Visits to suppliers

Some aspects of supplier performance can only be ascertained by visits (*see* Fig. 50). Visits to suppliers can be a source for debate and sometimes of misunderstanding with technical colleagues. Ideally, technical vetting of a supplier and supplies should be done by a technical man and commercial vetting by a commercial one. However, it must be accepted that because quality is usually the primary consideration the technical discipline is likely to prevail, for the initial visit at least. Terms of reference of Supplies staff should cover these matters. One solution is to establish that whoever goes on a visit should be briefed by and report back to the other. Each party should listen to the supplier's comments and note them.

All who make such visits to suppliers should be aware of the danger of inadvertently creating a contractual position, especially during informal discussions. For this reason it is good practice either to confirm the results of the visit in writing to the supplier or to get the supplier to do so. Apart from this, comments may lead the supplier to believe he has a commitment and to harden his approach in later negotiations. (*See also* Chapter 16.)

DIFFERENT CATEGORIES OF SUPPLIERS

Manufacturers

Whether to purchase from a wholesaler or direct from a manufacturer will be largely determined by the size of the order to be placed and the class of goods involved.

A manufacturer may give preferential terms for bulk supply. In that event he passes on to the purchaser a proportion of what could otherwise be the middleman's profits. He may also be prepared to give additional price advantages in consideration of an assured market. (If the purchaser bought through a wholesaler, there would be no guarantee that he—the manufacturer—would get the business.) A further advantage in purchasing direct from a manufacturer is that communication is then direct instead of through a third party. It may therefore be more speedy for such matters as progress-chasing, technical queries and inspection rejections.

However, many manufacturers will only supply through their distributors. Either simple economics or preferential agreements with middlemen may decide this.

Middlemen (intermediaries)

The stockholder or wholesaler makes his profits by acting as a "combining stores". He may increase his stocks if assured of continuing and substantial orders or a bulk demand from a customer, or arrange for goods to be shipped direct from the manufacturer to his customer and collect a price differential as his fee for the transaction.

He may be a much more important customer of the supplier than an individual purchaser could ever be and can thus have great influence upon delivery, price and even quality. Checklist 22 indicates some of the benefits which are claimed by middlemen to be advantageous to the buyer.

There are a number of points which are also of benefit to the middleman. For example, if the middleman arranges a contract for the goods to be shipped direct from the supplier to the purchaser, this may greatly strengthen his position in the trade, winning for him additional discounts on that or other products from his supplier. The astute purchasing officer should look out for such situations and negotiate with the middleman to share the benefits with his company by means of discounts and rebates.

There are other advantages of using a middleman. For example, a local stockist may be able to provide services such as the following:

(a) weekly or other topping up of the purchaser's stocks;

(b) maintaining and topping up of a bin at the purchaser's works;

(c) monthly single invoice to co-ordinate purchases;

(d) opportunity to streamline ordering techniques with benefits for the purchaser (*see* Chapter 15).

Kinds of "middlemen"

There is a wide range of middlemen. It will only be possible to enumerate a few, and it must be explained that the terminology used for these traders is rather indefinite. They include wholesalers, warehousemen, distributors, manufacturers' agents and others. The functions may vary from the title and should be checked before starting important negotiations so as to ascertain the nature and scope of the services offered. The latter may include technical advice and service, free delivery, special packaging, or other benefits referred to in the previous section and in Checklist 22.

Nationalised industries and government agencies

Purchasing from nationalised industries and government agencies is normally controlled by the special trading conditions laid down in the statutes which set up these trading bodies (*see also* Chapter 13). For this reason it is important that the purchasing officer should make himself familiar with their terms of trading. These may not be negotiable and in the event of a dispute it will be their terms which govern the contract.

However, while the area of negotiation is often very small or non-existent, there are some policies which the user company should consider for reducing the cost of services, including the following.

(a) Select the best tariff for the service.

(b) Avoid overloading the system.

(c) Improve load factor, utilisation factor and power factor.

(d) Use "industrial water" or other recovered materials.

(e) Collaborate with neighbouring firms for shared services.

(f) Consult consumer advisory councils, etc.

(g) Join or support consumer associations.

(h) Persuade authority to provide standby or duplicate service to avoid shut-downs.

(i) Investigate other alternative sources in private sector.

(j) Set up own service, generate own power supply, etc.

Monopolies

Purchasing from monopolies (*see* Chapter 13) is likely to be the most commercially unrewarding of a purchasing officer's activities. However, where a near monopolistic situation exists the purchasing staff should be no less diligent than in the competitive situation. Price and terms may be settled by the monopoly, who dictate them from a position of strength. The rest of the field is still open in matters of service, delivery, technical specification, tariff selection and so on (*see also* Chapter 13). It must never be overlooked that a monopolistic source may be self-induced by the purchaser, owing to the requisitioner, designer or other functional staff demanding goods from one specific supplier or of a particular brand.

Trade associations and cartels

Trade associations are being increasingly challenged. Governments and bodies such as the EEC look askance at anything which is thought to inhibit competition and free negotiation.

An appraisal should be made of the benefits, or otherwise, of buying within a trade association. Most associations claim to be technical only and not to fix prices, in compliance with enactments against restraint of trade and price rings. Many can provide useful advisory and technical services, others control specifications and standards of members, or carry out research, development and testing.

A number of trade associations and some professional bodies produce standard forms of tender and contract which can be of great advantage in highly technical or complex contracts.

Finally, an association may in certain cases help to clear supply bottle-necks by steering orders to members who have capacity available for production.

Consultants

As "suppliers" of advice these are considered in Chapter 5.

"Make or buy"

"Make or buy" is a matter of Supplies policy directed by company policy. Supplies staff should, however, understand the general principles governing the decisions of management in regard to this. Checklist 23 lists some of the many points to be considered in a make or buy decision. It is worth also looking at Checklist 24 (Importation) to gain a wider picture. A number of points affect both.

The results of purchasing research may lead the purchasing officer to suggest that components could be bought outside more economically than by manufacture in his factory's production line. Alternatively, the production load may be such that the approach is from production manager to purchasing officer for a supplementary source of supply. Quotations from outside suppliers should be compared with the firm's own cost estimates.

A detailed study is usually needed, involving engineering and design, production, planning and costing as well as purchasing.

Break-even analysis can be applied to "make or buy" problems (besides many others in Supplies) and Fig. 51 shows an elementary example. Where the lines cross at *P*, the costs of buying and making are equal (i.e. they break even where costs are £5,300 and number of units required 50,000). This assumes that the price per unit is constant as shown by line *O—D*. However, the purchasing officer should have already obtained a better price for a large quantity. Assume he does so at 40,000 units *(E)*. The cost per unit then changes direction and follows a new line *E—F* which crosses the "making" line *A—C* at Q raising the break-even quantity to 70,000 before it is more economical to make than buy.

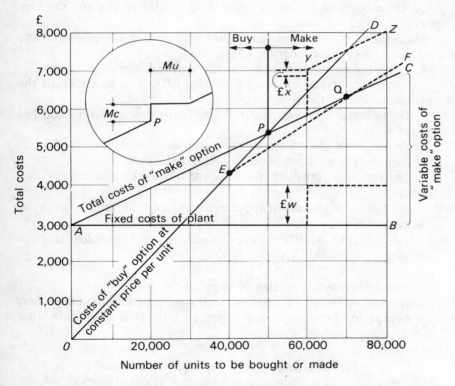

Fig. 51. *Break-even chart: applied to "make or buy" situation*
NOTE: For explanation of inset, *see* p. 264.

The following precautions are needed when applying the break-even principle to supply problems.

(*a*) Labour is no longer a fully variable cost. At one time it was hired and fired as necessary. However, circumstances have changed and, despite the drives against overmanning, various factors militate against this more profitable management philosophy, for example:

(*i*) fear of losing valuable technical staff to competitors;

(*ii*) redundancy costs and fear of action for wrongful dismissal;

(*iii*) changes in attitudes to human values.

(*b*) The purchasing officer must also be prepared for fluctuations from the norm in fixed costs. For example, in Fig. 51 at 60,000 units his firm may need to add £w to fixed charges for additional plant, and additional operators will be needed to man it at a cost of £x. It can be seen from the diagram that buying would in that case be the best option—for that output. (The slope of y—z may or may not differ from the slope of A—C depending upon the efficiency of added plant w.) A similar situation could have occurred at, say, 30,000 units on the "buy" option with similar results for the supplier.

(*c*) Labour content per unit is likely to reflect the effects of the "learning curve" (*see* Chapter 13).

(*d*) Storage costs are not necessarily constant per unit volume.

(*e*) It is important for the purchasing officer to consider all the options, including the following:

(*i*) maintain present output and supplement from another source;

(*ii*) improve plant utilisation by overtime or shift working;

(*iii*) modify existing plant to increase output;

(*iv*) redesign product to improve production methods and output;

(*v*) find new sources of supplies and/or new supplies to improve output;

(*vi*) improve quality control to reduce percentage lost through rejects.

Non-buying through recycling of supplies

Non-buying or re-use of materials can hardly be included anywhere else except in the chapter on where to buy. It is a reminder that

Fig. 52. Outline of some importation procedures
(1) Figures in circles indicate suggested sequence of operations. (2) "£" indicates *some* of the costs which may arise. (3) * In all cases check start and termination of contract for transit.

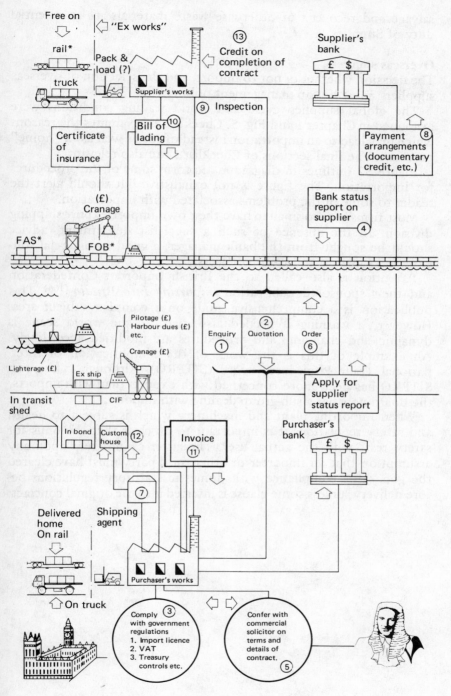

247

salvage and recovery of otherwise waste materials are an essential duty of Supplies.

Overseas sources

The decision whether or not to import, and the selection of overseas suppliers, must be top management policy.[100]-[105][138]

The global supplies cycle and world trading conditions were examined in Chapter 1 and Fig. 5. Checklist 24 examines the reasons which may lead to an importation instead of (or as well as) a "home" purchase. The final sections of Checklist 1 are also relevant.

Figure 52 outlines in diagrammatic form some of the procedures for importation. The figure is not exhaustive but should alert the reader to some of the problems associated with importation.

Most firms are too small to have their own import/export shipping division. In the absence of such a specialist department, advice should be sought from the bank manager, a good commercial solicitor and Customs and Excise officers.

Attention is also called to the British Importers Confederation and their sponsored publication *Importing Into Britain*.[106] This publication is a comprehensive guide on a complex subject area. However, a warning is needed also, because the world scene is dynamic and changing, and procedures are modified accordingly. An example of this is the work of the Simplification of International Trade Procedures Board (SITPRO). Although in the past SITPRO has been more concerned with exports than with imports, the Board now has a sub-group dealing with imports.

When importing plant and machinery which is subject to health and safety regulations it is important to be clear that the onus for safety rests with the actual user. The latter cannot rely upon any assumption that an importer or other third party must have cleared the goods for compliance with domestic statutory regulations before delivery, unless some clause is inserted into the original contract.

CHAPTER 13

Finance and Economics of Supplies

INTRODUCTION

Finance and economics stand at the heart of supplies management policy.[107]-[117][138] For an enterprise to be profitable it must ensure that its working capital turns over rapidly with the minimum injections of loan capital or cash—and this is a reflection of the physical movement of supplies themselves.

Intake of supplies in advance of production (i.e. conversion, *see* Fig. 49) means slow turnover of the cash which was spent in purchasing them. An unduly lengthy production period, due, for example, to re-working faulty goods or materials (provided by Supplies), has the same result. The analogy between physical stocks and money supply persists through to the final stages of manufacture and despatch. At this latter stage, any delays incur an unnecessary slowing-down in the flow of cash inwards from sales.

In conclusion, any inefficiencies in provisioning supplies is parallelled and reflected in slower cash flow, greater borrowing requirements and often higher interest rates, or the diversion of cash from increased production to pay for these inefficiencies.

Definitions

"Price", "cost", "value in use" and "value" require careful definition and use in Supplies. Although the broader definitions of the economist should be understood, those used throughout this book are given below.

Price is the amount, usually, but not always, in money, for which goods and services may be purchased—it is one component of cost.

Cost is often used carelessly as a synonym for price, but in Supplies its use should be confined to the sum of the price paid *plus* all other costs and charges for goods and services. It should also take account of value in use when comparing different offers.

Value in use and *value* include objective assessments which can be evaluated in cash terms. In addition, where practicable, they can take account of subjective aspects, such as social cost-benefits, which can only be evaluated by estimates or weightings. (For weightings, *see* Chapter 2, Table 4).

Relative costs will be in direct proportion to price paid but in inverse proportion to value in use. Thus, the lower the value in use the higher the relative costs. This gives rise to the fiction "you get what you pay for", which should be replaced by the following axiom.

AXIOM: You get what you deserve!

MAXIMISATION OF PROFITABILITY

Profitability is referred to frequently in this book. It is unusual for Supplies actually to make a profit, but all their efforts should be devoted to maximising "profitability", i.e. the ability to make a contribution to profits.[138] Maximisation of profit and profitability is vital to all businesses, not only for payment of dividends (in the case of private industry), but also for expansion and progress, the creation of a sound financial base—or even survival itself! However, there are important differences between the public and private sectors of the economy.

Public sector enterprises, such as nationalised industries, are usually enjoined "to make neither a profit nor a loss, taking one year with another" while local authorities, etc. are subject to public accountability disciplines including budgetary control and public audit. If the contributions to profitability of the various activities of a nationalised industry lead to a "profit" (i.e. a surplus of income over expenditure) the enterprise must take appropriate action, such as reducing prices, expanding and improving services, or repaying government loans. Other public bodies may be expected to make suitable adjustments to their subsequent budget from any surplus or shortfall in the current period.

Maximisation of service and quality in order to meet public demand or statutory obligations is always likely to be inimical to profitability, and may result in the ratio of costs of supplies to sales values increasing beyond the norms for private industry. Social cost-benefits must therefore be included by a purchasing officer when studying the profitability and prices of a public enterprise for the purposes of negotiations. (For areas which may provide scope for negotiations with public enterprises, *see* Chapter 12, nationalised industries and government agencies.)

In conclusion, disciplines in Supplies policies and actions require even closer control in the public than in the private sector. This is because the absence of measurable profit can make it difficult to ensure that every activity of a public enterprise is continually reducing costs and improving efficiency, output and service.

In private industry contributions to profitability can result in reduced prices to compete more effectively with business (or state) rivals, expansion, reducing loans, higher dividends to those who have risked their capital in the venture, and (more recently) bonuses and shares or other benefits to workers who have placed their services at the disposal of the company.

This chapter examines how "contribution" (in the financial management sense) can be won by the profitability gained through vigorous and successful Supplies activities (*see* Table 29).

SUPPLIES AND FINANCIAL CONTROL

Control over future commitments

The involvment of Supplies in company financial control and decision-making depends upon the policies of management towards its Supplies organisation, and this is influenced to some extent by the supplies/sales ratio and the delegation policies of management. It also depends upon the degree of awareness of those who control the financial commitments of the firm that such commitments ought to be controlled when the orders are placed instead of when the invoices are received—by which time it may be found that cash is not available! (*See* Chapter 2, financial supply control policy.) Control should be exercised at the requisitioning stage by the requisitioner and may be monitored by Supplies, or order copies sent to the financial control department for control as orders are placed.

Credit control

A seller's market permits suppliers to decide whether to increase sales without too much attention to credit, or to restrict credit to purchasers who pay promptly. Research by the British Institute of Management indicated that in 40 per cent of companies which have sales over £50 million, credit policy was determined by the financial department. In 20 per cent of the smaller firms this decision area was left to the selling function.

Clearly, control by the financial department can make negotiation more difficult for the purchasing officer because:

(*a*) the salesman is deprived of some of his authority to negotiate;

(b) the financial department may not understand the value of the customer or his orders and make decisions which may frustrate business.

Under seller's market conditions, purchasers must expect to be subject to credit control by suppliers.

Conversely, the purchasing officer may find that the finance department of his own company is withholding payment to suppliers with whom he is trying to establish good relationships to ensure continuity of supply, improved delivery, new development, stock arrangements and so on. It may be worth an appeal to top management for a policy decision to correct this.

CHARACTERISTICS OF PRICE

Table 28 lists the principal kinds of price, together with the conditions giving rise to them or components of them. When negotiating or considering offers, it may be helpful to bear in mind the many factors involved—some of which may lead to profitable negotiations. The table should also be related to:

(a) the actual price structure or "elements of price";
(b) the price network (*see* Fig. 56);
(c) discounts and rebates (*see* Table 30);
(d) value analysis and value engineering (*see* Fig. 55);
(e) market conditions and purchasing policies (*see* Fig. 57);
(f) areas of negotiation (*see* Fig. 59);
(g) negotiation/planning matrix (*see* Fig. 60).

Competition

Price is one of the main elements of competition. In 1958 the economic survey team of the Purchasing Officers' Association made the comment that: "Competition offers the best stimulus to industrial efficiency. The most beneficial price reduction from the national standpoint is that secured through buyers driving their suppliers to increased efficiency, yet at the same time buying at a fair and reasonable price."

NOTE:

In times of inflation it seems inappropriate to speak of price "reduction". However, the statement stands if the word "reduction" is omitted. At such times, every purchasing officer should negotiate for a reduced rate of increase! (*See also* requests for price increases, later in this Chapter.)

Articles 85 and 86 of the Treaty of Rome, establishing the EEC, ensure competition, while articles 87-9 give the Council of Ministers

252

TABLE 28. SUMMARY OF KINDS OF PRICE AND
CONDITIONS AFFECTING PRICE

Kinds of price	Conditions affecting price and components of price			
	Location of delivery[1]	Time of ordering settlement etc.	Statutory and legal effects	Trading conditions and terms
Cost	At or ex station	Contract price adjustment (CPA)	Bonded price	Cut price
Dumped			Customs duty	Discriminatory
	Basing point			
Economic		Deferred rebate	Drawback	Group price
	Cost insurance and freight ("CIF")			
Fair		Firm	Duty price	Loss leader price
Fixed		"Futures"	Excise duty	
	Delivered home		Price code	Loyalty rebate
Indifference		List price[2]		
			Value added tax (VAT)	Price fixing
Market	Ex warehouse	Overdue account charge		
				Price leader price
Marginal	Franco			
		Progress (stage) payments		
Monopolistic	Free alongside			Quantity price
Negotiable				Resale price
	Free on board ("FOB")	Prompt cash (= liquidity discount)[3]		Reported price
Premium				
Quantity	Free on rail			
		Quoted[4]		Ring price
Survival	In bond			
		Retention money		Trade price
Target	Landed			
				Transfer price[5]
	Loco	Seasonal		
	On site, erected, tested, commissioned	"Spot"		

253

NOTES:

(1) It is essential to communicate the precise locations of departure and arrival. Practice varies between different firms, trades and states. (2) Lists were at one time considered current until the next list was published. This obviously can no longer be relied upon. (3) "Prompt cash discounts" can be advantageous to the purchaser who is able to meet the invoices within the supplier's time limit (*see* Chapter 22). (4) Normally conditions of sale and quotation state that an offer is open for acceptance if instructions are received within thirty days from the date shown on the quotation. (5) "Transfer pricing",[118] if efficiently carried out, can provide valuable information for comparing profitability between company, group and departmental units. Objectivity is difficult to maintain where managers are trying to maximise the profitability of their own unit against that of others in the same company or group. Individual and corporate objectives need to be reconciled in a total company (or group) policy, with particular regard to prices charged for goods transferred between units.

power to issue Directives in the field of competition. The European Commission is responsible for supervising the application of such Directives, investigating any alleged breach and bringing it to an end.

Economic price and fair price

An "economic price" derives from a "fair price", which was defined as follows by the Purchasing Officers' Association survey team: "A fair price is one which allows a producer to pay fair wage rates, buy and use the correct materials, carry out adequate research, maintain adequate capital investment in plant and equipment, and earn a reasonable return on capital so invested." To this should now be added: "and maintain good working conditions in compliance with the Health and Safety at Work, etc. Act, and provide for indemnity against all relevant trading risks such as 'product liability'." [Auth.]

Price in the free market

Competition between suppliers in a free market should be expected to ensure keen prices, quick deliveries, more investment in industry, and increased innovation in design and development and improved production methods. However, *unrestrained* and "random" market forces may have other results for the supplies manager to cope with.

For example, competition may depress prices charged for goods and services to a level which is below the economic price. It may also develop to the situation where the number of available suppliers is reduced because of weak firms going out of business. It must not be inferred that weak firms are the least satisfactory suppliers. Their very weakness may be a result of their efforts to give customers a satisfactory service and meet demands for technical or other inno-

vation, thus involving them in heavy oncosts in technical administration and research resulting in loss of their profitability.

Uncontrolled competition may also lead to horizontal and vertical
mergers which may remove yet more suppliers from the purchasing
officer's source list. As the remaining firms strengthen their hold
upon the market they may call for intensification of protectionist
policies and/or impose monopoly prices. The precise causes of these
various phemonema vary and economic theory is widely debated. It
is with their effects upon supplies that we are concerned here, particularly when they occur during a recession or slump. In a time of
recession demand is weak, prices are likely to be depressed (or rising
less quickly), and lead times may be short (within the plant capacity which still remains after closures and short-time operation). It
then appears that the advantages are to the buyer. This may be true
in the short term. However, as time passes and the market becomes
oligopolistic it changes from a buyer's market to a seller's market
with the following results, most of which tend against the original
cause, i.e. competition.

(a) Price leadership (although illegal) may take place.

(b) Lead times tend to extend, sometimes artificially.

(c) An assured market reduces the need for research and development.

(d) "Captive customers" permit a cut-back in service so as to
increase suppliers' profits.

(e) Collective protectionism will be possible among the reduced
number of suppliers which have survived.

(f) Nationalisation may prove attractive on grounds of political
dogma or the plea of national security, or as a source of income for
the exchequer sometimes with prices manipulated to increase this
income.

In a "perfect" or "near perfect" market the effects of individual
buyers for normal size industries will make a very small impact
upon the national or international situation, although collectively
(even when there is no collusion between them) they may have a
great influence. However, the greatest influence of all upon the market is that applied by governmental action.

It would appear that both excessive government interference
with the market and an excessive dose of competition can be self-
destructive if permitted to persist too long or too uncontrolled.
Purchasing officers must therefore be alert as to where company
policies or government actions are leading in respect of main supplies. When prices are left to unrestrained market forces in a free
market economy complex movements take place as a result of a
combination of many factors, such as:

(a) competition;
(b) inflation, deflation, etc.;
(c) "what the market will bear";
(d) dominance of buyer or seller in the market place;
(e) "free collective wage bargaining";
(f) supply and demand.

The effects of the last mentioned upon price are frequently referred to by economists as "the *law* of supply and demand". However, the complexity of modern business makes it doubtful whether this phenomenon should now have any status higher than a mere "rule". Certainly in the case of industrial purchasing of purpose-made engineering products bought in the course of trade this may not, and perhaps should not, apply. For example, the price paid for industrial purchases should be the result of careful costing based upon factory expenses, labour, materials and profit, plus negotiations for the best bargain—the quantity being fixed by factory needs and not by fashion, price or market forces (*see also* Chapter 5, process plants).

Those who are scientifically inclined may care to study the axiom below.

AXIOM: The total market forces of the universe tend to total disorder. (With apologies to Newton's Law of Thermodynamics.)

For all these reasons purchasing staff should have knowledge of costs and costing methods. They then have an idea of the margins the supplier may be holding, and of the space in which to manoeuvre during negotiations. This knowledge is also important when the supplier claims a price advance. Similarly it is useful to know when a price reduction should be pressed for because of changes in the market position which could have reduced the supplier's costs.

Inflation

"Inflation" in its vulgar sense is used to describe merely a rise in prices.[119] However, since the time of earliest economic records prices have been generally rising as living standards have risen. The process has been accelerated by the growth of world trade, the demands of underdeveloped countries for an increase in their own living standards and working conditions, the depletion of natural resources, and the increasing direction of raw materials and supplies away from basic consumer goods and services or productive commodities and plant into luxury goods and high-cost outlets (space shuttles, nuclear warheads and so on) which consume resources without contributing to further wealth-producing processes.

Price-inflation is an area in which Supplies staff have a part to play by sheer resistance to each claim for an advance in price. Importance is added to such resistance by the increasing value of supplies as a proportion of product sales, usually far exceeding wage costs. However, emphasis is rightly placed by economists upon the effects of wages upon "inflation". The following statement, however, by a leading British Bank should be noted ". . . savings in bought-in [purchased] material and component costs, where achievable, are a less painful and more immediately effective economy than savings in labour—where redundancies may be required."

The fight against price-inflation does not end here. It passes back along the various stages of the total economic cycle to the original extractive industry with value-added savings to be made at each stage.

Demand-induced inflation depends upon the theory of "too much money chasing too few goods". However, this is a situation which is unlikely to affect normal Supplies activity in the industrial field. The purchasing officer is driven to make greater efforts in times of shortage and is seldom provided with "too much money" to obtain scarce supplies! Perhaps economists, politicians and others should distinguish the economics of distribution and domestic demand from those of the productive industries with their value-added content. Certainly, the bland assumption that an industrial purchasing officer merely accepts price increments should be untrue.

Accounting for supplies
The methods used when pricing and accounting for supplies, particularly stocks, can have direct effects upon final product price and profitability (or lossability) of the final product. Two methods are therefore outlined here.

"Current cost accounting" (also known as "inflation accounting") was put forward by the Sandilands Committee and adopted by the accountancy bodies in *Statement of Standard Accounting Practice* No. 16 in March 1980. The principal features are as follows.

(*a*) Monetary units should remain constant.

(*b*) Accounts should show the "value to the business of a company's assets at the date of the balance sheet". ("Value to the business" is defined as "the loss the company would suffer if it were deprived of the asset", i.e. in most cases its current replacement cost.)

(*c*) Profit for the year should consist of the operating gains but excluding any "holding" gains. Any extraordinary gains may be shown as profit but must be distinguished from operating gains.

(d) Accounts drawn up in this way should become the basic published accounts of companies. In addition the net book value of assets and depreciation for the year on an historic-cost basis should be shown in notes in the accounts.

The implications for Supplies and the need for further study should be clear from these very brief notes. Particular points to note are:

(a) costs of stock replacements;

(b) sales of plant and equipment—redundant, etc.;

(c) "special bargain lots" purchased which may not be replaceable at the same figure.

"Historical cost accounting", as its title implies, relates to past costs of, for example, materials, based on their price at the time of purchase, and does not take account of changes in value during stock-life or during the period between production, sale and payment e.g. "First-in, first-out" ("FIFO") stock valuation.

COSTS AND FINANCE OF STOCK

The main component costs of stocks are physical and financial.

Physical costs relate to the actual stowage and housing of supplies. These are examined in some detail in *Storehouse*. Broadly speaking, they cover buildings, stockyards, plant and equipment for handling and stowage, preservation and issue.

Financial costs include the economic costs of the physical aspects, but more than this, they include the cost of money represented by the stock itself, and "opportunity costs".

There have been numerous methods of pricing stock, but the one most used today is that covered by "current cost accounting" discussed earlier. Regardless of the financial methods for pricing stock for balance sheet and taxation purposes, there is a further important financial consideration when costing stocks for estimates and quotations. A company which prices its estimates by costing materials on the old "historical method"—first-in first-out ("FIFO") —on a rising market may find it has quoted such a low price that it is certain to get the order. However, if it has to buy material at the new price it is sure to make a loss because the replacement cost of stock has risen. Conversely, if prices of supplies fall (?!) it could lose the contract for the opposite reasons. If it was fortunate enough to get the work despite its unnecessarily high price it would reap a windfall profit at the expense of its customer who was not sufficiently alert to falling market prices.

Stock ratios

An important financial consideration of stock is the ratio of its value to that of the finished product. Reference should be made to Appendix III, Interfirm Comparisons, and in particular to ratios (12) material stocks/sales, (13) work-in-progress stock/sales and (14) finished stocks/sales.

Figures 53 and 54 showing the nature of stocks in the UK and the notes which follow are based on *Economic Progress Report* No. 122, June 1980, published by the Treasury (by whose kind permission they are reproduced here). The Treasury comments are

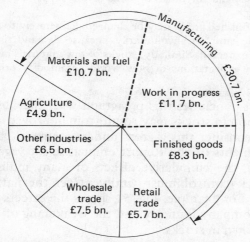

Fig. 53. Distribution of stocks
Book values of stocks and work-in-progress at end of 1978. Total £55 billion.
Source: *National Income and Expenditure 1979.*

quoted to highlight the difficulties and pitfalls in analysing statistics of supplies and in making the correct deductions from data. The comments apply nationally and also to company data.

The figures in the diagram are illustrative only. The distinction between different types of stock is not always clear. For example, some goods such as petroleum products or semi-finished steel may be classified as "finished goods" in the stocks of the firm producing them, and yet be classified as "fuel and material" in the stocks of the purchaser using them as inputs to his own productive process.

Changes in stock values. The book value of stock changes in two ways: through *physical increase* or *decrease* in stocks, and through *stock appreciation* (arising from changes in the prices at which stocks are valued and therefore representing the additional cost of replacing the same volume of stocks at a higher price). Calculation of the *value of physical increase* in stocks (the element of stockbuilding included in total demand) is possible only by indirect means—using assumptions about accounting practices as well as about stockholding patterns in conjunction with price indices to revalue book value data. The division of changes in book value between changes in volume and in stock appreciation is uncertain, particularly when accounting practice for stock valuation may be changing.

Changes in stock levels. The level of stocks held in the economy tends to rise as national output rises. However, the level can fluctuate considerably over a short period, largely because stocks and stockholders act as buffers between production and consumption and are usually the first sector of the economy to feel the effects of any anticipated or actual changes in either the level of demand for finished goods or the supply of fuels and materials for processing.

Stocks of finished goods may be changed deliberately to meet anticipated changes in demand, or involuntarily because demand rises or falls more sharply than expected. Similarly, stocks of raw materials may react strongly to changes in expectations of how world commodity prices are likely to move.

The Report concludes this paragraph with the observation that: "some reduction in stocks may result from improved stock control"! Some would consider this a gross understatement, for, whereas the previous comments of the Report emphasise the vagaries of natural market forces, the cumulative effects of many industries applying scientific stock control must vitally affect the national levels of stock carried. For example, Fig. 54 shows the effects in 1975 of the pressure on company liquidity and the weakening of demand which led to a run down in stocks.

Stockbuilding and the level of demand. Nationally (and individually) it is important to differentiate between the *levels of stocks* at any given time, changes in these levels, i.e. the *rate of stockbuilding,* and the *changes in the rate of stockbuilding.*

These can be tied to company policy as well as national data. The level of company (or national) stocks should be taken as basic. The ratio of stocks to production depends upon the degree of uncoupling and service-factor demanded along with financial policy for investment in stock. The rate of stockbuilding may increase because of changes in policy for uncoupling or service-factor to increase or because financial policy demands (or permits) it. On the other hand, it may decrease for converse reasons of financial policy.

However, the changes in the rate of stockbuilding should be examined. Too rapid a change requires investigation to ensure that it is not out of control. There are three important lessons to be learned by supplies managers of individual firms from the national figures quoted in the Report, as follows.

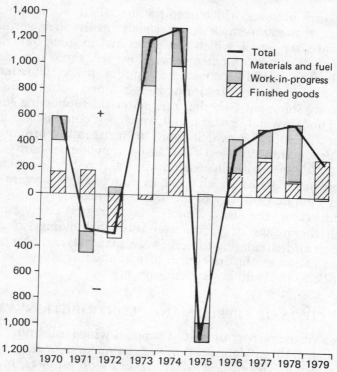

Fig. 54. *Physical changes in manufacturers' stocks*
£million at 1975 prices. Source: *Economic Trends*, April 1980 and Annual
Supplement.

(*a*) Every management should carefully analyse its stockholdings in the three classifications, "A", "B" and "C", and inter-firm comparison ratios (12), (13) and (14). The fact that these might approximate to the national mean should provide no assurance to management that all is well. Stock levels should be determined by statistical methods carefully checked with past demands and future estimates. These must then be translated into financial terms and budgeted accordingly and monitored continuously.

(*b*) Changes in basic levels, particularly the reorder level, should be planned in advance of needs, and also—as above—monitored continuously.

(*c*) Figure 47, supplies horizons, should be the basis for the continuous appraisal referred to above.

Stock investment policy
Elsewhere in this volume "policy stock" has been referred to as

those sections of stock which need the special attention of management, e.g. maximum stock levels which involve heavy financial outlay, and safety-stock which ties up capital in stock but which is idle except at times of emergency. However, there is a sense in which all stock should be considered "policy stock" whether lying in stores, at work-centres, in finished-goods store, or at the despatch bay awaiting shipment (whether raw materials, supporting goods or finished goods), which is static and which if it could be got moving might reap a profit (i.e. which could be spent in the promotion of further production or sales). The firm or public authority which ignores these aspects of financial control and policy is neglecting a major loss-making area which could be converted to increase profitability in a public authority or profit in a company.

In conclusion, the usual concept is to regard fixed capital as providing the means of production through buildings, plant and equipment, and circulating capital as raw materials and other stocks which are consumed in the course of manufacture. (*See also* Chapter 2, stock control and investment policy.)

COSTS OF SUPPLIES AND "CONTRIBUTION"

There is a further aspect of cost of supplies which must not be overlooked, namely the "contribution" it can make to profitability—or loss! Against a background of rising costs of supplies, managers must produce more goods, give better service and achieve greater sales without raising prices above competitors or reducing profits. The materials content of production thus becomes increasingly important in relation to overall costs.

Production costs
Supplies managers and their staff should be knowledgeable on production methods, costs and productivity. When analysing quotations or negotiating supplies it is useful to know about productivity bonus schemes, for example, and their effects upon prices of incoming supplies and upon the costs of the purchaser's own product.

However, there are pitfalls when considering production schemes and work study, because there are many processes where production time is determined by automatic cycle time (BS 5191 (2.6)) and/or by the characteristics of the materials used rather than by the efforts of the operative. There may thus be very little variation in the time taken to do the same job by different people, or considerable variation where the same task is manual compared with fully or partially automated.

Added costs

(*See* below, added value.) These may be reduced by lowering labour content through the application of cybernetics, ergonomics, automation or other means. If these succeed, the materials used become a yet more critical component of the total price. Savings in supply are then even more significant on this account. These savings can arise from a number of factors which are directly related to price, such as reduced price, discounts, rebates, etc. However, there may also be hidden supplies savings (*see* Checklist 25).

Contribution

Table 29 examines the "contribution" that savings in supplies can make to profitability. Savings are related to "profitability" rather than actual profit. The table brings out a number of points in financial accountancy which affect purchasing and supply.

It has been assumed that the supplies or materials content of the product is 50 per cent of the selling price which in this case is £100 per unit, line (*e*) (*see also* Table 5).

TABLE 29. "CONTRIBUTION" TO PROFITABILITY THROUGH SAVINGS IN COSTS OF SUPPLIES

	(1)	(2)	(3)	(4)	(5)	(6)
(*a*)	Savings on supplies: price, etc. (%)	nil (basic)	−2½	−5	−10	+5
(*b*)	Supplies (direct materials) costs	£50	£48.75	£47.5	£45	£52.5
(*c*)	Labour and other variable costs	£30	£30	£30	£30	£30
(*d*)	Total marginal costs	£80	£78.75	£77.5	£75	£82.5
(*e*)	Selling price	£100	£100	£100	£100	£100
(*f*)	"Contribution (*see* p. 000)	£20	£21.25	£22.5	£25	£17.5
(*g*)	Change in contribution from basic (%)	nil	1.25	2.5	5	−2.5
(*h*)	Fixed costs including profit	£20	£20	£20	£20	£20
(*i*)	Profitability change as % of fixed costs	nil	6.25 (gain)	12.5 (gain)	25 (gain)	12.5 (loss)

Savings on supplies line (*a*) and *costs* line (*b*) have been purely to direct materials and supplies. Beyond this accountancy discipline, every purchasing officer knows that he can make significant savings on indirect costs of his company's products, particularly in the fields of services and supporting goods for production, etc.

"*Variable costs*" at line (*c*) are those which vary with every marginal change in output. It will be noted that the labour and other variable costs have been shown as constant for each saving in costs

of supplies. This assumes that in negotiating a lower price the purchasing officer has not incurred any of the following disbenefits:

(a) depressed quality producing more rejects in production;

(b) poorer machineability, thus slower production;

(c) inferior packaging or less suitability at work-centre; shorter
shelf-life, damage in transit, etc;

(d) loss of other qualities listed under value analysis (see Checklist
25).

Where Supplies staff are production and profitability motivated,
it should be possible for them to make a contribution towards
reducing labour and other variable costs.

Added value is an important concept. This is included in the
Census of Production and has increasingly important implications
for Supplies. It reflects broadly what is done with, and what is
spent on supplies during their conversion through production into
the finished product. This is linked with the other statistics used
throughout this book, namely sales per employee. (*See* Table 5.)

Added value is a concept which represents the creation of wealth
and the rate of economic activity.[120][121][122] Of the various definitions currently emerging, the following by the British Institute of
Management is probably one of the most useful:

Income (output)   —   *expenditure* (input)   =   *added value* (all
(from sales or   (on materials and   operating expenses,
services rendered)   services)   taxes, profit, etc.)
                        [supplies]

The activities of Supplies with regard to "prices paid for input"
are clearly of great importance, but Supplies can also influence the
other side of the equation. The added value (wages) content (and
some other areas) may be reduced by providing more suitable tools,
plant, equipment, materials or other supplies which gain increased
output for lower unit labour costs per unit of output.

Marginal costs (BS 5191 (B1004) are particularly important
when investigating the economics of quantity orders. First the
make-up price or other cost must be divided into its fixed and
variable components. Having done this the fixed costs can be set
in place and the variable costs of labour and materials assessed for
one more (or one less) unit produced or bought, or not produced or
bought. Marginal costing allocates only those costs which vary with
the volume of output: line (d) in Table 29.

The inset in Fig. 51 shows the effect of adding one marginal unit
Mu at point *P* on the break-even chart at a cost of *Mc*. When using
break-even charts such as that in Fig. 51 (and other quantity or
volume related data) it is vital to remember possible sources of error

which apply particularly in this instance.

The selling price at line *(e)* has been assumed to remain constant per unit sold. However, the manufacturer may be forced to reduce his price to retain the market, or he may have told his purchasing officer to reduce costs of supplies so that he in turn can maintain his price. Alternatively, savings in supplies costs may enable him to reduce his price.

"Contribution" (line *(f)*), in the sense used by the financial accountant, is assessed through all savings made including those from improved supplies, lower purchase price, etc. "Contribution" is the difference between the marginal costs and the selling price and is so called because it provides contribution to meet the costs of fixed overheads and profit, line *(h)*. It must be appreciated that "contribution" can be achieved by improved prices and costs of materials, etc. and also by improved materials management by both Supplies and production staffs—a further powerful argument for the integration of Supplies with the remainder of any industrial undertaking!

"Fixed costs" at line *(h)* is used here in its accountancy sense, and is shown constant at £20. (*See also* variable costs at line *(c)*.) This is an important cost area and that portion of it which constitutes profit is clearly influenced by supply costs. Supplies executives should bear in mind that even accountants differ as to what should be included in fixed costs. For example, local rates may be the subject of appeal to the rating tribunal, insurance rates may be negotiated, improved tariffs may be adopted, etc. There may be scope for Supplies to challenge the very existence of fixed costs, or at least to mount a vigorous attack against their inflexibility.

"Profitability change", line *(i)* of the table, is the most important of all when considering savings through supplies. It shows the gain in profitability of each saving in supplies costs at line *(a)*, or the loss of profit in the case of column (6) where the price, or other cost centres of supplies, has increased.

VALUE ANALYSIS AND VALUE ENGINEERING

The basic elements of selling price (PD 6470 (1.2))
The question of "contribution" considered in Table 29 leads logically and directly into the field of value analysis. When the buyer purchases a material or product he pays a price which, as the selling price of the supplier, includes the following elements (unless the supplier sells at a loss or subsidises his price, for example from another product):

    (a) prime costs of labour and materials;

   (b) factory oncost;

   (c) office administration;

   (d) sales costs;

   (e) packing, transport and distribution;

   (f) royalties, patents, etc.;

   (g) taxes;

   (h) profit.

The above elements may also be influenced by the cost of money. The supplier's selling price becomes the buyer's prime cost of material. It is to this section of costs that value analysis applies.

The fact that negotiations are necessary between buyer and seller does not of itself reflect upon the estimating ability or the veracity of the seller. If a buyer calls for a new quotation because he considers a price is too high, the new selling price may be lower due to a change in one or more of the costs embodied in the basic price offered, such as the following.

   (a) Materials' prime cost. Use of more suitable, cheaper, or more easily manipulated materials.

   (b) Reduced labour costs. More efficient use of labour or machines. Lower setting-up costs.

   (c) Cheaper, or more efficient, use of energy.

   (d) Better/cheaper quality assurance and control.

Outside these direct costs the final price may be affected by a change in one or more of the considerations under review, such as unit loads, packaging and method of transport.

Purchasing research

Value analysis and value engineering affect "purchasing research", which also includes standardisation, simplification and variety reduction.[55]-[58] All should be involved at the design stage and should be continuing disciplines. In large companies they may be carried out by a value analyst, in smaller ones by a purchasing analyst or the purchasing officer, but always in a collaborative role. In so far as they both affect technical and commercial activities of a firm they should be regarded as "techno-commercial" in a recognition of their value to both areas of company activity.

The purchasing officer will be expected to make his own value analysis of every significant purchase in so far as the more obvious and less technical implications are concerned. However, the degree to which he becomes involved will depend upon (a) his technical ability (which is *not* the same as technical knowledge), (b) his interest in his company's processes and products, and (c) his terms of reference.

Formula for value analysis and value engineering (BS 3811)

A number of formulae have been produced for estimating and comparing the results of value analysis and value engineering. The author recommends the following:

$$\text{Relative value} \propto \frac{\text{suitability for use (``functional value'')}}{\text{total purchase price + life cycle costs}}$$

When carrying out value analysis of any plant or material the implications of the Health and Safety at Work Act are never far away — or should not be. Ignorance of safety matters is no defence. However, there is also a positive aspect. In his 1980 Report the Chief Inspector of Factories made the following comments: " . . . an economically disciplined approach to health and safety matters . . . . beneficially affects the whole performance of the organisation. In the long term, and taking into account the broader considerations, properly calculated expenditure on safety more than pays for itself." Although not specifically aimed at purchasing and supply the report is clearly relevant.

"Life cycle costs" in the formula above include "the total costs of an item including: initial price, maintenance and support costs" (BS 3811) [less disposal value Auth.].

BS 4778 (29) Fig. 4 calls attention to an important factor to be studied in value analysis (of plant in particular). This "factor" relates to what might be termed the "three ages of plant".

(29.1) *"Early failure period"* during which failure rate [and frequency of adjustment and servicing] usually fall rapidly. This is a period which should be covered in the contract by suitable maintenance guarantees, servicing and "retention money" arrangements.

(29.2) *"Constant failure rate period"* during which failures may occur at an approximately uniform rate. Supply arrangements should be made for spares, maintenance and servicing on a forward planned basis during this period.

(29.3) *"Wear out failure period"* is "that possible period during which the failure rate increases rapidly". Maintenance and service records may indicate when this period has been reached, also records of purchase orders for spares may give an indication of the need to increase priority action in future if "down time" is to be avoided.

Methods and results of value analysis and value engineering

Methods of carrying out value analysis and value engineering vary according to the firm and its needs, and may include the following.

(a) Formal, regular committees comprising representatives of sales, production, design, costing and Supplies.

   (b) Informal, occasional meetings when something goes wrong!

   (c) Include in "quality circles" technique *(see* below).

   (d) Appointment of value analyst or purchasing analyst.

   (e) Regular teams or *ad hoc* groups.

   (f) "Brain-storming" sessions.[123]

   (g) Reports, manufacture of prototypes, purchasing research, etc. may emerge.

Figure 55 illustrates the results of value analysis and value engineering. Curve *o-p* is drawn through a scatter diagram of a number of prices for the same article. At *o* the goods are offered absolutely free but may still be rejected by the offeree because they are totally unsuitable for purpose. At *q* a very high price is asked, and the goods may be of very high quality but still be rejected for reasons such as those given in note (2) to the figure. Variations in price change with changes in specification and these must be value analysed. (Points *a, b,* and *c* have other significances which are discussed later.)

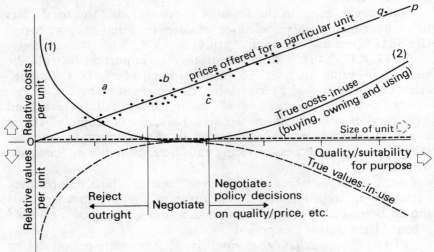

Fig. 55. Value engineering and value analysis curves

NOTES:

   (1) Rising costs as a result of poor delivery and spares service; more rejects; poor finish and packing; low efficiency and overload capacity. (2) Rising costs as a result of low power factor; more space needed; more capital invested; greater loss on obsolescence; replacement perhaps being inhibited by long life.

Suggestion schemes

A well-used suggestion scheme will throw up ideas over the entire field of a company's activities. All staff should be encouraged to participate, particularly those in Supplies.[24] Suggestion schemes act as "feedback" into a Supplies department.

Quality circles

This is a technique which has been introduced from Japan. The circles are small groups, normally eight persons, who do similar work in the firm. They meet regularly for about one hour per week or fortnight under a leader. They then identify problems, analyse their causes, recommend solutions to management and, where possible, implement the solutions themselves. It must be made clear that whereas value analysis relates to supplies, the quality circle technique is concerned with production problems and represents the development of participative management.

DISCOUNTS AND REBATES

In the following account, except where stated otherwise, a discount is to be understood as taken at the time of purchase whereas a rebate is normally deferred until the completion of an agreed period or when a target has been reached.

Neither must be looked upon by a purchasing officer as an act of disinterested benevolence on the part of the supplier—although he may be expected to represent it as such. It must be borne in mind that before negotiations commence the sales department of the supplier will have briefed the salesman on how much discount to offer and how much to keep "up his sleeve" in case negotiations move adversely. (*See also* Checklist 26.)

When examining either discount or rebate steps it is worth checking the consistency of the discount or rebate structures. Such an examination may reveal a drop in discount or rebate or an increase in price—sometimes even for the most popular unit in a range! For example, a supplier, knowing that size x or goods y are in short supply and/or in big demand, may inflate the price. This premium price may be concealed in the overall price structure, either in the basic price or in a complex discount/rebate arrangement.

The basic expected price for supplies may be assumed to be based upon size, capacity or other measure. However, on plotting the net prices (after allowing for rebate, etc.) deviations from expectations may be found. Referring back to Fig. 55, it could transpire that a was a popular size in short supply, b was an exceptional price because the size was cut from a larger unit with no allowance by the supplier for the offcut, and c was a straightforward estimating error (the unusual feature here was that it was an underestimate).

Discounts

"LOYALTY DISCOUNTS" are given in some trades in consideration of the purchaser entering an arrangement to purchase exclusively, chiefly or continuously from that one source. Such arrangements are of a dubious nature commercially and legally under present and future UK and EEC legislation designed to foster competition.

"SETTLEMENT DISCOUNTS": *see* Chapter 22.

SLIDING SCALE DISCOUNTS may be given against either quantity or value of the order. This applies where goods are in regular supply and the margin varies according to the size of order.

MULTIPLE DISCOUNTS: in such cases, it is essential to establish whether the discounts are calculated serially or cumulatively. Consider a discount of 10 per cent for a large annual contract *and then* a further 5 per cent for bulk deliveries.

Serially: £100 − 10% = £90 and £90 − 5% = £85.5
Cumulatively: £100 − (10% + 5%) = £100 − 15% = £85.0

The difference on a large contract could be considerable.

RETROSPECTIVE DISCOUNTS may be given in a period based on the amount of trading in the previous period. If a bad year follows a good one, the buyer gains because a high discount rate will apply to all purchases in the following bad year. If heavy purchasing follows a lean year, the seller will gain, as low discounts will apply to bigger demand.

Rebates

REBATE SCHEMES can be fair to both purchaser and seller particularly where the amount of future business is not known.

Rebates fall into three main classes: flat, progressive and stepped. A flat rebate is fixed and paid on the whole amount of business transacted with or without a target. Both progressive and stepped rebates are on a sliding scale which depends upon the amount of business transacted, usually related to a time scale of, say, twelve months. In a stepped rebate the purchaser receives the rebate due directly each step is reached. In the progressive rebate he must wait until the end of the agreed period, but will then probably receive more cash. An example is shown in Table 30: it has been agreed to pay rebate at the rate of 2.5 per cent for each £1,000. As can be seen, the stepped rebate results in a total of £250, whereas the progressive rebate results in a total of £400.

The purchasing officer must decide which is the better: less cash soon or more later. He must also make sure in negotiation which rebate is intended. On all large contracts, records (*see* Chapter 3) should be checked regularly, especially in the early stages, to ascertain if targets are likely to be reached (*see also* Chapter 18, progressing).

FIRM AND ADJUSTABLE PRICES: THE "PRICE" NETWORK

Figure 56 illustrates the "price network", which is explained in the following notes.

(1) BASIC PRICE is that quoted by the supplier.

(2) NON-NEGOTIABLE and partly negotiable aspects arise from state industries, price controls, etc.

(3) NEGOTIABLE aspects (*see* Checklist 25).

TABLE 30. EFFECTS OF PROGRESSIVE AND STEPPED REBATES

Amount of business transacted	Rebate rate applied	Results of application of the different methods				
		Progressive rebate		Stepped rebate		
		Amount of business	Total rebate due at end period	Amount of business	Rebate due at each step	Cumulative amount due
£	%	£	£	£	£	£
Under 1,000	nil	nil	nil	nil	nil	nil
1,000	2.5	1,000	25	1,000	25	25
2,000	5	2,000	100	1,000	50	75
3,000	7.5	3,000	225	1,000	75	150
4,000 and over	10	4,000	400	1,000	100	250

(4) FIRM PRICES are attractive because they:
  (*a*) tend to stabilise company (and national) price structures;
  (*b*) encourage a sense of responsibility when tendering;
  (*c*) tend to improve advance planning;
  (*d*) should therefore lead to fewer delivery delays;
  (*e*) should assist companies in economic planning and stabilisation.

Firm prices offered too glibly and accepted too readily may result in subsequent applications by the supplier for price increments. Alternatively, the supplier may have had foreknowledge of an easing of inflation—or an actual fall in price—at the time he negotiated his firm price for the contract. In this case he gains a windfall profit at the expense of the purchasing company. How firm prices may react against the buyer in a falling market and against the seller in a rising one should be clear from Fig. 57.

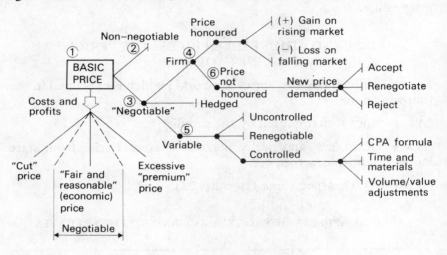

Fig. 56. The price network
Numbers in circles refer to notes in text.

(5) VARIABLE PRICES are almost inevitable in a free market economy—nor are they always absent in a controlled one! An alternative view to the "firm price" theory is to accept that prices must change and to seek to control them by challenging them, costing to make allowance for them, or applying formulae such as "contract price adjustment" (*see* Chapter 22).

Few purchasing officers are authorised to speculate with company cash but it is clear that speculation is inevitable when making the decision whether or not to accept a firm price. Purchasing officers are seldom true entrepreneurs although they are expected to display entrepreneurial skill. The following axiom applies to all purchases in matters of price, delivery, quality and other features.

AXIOM: Every purchase order *is* a speculation.

(6) "DISHONOURED PRICE" is a stricture which can be legitimately and objectively applied to a request for a price increase made during the currency of a firm-price contract. The "sanctity of contracts" has perhaps been less evident in recent years than formerly in regard to price, delivery and even specification. This is an area to test the professional skill and business acumen of whoever does the buying

to raise standards and stimulate suppliers to reduce costs rather than merely try to pass them on to the purchaser as price increase claims.

MARKETS AND MARKET TRENDS

Figure 57 shows how to mitigate the ill-effects of a falling market and to take advantage of a rising one by adjusting order quantities (*see* Chapter 10). Alternatively, use can be made of "futures" markets. Market variations can have all the characteristics observed in the patterns of demand (*see* Chapter 8). Markets must be carefully watched by the purchasing officer, since a small change in supply or demand can have a very disturbing effect on availability, price and profits."Hedging" may be essential.

AXIOM: "Not to hedge a risk *is* to speculate." (David Sheriden.)

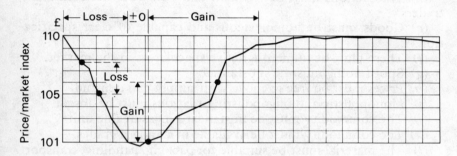

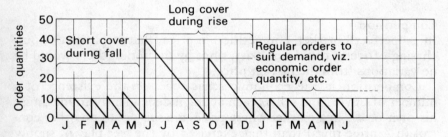

Fig. 57. *Market conditions and purchasing policy*

Market buying

"Market buying" requires special skills and needs to have control from board level. Two methods of using the market forces in solving market problems where buying is extremely heavy are:

   (*a*) volume timing;

   (*b*) budget-equalised purchasing.

273

These techniques cannot apply where usage is a fixed quantity or is tied rigidly to production demands. For further information see *Purchasing and Materials Management*.[23]

"Perfect" markets

A "perfect" market is one where economic conditions are such that in the same market at the same time there is only one price for the same kinds of goods to the same identical specification. The economic conditions referred to are interesting though purely academic, because to some extent they provide a list of guiding principles for purchasing officers, as follows.

(a) Communications between buyers and sellers must be efficient.

(b) Information (data and statistics) on supply and demand must be as complete as possible.

(c) There must be free competition between buyers and sellers.

(d) Transactions must be frequent and numerous between many traders.

(e) Goods must be homogeneous and capable of clear specification.

(f) There must be numerous active speculators in the market.

(g) Spot trading must be substantial.

(h) Prices must be free to move with supply and demand.

(i) Monopolistic and oligopolistic situations must be absent.

(j) The commodity must be in standard measureable units.

(k) The commodity must be available in standard grades.

(l) The material must be suitable for packing, handling, transport and storage.

Competition

In a "perfect" market, competition in price (that staple diet of purchasing officers) could not exist, since by definition there would be no variations from the market price.

Competition in the economic sense relies on the existence of a number of buyers and sellers each acting independently to maximise his own profit in a market where prices are subject to no other control (e.g. price rings) than that exercised by the free play of supply and demand.

Like markets, competition is never "perfect", but on the other hand it is rarely absent. Even in a monopolistic situation there is usually some element of competition, and therefore of "negotiability".

Monopolies

Few markets are completely monopolistic.[138] Outside the private industry sector some nationalised industries are monopolies for their own trades, while others are not fully monopolistic. For example, even in the case of nationalised electricity, the user can change to another form of energy, or even generate his own and sell any surplus to the Electricity Board. Price structures in these industries tend to be rigid, partly because of their public accountability and partly to avoid showing any favouritism to particular customers. Public accountability emphasises the need to control costings closely and this becomes more difficult if the rates are diversified. (*See also* Chapter 1, stage 10: industrial infrastructure.)

THE OBJECTIVES OF MONOPOLY are to maximise profit by holding a major portion of the market. This does not necessarily imply high prices. The monopolist knows that if he inflates his prices too far a competitor will emerge.

EFFECT OF MONOPOLY ON PURCHASING. The monopolist seeks to hold the market against all comers. His price policy is likely to harden in negotiations with purchasers, unless competitors emerge. He may also regulate output to maintain a high price by restricting supply.

The following real-life example of a monopoly situation should assist the reader to appreciate the practical implications of monopoly for supplies management.

A monopoly supplier of chemical x found himself under attack from three directions:

(*a*) investigations into his trading terms and contract conditions by the Office of Fair Trading;

(*b*) low-cost imports arriving from another continent;

(*c*) moves by the home government to remove a protective tariff of 10 per cent on chemical x for low-cost imports.

Chemical x is a class "A" raw material in glass, soap and detergent industries and widely used in smaller quantities by a large section of the chemical industry. Originally the supplier's contracts were of an indefinite duration, required two years notice of termination and included a sole supplier clause. Moreover, the supplier had the only dockside equipment in the UK which could handle chemical x in bulk.

Eventually, the intervention of the Office of Fair Trading resulted in the supplier providing customers with a range of five contract options and the removal of restrictive clauses from the old contracts.

CONTROL OF MONOPOLIES. Under the Fair Trading Act 1973, the Monopolies and Mergers Commission investigate monopolies referred to them (*see also* Chapter 16). The Office of Fair Trading is empowered to refer to the Monopolies and Mergers Commission any anti-competitive practice for a six-month investigation.

BUDGETARY CONTROL OF SUPPLIES

Closely associated with price are budgetary control, capital project sanctions and commitment accounting.[124][125](BS 5191 (B1006).)

Price statistics are needed for budget estimates and should be available from Supplies or the budgetary control staff may tell the purchasing department at which price targets it must aim in order to achieve the results upon which the budget was based.

The methods and applications of budgetary control vary widely. The control may be confined to (a) basic raw materials, (b) production, (c) each department or (d) work-centre. The complexity of the system will vary accordingly and the degree of involvement of Supplies depends upon the points at which the control is applied. In a large and well-controlled unit discipline may be applied before the ordering stage is reached. Warning levels may be set as in the case of normal stock control, to warn those concerned when expenditure or usage is too great.

Control is most effective when applied at the requisitioning stage or the order stage at the latest, as in commitment accounting. An inherent weakness of many budgetary systems is the "end-of-term spending spree" that can occur towards the close of the budgetary period unless restraints are applied. Some solutions (where Supplies operate a supply budget) are for management to instruct that:

(a) invoice payments shall not be brought forward in the tail-end of the period (and paid before their due date to boost budgeted expenditure!);

(b) "warning signals" and not actual amounts be divulged to heads of departments, except through management;

(c) "carry-overs" shall not be permitted;

(d) continuous monitoring be applied to every budget.

Financial management of capital projects

The financial manager of a company is responsible for the financial statements which are themselves mathematical models of the company's assets in written form. The supplies manager is responsible for physically acquiring the actual assets themselves and for their safe keeping if and while they are in the custody of his department. The following paragraphs do not give advice on financial management but merely examine how financial policies may affect and interact with Supplies policies and activities.

The factors which may lead to capital projects being put in hand include the following.

(*a*) Expansion of production output or process throughput.

(*b*) Replacement of plant, equipment or buildings to a life-cycle plan.

(*c*) Modernisation to reduce losses, improve efficiency or restore competitiveness.

(*d*) New plant to improve product design and performance.

(*e*) New products, or diversification of product.

(*f*) Change of plant to suit new materials.

(*g*) Major disaster which has destroyed the plant.

In every case profit (or in the case of state industries, profitability) is a key objective. Closely allied to profit and profitability are the costs of materials supplies which will be used in the plant (*see* Table 29). This should be considered when embarking upon any new production. From the point of view of supplies management, considerations are "first price", "life-cycle costs" and "value analysis", and in some cases "value engineering".

Normally, except in the case of a disaster (*see* (*g*) above) the project should follow fairly predictable stages in its preparation. Stage one may be confined to practical and overall financial considerations along with company policy. Supplies staff may not even be aware of the discussions taking place (but *see* Table 10 and text).

Assuming that stage one results in a definite proposal for a project to be developed, a more detailed examination may then be made involving a feasibility study. At this stage management would be most remiss not to involve their Supplies team in the following areas:

(*a*) enquiries for plant, equipment and buildings;

(*b*) negotiations (or at least share in negotiations);

(*c*) detailed arrangements for contracts;

(*d*) practical administration of contracts—purchase procedures;

(*e*) physical aspects of materials management for project: handling, transport, etc.;

(*f*) information feedback on suppliers and supplies.

How management carry out their feasibility study is beyond our scope here, but supplies management policy and purchase contracts for the company may depend upon how the project is financed. Some methods of financing are therefore briefly outlined below.

(1) OWN RESOURCES must be first choice where the cash flow is adequate. This may result in lower first prices by reason of cash purchases and will of course avoid interest charges. The only possible disadvantage could be the opportunity cost if there were other and possibly rival claims in the firm for the use of the cash. For example, an important consideration is that the drain on cash flow should not inhibit the flow of raw material, prevent advantage being taken

of seasonal or other price benefits, or reduce marketing efforts.

Own resources may be generated internally as follows:

(a) retaining profits;

(b) reducing credit to debtors; demand prompt payment;

(c) delaying payments to creditors;

(d) increasing limits allowed by creditors;

(e) reducing stock-holdings;

(f) reducing and liquidating surplus stocks.

(2) BANK'S RESOURCES are usually available by loan in preference to an overdraft limit on the current account of a company. A bank will not as a rule lend 100 per cent of the total cash but such amount as seems reasonable to the manager in the light of the borrower's liability to the bank at the time and past performance.

When approaching the bank a carefully prepared proposal is essential. The questions asked by the bank manager may be of value to both parties, namely:

(a) reasons for the selection of particular plant, type, make, etc.

(b) exact amount of finance needed;

(c) all aspects of cost of installation;

(d) methods of repayment;

(e) financial strengths and prospects of the company.

The advantages of a bank loan may include the following.

(a) It is a relatively cheap source of money compared with some other loan sources.

(b) It can be easily controlled by a separate loan account providing a ready means of monitoring progress of the scheme, amounts paid for purchases and so on.

(c) For large schemes separate accounts can be opened for each section of the project.

(d) Interest is paid only on the outstanding amount of the loan and can be either added to the principal sum outstanding or debited to current account.

(e) Payment terms can usually be negotiated with the bank manager and arrangements for an earlier repayment than planned do not involve a surcharge as sometimes occurs with other loans.

(3) LEASING provides a source of 100 per cent of cash for project, thus releasing cash flow for other purposes such as raw materials needed for the setting into production the completed scheme, and sales promotion and other essential purposes which may be relevant to the project. Whereas interest rates on bank loans or hire purchase may fluctuate, leasing rentals are constant and at a known rate and for an agreed (negotiated) period. Rents payable are allowed as a business expense for tax purposes in the UK. This tax relief is of

APPLICATION FOR CAPITAL AND SPECIAL EXPENDITURE SANCTION		Sanction No. _____ Date _____	
Department _____			
To: General manager (Circulation as at foot of form)			
Approved by general manager_____		Date_____	
Approved by Board_____		Date_____	
(a) Particulars of items required:			
(b) Reasons for application:			
(c) Estimated savings per annum:			£
(d) Other supporting details:			
(e) Estimated/quoted cost:			£
(f) Replacing:	Plant No.	Year	
(g) INSTALLATION COSTS			
(h) Foundation:		£	
(i) Building alterations:		£	
(j) Services:		£	
(k) Additional services:		£	
(l) Sub total:		£	£
(m) Total cost_____			£
(n) Completion date (estimated)			
CIRCULATION			
1. Originator_____ Date_____ (head of dept.)			(Complete lines (a)–(d).)
2. Plant engineer_____ Date_____			(Complete lines (e)–(n).)
3. Chief engineer_____ Date_____			
4. Chief purchasing officer_____ Date_____			
5. Chief accountant_____ Date_____			
6. Solicitor_____ Date_____			
7.			

Fig. 58. Finance application form
Based on a number of industrial forms and other layouts available from the
British Institute of Management.

particular value where for any reason the lessee cannot take full advantage of the first-year capital allowances available for plant and equipment. For example, profits in the first year can often be very small or promotional costs exceed estimates. When negotiating terms the lessee should look for an option to renew the lease at a nominal rent for as long as he pleases after the primary period has expired.

(4) INDUSTRIAL HIRE PURCHASE involves the purchase of the plant and equipment by the hire-purchase company which then rents it to the user. At the conclusion of the contract period the user can purchase the plant and equipment at a pre-agreed (nominal) price. An initial deposit is usually called for with repayments up to an agreed number of years. As with other forms of loan, hire purchase releases cash for more profitable uses and enables the hirer to obtain first-year capital allowances.

It should be clear from the foregoing that Supplies should be involved at a number of stages throughout, and in particular may become involved in the issue of letters of intent in order to get projects underway.

Capital sanctions

Capital project sanctions are within the province of top management. Usually a standard form, such as the example shown in Fig. 58, is employed for communication, control and record of the operation. The form should be so designed that there is little chance that any vital stage will be omitted. Action needs to be taken by responsible members of the executive staff, who should be named on the form as in Fig. 58 (the production manager was omitted on the assumption it was he who initiated the form).

The following are further possible signatories whom management might consider adding to the circulation list.

(a) Health and safety officer for statutory regulations as they affect workers and staff.

(b) Industrial relations officer; for "acceptability" from the start instead of a "stoppage" at the end.

(c) Works Council, or worker member of the Board.

The procedure may be streamlined by giving heads of departments certain value without going through the whole procedure. The managing director may himself have a further point up to which he can put work in hand, but beyond which the Board must give authorisation. Where the control is applied in detail the management will wish to see the summary of alternative estimates, with reasons if the lowest was not accepted.

Financial aspects of quality assurance and quality control in supplies
Costs of quality assurance and quality control, (QA and QC), like freightage, tend to be concealed in suppliers' price structures and are thus difficult to ascertain.

Purchasing officers when considering offers or making value analyses should bear in mind that a supplier's financial staff may look upon inspection (for example) as a loss centre. The supplier may therefore seek to increase his profit by its reduction—or even by its elimination. The buyer must then apply the quality control by his own inspection—or use! Costs of this—particularly the latter —should be allowed for in the value analysis. The degree of quality assurance demanded depends upon; specification, design, practical requirements and, above all, the economics of production. The degree of QA and QC called for is a major component in the value analysis curve Fig. 55, BS 6143 Fig. 1 and PD 6470 Fig. 1. "Failure costs" should be plotted against "prevention and appraisal costs" and added to give a curve of total resultant costs of QA and QC. The economic balance will not necessarily be at the intersection of the cost lines. This is because "failure costs" fall and "prevention and appraisal costs" rise exponentially. BS 6143(0) points out that "Effective quality management can provide a significant contribution to profit, since evidence shows that resources deployed to identify, reduce and control failure costs give a commensurate benefit in terms of improved quality, increased profitability and enhanced competitiveness".

Requests for price increases
(*See* Fig. 74, Chapter 22 and Checklist 27.) The causes of price increases should be examined by purchasing officers as part of their "diagnostic activities". World economic trends provide guide-lines for anticipating price changes, particularly in "sensitive" raw material markets.

The purchasing officer must identify the reason for, and the validity of, the increase. For example, a supplier may ask for a price increase of 5 per cent due to a 5 per cent rise in the cost of basic material. If the material content of the product is 50 per cent he would in fact be attempting to pass on 200 per cent of the increase (i.e. if selling price is £100, 5 per cent on cost of material is £2.50, but 5 per cent on selling price is £5).

Similar effects can result from governmental directives, etc. These may set a maximum price or general trend in price (or "norm"). In either case suppliers usually try to apply the maximum price or follow the top of the trend. The purchasing officer owes the same duty to his company to question such action as the supplier's sales department did to theirs when they applied it.

Investigations should not be restricted to price increases but applied also to established prices. In one case the long-established price of an article was queried merely on the cost per kilogram of a ferrous casting. The supplier halved his price! In another instance, a state railway checked prices for locomotives by comparing these on the basis of price per tonne per unit tractive effort.

A demand for a price increase should also lead to the following questions being asked.

(a) Can the purchasing firm itself absorb the increases?

(b) Must it pass them on in turn to its own customers?

(c) If passed on, what effect will they have on sales and therefore on stocks and purchases?

(d) Can supplies or suppliers be changed?

The introduction of synthetic materials, for example, can have a stabilising effect on markets by first of all providing an alternative source to the natural or traditional product, and later competing with it, thus to some degree controlling its price.

See also Chapter 20, transport costs.

Depreciation

The method employed for depreciation allowance must be a matter for company policy and is beyond our scope here apart from the following general points.

Depreciation, in most cases, is made up of two main factors: (1) obsolescence and (2) use. Where, because of the speed of techno-logical advance or other causes, the rate of obsolescence is high, a greater percentage of depreciation should allow for this is in the earlier years of use. Where this does not apply, an annuity method may be introduced which provides for increasing contributions in the later years as replacement time approaches. This is to meet the general rise in plant and machinery costs, and to enable the firm to be in a position where it can purchase the most up-to-date replace-ments when the time comes. In other cases the depreciation may be covered on a straight-line basis, so that the contributions are the same each year.

An alternative strategy to avoid obsolescence is hire or lease of plant. In this case the problem is passed to the lessor who must make provision for obsolescence and depreciation when managing his finances. He will of course recover these costs from the purchaser.

For plant the total annual costs in relation to depreciation depend upon the following:[126]

(a) rate of physical deterioration;

(b) rate of technological advance in the industry;

282

(c) rate of technological advance in the plant used;

(d) capital cost of the plant initially;

(e) replacement cost of plant (increases vary);

(f) rate of interest;

(g) load, utilisation, space and other factors;

(h) expected replacement cost at end of life cycle;

(i) maintenance costs (may fall after running-in then rise with age). (See value analysis.)

Other methods include "pay back" and "discounted cash flow".[127] Clearly, the whole question of depreciation must be taken into account when subjecting offers for plant to a value-analysis operation.

THE "LEARNING CURVE"

The "learning curve", also known as the "improvement technique", is an important element of price.[128] It postulates a relationship between quantity and price governed by a "learning" factor referred to here as "Lc", a major component of which is setting-up cost.

The value given to "Lc" varies directly with operating time and setting-up time, but inversely with the degree of mechanisation or automation. The degree of labour intensity of the industry is thus a good, but by no means infallible, guide. In any case it should, in most applications, be used as a guide-line rather than dogma.

The method is usually to take quantities produced (and bought) as a geometrical progression, i.e. 1, 2, 4, 8, 16, 32, 64, 128, 256, etc. The price for each succeeding step is then found—or checked—against the "learning curve" by the multiplication of the last previous price by the factor "Lc".

Over certain broad categories of supply "Lc" varies as follows.

(a) Materials from process plants which are highly materials-intensive and low in labour content: 0.96 to 0.99.

(b) Piece parts, with medium materials and labour content and may be automated: 0.92 to 0.98.

(c) Subcontracted items: 0.78 to 0.95.

(d) Assemblies, likely to be more labour intensive: 0.63 to 0.84.

The figures taken must be a matter of judgment and suppliers are unlikely to divulge their costing secrets. On the other hand, analysis of quotations from the same firm may provide a guide enabling "Lc" to be established and/or checked.

Like most other techniques, "Lc" must not be over-played. It can, however, be used in checking prices from new suppliers against existing ones, negotiating with suppliers on increasing quantities and fighting against price increase demands.

The probable effect of the learning curve can be visualised by reference to Fig. 39, reading the upper (full) curve. It will be seen that the effect dies away as each increment in time is doubled. This is similar to the anticipated effect of a learning curve with the factor Lc given a value of 0.5 and indicates a high gain in improvement at the initial steps. It will also be seen that the secondary or differential effect shown dotted in the lower curve of the same figure leads one to suppose that the maximum benefits accrue in the earlier stages. There is no certainty in this, but when applying the learning curve a break-even point must be looked for (*see* Fig. 51), but bear in mind that the graphs will be curved and not straight). A situation is most likely to arise where the benefits of scale or quantity are outweighed by other factors such as costs of administration, capital tied up, storage capacity, or even shelf-life.

FINANCIAL RISK MANAGEMENT IN SUPPLIES

Risk management in Supplies covers such a wide area that it would be unwise to propose a dogmatic policy to cover all contingencies. There are, however, the following main areas of risk.

(*a*) Physical risk, i.e. supply failure, defective materials, deterioration and other factors discussed elsewhere in this volume.

(*b*) Financial risk, i.e. after the acquisition of a large volume of stock, demand or prices may fall and investment in stock becomes a loss-maker, or new, better or cheaper materials may render existing stocks obsolete.

(*c*) Plant may be rendered obsolete by new and more efficient units.

Some physical risks such as non-availability of materials owing to supply failure can be insured against by increasing financial commitment in terms of increased stock investment. As with "safety-stock", the financial costs of avoiding risk should break even with the costs which may be expected to arise if the risks materialise. As hinted earlier in this chapter, a supplies manager can look upon the financial resources of his company as a "stock of cash". Cash, like supplies, flows and like supplies it can build up excessively (over-investment) or it can flow so fast as to result in a "stock-out" (bankruptcy!). The failure of managements to perceive this important analogy or its mirror image in physical stocks has resulted in the demise of many a promising company.

The natural instinct for self-preservation leads men and companies to seek to avoid risk by paying high premiums and seeking to avoid any speculation or speculative actions. Before examining how to avoid risk it may be opportune to question if it is wise or even ethical to take excessive avoiding action and how far to go in this? Risk appears to pervade nature and the human condition. Perhaps it is best to accept it and react with it instead of against it? Over-reaction in large-scale industry and public bodies often leads to costly bureaucratic control resulting in high costs and loss of productivity. This is admirably summed up by Professor David Farmer in an article, "Buyers and Risk", *Purchasing and Supply Management*, February 1980:

> . . . organisations which are what we might call "risk avoidance orientated" lose their competitive edge. Furthermore while some of the risk-avoiding decisions are justified no one is aware of the "insurance costs" associated with them. In many such situations the organisation adopts formal or in-formal policies. Because these are accepted by the decision-makers they remain unchallenged even when circumstances change. Even when the decision remains relevant the efforts put into reducing insurance costs are minimal because they are largely unknown.

Since we are here concerned with financial and economic aspects of supplies management, some typical risks, their financial aspects and their avoidance are examined below.

(a) Variations in prices of supplies can be examined by a study of probable trends. The width of the band variations a-a and a_1-a_1 in Fig. 38 gives a measure of the expected range of variance. The application of contract price adjustment may be a solution.

(b) Variations in availability of supplies can be similarly studied, and dealt with by adjustments to stock levels to meet the contingencies.

(c) Variations in demand should be more easily predictable since these are related to the actual, potential or expected promotion of sales. The financial implications, however, can be fraught with disaster. Immediate requirements for cash for supplies may exceed available liquid cash resource and a bank or other loan may be essential.

(d) An approaching end of product-life with sales falling rapidly (*see* Table 10, event 20) requires particularly careful financial treatment so that supplies commitments can be controlled and contracts and subcontracts run down without incurring compensation to the suppliers, or other losses such as surplus stock, scrap and waste.

CHAPTER 14

Enquiries and Negotiations
for Supplies

INTRODUCTION

A cynic may suggest that "negotiation for supplies is the art of the unscrupulous pursuing the unwilling to persuade him to perform the impossible immediately—at a loss". More accurately it can be defined as: "Bargaining or conferring with others for the purpose of coming to an agreement or making an arrangement which is freely acceptable by all parties concerned." [Auth.] [129]

The principal areas in which negotiations for supplies take place are illustrated in Fig. 59 (see also Fig. 60 and Checklist 28). The areas can be divided into:

(a) those which the buyer must control;

(b) those which the buyer's technical advisers and functional users must control;

(c) those over which (it is hoped) the supplier will have control.

The place of negotiation in the supplies cycle

Before studying negotiation it will help to consider Table 33 (Chapter 16), the mechanics of ordering.

Enquiries and negotiation are links in the external supplies cycle as regards both the cycle of operations and the relationships between buyer and seller, for one firm's output is another firm's input until the final user is reached. (See Fig. 4.)

NEGOTIATIONS

Internal and external negotiations

Negotiation is a continuing main function between the purchasing officer and the outside world. It is not confined, as many suppose, to price, but covers a much wider field. Neither is it only in an outward direction to suppliers but extends inwards, i.e. with colleagues within the firm.

Referring to Fig. 59, negotiation, or at least discussion, should be regarded as normal at the following stages of negotiation for supplies.

(a) *With the user,* before an enquiry is sent, regarding the areas W and X to settle a specification which will attract the best offers.

(b) *With the supplier* who, on receiving the enquiry, seeks a change in specification.

(c) Reference of this back to the *user* via the purchasing officer or direct.

(d) In the latter case area W must be referred by the user to the purchasing officer who may wish to amend the enquiries to other suppliers.

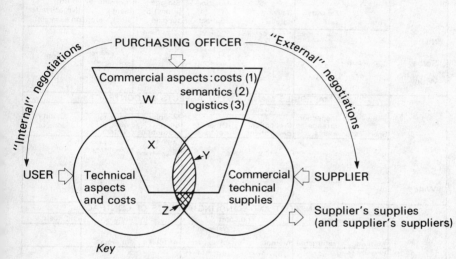

Key

W = Commercial/economic areas negotiated by Supplies

X = Area with some technical content but where economic/commercial aspects are dominant

Y = Areas where technical considerations are dominant

Z = Areas of high technical content entirely in the province of technologists

Fig. 59. Areas of negotiation in Supplies

(1) Total concept of value, taking account of price and all other factors using VA/VE techniques. (2) Specification and accuracy and completeness of instructions. (3) Quantities, stock levels, transport, handling, storage, issues to work-centres, etc.

Scope for negotiation	**1. FINANCIAL ASPECTS OF CONTRACT**						
	PRICE			If progress (i.e. stage payments) acceptable	If "liquidated damages" are to be included	If "retention money" is to be arranged	Settlement terms: monthly account, prompt, etc.
	"Target" for basic price	If price is variable:					
		Method for adjustment	If increase recoverable from customer				
Nil ⇨				n.a.		n a	
Some ⇨	limits +5% £10/tonne	C.P.A.	has agreed C.P.A.	–	lost Production £1,000/day	–	negotiate if possible for 2½% ma/c
Wide ⇨				–	–	–	

	2. SUPPLIES ASPECTS OF CONTRACT						
	Quantity		Delivery date	Duration of contract	Storage (if any) by supplier	"Consign-ment stock", etc.	Quality control (Negotiate for on contract)
	Total	Delivery rate					
Nil ⇨		50 tonnes per day minimum	1/1/80 (see 1.g: damages)		500 tonnes reserve stock		
Some ⇨	+10% overdelivery	accept +5%		12–24 months		if possible 500 tonnes	✓ see section 3
Wide ⇨							

	3. MATERIALS MANAGEMENT ASPECTS OF CONTRACT						
		Inspection arrange-ments	Co-ordination with		Storage		Quality control
	Specification		Production department	Other contracts	Modular or other restrictions	Issue to work-centres	
Nil ⇨	exact to BS 12345	weekly at suppliers work	✓	none	2 tonne containers palletised	in same containers	Full
Some ⇨	no						Some latitude
Wide ⇨	nc						

	4. TRANSPORT AND HANDLING ASPECTS OF CONTRACT						costs
	Packaging		Transport		Handling		
	Method	If returnable	Method	Vehicle, limits of size, etc.	At intake	In works	
Nil ⇨	containers (palletised 2 tonne)	yes	suppliers vehicle	10 m' artic maximum			(See Chapter 20, transport costs)
Some ⇨					Fork truck or crane hooks	Fork truck or crane hooks	
Wide ⇨							

Fig. 60. Negotiation/Planning matrix

(e) If the lowest offer does not embody an acceptable specification, *with the supplier* to improve the specification—at the same price, of course.

(f) And/or *with the user* to see if the specification can be adjusted or made less stringent.

These are all areas where the purchasing officer's technical ability is important—and essential in higher technology industries. Not only will it make him sympathetic to the outlook and needs of technical colleagues but it will also enable him to lead the supplier to raise his specification, to know when a supplier is "pulling technical wool over his eyes" and above all to know how to meet the final problem suggested here, namely when suppliers offer new lines. There is sometimes resistance to change on the part of the user as a result of his "brand loyalty", "sales pressure" upon him by suppliers, or "simple prejudice".

Legal aspects must be kept in mind. While a contract is "an agreement and promise enforceable at law" (Judge Pollock), one of the fundamental components of a valid contract is the *consensus ad idem.* Negotiations are incomplete until they achieve this.

Areas of negotiation

Although Fig. 59 outlines areas of negotiation, these cannot really be so easily confined. There are many strands but few boundaries to negotiation. A most vital strand is that of quality, i.e. "suitability for purpose", leading to quality assurance and quality control. Suppliers should be expected/asked to detail their arrangements in these important matters when making their offers.

As regards actual contents of enquiries and offers, there can be no limit. Checklists 25, 27 and 28 should be regarded purely as "short lists" of areas which may need to be covered.

Others are shown on the "negotiation/planning matrix" in Fig. 60 which is intended as an *aide-memoire* for those conducting negotiations. Whether it is in writing or not depends upon the capacity of a purchasing officer to remember all the negotiating points he needs and whether he intends to hold a pre-negotiation meeting with colleagues to decide any vital or practical points. Some points have been jotted in on the example. The example is not intended to be exhaustive and if the reader decides to use a "planning matrix" he should provide space for other matters which may arise either at the pre-negotiation meeting or during the actual negotiations.

The matrix could be the basis for automated negotiations between companies through on-line computers. However, the program and computer time would probably prove more costly than the use of human Supplies negotiators! Moreover, the computer system having zero IQ could introduce no intelligence into its decisions other than "yes/no" answers written into its program.

Elements and techniques in negotiation

It was suggested in the Introduction to this volume that there is no technique or technical skill unique to purchasing and supply. On the other hand, no one who lacks the ability and skill to negotiate can expect to reach the top of the Supplies ladder—or stay there! This ability and skill is chiefly, but not exclusively, confined to the commercial and economic areas of Supplies activities. It extends into the technical fields as "technical ability".

Certain elements must be present if negotiations are to be successful. These are summarised in the following guide-lines (*see also* Checklist 28).

(*a*) There must be intention to establish a *consensus ad idem.*

(*b*) Define the areas of negotiation: specification, terms, price, delivery, etc.

(*c*) Seek areas of agreement and expand these.

(*d*) Ascertain fundamental requirements.

(*e*) Before commencing negotiation ensure the other party can comply with (*d*). His company may not specialise in the goods required or even make or supply them!

(*f*) Maintain ethical standards, otherwise there may be no valid contract.

(*g*) Select appropriate technique from the following.

(*i*) *Logical:* each step leads to the next in logical sequence.

(*ii*) *Step-by-step:* tackle each problem sequentially (may or may not be in logical sequence).

(*iii*) *"Exam technique"* or *"queuing theory":* tackle the easiest points first.

(*iv*) *Pragmatic:* "opportunist" or "playing by ear".

(*v*) *A tactical campaign:* by the purchasing officer to match that of the supplier.

(*h*) Start with lower quantities than the known requirements. From, say, 25 per cent of the expected or known needs, build up step by step rather than the reverse. Otherwise, the "learning curve" cannot be applied with any degree of certainty that it will reflect the true selling strategy of the supplier or his true costs.

(*i*) Use diagnostic skill to discover the supplier's tactics and plan. A purchasing officer who lacks a plan, or this skill, may find himself being led unwittingly to his doom!

(*j*) Maintain a dominant, persuasive role rather than an aggressive and domineering one.

(k) Plan strategy to gain position of strength when faced with powerful negotiators such as a large company or consortium of suppliers.

(l) Maintain objectivity, particularly when faced by a euphoric salesman promoting a new product or an enthusiastic colleague who wants to try it!

(m) Do not ignore or dismiss subjective aspects, e.g. preference of operative for traditional tools, even when misguided (e.g. preference of linesmen for leather safety belts rather than the safer synthetics).

(n) Develop a good command of language and the following skills.

(i) Clarity of thought, diagnostic skill, objective and impartial outlooks.

(ii) Numeracy and agility with statistics and "raw" data, commercial agility.

(iii) Integrity, tact, determination, patience and diplomacy.

(iv) Dynamism: enthusiasm and persistence.

(v) Knowledge of prices, costs, economics, plus financial and commercial ability.

(vi) Use of correct terminology without using jargon.

(vii) Knowledge of own products plus "technical *ability*" (not the same as "technical *knowledge*").

AXIOM: "A little knowledge is a dangerous thing" (Alexander Pope)—but even a little technical *ability* is a good thing.

Who shall negotiate?

Who shall conduct and/or participate in negotiations for supplies should be clearly established in terms of reference, job descriptions, etc.

Few functional chiefs will admit that a trained negotiator could do better than they. There is, moreover, a certain glamour attributed to the job of negotiation and this is jealously guarded. To transfer this task to a professional negotiator, such as a purchasing officer, is likely to lead to emotional conflicts with those who previously negotiated. There is also a natural fear on the part of the functional man that a new negotiator may wish to interfere with his activities on specification or erode his authority. It must be admitted that sometimes the purchasing officer builds up the same jealously guarded frontiers.

The happiest situation occurs where the functional staffs accept and respect the principal of central commercial negotiation, and where the purchasing and other Supplies staff accept and respect the specialist areas of functional colleagues.

Purchasing officers must not (unless their terms of reference so permit) make unilateral technical decisions. Technical colleagues, however, are paid to do so. Nevertheless, a word of warning is given here for those who tell suppliers direct of specification changes without giving their purchasing officer time or room to manoeuvre. Unless exigencies demand otherwise, all amendments to enquiries —and certainly to orders—should be communicated through the purchasing department. The sales policy of the supplier will harden if he knows the purchasing officer is powerless to negotiate through a prior commitment (or semi-commitment). In fact, the strength of the technical staff is increased, not weakened, if they can tell the supplier that "the technical decision is subject to satisfactory negotiations through *their* purchasing department". (*See* Chapter 4, terms of reference.)

AXIOM: Specification changes should be expected to change costs.

With whom to negotiate

The question "With whom shall the purchasing officer negotiate?" is often answered for him by the degree of importance the selling firm places on its own Supplies activities. A purchasing officer may be confronted with a *manufacturer's agent* who runs a number of lines for different manufacturers and may know very little about all the goods he handles. At the other end of the scale he may be confronted by a *sales director* who is interested chiefly in policy and less in the problems of day-to-day "grass roots" business. A wide variety exists between these two extremes of sales staff. For example, a *technical representative* may have little interest in the commercial aspects of his product and may tend to ignore the purchasing department in the hope of securing an order through contacts with technical staff. *Sales representatives* on the other hand should combine the technical and commercial aspects in their activities and may be of great assistance to the purchasing officer.

There are occasions when instead of an individual the purchasing officer is faced with a *consortium* or *committee* with whom he must negotiate. Powerful organisations such as these require either a man of exceptional stature or a committee to negotiate with them. Forces should be concentrated and deployed accordingly.

Group-company negotiations may be carried out on behalf of the group by the chief purchasing officer of the group, or by the purchasing officer for the largest user in the group, or by a committee representing the interests of the various constituent members of the group. Obviously the larger the bulk demand from such a group, or the more technical their requirements, the greater will be the need for strong representation at the negotiating table. In fact, for classification "A" materials the inference is that the Board should be directly represented.

Ethics in negotiations

The application of good ethics and sound business practices are essential to successful negotiation. (*See also* Chapter 2, supplier relationship policy, Checklist 2 and Appendices I and II.)

The purchasing officer who pursues firm, vigorous, sound and ethical policies places himself in an almost unassailable position when negotiating. But he should remember that if his company becomes involved in litigation the law will tend to protect the seller who was the original possessor of the goods. The court will seek to find the "intention of the parties" and the adversary's counsel will be looking for weaknesses. In the case for the purchaser, unethical activities can be one of these. Examples of such activities are given below, varying from "black" to "grey".

(1) INFLATED QUANTITIES may be given by functional departments to the purchasing officer, either as a result of enthusiasm or to obtain an attractive price on an enquiry. If his relationships are good the purchasing officer may tactfully query the quantity. If not, he would be well advised to ask the suppliers to quote for the quantity specified and, either on the same quotation or separately, for lesser, more realistic quantities. He can then make sure that his colleagues note the various prices available. If the situation is very delicate or there is a possibility of further harming relationships, the purchasing officer should consult his management before negotiating.

(2) AN ENQUIRY FOR INFLATED QUANTITIES may be given direct to a supplier's representative by a member of non-purchasing staff, perhaps during a technical discussion. This is more difficult to correct. The purchasing officer should confer with his colleagues and endeavour to improve the rapport so that in future more realistic quantities are given and/or made subject to adjustment at the formal enquiry stage (*see* Chapter 16 "inadvertent commitments").

(3) A DELIBERATE COMMITMENT TO INFLATED QUANTITIES by non-purchasing staff is an even worse situation than that described above. The purchasing officer may find himself in the embarrassing position of having to explain to a director of the supplier why (for example) the commitment of ten fork-lift trucks for which he gave a discount of 10 per cent differs from actual needs for five fork-lift trucks.

(4) AN INADVERTENT COMMITMENT by any staff member—but particularly by non-purchasing staff—is the worst situation of all (*see* Chapter 16 "inadvertent commitments").

(5) FICTITIOUS BIDS invented to deceive the supplier into reducing his price are a temptation to which many a hard-pressed purchasing officer (or others) may be subject, sometimes under pressure from management, as in the following example. Three quotations were received: Firm "A", £100; Firm "B", £85; Firm "C", £80. "C" was called in and told that the purchasing department knew where they could get a price of £75. "C" believed this. (He had not had previous dealings with the purchaser and did not know his trading methods.) To avoid losing the business "C" requoted and took on the job at £74. "B", who was the usual supplier, had a little margin and could have reduced his price to £82.50, thus providing at least one economic alternative source of supply.

In 12 months' time the purchasing firm again went out for quotations. "B" had now filled his order book with more profitable business to replace what he had lost to "C". Firm "C" had discovered that he had been "fleeced". His market-research team ascertained that "A" was still operating in a premium-priced market, and that "B" was now too heavily occupied to be a serious competitor. His team pursued their investigations and found that "A" was willing to quote at £101 on this occasion. ("A", who was the price leader at the top of the market, had an interest in maintaining the general level of prices.) It was agreed therefore that "C" should quote £99, while "A" quoted £101.

The buying firm had now:

(a) lost the source of supply "B", who being a "thruster" now had a full order book;

(b) induced a price protective manoeuvre between "C" and "A";

(c) been forced to buy in a higher price market.

If the buying company needed a lower price, they could have sought it by a revised specification. If there was reason to suspect that the prices were not "fair", they should have (a) spread the enquiry net wider, or (b) tried to estimate the costs, checking them against the estimates received, (c) explored the market more thoroughly, (d) pursued a more ethical policy, (e) upheld scrupulously the same policy for others as they no doubt expected others to adopt towards themselves.

(6) "SPECIALS" CALLED FOR WHERE "STANDARDS" ARE AVAILABLE is a policy rather than an ethical problem and may arise because of the requisitioner's prejudice or because he is unaware of newer and more suitable products. He may specify a brand name or named supplier for the same reasons.

It must be recognised that "suitability for purpose" is the main criterion. This may justify the requisitioner's restrictive specification, or the quantity may be large enough at least to break even with the price of an existing standard and give better suitability in this instance.

However, if these criteria are not satisfied the company is likely to sustain a continuing loss by the specification of non-standard items. (The methods and policies of Supply staff in coping with all the problems so far discussed were looked at briefly in Chapter 6, specifications.)

(7) DRAWINGS AND SPECIFICATIONS OF ONE SUPPLIER SENT TO OTHERS is a form of mean parsimonious dishonesty through which the purchaser avoids his task (or that of technical colleagues) of preparing the drawings, bills and specifications. Only those who, like the author, have seen their drawings (upon which they have lavished many hours of work and skill) lying on the desk of a prospective customer attached to the quotation of a competitor to whom he has sent them with his enquiry, can appreciate the feeling of impotent fury at being so cheated. "Impotent fury" because the "victim" knows that if he raises the matter he will almost certainly not get the order, and "cheated" because he realises that the competitor has an unfair advantage through not having to spend expensive drawing-office time in preparation of his quotation. Both parties must, of course, know that the practice is open to legal action although the purchaser realises that the seller is unlikely to take action because the costs of litigation would doubtless exceed any hoped-for profit and lose his future custom.

We are not concerned here with what action the "victim" may take. On the other hand, the purchasing officer may find that the practice has been brought to the notice of his managing director who may not be too happy to condone it.

However, it is worth examining a few alternatives to this breach of copyright, as follows.

(a) When submitting enquiries inform suppliers of intentions, e.g. "*Note*: Any drawings or specifications resulting from this enquiry to be the property of this company".

(b) Seek permission or negotiate the "purchase" of the right to use drawings and specifications.

(c) Ask the supplier to itemise any patent or copyright attached to their quotation.

(d) Make sure own staff colleagues are aware of the legal implications.

(e) Negotiate a "design and development" contract.

(f) Arrange for own technical staff to produce at least outline drawings and specifications.

(g) Discuss with top management for a policy ruling.

(8) ADMINISTRATIVE INTEGRITY is an area which is included at this point although it can scarcely be dignified by the description of ethics or policy. However, a tough ethical line is unlikely to be fostered with suppliers if it is not evident within the firm itself. There are some administrative arrangements which may ease the problem and even encourage a concerted effort towards profitability.

(a) Improved veracity of details given on requisitions, by demonstrating to users that when they specify a "date required to use" the purchasing department will act upon it. Ensuring that requisitioners do not mark every requisition "urgent" or "as soon as possible" which might cause delivery too soon! (See Fig. 49.)

(b) Equality of good service given by Supplies staff to all departments and not only their "best customers" (usually production).

(c) Building up confidence of users in the ability of the Supplies department to obtain goods of satisfactory specification so that they do not need to stick to brand names, refuse to accept standards or try new supplies or sources.

In concluding this section on ethics and policy in negotiation, the reader's attention is called to the ethical code of the Institute of Purchasing and Supply in Appendix 1, and to the following comment: "Do not attempt to impose a standard of business behaviour upon others which you do not expect to uphold scrupulously yourself when conditions move against you" (Sheridan, *Modern Purchasing*, April 1980).

Pressure by suppliers

Pressure by suppliers to obtain orders is natural, legitimate, and even laudable as an indication of industrial and commercial vigour. The antidote is not retreat *but equal pressure* by the purchasing officer. Some of the "pressures" exercised by salesmen are pinpointed in Checklist 29.

Supplies staff must never have (undeclared) financial interests in suppliers. However, the possession of a supplier's annual company report can be invaluable when negotiating with a supplier who is reluctant to reduce his price or who is seeking a price increase. A copy of the *Financial Times* or a report from the company's bank are alternatives. A bank report may also divulge who owns whom. This can save the embarrassment of discovering that the new supplier is a major and vigorous competitor, or that a particularly hard line has been taken with a principal customer!

On the other hand, if a purchasing officer is a shareholder in his own company this may give him an added edge in his negotiations with suppliers. The fact that shareholders are entitled to attend and ask questions at shareholders' meetings can be a salutary discipline on suppliers if they know of the purchasing officer's financial interest in his company, and that he attends shareholders' meetings.

Other forms of pressure which occur from time to time (chiefly but not exclusively in the domestic market) are "tie-in sales" and "full-line forcing". Both activities may be in many cases illegal or at least unenforceable and should, unless advantage to the company is assured, be totally rejected by the purchasing officer.

ENQUIRIES

Origins of enquiries
Enquiries can arise from:
   (a) normal day-to-day needs;
   (b) advertising or other promotions;
   (c) the purchasing officer's discovery of something new on the market, which he may wish to bring to the notice of his colleagues;
   (d) colleagues noting new lines and asking the purchasing officer to obtain quotations (Fig. 8);
   (e) suggestion schemes producing new supplies, or suppliers;
   (f) new equipment being sought by the firm.

Multiple-stage enquiries
Where major requirements arise for which no clear specification is immediately available, the stages of enquiry are suggested below.

STAGE (1). A preliminary specification, with performance requirements and possibly outline drawings, is submitted to a wide range of possible suppliers who are asked to quote approximate prices and offer their nearest available standards, if any.

Maintain a sound position for the next stage, e.g. by inserting "use of information" clauses (see above). This may lead to secondary negotiations with some suppliers for use of information they provide.

It may be in the mutual interest of all concerned to agree a suitable development charge, with the option for a "development contract" at a later stage (or at the outset) for large projects.

STAGE (2). This involves the preparation of a further enquiry with more complete (or final) details, circulated to short-listed firms.

STAGE (3). For larger projects there may be a third stage when the final short-listed suppliers are called in for discussions on detail and policy.

COPY ④

No.	SUPPLIER	COMMENTS	URGED		REC.
1	... ... Co		8/2	15/2	26/2
2	Soreres Ltd	X		15/2	NR
3	Pierre qui roule	O		15.2	20/2
4	Careck Fire bal.	X O	8/2		13/2
5	Globe Industries	N/app		—	6/2
6	Triconiums Ltd	ⁿ 4444/13		—	8/2
7					
8					
9					
10					

Ref: 14/4444
Date: 1.2.-9
Closing
Date 22.2.-9

ENQUIRY

(Note: This is *not* an order)

To:

Triconiums Ltd.,
Biggleswade,
Beds.

From THE PANEGYRIC CHEMICAL CO. LTD.
(Head Office) 5 DOCK GREEN,
YATTON, SOM.

Delivery carriage paid to: ⑤

The Panegyric Chemical Co. Ltd.,
No. 2 Store,
Portsea Road,   ①
Pill, Somerset.

Ref: 14/4444
Date: 1.2.-9
Closing
Date 22.2.-9

⑥ Vendor
rating: Z

Notes
(a) Basic price with discounts and settlement terms to be given.
(b) Please return drawings with quotation.
(c) This enquiry is open for 10 days unless stated otherwise above.
Let us know if you require extra time.
(d) Where carriage is not paid we require an estimate of delivery costs.
(e) Quote *also* your own standards if near or equal to our specification.
(f) The person to contact in connection with this enquiry is
ON BEHALF ON THE PANEGYRIC CHEMICAL CO. LTD.
(g) Our normal conditions of purchase apply and are shown on the reverse.

Date required ___9.4.-9___ (ii) A firm date must be
given if the above date cannot be met.

Containers: (in the absence of other instructions
state if: FREE, RETURNABLE, HIRED, ETC.)

ITEM	DESCRIPTION	QUANTITY
A	Triconiums to our drawing 4A176000 issue B, specification PG/24/66	20 off

In view of the urgent delivery date please put work in hand.
Order number H/14/23456 has been allocated to this job.
The order endorsed "confirmatory" will be released directly we
agree your quotation.
Please confirm that work is in hand when you quote.   ②

With reference to note (d) above, please also quote ex. works
loaded to our vehicle. ⑤

NOTE: To save paperwork you may return this
Enquiry Form endorsed with:

PRICE...
DISCOUNT............Normal Settlement Terms.....
Prompt Cash " " ....   ③
DELIVERY..........................(Date............)
VAT No. ....

Enquiry
working
and file
copy.

Enquiry
original
(or copies)
to suppliers

signed _____

Fig. 61. Enquiry and working copy

NOTES TO FIG. 61:

(1) Delivery address only needed for multi-plant units.

(2) *See* Chapter 15, "enquiry proceed".

(3) The rubber-stamped endorsement on form is a time-saving device for smaller enquiries. It may speed up replies from large bureaucratic suppliers by avoiding full quotations procedures.

(4) Suggested method of using the file copy of enquiries to chase quotations explained below. This can also be a useful record for further use without involving extra clerical work apart from the actual progressing of the enquiry for quotations.

(a) The Paper Ball company were late in quoting and required several reminders. (Investigation of their place on the vendor rating scheme may show they were low on the approval list.)

(b) The "X" indicates that the enquiry was returned marked "gone away". The supplier list should now be endorsed accordingly.

(c) The "O" indicates "not quoting on this occasion".

(d) The "XO" indicates "not in our line of manufacture". Supplier or commodity lists need updating.

(e) "N/app" indicates "not approved". This may warrant further purchasing research or discussion with functional users.

(f) The entry "O/N 4444/13" indicates that this is the thirteenth order for commodity code numbered "4444" and was placed with the actual manufacturers, Triconiums Ltd.

(5) Add these particulars where applicable calling the suppliers' attention to them where specially important, e.g. if transport estimates are essential.

(6) Insertion of the vendor rating code of each supplier at a suitable reference box or special location may stimulate his interest to improve his vendor rating status, or at least enquire about it.

Cost of enquiries

An enquiry adds to acquisition costs which must be weighed against possible savings such as:

(a) a lower price than would have been paid if a single offer had been accepted;

(b) use of enquiries and quotations as records (*see* Chapter 3);

(c) discovery of new sources of supply.

Assume an enquiry costs £1 to process and that there is a 5 per cent saving by having gone through the enquiry procedure. The value of the order where it just pays to follow the enquiry procedure would be £20 (5 per cent of £20=£1). This assumes that the supplier did not (as some suppliers claim) inflate prices to cover the costs of preparation of quotations.

The selection of incorrect techniques may add unnecessarily to acquisition costs, the price paid and lead time. It is a basic skill of the purchasing officer to select the appropriate method and also to know the best suppliers.

Format of the enquiry
The format of the enquiry and the number of people to whom it is sent is worth a little thought. As with most routine operations, the use of a standard form helps to keep communications flowing smoothly and accurately with the minimum of clerical labour for both purchaser and supplier (*see also* Chapter 3).

The enquiry form should be clearly overprinted to show it is an enquiry and not an order. Sales offices have been known to "overlook" the fact that the document is an "enquiry" and pass it to the order section, with shipment taking place before the buyer even receives the quotation!

An enquiry should indicate the terms and main conditions the purchaser wishes to apply to his order. If a definite delivery date is needed, it should be stated. As with requisitions, such phrases as "earliest delivery" or "as soon as possible" should be avoided. Other points of detail are covered in Fig. 61 and notes.

ENQUIRY BY LETTER, or an accompanying letter, may be needed for long, complex or highly technical enquiries. Where this is the case, it is recommended that letters, drawings, specifications, etc. be "attachments" to a normal enquiry form, with a list of such attachments being included on the main form—in a similar manner to the procedure where purchase orders are accompanied by other papers. This harmonises the enquiry with the normal system and enables procedures to be followed which are efficient and compatible with Supplies routines, administration and legal requirements.

If enquiries may be of importance to functional colleagues, it is a good practice for a spare copy to be circulated for comment or information.

TENDERING PROCEDURE may be employed for large-value contracts and for public authority work. A notice may be inserted in the Press asking those who are interested to apply by a certain date for tender forms. These are then sent with a closing date and time for receipt of tenders. On the day appointed the tenders are opened and recorded at a formal tendering panel.

In theory this method of enquiry and quotation provides for complete security for all concerned. In practice it is cumbersome and it is not unknown for fresh enquiries to be issued as a result of the tenders, sometimes with a change in specification. Some would question whether tendering formality and secrecy (*a*) permits the exercise of entrepreneurial and negotiating skills needed for major projects and supplies, (*b*) inhibits commercial value analysis and (*c*) gives the degree of security which can be provided by purchasing staff of high integrity.

How many suppliers?

The number of suppliers to whom an enquiry is sent depends upon its nature and value. Where a small enquiry is involved, three suppliers is a good basis. (How big is "small" in this case must be determined in the light of company policy and the importance of the goods "enquired for" to production. Some firms set a financial limit, such as £50—£500. Where the value is around £500 and over the market is then explored over a reasonably wide field.)

Where a new and unknown field is to be explored the net can be cast widely. In this case a trade association may give a list of suppliers, but it will be unlikely to list those who do not subscribe to its policies, and the competitive position may be weakened if restricted to association members only.

Discussion with visiting representatives from those who had the enquiry may lead them to divulge the names of rivals. (It would obviously be useless to seek this information too pointedly, but the flattery which is frequently offered to the buyer may be turned on the representative to good effect.)

Follow-up

Unfortunately the issue of an enquiry does not necessarily result in a quotation and it may be necessary to follow it up after a reasonable time. A standard note may be used asking the supplier to return it suitably endorsed, saying "if" and "how soon" he expects to quote. Bad performers at the enquiry stage are generally inefficient at the production stage.

Following the enquiry and hard on the heels of the quotations— or even before them— representatives may arrive. The purchasing officer may be well advised to see them. Queries at this stage often arise. He must decide who else shall be present at such interviews.

Estimates, quotations and tenders

Differentiating between these terms (referred to in the text collectively as "offers") is no mere academic exercise. Misunderstanding of them can result in actual financial loss. The original request by the purchaser should make clear which is required. If an estimate only is needed a wise precaution is to ask the supplier to indicate a range of variances above and below his estimate, or what price adjustment formula he applies. Tenders, which are usually reserved for very major works and public undertakings, should be carefully handled, especially in regard to stage payments, escalation clauses and administrative procedures. In all cases where financial clauses may effect the methods and amount of final payment or retention money, these must be agreed at the time the contract is made and written into it, showing any formulae or contingencies.

Analysing offers by suppliers

When offers are received, they are assembled and studied by preparation of a summary sheet (*see* Fig. 62). There may be points to be referred to the engineers or other functional divisions.

It is an important discipline to compare and present objectively the summary of quotations, estimates and tenders. Strictures are sometimes made, e.g. "When pricing a job, buyers compare 'like with unlike', that is they line up prices by companies selling machine-time with those also selling technology. Assessment of the value of technology is, however, almost impossible to quantify and the buyer is expected to select the optimum bid" (NEDO). The purchasing officer should, however, avoid such problems by ensuring that technical evaluation of the offers is carried out in collaboration with those who are responsible for the technical aspects of the requirement.

The "value analysis" which results may show startlingly different results from the net prices. For example, the friction, heat or other losses on different machines can be capitalised over the expected life of the plant and added to the net basic price to give a true cost comparison. This may show the lowest price offer to be at a serious disadvantage.

How far the work of collation of offers will fall within the duties of the purchasing officer depends upon his technical ability and the confidence placed in him by his technical colleagues. The latter should, subject to final assessment by management, be able to put values on the various features required and offered. Some examples of the points to evaluate are shown in Checklist 25. As far as possible these should be covered in the enquiry. Too rigid a specification, on the other hand, may prevent suppliers from producing their best design.

NEW PRODUCTS

When negotiating for supplies required in production of a new line for manufacture and/or sale by the company, the following factors need consideration (*see also* Table 10):

(*a*) If, as is usually the case, the sales and marketing department hope for rising sales, the purchasing officer should negotiate for reducing forward prices as expected demands increase.

(*b*) It is usual for tooling costs to be written off early in the life-cycle of sales so that profits can be enhanced as early as possible. This may provide some latitude on price if a competitor intrudes into

OFFER SUMMARY SHEET ⑥ ˣ

ENQUIRY REF: ....

Vocabulary ④

BUSH, STEPPED, M.S.

File Ref: *14/33/3*
Reg. No: *RTA 6730*
Order No: *MS 4949*

Drg. No: *21356 issue C*
Dated: *2 - 9*
Dated: *22.2.-9*

*Eight mild Steel, Self finish
tolerances ± 0.5mm on all dimensions
O/L dimensions: 20mm dia. × 12 mm
long × 6 mm bore.*

⑤

ˣ   ˣ

Quotation details			Delivery (weeks)	Net price per unit ①		Delivery costs	Other costs	③
Dated ②	From	Ref		For 1,000	For 10,000			COMMENTS
14.2.79	Blenkinsop	P47650	2	4p	3.8p			
15.2.79	Appleton	JM 6/32/1	3	3.7p	3.5p			
15.2.79	Sumit	JM/8/04	1½	2p	1.9p			NEW SUPPLIER
18.2.79	Sandlop	AR/F8/1	6	2.2p	2p			
21.2.79	McSmithers	Q5066	4	3.1p	3p			

Fig. 62. Offer summary sheet
Numbers in circles refer to notes below.

NOTES TO FIG. 62:
The summary sheet may be a separate document from the original enquiry form or may be reproduced on the reverse side of the latter. (1) Net prices per unit of quantity or measure should be calculated by the clerk who collates the quotations on the form. (2) The date of the quotation rather than the date received is recommended. (3) Comments, e.g. "no prompt cash discount", "vendor ratings", etc. (4) Vocabulary should be one of the first, not last, aspects of supply to be dealt with. (5) A thumbnail sketch of the component is a debateable refinement. Where, however, the firm uses many thousands of components the filing of summary sheets by shape of component may be advantageous. (6) Other details in the box x-x-x may be omitted in many cases, provided the enquiry reference is given.

what is expected to be a profitable area. Tooling policy may thus affect Supplies policy.

ACCOMMODATION FOR INTERVIEWS AND NEGOTIATIONS

Accommodation for interviews and negotiations should be carefully planned. It will be noted that in Fig. 10 (Chapter 3) a waiting (or interview) room is shown. Representatives reach this without passing through the main office thus avoiding distracting the staff or possibly their gaining confidential information en route! For unscheduled visitors the room provides a means of expeditious interviewing. For regular or pre-arranged interviews the privacy of the office of the purchasing officer is better than in an open-plan office or interview room if others are present. In such cases the interviewee may well be inhibited from fully presenting his case for fear that someone—possibly even a competitor—may overhear his company's plans, policies, offers and so on. The interview room may also be used for meetings where fewer interruptions are likely than in the buyer's office. The accommodation should be normal office standards giving an air of efficiency without ostentation.

CONCLUSION

Negotiations and enquiries are the shop window of the purchasing company and must be conducted in such a manner as to inspire confidence of the supplier in his customer. In addition to ethical policy, consideration must be given to the development of sound supplier relationships. Important prerequisites for this are good firm ethical business practices, complete impartiality and absence of any favouritism. For example, if one firm is allowed to requote then all must be invited to do so; if the price of any is divulged it should be with their agreement and to *all.*(*See* Checklists 2 and 28.)

A similar consideration is whether or not unsuccessful offerors should be told of their failure. There is no legal obligation for this and it adds to acquisition costs with benefit almost entirely to the supplier. However, the following points should be borne in mind.

(*a*) The supplier may have provisionally reserved production space in his programme and this may extend delivery offered on a later enquiry.

(*b*) If one supplier is told then all should be told.

(*c*) Suppliers frequently ask to be told the prices they are competing with. A stock reply can be in the form of another question: "Would your managing director like me to divulge to your competitors your prices upon which you spent so much loving care?" If the answer is "yes" it may still be advisable only to tell them whether they were "very wide", "wide" or "marginally wide" of the best or target price. (*See* Checklist 2.)

AXIOM: 'A bad bargain!' says the buyer to the seller, but off he goes to brag about it." (Proverbs 20, v. 14.)

CHAPTER 15

Ordering Methods and their Management

INTRODUCTION

A purchase order is not itself a contract but evidence of intention to make an offer to enter into a contract. The acknowledgment, delivery or other action by the supplier, with or without a formal acknowledgment, is agreement. Acceptance of and payment for the goods is the final discharge of the contract. The purchase order is a document of communication, specification, control and instruction, and is known to lawyers as a "document of record". (*See* Chapter 1, external supplies circle.)

A purchase order is a deliberate act committing the company in the establishment of valid contract. Who is authorised to sign purchase orders is therefore important and a number of references are made to it throughout this volume.

VITAL COMPONENTS OF AN ORDER

Accurate specification and quantity are the most vital components of any order. Important means for ensuring such accuracy are the use of a comprehensive stores vocabulary, its associated commodity codes and sets of specifications. The following comments taken from a copy of *The Manager*, although dated 1955(!), are still apt: "A customer rarely, if ever, orders commodities in terms that are either accurate or technically adequate for manufacturing purposes and consequently someone at the receiving end has the responsibility of translating the terminology in customers' orders to avoid supplying the wrong articles: or, more positively, to ensure the right articles are supplied."

On preparation of a stores vocabulary, it was found that the simple bush illustrated in Fig. 62 had thirty-six different names in the works. (See also *Storehouse*, commodity coding.)

Components of purchase orders are summarised below.

(*a*) Insertion of commodity code numbers. (BS 5729 Part 5, Table 2(2) calls for the relevant code numbers to be stated on each purchase order and other documentations.)

(*b*) Instructions regarding inspection, tests and procedure for release.

(*c*) Packaging, size of package, provisions for handling, transport, etc.

(*d*) Marking of packages, and other documents with order number, commodity codes, shipping marks, etc.

(*e*) Statement whether the price includes delivery, VAT, duties, etc.

(*f*) Routeing of advice notes and invoices to be made clear if the destination for these is not obvious.

(*g*) Printed terms and conditions. (Should be kept to a mimimum and be vetted by a commercial lawyer before issue.)

(*h*) Reference to the supplier's quotation, if any, or alternatively the previous order number.

(*i*) Plant and serial number of the existing machine, and maker's part numbers where spares are involved.

(*j*) Discounts, settlement terms and price.

(*k*) Where the purchase relates to an importation a large number of further details have to be given. These include the import licence number and period of validity, method of payments, shipping marks, etc.

(*l*) Signature: there should be no doubt who is authorised to do this. The official should sign not in his own right but "on behalf of" the company. Without this proviso he may find himself liable at law for the contract which, of course, is intended to be between his company and that of the supplier. (*See* Chapter 16, purchasing officers as agents.)

(*m*) Amendments, variation orders and cancellations (*see* below) should only be communicated officially by the purchasing officer, thus leaving him room to manouevre or at least safeguard the company's negotiating strength (*see also* Chapter 14, who shall negotiate?).

Design and layout of purchase order forms

Some general guidance is given in Chapter 3, while the subject is dealt with in greater detail in the book by Baily and Tavernier[31] (*see also* Fig. 63, and *Storehouse*, design of forms).

An interesting design which may be of particular interest to smaller firms, i.e. below 200 employees, is illustrated on Fig. 69. It is part of a composite single document for smaller companies to replace

ORDER FROM
THE PANEGYRIC CHEMICAL CO. LTD.
(Head Office) DOCK GREEN,
YATTON, SOM.

Order No. X 10001
Date 20th December 19-8

Supply to depots at:

1: 123 Smith Rd., Bristol, 1 (tel. 3425)
2: 402 Circle St., Birmingham (tel. 1234)
3: 456 Cherry Ave., Newport (tel. 5678)

To:
Supplier:
Solvents Ltd.
River St.
Wigan (tel. 0404)

Ref: 14/5 Supplier's ref. AEC/XYZ dated 12th December 19-7

This is a forward contract for supplies from 1st January 19–9 to 31st December 19–9.

Deliveries to be made as and when required in accordance with call-off orders from the above depots.

Drums to be delivered on standard pallets 1,200 × 1,000 mm. Invoices to be rendered to our Head Office.

Items	Description	Price
A	Solvent "X" 27,300 litres per annum delivered at 2,275 litres a month ± 20% according to draw-off orders	10p per litre (see below)

Notes (*To depots*)
(1) This material is supplied in 200 litre returnable drums.
(2) Solvent "X" is highly flammable and must be stored in an outdoor stores compound shielded from bright sunlight.
(3) It is a condition of this order that any commercial negotiations regarding it shall be undertaken through the Purchasing Department.
(4) The supplier requires 7 days' notice for normal requirements. In the case of urgency phone Wigan 0404, Extn. 10.
(5) For technical data sheet see the chief engineer's instructions below.
(6) Progress direct with supplier unless help is needed from HQ.

British Standard	Engineering instruction	Empties	Carriage	Discounts	Settlement terms
BS 12345	Chief Engr. 31st Dec. 19-7 FWL/ZAB	Returnable £5	Free on 5 barrels and over	20%	Net M/Ac 5% prompt cash 7 days

Note to Staff. The terms of this order are strictly confidential. Terms and other details of this order must not be disclosed outside the company. Complaints regarding the performance of this order should be made promptly to the purchasing department.

....
ON BEHALF OF
THE PANEGYRIC CHEMICAL CO. LTD.

Fig. 63. Order for a firm annual contract

the numerous forms which multiply along the "admin. network" as a firm grows. It has several applications, but is particularly useful for progressing (*see* Chapter 18).

Amendments, "variation orders" and cancellations

Amendments to orders should preferably be on a distinctive form if the number warrants this. If the normal order is used, it must be clearly marked to show that it is an amendment.

Some consider that any amendment must repeat the entire ordering details. However, it is preferable to use the "exception principle" here. After giving identifying heading, such as six words of basic description, the amendment should state the variation from the original. This avoids inadvertent duplication of the order which can occur if the full description is given. Similar remarks apply to cancellations of orders.

Amendments and cancellations must always be prompt and include a request for an acknowledgment which must be insisted upon.

Generally where the circumstances are reasonable and the seller has not already been put to expense, cancellation will be accepted, otherwise payment may be demanded.

Cancellations and amendments should be notified internally to interested parties. This is best assured by normal order copy circulation.

(*See also* Checklist 9, "variation orders", and Chapter 16, verbal orders, communications and instructions.)

USE OF BEST ORDER METHOD

Whatever the form of order used it is important always to minimise acquisition costs without loss of commercial benefit, control or records of the transaction. Examples of some new ordering methods are discussed at the close of this chapter. With these and similar methods there is usually a risk of losing control and/or records. The work saved in the purchasing department of the buying firm may be transferred to the supplier who will (sooner or later) recover the costs transferred to him, thus nullifying any savings.

The varying needs of most firms determine the pattern of ordering that will predominate. These are usually related to the shape of the "A.B.C." analysis curve and will depend upon the following:

(*a*) fixed commitments in bulk;
(*b*) fixed commitments in small lots;
(*c*) variable commitments in bulk;
(*d*) variable commitments in small lots;
(*e*) random demands for own production and use;

(f) random demands for resale and service to customers, etc.;

(g) random demands for capital projects;

(h) demand for services—power, transport, etc.

With these points in mind it is necessary to consider next:

(a) whether the supplies are high technology and call for special procedures;

(b) whether one form of purchase order may obtain a better price or delivery than another;

(c) whether a running contract of some kind can ensure better delivery;

(d) what type of contract is warranted in the light of the value of the goods, guarantees of performance and so on;

(e) whether the price, nature and size of the article make it unsuitable to buy and store in bulk so that individual orders are essential.

Table 31 lists many forms of purchase order in common use. Explanatory notes on some of the more common types of order are given in the text which follows.

(1) Contracts and (2) general orders

Classification "A" main materials and large-value items warrant contractual arrangements. These safeguard continuity of supply, obtain the best price, and stabilise the price as far as possible. Annual contracts may be negotiated with one or more suppliers for a fixed total quantity of materials delivered according to a preplanned programme, by schedule or other means.

The preparations and negotiations for contracts are usually time consuming and therefore costly. It is important to avoid costly administration. For example, some executives insist on a "stock letter" for each intake. This is not only more costly than a simple draw-off order, but may also defeat the entire order sustem, unless many copies of the stock letter are made for the various control centres such as stores, goods inwards, accountants, production control and supplies, as with normal purchase orders.

A typical contract is shown on the order form in Fig. 63. The layout is intended to be suitable for circulation to the various works and depots as well as to the supplier. It gives full instructions, not only to the supplier but also to the buyer's depots/branches, about the method to be employed for calling up supplies. (It may also be helpful if the supplier sees what internal arrangments the buyer makes within his own company.)

There may be confidential instructions to staff or lists of alternative suppliers or supplies. These may be located where they can be cut from the supplier's copy or rendered indecipherable. All contracts

TABLE 31. SUMMARY OF KINDS OF PURCHASE ORDER

(1) Contracts, Classifications "A" and "B"	(2) General orders, Classifications "A", "B" and "C"	(3) Production-related	(4) Customer-related	(5) Miscellaneous needs, "C" and "B"	(6) Informal	(7) Quasi-contracts	(8) Projects	(9) Special, non-standard
(a) Forward supply	(a) General	(a) Loan	(a) Free-issue	(a) Small-value orders	(a) Verbal	(a) Forward supply arrangements	(a) Serial contracts	(a) Supplier's pre-printed schedule
(b) Bulk	(b) Forward supply	(b) Sale-or-return	(b) Reciprocal trading	(b) Local-purchase orders	(b) Supplier's order form	(b) Letters of intent	(b) "All-in", "turn-key", "design and make"	(b) Cheque order
(c) Blanket	(c) Draw-off	(c) Self-regulated		(c) Petty cash	(c) Delivery note acceptance	(c) Sample orders	(c) Sale and lease-back	(c) Barter
(d) Futures	(d) Standing orders	(d) Material schedules			(d) Requisition-order	(d) Enquiry-proceed	(d) Parallel working	(d) Counter trade
(e) Consortium	(e) "Model" "master"	(e) Production reservation			(e) Unintentional/inadvertent		(e) "Run-on" contracts	(e) Sole supplier
(f) Group	(f) Periodic/batch	(f) Consignment stocks					(f) Incentive contracts (see also "penalties")	(f) Hire
(g) Long-term	(g) Amendment/cancellation	(g) Sub-contracts					(g) Design and development only	(g) Service
	(h) Dye-line	(h) In-plant stores					(h) Cost plus	(h) Hire purchase
	(i) Computerised							(i) Leasing
	(j) Automated							(j) Back order*
	(k) "On-line"							(k) Importation
	(l) Schedule							

*BS 5191 (B 1006)

are, of course, confidential, but notes to staff as indicated at the foot of the form may be advisable for security and confidentiality.

(1(a)) Forward supply contracts and (7(a)) Forward supply arrangements

Where the forward (i.e. annual) usage is known with some confidence a forward supply contract is appropriate with a fixed total commitment (*see* Fig. 63). Where confidence is lacking the less binding form of order known as a "forward supply arrangement" is more suitable with target figures or approximate expected demands only given if these can be forecast. Withdrawals from the forward supply contract *may* be by regular fixed scheduled deliveries. In the case of a forward supply arrangement this is seldom practicable and withdrawals must be made by draw-off instructions as needs arise. This is also in fact necessary with most forward supply contracts because few plants can schedule fixed quantities over more than four to twelve weeks ahead of production.

The following are some of the benefits of forward supply contracts.

(a) Advantageous trading terms, price, discount, rebates.

(b) Continuity of supplies.

(c) Staff use selected and approved suppliers.

(d) Suppliers (particularly wholesalers) may carry (reserve) stock earmarked for the purchaser.

(e) Supplies have had technical approval by the appropriate functional department at the purchaser's factory.

(f) It should be an encouragement towards standardisation and an indication of such progress.

(g) Savings in administrative costs may be considerable: records and controls may be simplified and computerised.

(h) Operatives may learn the cost of the supplies they consume. (Opinions are divided as to whether shop-floor staff should be told prices of supplies. Objectively, this must depend upon the extent of staff and worker participation, their degree of responsibility and attitudes, and above all the amount of feedback which Supplies wish to generate.)

(i) The supplier becomes (indirectly) part of the purchaser's Supplies system.

A forward supply arrangement may be open as regards quantity and/or time during which it remains in force. It provides most of the benefits of a forward supply contract listed above with the addition of the following.

(a) Its informality puts no restraint upon Supplies from carrying out supplies research.

(b) It gives the supplier some assurance that he will continue to receive the business, provided he maintains quality, price and service.

(c) The supplier cannot sue for breach if the arrangement is terminated prematurely.

(d) The supplier cannot therefore afford to become complacent by having a "tied customer".

(e) The supplier is not inhibited from suggesting new lines.

(1(*g*)) Long-term contracts

Long-term contracts (generally those of over two years' duration) may have the advantages (+) and disadvantages (−) listed below. (Most of these also apply to forward supply arrangements.)

(a) Price reduction for long-term horizons (+).

(b) Security of intake through long-term programme (+).

(c) Continuity of design and performance through single initial specification (+).

(d) Difficulties in changing specification (−).

(e) Administrative benefits: fewer suppliers, orders, etc. (+).

(f) Purchasing research may be discouraged (−).

(g) Difficult to plan on long horizons (−).

(h) Changes in demand (or supply) may not have been contemplated (−).

(i) Changes in financial policy of supplier or purchaser (−).

(j) Market changes, collapse, inflation (−).

(k) Weather may upset long-term plans of either party (−).

(l) A "sole supplier" may become a "sleeper" (−).

(m) Purchaser is inhibited from exploring new sources (−).

(n) Changing a source may involve cancellation costs (−).

(o) Only the supplier profits unless contract is skilfully drafted (±).

(2(*c*)) Draw-off orders from forward supply arrangements and contracts (BS 5191 (42))

SVOs and LPOs (*see* (5(*a*)) and (5(*b*)) below) can be used by local sources on a forward supply arrangement or contract, provided the financial limits are not exceeded. If for control purposes the full routine is needed, or the sources are remote and the value above the LPO and SVO limits, use should be made of a full order set or one of the other methods listed below.

(a) Pre-printed (or duplicated) order with all details except the variables such as quantity already shown or use a word processor.

(b) "Master" or "model" order which can be copied by a clerk (2e).

(c) Pre-printed parts schedule or drawing schedule attached to order form (2h).

(d) Copy of process control chart for a process plant.

(e) Linked computer terminal at supplier's works (2i, j, k).

(2(e)) Model orders

In their most sophisticated form model orders may be linked with a word processing system. Whether manual or automatic operation is used the following benefits are to be gained from using model orders.

(a) Eliminates detailed preparatory work.

(b) Speeds editing, typing and checking.

(c) Ensures accuracy, reduces errors.

(d) Content of orders is clear and consistent.

(e) Avoids queries at acknowledgment stage and later.

(f) Supplier becomes familiar with orders: speeds supplier's internal work.

(g) Junior labour can be used: releases senior staff for purchasing research, etc.

(h) Reduces internal and external lead times.

It may be useful to attach a copy of the model order to the company standard for the supplies which it covers.

(3(a)) Loan orders

Loan orders used when the factory borrows tools or equipment have the advantage that both parties have records of the loan. The loan order may state the expected duration of the loan. In this case the progress sections can check the return of the goods.

(3(b)) Sale-or-return

An invoice may follow or may arrive with the goods, in which case it must be held. It seems logical that purchasing should hold the invoice with the sale-or-return order until the agreed date arrives, or the department wanting the goods decide to retain or return them. Where the goods are for resale the arrangements may be part of a general consignment-stock contract (see below). Details in this case will be more complex, but in principle follow the same general plan.

(3(g)) Subcontract orders

A subcontractor can be regarded as an extension to the production line of the main contractor. This applies whether the main contractor is engaged upon manufacture of goods, assembly of parts or on construction projects. The phasing of delivery with the main operation is usually vital, and may involve complex sampling, inspection, approval of drawings, test-room runs, on-site erection, on-site tests, commissioning, etc.

Subcontracting and subcontract orders tend to be complex and highly specialised—so much so that in very large industrial units subcontracting is often attached to the main production unit or is a separate function from Supplies.

The soundness of both of these arrangements is questioned. The commercial aspect of subcontracted work is no less important than for raw materials and general supplies. If Supplies are not able to secure satisfactory subcontracted goods they are unlikely to succeed in other fields either.

Whether the firm issuing the subcontracted order is large or small, similar problems will attach to the order for the work. Where subcontract orders are very frequent a standard form of order can be used to ensure that all the main points are covered.

The policy of an undertaking in regard to those who subcontract for it should be reflected in the terms of the subcontact orders themselves. In production it is a good policy to keep subcontractors informed of the ups and downs of demand. They may be warned of this by a clause in the order relating to planning, progressing and delivery. In a similar manner it may be advisable to arrange some form of "break clause" so that if a customer—particularly a government department—holds up or cancels a main contract the subcontracts can be dealt with, without recourse to legal action.

The administration of subcontracts may involve the provision to the subcontractor of materials, parts or other goods (*see* free-issue), tools, templates, equipment, gauges, fixtures and handling or packaging units. Certain precautions are essential in such instances. If the subcontractor goes into liquidation while in possession of the above goods belonging to a purchaser the latter may have two major problems on his hands. In the first place his source of supply is lost or is at least in jeopardy. No less serious may be the fact that until the receiver had held meetings with all the creditors he may not be able to retrieve the goods, even though he can prove title to them. This also applies to part-finished and fully finished goods both of which will need the authority of the receiver for their release. Conditions in the original contract will only provide evidential help.

Partial solutions are to insist upon the return of all property between contracts, and where practicable to appraise the day-to-day situation through the local "grapevine" where the subcontractor is situated.

(4 (*a*)) Free-issue orders
A customer may supply his own materials or embodiment parts for incorporation in the finished product. If so, there is often merit in raising a free-of-charge or free-issue order set for internal use at least,

314

even if the original is not sent to the customer. If the customer agrees to accept the system of free-issue orders, the whole routine of progressing, intake and administration is brought into line with normal supplies procedure at both the customer's and the supplier's works.

(5 (a)) Small value orders (SVOs) and (5 (b)) local-purchase orders (LPOs)

Classification "C" goods and materials are the most difficult to handle economically. Unless care is exercised the cost of aquisition and control may exceed the cost of what is purchased. Some small factory consumable items may be bought through petty cash (5 (c)), although small-value orders are more cost-effective having regard to the disciplines and control which they afford (see Fig. 64). Controls must be kept to the minimum whilst noting the following points.

(a) All users must be told of their responsibilities for SVOs and LPOs.

(b) A list of authorised signatories must be published under the authority of the chief purchasing officer.

(c) A list of pad numbers should be kept, together with a note of to whom they have been issued.

(d) A copy of each SVO and LPO is sometimes insisted upon by the purchasing officer. This may reveal his inability to delegate, to trust staff or to select trustworthy staff (where they are in his area).

(e) Stubs of completed pads, however, should be sent to the purchasing department *as they are completed.* This gives the opportunity

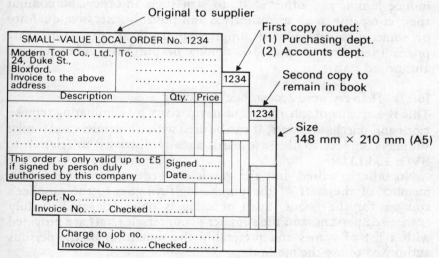

Fig. 64. Small-value or local-purchase order

315

for the department to see whether there are any areas where commercial advantage could be gained by purchasing research, or of course, where irregularities have occurred.

(*f*) The signatories of these orders should understand their responsibilities for the orders they issue and exercise due care and discrimination in their use. This can produce within the company a healthy "Supplies outlook" to the great advantage of all concerned and the economic functioning of the company.

(*g*) It must be clear to all that the purchasing officer has the right of scrutiny on demand.

(*h*) It must also be understood that the ultimate responsibility lies with the chief purchasing officer and that he has the right to intervene in any purchase on SVO or LPO.

The object of all these arrangements is not to spy on those using the orders, but to retain control and provide information in regard to demands and whether these are likely to lead to an advantageous forward supply arrangement. If the demands upon a single supplier are fairly continuous, he may then be told to render a combined invoice at the end of each month, saving bookings, invoices and cheques. This may also result in improved terms.

(6(*b*)) and (9(*a*)) Suppliers' orders

Suppliers' order forms are sometimes presented by salesmen for signature. These may deprive the buying firm of records and also puts the purchaser entirely in the hands of the supplier. The system is also liable to gross abuse by unscrupulous salesmen who may induce junior, and other staff, to sign such an order and commit their company to an unauthorised and possibly excessive quantity of sometimes substandard supplies, perhaps at an extortionate price! (*See also* Chapter 16, signing of purchase orders by unauthorised staff.)

(6(*c*)) "Delivery note-acceptance" ordering

This is a means of cutting acquisitions costs by eliminating requisitions and purchase orders. It can be used with wholesalers and similar suppliers subject to the safeguards already discussed in relation to SVOs and LPOs.

No order is raised, but the goods are ordered by telephone. A member of the staff of the purchasing firm goes to the supplier's counter for the goods. Such ordering is only delegated to duly authorised persons, and the supplier's countersales staff are provided with a list of names and preferably the signatures of the persons authorised to use the method.

The materials and goods are then taken (or delivered) under

cover of a specially printed delivery note set made out by the supplier. The set comprises:

    (*a*) supplier's office copy;

    (*b*) invoice copy;

    (*c*) delivery note copy (1);

    (*d*) delivery note copy (2);

    (*e*) goods received copy.

The second copy (*b*) is sent to the purchaser's accounts department for payment. The third copy (*c*) is the equivalent of the purchase order. An invoice will only be accepted where one of the persons authorised to do so has signed both delivery note copies (1) and (2). Delivery note (1) is returned to the supplier and copy (2) retained by the purchaser for checking against the invoice.

Such a method of ordering is suitable for goods for resale but should not as a rule be employed for general stock items. The purchaser is entirely in the hands of the supplier who may be above reproach, but cannot answer for the misdeeds of his employees acting with or without the collusion of the employees of the purchaser.

(6(*d*)) Requisition ordering systems

Such systems involve the use of the requisition as a purchase order. It must be prepared legibly by the requisitioner and passed to the purchasing department for processing and passing on to the supplier. It is a form of streamlining which shows marginal savings only.

(7(*b*)) Letters of intent

Letters of intent can be used where the issue of the order on a particular supplier is practically certain and the demand urgent. The supplier is given the order number which will be issued if the order proceeds and is told that it will be issued subject to agreement of his quotation and delivery. He is also told to note that the letter is only valid to a stated expiry date. He should be asked to confirm that he has put preliminary work in hand and to state his delivery date. The letter of intent has advantages over unpriced or open orders in that it:

    (*a*) keeps the commercial aspects in mind;

    (*b*) will be followed up from the initial stage;

    (*c*) enables any queries to be ironed out before the formal order is placed.

Letters of intent can be a source of commercial disaster and loss if not kept under continuous surveillance and control. The progress section with its contacts within the company can be a useful "watchdog".

As in the case of the enquiry with instructions to proceed ($(7(d)$) and *see* below), it is important to send a copy of what has been written to the person responsible for the need. He should be asked to be sure to note on his requisition that the supplies have already been provisionally covered by allocated order number X.Y.Z.

A typical letter of intent is shown in Fig. 65.

The letter of intent should never be used without the authority of top management. Although a letter of intent is not a contract, it can easily develop into one. In any dispute the judge would look for the intentions of the parties and assess these intentions by the actions taken. For example, the question may arise whether development work carried out during the pre-contractual stage should be

---

The Panegyric Chemical Company Limited

To: The Refinery Plant Company Limited
Ditchem on the Fosse
Devon

Your Ref. ABC/1234/MCC
Our Ref. Cap.6.65./C665
Date: 31st December 19-5

Dear Sirs

New degurgitating plant. Preliminary drawing 19999.
Depot number six. Quotation 1234 dated 11th December 19-5.

Please accept this as a letter of intent to place on order the above equipment in accordance with your provisional drawing and quotation mentioned above and subject to finalisation of details within the validity period of this letter.

Order number C.665 has been provisionally allocated and delivery is required with completed installation by 31st March 19-6 and commissioning by 14th April 19-6.

We reserve the right to cancel this letter in the event of the work not proceeding for which this plant is required or if negotiations fail.

This arrangement is subject to confirmation in four weeks from this date unless otherwise extended or cancelled.

Will you please acknowledge this letter as soon as possible, indicating what action you are taking and what additional information - if any - is required by you?

Yours faithfully

R. Humphuer.

Chief Purchasing Officer
On behalf of The Panegyric Chemical Company

Fig. 65. Letter of intent

part of the main contract. This may occur whether there has been a letter of intent or not. A relevant leading case was *Trollope and Colls Limited* v. *Atomic Power Constructions Limited.*

The facts of the case were complicated, but the main issue was simple: "Did the contract cover work done in anticipation of it before it was signed?" Mr Justice Megaw held that it did. He said: "I am satisfied from all the circumstances that both parties in all that they did in the course of the negotiations. . . were doing so on the understanding and in anticipation that, if a contract were made and that whenever it was made, that contract would apply to and govern what was meanwhile being done by the parties."

(7(c)) Sample orders (for goods on trial examination, etc.)

The use of "sample orders" removes any doubt as to who does what. It also gives the goods-inwards section and stores a clear indication of what goods to expect and of their final destination. This is important in the case of a large industrial (or commercial) unit with many departments, especially if the firm supplying the sample is new to them. The supplier's personnel in this case are probably not familiar with their new customer's internal supplies arrangements and label or consignment instructions are likely to be vague.

"Thrusting" suppliers and keen technical, production and other staff may lead to the offer and procurement of free (?) samples. In large organisations and those with multiple production units it can be important that such goods and the resulting tests shall be co-ordinated and controlled through a central office. This avoids duplication of action in a number of departments or at a number of work-centres, although, of course, the tests may not be confined to a single-centre or field trial. A minimum of central control enables data from tests to be collected, collated and disseminated through the company's communication network. Where, for example, the Supplies department issues a regular "Supplies Bulletin", this can be a useful vehicle for such dissemination.

(7(d)) "Enquiry proceed"

(*See also* Fig. 61.) As this has similar quasi-contractual implications to a letter of intent, the comments made above are generally applicable, except that the sums involved will be very much smaller than those for a letter of intent.

(8(a)) Serial contracting

This is a method used by, for example, local authorities, where a series of schemes are given special terms for the jobs to follow on subject to reappraisal at each stage. It could be worthy of consideration for large industrial undertakings with large plant programmes.

(8(b)) "Design and make", "all-in" and "turn-key" contracts

In this case a formal contract is made for design, development *and* manufacture. Costs may be controlled as follows.

(a) A ceiling price may be established.

(b) Work may be on a time and materials basis.

(c) As (b), with time sheets submitted for agreement and signature.

(d) Progress payments as work proceeds.

A clause should be inserted stating who owns the design, etc. Protection must be written into the contract against patent and copyright infringements, and agreement reached as to who shall own the patents, etc., and who shall own tools, patterns, dies, etc.

(*See also* Chapter 14, multiple-stage enquiries, and (8(g)) below, design and development.)

(8(g)) Design and development only

In this case the supplier may be used purely as a consultant and any order must show this clearly. Particular attention must be given to the relevant sections of "design and make" contracts, especially if prototypes, tools, drawings, etc. are involved. (*See also* Chapter 14, ethics in negotiations.)

(9(f)(g)(h)(i)) Hire, service and leasing contracts

Hire and leasing contracts differ from most other forms of order and require closer study. Hire and leasing depend upon the separation of ownership from possession and use. They make it possible to have the use of a service, labour or plant without expending capital, thus earning profit on someone else's capital and paying for the present use from future profits.

In the case of simple hire (9(f)), service (9(g)), and hire purchase (9(h)), the hirer will usually be expected to sign a contract form provided by the supplier. This must be given especially careful scrutiny in regard to terms and conditions of hire offered which can be assumed to give the supplier maximum protection from all eventualities and from all claims by the hirer for any indemnity. The following safeguards can be considered.

(a) Check the terms and conditions with the contracts book [135] of the Institute of Purchasing and Supply and with Table 32.

(b) Check the supplier's membership of a trade association and his terms and conditions with those of the association.

(c) Insist that the supplier accepts confirmation on the company's official order with a note on the face that any abnormal terms and conditions must be pre-agreed with the company before the hire commences.

(d) Check that plant is returned promptly when finished with (see Table 34).

"Leasing" (9(i)) in various forms from finance companies is a much more complex matter than simple hire. The publication, *The Lease-buy Decision*,[130] gives some useful guide-lines. The application of break-even analysis can be helpful, although it can only provide a rough yardstick because of the number of unpredictables which usually surround the problem. The major considerations are those surrounding the general philosophy of hire and use of capital—and its saving. However, from this point the practical applications differ radically.

The user of the plant or equipment will usually be expected to:

(a) negotiate with the maker or supplier;

(b) select equipment which is suitable for his purpose in every way;

(c) place his own purchase order and proceed in the normal manner through to intake;

(d) be responsible for maintenance and all other normal liabilities as if he were the owner.

TABLE 32. FACTORS TO BE CONSIDERED WHEN HIRING

Part 1: Advantages to the user which may be put forward by the hire company

(1) No capital outlay by the hirer, hence minimum disturbance to cash flow.

(2) User is not committed to a particular piece of plant which he may later find is not so suitable for purpose as another, possibly later or improved, model, and he should be able to change.

(3) Obsolescence is avoided, company can (regularly/periodically) update their equipment.

(4) Hire company has a vested interest in the maintenance of its equipment.

(5) The hire company may work on a "short life and replacement" basis. If so, the user *may* be assured of the latest model always being available.

(6) Hire company will wish its plant to be properly used, and may therefore provide training in its operation. (Training of operatives by plant suppliers is often very poor.)

(7) Plant companies claim that their standard hire conditions protect the hirer. (But *see* (11) in Part 2.) Principal forms of agreement are those of the Contractors' Plant Association and the Federation of Civil Engineering Contractors.

(8) Under common law "Where a chattel is hired there is an implied warranty that it shall be fit for the purpose for which it is hired as far as reasonable care and skill can make it": Judge Lewis in *Read* v. *Dean* (1949) KB 1880. (But *see* (13) in Part 2.)

(9) Plant hire firm will hold spares, and provide standby for breakdowns.

(10) Plant hire firm may be able to augment capacity at short notice.

(11) Hire company may have other services available to help at times of break-down or heavy overload of capacity.

TABLE 32. FACTORS TO BE CONSIDERED WHEN HIRING (*continued*)

(12) Records may be kept in detail by hire company thus saving clerical work by hirer.

(13) Hire avoids some acquisition cost, e.g. spares stocks/orders, etc.

(14) Hire company may provide technical/practical advice.

(15) Hiring and leasing are flexible forms of funding and negotiations should not be lengthy.

Part 2: Points for consideration by the proposed hirer

(1) Is capital available for purchase?

(2) Is a government grant available?

(3) Could capital be better used in another part of the plant?

(4) Does expected cash flow from purchase after all allowances and costs exceed costs of hire on a comparable basis of use?

(5) How much of the hire company's hire charges represent its oncost *and profit*? Are these reasonable?

(6) Is the hire company reasonably near at hand?

(7) Does it always give prompt service in the event of breakdown?

(8) Do risks of non-availability exceed costs of owning?

(9) Ownership usually involves the costs of carrying spares.

(10) *But*, hire may also involve the hirer in the cost of carrying spares; this must be part of the negotiations.

(11) Standard forms of hire companies are mostly designed to protect their own interests and exempt them from common law liabilities. Always obtain legal advice for major hire agreements.

(12) Ownership may assist in the general diversification of plant, in loading and in diversifying the end-product.

(13) Plant must comply with Health and Safety at Work Act and all the commitments which arise from it. Ownership does not avoid this nor does hire.

(14) Ownership confers rights of alteration, transfer, sale and scrapping of plant.

(15) Ownership makes the user independent of the hire company which may not always have plant available.

(16) Is utilisation factor of plant increasing? At what rate?

(17) Is utilisation factor decreasing? At what rate?

(18) Is size of plant offered and available adequate for needs now and in the future?

(19) Negotiations for hire at irregular intervals may be as costly as those for purchase on a once-only basis.

NOTE:

For further considerations regarding hire of accommodation for stores, etc., see *Storehouse*

During the currency of the agreement with the finance company the ownership rests with them, and they, as owner, receive any statutory reliefs or grants which the lessee should make sure are reflected in the rates of payment. Other points to consider include the following.

(a) Would higher payments in earlier years be warranted so that more cash would be available in later years for maintenance or extra stock to meet increased production?

(b) In the case of conventional leasing or lease-purchase what are the arrangements for disposal or extended reduced rates when a conventional lease is terminated, or in the case of lease-purchase the final fee for transfer of ownership from the finance company to the user?

As in the case of "liquidated damages" (see Chapter 16), keen foresight is essential.

OTHER DEVELOPMENTS IN PURCHASE ORDER METHODS

What of the future pattern of ordering? Can acquisition costs be cut without losing control or destroying communication and record, and above all without destroying competition? Supplies should always be on the look-out for new ideas and the following are some which may be worth a thought. (Numbers refer back to Table 31.)

(9(b)) BLANK-CHEQUE ORDERING SYSTEM. A large American plant places its orders up to about £350 value in this manner. Each purchase order incorporates a blank cheque made out in favour of the supplier. On executing the order he fills in the value and deposits the cheque in his bank. It should be pointed out that banks in most countries do not favour this style of business transaction.

(3(b)) IN-PLANT STORES, a scheme also known in the USA as the "honour system", is now operating successfully in the UK. Special security arrangements may be needed and checks made on the amounts invoiced claiming for "kinds and quantities" of supplies it is stated have been consumed.

Under this scheme the vendor's salesmen visit the customer's stores at regular intervals, top up the bins, and initiate replenishment orders for those which have been replenished. This method can make savings in acquisition costs. While it could easily be open to abuse, this can be checked by an overall control on the value of goods taken into the stores.

It is essential when managing this type of arrangement to ensure that stock levels are agreed initially with the supplier and that during its operation the supplier does not inflate stock-holding without prior agreement with the purchaser.

(3(*f*)) "CONSIGNMENT STOCKS" is an increasing practice amongst larger users of supplies. As in the case of "in-plant stores" and "sale-or-return" goods (3(*b*)), it gives the purchaser possession of supplies on credit against use, except, of course, that "sale-or-return" is usually confined to the domestic market—few suppliers of industrial supplies would welcome their return!

The following are some of the advantages (+) and disadvantages (−) of consignment stocks, in-plant stores and sale-or-return.

(*a*) Purchaser obtains free credit. (+)

(*b*) Purchaser has assurance of availability. (+)

(*c*) Schemes may help to stabilise prices. (+)

(*d*) Purchaser becomes bailee for supplier's goods. (−)

(*e*) Purchaser must also meet storage costs. (−)

(*f*) Purchaser avoids interest on outlay for stock.(+)

(*g*) Supplier pays interest on stock.(!) (+). . .

(*h*) But, supplier may try to recoup interest in price. (?)

(*i*) Access must be given to supplier for inspection of his goods at reasonable times. (−)

(*j*) Supplier gains a "captive" customer. (−)

(*k*) Supplier assured of sales. (±)

For the privileges (*e*), (*j*) and (*k*), the purchasing officer should extract some cash benefit for his company.

(2(*i*), (*j*), (*k*)) ON-LINE COMPUTERISED ORDERING is a cost-cutting technique for purchasing. It can be used between two or more firms with on-line computers and computer terminals. In this case arrival at the reorder level automatically results in the issuing of the order, thus virtually eliminating order lead time.

CONCLUSIONS. The trends suggested by these methods lead towards a reduction in the number of suppliers, fewer purchasing staff, and the shifting of the load on to the supplier's shoulders. This latter point may mean that the supplier adds to his cost by taking on extra staff. The purchasing department loses control of the commercial position and initiative passes into the hands of the supplier, together with the possibility of the supplier increasing his profit at the purchaser's expense.

CHAPTER 16

The Law on Supplies and Materials Management

INTRODUCTION

Constraints

Supplies and materials management embraces such a wide area that it is impossible to do more than mention a few of the points of law which are relevant. The constraints which prevented wider treatment of the subject may themselves be helpful to readers in avoiding legal pitfalls. Some of these constraints are therefore listed below.

(a) Overseas readers should note that mostly English law is quoted in this volume.

(b) Home readers should take nothing for granted: plant may comply with overseas but not with UK laws, regarding pollution, safety, etc.

(c) Do not assume laws are uniform throughout a state, e.g. Scottish law differs from English.

(d) State laws may be supplemented by local laws, e.g. planning.

(e) Laws are changing rapidly to meet technological and social needs, and as a result of internationalisation: e.g. Law of the Sea, UN Conventions, EEC Directives.

(f) Much recent legislation is intended primarily to provide consumer protection, not to protect business buyers.

(g) The scope of legislation has been widening to protect consumers, workers, users and the public.

(h) Ignorance of the law has never been any defence.

(i) Where any contract relies more than usually upon statutory provisions, it is prudent to make clear reference to them on the order documents.

(j) Nothing in this book should be construed as giving legal advice or interpretation of the law.

It is emphasised that no amount of reading can replace consultation on legal matters, but those engaged in supplies and materials management should have a basic understanding of the matters covered in this chapter. References to legal aspects are also made in the specialist chapters (*see* index under *law*).

Sources of information

Journals such as *Purchasing and Supply Management* (monthly) and *Procurement Weekly*, both published by the Institute of Purchasing and Supply, give space to legal matters relating to Supplies. Those requiring more detailed and broader information on legal matters should refer to specialist publications such as *The Buyer*, published by Monitor Press and *Current Action*, published by Sweet and Maxwell.

All engaged in supplies and materials management, particularly those in smaller firms lacking specialists in this area should be encouraged to make use of officers in the public services: local inspectors of the Health and Safety Executive, fire officers, police, local authority surveyors, planners and engineers. All are usually anxious to co-operate and give advice—much of which may have legal implications.

Guidance is also provided by some professional bodies such as the Institute of Purchasing and Supply (*see* Appendix I).

LAW OF CONTRACT

The law of contract [131][132][133][138] leans heavily upon the Sale of Goods Act (1893), now consolidated into the Sale of Goods Act 1979, which came into force on 1st January 1980.

The following rules are some of those vital for the existence of a binding contract.

(*a*) The parties must communicate their intention. "This may be in writing (with or without seal) or by word of mouth, or partly in writing and partly by word of mouth, or may be implied from the conduct of the parties."

(*b*) There must be an "unqualified offer and acceptance" by both seller and buyer, a *consensus ad idem.*

(*c*) There must be "consideration", i.e. money or money's worth must pass in settlement of the contract. Mere "procurement" does not necessarily imply the "passing of consideration" and may therefore lead to complications if treated as a contract.

(*d*) There must be "intention" to create contractual relationships and action.

(*e*) The objectives, etc. of the contract must themselves be legal and possible.

Verbal orders, communications and instructions

A party to a verbal (or other unwritten) contract may find he is bound by conditions habitually included in the supplier's written contract or acknowledgment. (This commitment may apply even though the buyer has not done sufficient business with the supplier for it to be deemed "a course of dealing".)

There is, however, a further warning needed regarding verbal (or written) comments relating to an order already placed. A Supplies or functional staff member may suggest a minor modification and imply that the supplier shall proceed accordingly. In the absence of documentary evidence to the contrary the verbal instruction is likely to prevail, even though the "minor" modification is found later to involve a major change in price.

The problems of verbal communication apply with special force to the comments and communications made by a purchasing officer, because he is the company's official "agent" and thus bears a special responsibility in this matter (*see also* below).

AXIOM: Verbal communications bind.

Purchasing officers as agents

The legal implications of "agency" should be made clear by management to all staff, but particularly to Supplies staff and purchasing officers.

In *Sika Contracts* v. *Giloseglen*, Mr Justice Kerr said that: "A person who is in fact an agent in the sense that he has someone standing behind him such as an employer or a principal can nevertheless enter into a contract in such a way that he becomes personally liable to the other contracting party." This case concerned an actual commitment through a purchase contract initiated by an exchange of letters in which the defendant (who made the commitment) made no reference to the fact that he was acting on behalf of his principals, and found himself personally liable for the contract.

Purchase order forms should be printed with a suitable endorsement beneath the signature space, such as "for and on behalf of X.Y.Z. Ltd.".

However, what is the position if the document is not an order but a chaser letter, or bringing forward delivery, or making some other change in the contract? Greville Janner *Purchasing and Supply Management*, April 1978) suggests that: "The element of personal responsibility should of course make you doubly careful when you instruct others (a supplier, for example) to act on your behalf. The company delegates to you and must avoid giving you an implied or apparent authority which you should not have."

When signing the contract form of a supplier it is particularly important to study the small print to ensure that it does not include a clause which may attach personal liability for the contract to the person who signed it.

Inadvertent commitments to contract

There are numerous ways in which a firm may commit itself to a supplier without intending to do so, or in which an unscrupulous supplier may make such a commitment leaving the reluctant purchaser in a very vulnerable position with little means of escape. Some examples are given below: these apply whether written or verbal.

(a) Use of supplier's order form (*see* Chapter 15).

(b) Change in specification by technical or other staff.

(c) Delivery date commitment by progress staff.

(d) Lengthy negotiations with work carried out at experimental or prototype stages.

(e) Unguarded comments or remarks made during a discussion at supplier's works, on site, or elsewhere.

Lord Diplock (*Manchester City Council* v. *Gibson*) stated that: "There may be certain types of contract, though I think they are exceptional, which do not fit easily into the normal analysis of contract being constituted by offer and acceptance: but a contract alleged to have been made by an exchange of correspondence between the parties in which successive communications other than the first are in reply to one another is not one of these." Despite this apparent weakening of "contract by inadvertence" the prudent purchasing officer should insist at the outset of any sequence of correspondence that no binding agreement shall arise until all the terms have been incorporated into the formal contract documents.

Signing of orders by unauthorised staff

This practice facilitates "trick selling". A note on a company's purchase order form that "only orders signed by the purchasing officer are valid" has little effect when the trick salesman presents his own company's order form to an undesignated and unauthorised member of staff for signature. The discipline must be applied internally so that only authorised staff sign purchase orders—a notice in the waiting or enquiry room stating this may suffice.

A salesman may present an order form for what he may state is "only a sample quantity at a nominal price" but which turns out later to be six years' supply at twice market value! A gift may accompany the transaction, and once completed the salesman will return later and seek to relieve the possible embarrassment of the

employee by extracting a further order and offering a larger gift—
and so on.

Once the salesman's order is signed the company is in an extremely vulnerable position in regard to the formation of a valid contract.
The law gives little protection in a business transaction as distinct
from a domestic or retail sale.

If the ruse is discovered in time—which is unlikely—the document should be cancelled at once and the firm given the information
quoted earlier. If too late because the goods have been delivered,
these should be impounded and the firm told that they must come
and collect them and that storage charges will be made until they
do so. They may also be told that if they do not collect them in a
reasonable time they will be returned carriage forward. However,
there is a risk that if they are returned the firm will either deny
they were received or say they were received "damaged". Recorded
delivery of some kind is essential.

General comments

(1) INTENTIONS. In settling disputes, lawyers look for the intentions
of the parties. Written evidence in the form of orders *and* amendments may be vital. Clarity, completeness, and accuracy of orders
are therefore essential as "documents of record".

(2) PENALTY CLAUSES. Courts will not enforce conditions which are
designed to inspire "terror" such as penalty clauses. Foreseeable
losses should be written into the original contract as "liquidated
damages" agreed in advance.

(3) EXPENSES incidental to making delivery fall on the seller (unless
otherwise arranged), those of preparing for unloading and receiving
at intake usually fall on the purchaser.[134]

(4) CAVEAT EMPTOR. Stemming from ancient case law to protect the
weak from the strong, there is a tendency for mercantile law to
protect the holder of property and hence to protect the vendor
rather than the buyer, thus *caveat emptor*. (*See* Chapter 15, subcontract orders.)

(5) CAVEAT VENDITOR (let the seller beware) could be the implication
of much recent legislation, but a warning is given to industrial and
other business buyers against making the assumption that the legislation has been drafted in every case to protect them. Far from this
being so, many of the new statutes are explicitly restricted to consumer sales. It is essential, therefore, that the purchasing officer
seeking advice from his lawyer or reading articles and books on the

subject makes a clear distinction between a "consumer sale" and a "business sale". Unfortunately, the distinction is none too clear in the various Acts themselves and probably the best explanation (by implication) was that given in the Supply of Goods (Implied Terms) Act 1973, s. 4(7) which read as follows (note especially the words in italics).

> In this section "consumer sale" means a sale of goods (*other than a sale by auction or by competitive tender*) by a seller in the course of a business where the goods:
> (a) are of a type ordinarily bought for private use or consumption; and
> (b) *are sold to a person who does not buy or hold himself out as buying them in a course of a business.*

(6) "MERCHANTABLE QUALITY" AND "STATEMENT OF SUITABILITY FOR PURPOSE" are covered by the Sale of Goods Act 1979. A statement by the purchaser of his intended use of the goods now shifts the onus of suitability on to the seller. The latter could, in the past, escape this commitment by merely telling the purchaser that he rejected any liability in this respect. Recent legislation denies him this escape in the case of a consumer sale. In a business sale, however, an exclusion clause is still permitted but is ineffective if it is neither reasonable nor fair to allow the seller to rely on it. (*See* Unfair Contract Terms Act 1977.)

It is clear that those who manufacture and sell for the consumer market will be committed to "merchantable quality" and "suitability" clauses for the consumer but may find themselves unprotected in this regard from their own suppliers. Attention is also called to the Consumer Safety Act 1978 (*see* below).

"Merchantable quality" is given a statutory definition by the 1979 Sale of Goods Act: "Merchantable quality [means] fit for the purpose or purposes for which goods of that kind are commonly bought and as it is reasonable to expect having regard to any description applied to them, the price (if relevant) and all other relevant circumstances" (s. 14(6)). A related provision is the implied condition that goods will be "reasonably fit" for the particular purpose which a buyer has indicated to the seller *before* the agreement was entered into (s. 14(3)).

TERMS AND CONDITIONS OF PURCHASE

Terms and conditions of purchase (or contract) are of less importance to the seller than his own terms and conditions of sale which he will seek to impose.[135] It is essential to bear in mind the risks to any contract if purchasing terms and (particularly) conditions

TABLE 33. THE MECHANICS OF ORDERING: GENERAL AND LEGAL EFFECTS
(Superior figures refer to notes which follow.)

	Action	By	General effects	Legal effects
1.	Advertisement or mail shot, etc.	Seller	Offer of wares or services to all comers.	Nil—provided the advertisement and its contents are legal.
2.	Enquiry to seller	Buyer	A "prod" to the seller to prepare prices and quote (verbal or written).	Nil—unless some other intention is shown, e.g. "enquiry-proceed" (*see* Chapter 15).
3.	Quotation, or price tag in a shop	Seller	"Information" and offer to treat (negotiate).	Usually nil unless and until the buyer takes positive action.
4.	Negotiation, offer and counter-offer	Buyer and seller	Buyer and seller reach a *consensus ad idem.*	Nil until both parties reach "unqualified agreement".
5.	Communication, order to the seller (written or verbal)[2]	Buyer	Offer, or "unqualified acceptance"[1] of the offer of the seller.	Notice of intention to enter into a contract.
6.	Acknowledgment of order (verbal or written)[2] or any work done by seller on "specific" or "unascertained" goods	Seller	Acceptance of order and recognition of creation of contract.	Contract legally established provided acceptance by both parties is unqualified.[3]
7.	Amendments to order[2]	Buyer	May radically change the contract in substance, terms or conditions.	Binding on all parties when agreed whether written or verbal once there has been acceptance.
8.	Progress chasing[2]	Buyer	Keeps prodding the seller: is delivery "of the essence" of the contract?[4]	Places the onus on the seller to deliver and on buyer to accept.
9.	Supplies delivered or notified ready for delivery, and invoiced	Seller	"Performance"[5] by seller of his part of the contract (conditions of contract must make this clear).	Full legal protection of seller if he has given satisfactory "performance" of contract.
10.	Packing of supplies (includes containerisation, etc.)	Seller	Covers transit only unless contract covers other aspects.	Must be suitable for safe arrival at buyer's works

TABLE 33 contd. THE MECHANICS OF ORDERING: GENERAL AND
LEGAL EFFECTS
(Superior figures refer to notes which follow.)

Action	By	General effects	Legal effects
11. Transit and tendering of goods at intake point[7]	Seller or his nominee	Off-loading by, or assistance from, buyer.[6]	Seller must select suitable transport.
12. Receipt and inspection	Buyer	Commits the buyer to accept or reject and notify supplier in a "reasonable time".	Law now protects the buyer provided he is not in breach and notifies supplier.
13. Work on or use of any kind of the goods	Buyer	Commits the buyer to complete contract.	Property passes when the parties intend, or when the buyer performs any act inconsistent with ownership by the seller.
14. Invoice sent to buyer[8]	Seller	Calls upon buyer to complete his portion of the contract.	Obliges the buyer to complete his portion of the contract provided the seller has made a satisfactory "performance".
15. Payment (passing of "consideration")	Buyer	Absolute discharge of contract by buyer.	But contract can also be discharged in other ways.[9]

NOTES TO TABLE 33:

(1) Whether "offer" or "acceptance" depends upon the angle from which the transaction is viewed, i.e. from Seller or buyer. However, in either case there must be "unqualified agreement" by all parties for the contract to be valid.

(2) Again it should be noted that communications are binding whether written or verbal and may change the character of a contract during its currency. In all cases the onus is liable to be upon the purchaser to ensure that the communications are clear and are understood by the recipient.

(3) The onus is upon the buyer to check the terms and conditions of any seller's acknowledgment (see Chapter 17). Unless he communicates any disagreement with them to the seller, the buyer will be deemed to have accepted them, regardless of his own terms and conditions excluding this (unless he is a statutory body).

(4) The Sale of Goods Act 1979 states merely that "Any stipulation as to 'time is of the essence of the contract' depends upon the terms of the contract." It is essential, therefore, on contracts where delivery is crucial to communicate this *and* to ensure that the supplier understands and accepts this condition.

(5) "Performance" of the contract includes all work (or service) started or carried out in compliance with the contract. "Performance" is the term used for the completion of the obligations by the seller to the other party to the contract.

(6) The supplier "tenders", i.e. "holds out goods" at the intake point for the buyer to "take". Where there are any special requirements (e.g. for cranage, low-loaders or fork-trucks) these must be made clear in the contract, since the buyer is normally responsible for off-loading arrangements.

(7) The intake point must be made clear at the time of making the contract. Unless other intentions are agreed "the place of delivery is the *seller's* place of business" (Sale of Goods Act 1979, s. 29).

(8) Invoice must agree with the contract and must not contain any change which has not been previously notified and agreed with the buyer (*see* Chapter 22).

(9) Contracts may be "discharged" in the legal sense by "frustration" (e.g. goods no longer exist), cancellation and so on.

conflict with those of the seller so that an "unqualified agreement" between both parties is prevented.

The "mechanics" of ordering and their general and legal effects are summarised in Table 33.

General comments

(a) If terms and conditions are given elsewhere than on the face of an order, a note calling attention to their location must appear on the face of the order.

(b) Clauses which are likely to be rejected by suppliers should be avoided. If they are important, they should be negotiated and the facts stated on the face of the order.

(c) Exceptional requirements should always appear on the face of the order. This applies with extra force to any having special legal implications.

(d) The supplier should not be expected to wade through thirty clauses of small print in feint type on the reverse of the form only to discover that "the customer can receive goods only on certain days at certain times of the day", etc.

(e) Clauses which are contrary to "customs of the supplier's trade" should not be included. For example, most carriers of liquids use their own dip-stick carried on the vehicle and calibrated for that tanker. Conditions by a purchaser calling for the use of his own dip-stick would conflict with the supplier's terms and conditions and the practice of his trade and would require negotiation.

(*f*) Clauses which merely repeat terms for which enactments already give statutory protection should be omitted.

(*g*) It is worth including:

(*i*) an omnibus clause stating that the company requires its suppliers "to comply with the Sales of Goods Act and all relevant statutory obligations, including the Health and Safety at Work Act, and EEC Regulations";

(*ii*) a clause stating that "any amendment (or cancellation) must be regarded as invalid unless confirmed on an 'order amendment form' signed by the company's purchasing officer, whether or not the amendment is accompanied by any other communication" and "a written acknowledgment will be required from the supplier in all such cases".

(*h*) On important contracts the supplier's terms and conditions should always be checked with those of his trade association, if any.

AXIOM: Only fools ignore small print.

OTHER LEGAL REQUIREMENTS

Some other Acts and judgments are given below, quoting briefly points applicable to Supplies. Reference should always be made to the full text for details.

Law Reform (Frustrated Contracts) Act 1943

Loss of profit arising from contractual arrangements can be claimed and is not infrequently awarded. However, in such cases the buyer is obliged to reduce his loss by whatever reasonable means are open to him. The buyer is expected to be fair to the other party even though the latter may be the wrongdoer. The 1943 Act lays down the parties' rights to recover moneys paid and compensation for partial performance. It only applies where a contract which is subject to English law has become impossible of performance or has been frustrated, the contracting parties as a result being discharged from the further performance of the contract. The date of frustration is crucial to any claim.

Arbitration Act 1950

This act governs mercantile disputes where they are referred to arbitration in the following ways:

(*a*) by consent of the parties, i.e. because there is a clause in the contract;

(*b*) called for by statute in certain cases;

(*c*) order of a court.

Arbitration proceedings can save time which would otherwise be protracted if normal processes of law were followed—provided the arbitration is successful. If it is not, then lawyers' time must be added.

The Health and Safety at Work etc. Act 1974

This Act is probably the most important legislation in the safety field and has counterparts in most countries of the developed world and, increasingly, in the developing world.[136] The principal change is an emphasis upon the responsibility of all concerned with the management and use of materials and equipment and their effects upon not only workers but also the general public. The new Act co-ordinates existing statutes and sets up machinery to enforce them more vigorously than hitherto. (*See Storehouse* for the practical implications of this Act.)

The Road Traffic Act 1974

This Act affects materials management in so far as it controls the conditions of vehicles which transport materials and goods. However, purchasing officers must not overlook its more direct implications upon their work where it covers tests on vehicles and spares and their specification and use. EEC regulations should also be studied if goods are either brought in from, or shipped to, mainland states in the EEC.

The Control of Pollution Act 1974

This Act has implications for supplies and materials management outside the negative aspect of controlling pollution. Local authorities are required to examine ways of promoting reclamation of waste and are given a wide framework of powers for this purpose (*see also* Chapter 25). Local By-laws should also be studied.

Restrictive Trade Practices Act 1956

Restrictive trade practices[138][139] are covered by an Act of 1956 and subsequent enactments provide for:

(*a*) the appointment of a Registrar of Restrictive Trading Agreements;

(*b*) the setting up of a Restrictive Practices Court.

Agreements such as the BEAMA price variation clauses are registered with the Registrar.

The Secretary of State for Trade may, by order, apply the provisions of the Act to *any* class of "information agreement" which aims to provide information between firms of "prices charged, terms of supply, costs, quantities or description of goods, processes of manufacture, or persons and places supplied".

There are a number of exemptions, such as agreements for supply between two persons who are not members of or do not constitute a "trade association". Wherever purchasing officers suspect that an "information agreement" is in action they should seek legal advice to ensure that competition is freely maintained.

The Monopolies and Mergers Commission, when investigating complaints regarding a company's price and supply policy, look for "evidence of the company having sought to build up or maintain a monopoly position by, for example, acquiring competitors or by systematic predatory trading practices aimed at the prevention or removal of competition" (*Commission Report*, February 1981). Other practices which might be deemed to be against the public interest include requiring distributors of the main product:

(*a*) to purchase ancillary equipment for use with the main product from the same company;

(*b*) not to handle the main product from other suppliers for a specified time after the contract itself has ended.

The Restrictive Practices Court has a strong "moral" effect upon trading as the following example shows. The Institute of Purchasing and Supply was vigorously involved in objections to a scheme which a manufacturer's association drew up in 1977, whereby its members agreed minimum prices and quotas based upon past market shares. The Institute claimed that:

(*a*) the scheme prevented buyers from choosing freely;

(*b*) orders given to one supplier might be executed by another;

(*c*) delivery dates could be extended so that a supplier could by this means avoid exceeding his quota, under the trading agreement.

Upon being called to defend the agreement before the Restrictive Practices Court the manufacturers' association withdrew its case. (It should be borne in mind that the onus is upon the defendant in such cases to show that the agreement is "not against public interests".)

Misrepresentation Act 1967

This Act curtailed attempts to exclude liability for misrepresentation —though not of breach of contract. Provisions relating to exclusion clauses were later repealed and re-enacted in the Unfair Contract Terms Act 1977.

Finance Act 1971

Section 45(1) establishes the principle of leasing to business and industry where the lessee will ultimately become the owner of the subject of the lease (i.e. machinery, plant, etc.) and states that in such an event "these shall be treated as belonging to him". It is important when negotiating any of the numerous forms of lease, e.g.

hire, "finance lease", "open-ended lease", "sell and lease back", "purchase lease", etc. that the purchasing officer shall establish his company's commitments in the terms of this Act. (Where the ownership will never pass to the hirer the scheme is a rental.)

Supply of Goods (Implied Terms) Act 1973

Clauses in this Act excluding liability for breach of the terms implied into sale of goods and hire-purchase contracts have since been re-enacted in the Unfair Contract Terms Act 1977.

"Retention of title"

An important principle for buyers was laid down in the famous *Romalpa Case,* which was upheld by the Court of Appeal in 1976.[137] Retention clauses provide for the following.

(a) Title to goods remains with the seller until goods have been paid for in full.

(b) The seller may recover the goods, or the proceeds of sale if the buyer sells the goods before payment in full has been made. This can apply whether the goods are sold separately as received, or have been embodied into an end-product. However, if the supplier of goods wishes to retain title in goods which he knows will be used in a manufacturing process, he must write an express term to that effect into the contract (Lord Justice Bridge). (*See also* later cases.)

Loss and damage

Loss and damage were ruled upon by Lord Justice Scarman in 1977 in regard to s. 14(1) of the Sale of Goods Act 1893. The principle to be applied was that once loss was within the contemplation of the parties the amount of damages should not be restricted merely because the precise degree of loss could not have been anticipated beforehand. Lord Scarman ruled that this principle shall apply not just with physical injury but also to cover the loss of market or profit.

Consumer protection

The Consumer Transactions (Restrictions on Statements) Order 1976 (SI 1976 No. 1813) came into effect on 1st November 1978. Although not concerned with trade between businesses, the Order means that it is important to ensure that designers do not call for, nor Supplies staff procure, supplies which would need some "restrictive statement" when the goods are ultimately sold to the consumer.[138]

Unfair Contract Terms Act 1977

This Act extends certain irrevocable rights to consumers, but also has an important implication for industrial and commercial buyers. In a business sale, although an exclusion clause is still permitted to the seller, it is ineffective if it is neither fair nor reasonable to allow the seller to rely upon it. This Act also applies to transactions between businessmen where the standard terms and conditions of one of the parties have been accepted by both for the purposes of the contract. In that case, subject to the test of "reasonableness", the other party may not set such terms and conditions aside at a later date.

Documents

Documents associated with contracts must be referred to upon the face of the contract document (i.e. the purchase order). A suitable form of words would be as follows: "The goods shall comply with specification X.Y.Z. attached." No enclosures of standards, and particularly drawings, however important, may be legally binding with the contract document (e.g. purchase order form) unless actually and clearly referred to upon the face of the document.

Notice particularly that if a supplier introduces a clause after a binding contract has been made such a clause is void without agreement having been made with the purchaser.

European patent law

European patent law is embodied in the following two conventions.

(a) The Convention on the grant of European Patents.

(b) The Convention for the European Patent for the Common Market (the Community Patent Convention CPC).

The CPC is intended to create a unitary patent law within the Common Market and also to harmonise certain aspects of national patent laws. Those buying goods from abroad need to check any patents against the new rules: similarly, the purchase of patented embodiment goods for shipment overseas may need careful scrutiny for protection.

It can be presumed that buyer and seller understand the restrictive effects of patent and copyright law. Negotiations between them should explore and cover these matters where relevant. However, they must also both be alert to possible third party implications—numerous cases have arisen where a third party has successfully sued for infringement.

Performance bonds and guarantees

Performance bonds and guarantees may have important implications in major contracts where continuity of supply, quality or other aspects are vital to the purchaser. They are frequently employed in the USA, EEC and EFTA states, and local authorities in the UK. The Confederation of British Industry has produced a "CBI Brief" which explains the use of performance bonds and guarantees.[140] It also gives examples of their use.

Since the reader may find his firm at the receiving end of such arrangements he should investigate how they may affect his own contracts with suppliers.

Product liability, Consumer Safety Act 1978
Legislation dealing with product liability[141] has been almost inevitable since the Law Commission, the Pearson Commission and the European Economic Community all advocated such measures. Apart from the UK legislation, an EEC Directive came into operation in 1979.

Under the new laws it should be possible for the consumer to sue for any injury against the manufacturer if the cause can be traced back to his product.

Legal action will require knowledge of the chain of supply throughout the whole manufacturing process. A heavy responsibility may thus be laid upon Supplies and production staff to keep records of identifications of supplies embodied in products. Close liaison with design staff and other specifiers of supplies will also be essential.

Insurance cover against product liability may be essential where the manufacturer sells direct to the user and has strict liability under the Sale of Goods Act 1979 to supply goods of merchantable quality and fit for a particular purpose, or where he is liable to the ultimate user in case of his negligence even where there is no direct contractual relationship between manufacturer and user. However, there is a strong possibility that the insurance company may insert an exclusion clause in respect of many forms of claim. It is therefore good practice to employ an insurance broker to check the cover provided and to see that there is no loophole through which the insurance company may escape the very liabilities which the insured wishes to cover.

Competition Act 1980
This Act aims to control anti-competitive practices, which are defined as "courses of conduct which have, or are intended to have, or are likely to have the effect of restricting or distorting or preventing competition in connection with the production, supply or acquisition of goods in the UK". Possible examples which may result in investigation by statutory bodies are "tie-in sales", "full-line forcing", "rental only contracts" and possibly "long-term supply contracts".

Supply of Goods and Services Act 1982

In the past it had been held that where the supplier actually performed a service (such as construction) in addition to the supply of materials, the contract was "for work and materials" and not a "contract for the supply of goods" so that the Sale of Goods Act did not apply. The Supply of Goods and Services Act remedies this deficiency.

The contractor is required to supply goods which conform to the contract description and which are of merchantable quality and reasonably fit for their purpose. In business transactions these clauses may be subjected to a "reasonable" exclusion clause agreed between the parties.

Contracts for the supply of a service are subject to the following three rules.

(a) Where no time is specified for completion, it must be in a "reasonable" time.

(b) Where a price has not been agreed beforehand that charge must be "reasonable".

(c) The supplier is expected to perform his task with "reasonable" care and skill except "where some higher duty is imposed" such as where the contractor gave a firm guarantee of suitability for purpose.

Throughout this chapter and this volume the term "reasonable" is used in its legal sense and refers to "a question of fact" as determined by a court of law when taking account of all the relevant facts applying to a case.

CHAPTER 17

Order Acknowledgments

INTRODUCTION

An order acknowledgment is a key document in a contract. Because of this, some purchasing officers insist that an acknowledgment shall be obtained against every purchase order. However, such tight control is wasteful and should be unnecessary (*see* Chapter 3, Introduction).

WHEN TO REQUIRE ACKNOWLEDGMENTS

Immediate goods
On routine or ex-stock orders, "middlemen" do not send acknowledgments. Nothing is gained by chasing for these except frustration, increased costs, and loss of good relationships. (*See* below, legal implications.)

Future goods
Urgent, difficult and costly orders for "future goods" should always be acknowledged and always incorporated into the progress procedure at the order stage. Complex, high value and technical orders need careful checking at an early stage to ensure that all is according to plan.

Acknowledgments of amendments and cancellations
In Chapter 15 it was pointed out that special attention should be given to these. They are all "documents of exception" and can easily fail to alert those engaged in the production of goods. For this reason the amendment or cancellation should bear a note asking the supplier to confirm receipt and acceptance. If all acknowledgments pass through the progress section, this will avert the unfortunate consequences—not unknown—of a progress chaser urging a cancelled

order! The progress section should follow up all amendments and cancellations for the necessary acknowledgment.

However, there is a further implication of a serious nature. If the supplier acknowledges an amendment or cancellation and wishes to claim amendment or cancellation charges, he must do so in a reasonable time, otherwise he is likely to lose the right to claim.

Special action
Special attention should be given to ensure that satisfactory acknowledgments are obtained for the following.
 (a) "Exceptional" orders of all kinds.
 (b) Orders planned on long horizon, FSAs, etc.
 (c) High-value orders.
 (d) Highly technical and complex requirements.
 (e) Overseas goods.
 (f) New suppliers, terms and conditions, etc.
 (g) Letters of intent.
 (h) Urgent orders.
 (i) Amendments and cancellations.
 (j) Production reservation orders (see Chapter 18).

LEGAL IMPLICATIONS OF ACKNOWLEDGMENTS

There is no legal obligation on a supplier to send a formal acknowledgment of an order. In fact, the supplier acknowledges his contractual obligations directly he undertakes any work in relation to the goods ordered (for example, in taking them from his stock bin and transferring them to his despatch bay, see Chapter 16, Table 33).

Where "future goods" are involved there may be a considerable lapse of time before there is any tangible evidence from the supplier that he has accepted any contractual liability. In such cases a formal acknowledgment can be very important. It is the view of some authorities that an acknowledgment is essential for a legally binding contract to be brought into existence. This, however, is not the case. In fact, the submission of such a document may "at a stroke" either render voidable or even void the whole contract if the terms and conditions of the acknowledgment are at variance materially with those on the order. They may then destroy the consensus ad idem without which a binding contract cannot exist.

However, usually the supplier will wish to ensure that his contractual position is satisfactorily established and will have noted that the purchaser has no doubt included terms and conditions which are greatly to his own advantage and to the disadvantage of his supplier.

If the supplier fails to tell the purchaser of his disagreement by acknowledgment or other form of communication a court may well decide in favour of the purchaser in any subsequent dispute regarding the contract and its terms and conditions.

In any case the court will look for "reasonable" implications in the contract and above all the "intentions of the parties". Their conclusions may or may not favour the purchaser. It must be remembered that the law tends to protect the holder of property against powerful claimants who may or may not have good title.

On the other hand, the court may decide that because of his long association in the past with the supplier, a "course of dealing" has been established and the purchaser could have been expected to know the terms and conditions of the supplier without waiting for a formal acknowledgment.

Finally, the court must also have in mind the Unfair Contract Terms Act. For example, it is important to make sure that no additional clauses in favour of the supplier have crept into the contract at the acknowledgment stage. An "exclusion clause" which may be reasonable to the supplier can render the goods "useless for purpose", e.g. the supplier might add at the acknowledgment stage a clause stating that: "There is no implied condition that the equipment which is the subject of this acknowledgment will perform satisfactorily in a corrosive environment." (*See* Chapter 6, corrosion technology.)

PROCEDURES

Methods of obtaining acknowledgments

(1) TEAR-OFF SLIP. Some purchasing officers incorporate a slip on the order form to be torn off, signed, and returned as acknowledgment by the supplier who usually carefully deletes any portion which obliges him to accept the purchaser's terms and conditions and attaches a copy of his own terms and conditions of sale. If the purchaser can persuade the supplier to sign and return his (the purchaser's) "acknowledgment of order" slip he may well be in a strong position to enforce his own terms and conditions instead of those of the supplier (*Butler Machine Tool* v. *Ex-Cell-O Corporation* (1979)). However, the most satisfactory results are obtained where the terms are agreed at the outset of the contract and nothing is left to chance or lawyers.

If the supplier "forgets" to return the form the purchaser must follow up his acknowledgment slips—a time-consuming and wasteful procedure.

(2) RETURN COPY. Some firms send an extra copy of each purchase

order for initialling and return in acknowledgment. This procedure is not recommended, because there is always the possibility of duplication taking place, even if the form is clearly marked, e.g. "copy for acknowledgment only, please return".

(3) DUPLICATE CONTRACT FORMS. Another method (especially where services are provided under a period contract) is for the supplier to submit duplicate contract forms to the customer, who is expected to sign and return one copy, retaining the second copy for file. In all such cases it is vital for the purchaser to scrutinise the supplier's terms and conditions because by signing the copy he has committed himself to them. One antidote is for the purchaser to attach a copy of his firm's order to the supplier's contract and endorse it with a note such as: "Unless you refer back to us we shall assume that for purposes of this contract you accept our terms and conditions".

Form of acknowledgment
A recommended form of acknowledgment is a copy of the instructions the supplier has issued to his own works or warehouse, i.e. a copy of the "works order" or warehouse "release note". The supplier's acknowledgment obliges the purchaser to accept the goods and pay for them—provided the quality is up to specification. If the goods as described on the acknowledgment are not what the customer *thought* he ordered, he may still be obliged to accept delivery if he takes no early correcting action. The purchaser must check the acknowledgment and tell the supplier of his disagreement regarding its description of the goods covered. It will be seen, therefore, that careful study of the acknowledgment is vital, and the tear-off slip or copy order give little or no protection if a mistake or change has been made by the supplier or the purchaser.

Follow-up arrangements
Follow-up arrangements for acknowledgments (where these are essential) should be incorporated into the normal procedure. The order copy for "progress" may be suitably coded where this is necessary, or the progress chaser may be left to use his own initiative—or to back up the instruction using his own experience.

Checking acknowledgments
Who shall receive acknowledgments and what they shall check can be a matter for debate. The following arrangements are suggested.
    (a) Pass to:
        (i) the progress chaser; and/or
        (ii) the purchasing officer;

(iii) the originator of the order if there is neither of the above.
(b) Check acknowledgment details with order, namely:
(i) delivery;
(ii) description;
(iii) quantity;
(iv) price;
(v) terms and conditions.

"Progress" have a primary responsibility for *(b)(i)*, but it is useful if they can be given a watching brief over *(b)(ii), (b)(iii)* and *(b)(iv)* as well.

Where there is any doubt as to the agreement of the acknowledgment with the order they should "fail safe" by referring it to the purchasing officer (or the originator of the need, if there is no purchasing officer). They should refer back in particular any acknowledgments for orders which fall within the categories listed above as requiring special action. There should of course be instant reaction if a supplier "forgets" to mention delivery!

Records of acknowledgments

Records of acknowledgments should be unnecessary as the document is already one of "record". However, copies of suppliers' terms and conditions of sale, which usually accompany acknowledgments, can be useful and should be checked on major orders by an appropriate member of staff against the copy in the "supplier file" (*see* Chapter 3, supplier records). In the case of regular suppliers it is most advisable to check on a regular, periodic or random basis that they have not changed their trading terms and conditions without notice—due to a merger, for example.

CHAPTER 18

Progress and Planning

INTRODUCTION

The function of progressing is referred to by the Americans as "expediting". Strictly speaking, this means "hastening" (delivery). Most of the effort of the average progress department, however, is fully absorbed in keeping deliveries "on time"!

The numbering of production periods in the manufacturing cycle of supplies can be a source of misunderstanding as regards delivery dates and promises of delivery. It is recommended that British Standard BS4760 "Numbering of weeks", be followed.

DELIVERY DATES

Experience shows that when a supplier says he will deliver in a particular period he means at the *end* of that period. This is not surprising when it is realised that most production managers are striving to achieve a production target by a certain date. Deliveries tend to be geared to this. It is one more variable which the stock controller must take into account.

So much confusion has occurred in the use of the words "despatch date" and "delivery date" that the National Economic Development Council has given the following definition.

"Delivery" should be interpreted by suppliers and purchasers as the date when *receipt* is required at the location of the purchaser. "Despatch" should always be interpreted as the date when the goods *leave* a certain specified location.

Causes of late delivery are discussed in Chapter 7, effects of external conditions.

DUTIES OF PROGRESSING AND INTEGRATION WITH PLANNING AND PURCHASING

Table 34 lists duties within the sphere of progressing or associated with it. The progress section may not carry out all these directly, but will need to be involved.

The work of progressing varies in importance as the materials become a higher percentage of total works output and the risk of losses due to stock-out become greater. It becomes more onerous, and more vital, in a seller's market where buyers—possibly in the same firm—are competing for supplies.

The job of progressing demands persistence, tact and a certain measure of of administrative ability (*see* Table 6). It calls for moral courage to keep users informed when the news is bad. There is always a tendency to delay "telling the worst" because it involves some loss of face, and one always hopes that things "may come right in the end"! This is the worst policy a progress section can follow. The production manager who knows in sufficient time that supplies will be delayed may be able to substitute other work or obtain and use substitute materials. If he is kept in ignorance, loss of production may be inevitable.

Like stock records, progress records are models of production, transport and delivery from the supplier. The staff employed must be dynamic—unlike the progress chaser who told the production manager he had "not chased the materials as requested because they were not due for chasing"—his chance to do so never recurred!

A major discipline is the exercise of diagnostic skill by the progressor to sort truth from fiction, the mere "put off" and excuse from the genuine problem—often at a distance of several hundred kilometres over an indifferent telephone line! It is hoped that Checklist 30 may assist in this process.

ORGANISATION OF PROGRESS SECTION

Staffing

The number of progress staff needed depends upon the number of orders which are "live" at any one time; the performance of suppliers; and the degree of importance to the firm of delivery in relation to the production plan. (*See* Figs. 12 and 13.)

Progressing may not be in the hands of Supplies staff but there are good reasons why it should be.

(*a*) The buying sections are automatically kept aware of the performance of suppliers.

(*b*) The purchasing department have orders to place, and delivery

347

TABLE 34. INTEGRATION OF PROGRESSING WITH PLANNING AND PURCHASING

Activity	Possible involvement of progress section
Requisition	Requisitioner may discuss reliability of suppliers' deliveries.
Enquiry	Purchasing officer may compare deliveries offered with past performance of suppliers who have quoted.
Letters of intent	Follow up for expiry of validity, renewal or cancellation.
Orders placed	Copies to progress section for progressing.
Acknowledgment of order placed	Progress to follow up for acknowledgment.[1]
Changes in delivery requirements	Deferring delivery ("de-progressing"), rescheduling, etc.[2]
Pre-urging	Progressing prior to due date to ensure programme is kept.
Normal progressing	Follow up on due date, etc.
Transportation	Co-ordinate orders to assist transport scheduling, return loads, etc.
Handling	Liaison on materials handling: off-loading, internal transport, etc.
Supplies' reports to management	Provide information on suppliers' performance.
Goods inwards	Progress section must be kept up-to-date to avoid "over-progressing" after goods have been received.[3]
Inspection of goods inwards	Progress ensure goods go forward for inspection or follow up for inspection at supplier's works.
Claims (goods inwards)	Progress ensure claims go forward urgently.[4]
Replacements of rejects, shortages, at intake	Progress follow up for replacements on an urgent basis.[5]
Stage payments	Confirm goods/plant delivered, work done, etc.
Test and commissioning	Progress ensure arrangements are satisfactory.
Rebates	Follow up for claims for payment, credit notes, etc.
Retention moneys	Progress follow up for clearance.
Hire of plant	Progress prompt return of plant which is finished with.
Return of equipment loaned to suppliers	(*See* Chapter 3, pattern, die and tool records.)

NOTES:

(1) Progressing for acknowledgments can be a useful progressing function (*see* Chapter 17, follow-up arrangements, and below, initiation of the progressing operation). (2) The progressing operation also includes "de-progressing" or deferment of supplies. Progress personnel should know the load on suppliers and delivery periods. On the other hand, negotiations for deferments should be in the hands of the purchasing officer. They represent a near (or actual) breach of contract and may require delicate handling. (3) Sometimes goods and equipment are left idle for long periods after they have been received. This may have bad effects on (*a*) the supplier (if he finds out), (*b*) the progressor (who loses his sense of urgency), and (*c*) the requisitioner (who becomes increasingly careless, and may tend to allow insufficient time for the supplies operation in the future). (4) Claims arising for non-arrival of goods and those which arrive damaged may be handled by the progress section, who have an important interest in keeping supplies moving. (5) Following up delivery of replacements for rejects may be within the ambit of the progress section, since these affect the overall delivery position, and for similar reasons the progress section should be kept informed of rejections at the inspection of goods inwards.

is often a valuable bargaining point.

(*c*) Where Supplies either control or are closely associated with transport and handling they can improve productivity by increasing the speed and efficiency of intake and handling.

(*d*) If properly integrated, Supplies should operate from the receipt of the requisition to the price check on the invoice. Progressing is obviously included within this cycle.

When the firm is small, progressing may be one of the many jobs done by different members of the staff. As the firm grows the progress job will normally be passed to the purchasing department. When growth passes a certain level, specialisation may further develop and progress and material planning may become an entirely separate function. It must, however, remain closely allied to Supplies and many consider it is better operated and controlled if it remains within the Supplies organisation.

Delegation of progressing

Progressing may with advantage be delegated in the following cases to the point of origin of the instructions or purchase orders.

(*a*) LPOs and SVOs should not require formal progressing.

(*b*) Call-off orders against FSAs and FSCs.

(*c*) Intakes to process plants: process control may be adequate.

(*d*) Depots and branches remote from a central purchasing department.

Centralisation of progressing

Centralisation of progressing has the following advantages.

(*a*) Reduction of time spent by executives in chasing supplies.

(*b*) Avoidance of success depending upon the loudness of the individual outcry of functional staff.

(*c*) Prevention of executives duplicating one another's efforts, cancelling one another's instructions, or competing with one another for the same supplies.

(*d*) Centralised progressing can co-ordinate efforts, plan, and follow a deliberate policy.

(*e*) An objective approach can be maintained both to own company needs and to the problems of suppliers.

(*f*) Can develop techniques which are suited to each supplier.

(*g*) Suppliers know with whom they must deal.

(*h*) Lines of communication are shortened and made more direct.

Allocation of work

Progress chasers may be allocated to groups of supplies. They then tend to become attached to the buyers for their group of supplies, which gives them short, direct lines of communication, and also the ability to provide a rapid picture of the delivery position of each group of supplies. There is, of course, the risk of departmentalisation and the disadvantage that the supplier of a wide range of materials and goods may deal with a number of progress clerks and play one off against another. However, since most suppliers tend to specialise, this danger may be more apparent than real. Nevertheless, there are valid arguments for making a switch occasionally as this can broaden and stimulate healthy competition between progress staff. It can also avoid complacency on the part of suppliers, who will then be confronted with a different progress chaser who has not yet been subject to their "softening-up process", their excuses and so on.

Alternatively, progress personnel may be assigned to suppliers. This has the disadvantage that the same materials, but from different suppliers, are dealt with by different progress clerks. In this case an overall picture of the supply position for individual supplies may be more difficult to obtain. (*See* Chapter 12, vendor rating.)

RECORDS, REPORTS AND CORRESPONDENCE

Reports and correspondence arising from progressing may be of more than transitory value because they can influence negotiations, investigation of production hold-ups, supply failures, vendor ratings and so on. In regard to vendor ratings, it is important to know the capacity of suppliers and their ability to fulfil "promises" of many kinds—including, of course, "delivery". Records of past performance can prove invaluable in this. The problem is how to collate the data without spending any time and money! Methods vary from the simplest to the highly complex using EDP. A few are listed below. (*See also* Chapter 3.)

(*a*) File reports, progress copies of orders and letters (which should otherwise be disposed of) in a "supplier file" (*see* Chapter 3).

(*b*) Record on "A–Z" supplier cards the number of orders delivered late. (Restrict this to main suppliers, bad suppliers and essential supplies.)

(*c*) As (*b*) but divide the total number of such orders by the total in a given period (e.g. twelve months) to give a "performance rating".

(*d*) As (*c*), but summate the number of weeks overdue and again divide by the number of orders to provide a "mean lateness factor" for each supplier.

(*e*) Calculate a monthly ratio of the total number of orders in the progress file which are overdue at each review date to the total number of orders in the "live order file". This can be a simple yet useful guide-line as to the performance of suppliers and also to the effectiveness of progressing.

It is also important to remember that a supplier who produces an accelerated delivery on request should be noted on the credit side of the supplier's record for improved vendor rating.

Example of varying lead times and their effects

The last ten deliveries which took place over a period of eighteen months were found to be as in Table 35.

TABLE 35. VARIABLE LEAD TIMES

Delivery number	1	2	3	4	5	6	7	8	9	10
Lead time for	4	5	6	3	4	4	5	10	4	5 (=50)
each delivery	(a)				(a)	(a)			(a)	

NOTES:
(1) Mode by inspection is 4 at (*a*). (2) Mean $= \dfrac{\text{total } 50}{\text{results } 10} = 5.$

These are plotted in Fig. 66 to ascertain if any trend is apparent, and on the adjoining frequency chart to observe the pattern. It is clear from the graph that the supplier is an unreliable performer. When the first exceptional lead time of six weeks occurred, the progress chaser's efforts met with an immediate improvement to three weeks on the next delivery, which was better than the mode. (The mode was 4, which was better than the mean of 5.) If maintained this could have enabled the firm to reduce their stock, but, as can be seen, the deliveries crept up and reached a record high level at delivery number eight. Following this, and the row which took place, a slight improvement is noted. But the last delivery again showed an increase. On the other hand, there does not appear to be any general, well-defined trend. If the exceptionally long delivery of ten weeks can be avoided in the future, the frequency chart could indicate a reasonably stable pattern.

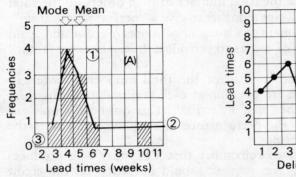 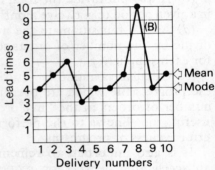

Fig. 66. (a) Frequency chart for variable lead times (b) Curve of lead times for ten consecutive deliveries

(1) Skewness of curve shows that deliveries tend to have greater variability beyond the mode. (2) This portion horizontal to show that lead time may lengthen indefinitely. (3) This portion shown dotted as an extrapolation, and vertical because lead time never falls below three weeks.

Investigations should therefore be made to ascertain if there were any exceptional factors. Was the ten weeks' delivery due to conditions of transport, or supplier's problems of supplies? It is useful to note the following points.

(a) The negotiation of deliveries shows the need to integrate the purchasing, stores and transport functions into a co-ordinated Supplies operation.

(b) It is important for Supplies staff to question all points concerning supplies, including in this case the pattern of deliveries by suppliers.

(c) Supplies staff, particularly progress staff, need to develop diagnostic skill and a strong sense of urgency.

If the result of the investigations and the efforts of the purchasing department to improve the supply should fail, what action must then be taken to ensure supply in this example?

(a) If the reorder level is fixed at a quantity to cover ten weeks, based on present lead time and constant usage, there will be no stock-out for a very long period but this security is purchased at the expense of high stock levels.

(b) Apply forward balance column (see Fig. 31).

(c) Apply more rigorous and continuous stock-control methods.

PLANNING AND PROGRESSING OPERATIONS

Initiation of the progressing operation

This can begin even before the order is placed, i.e. at the enquiry stage (see Table 34 and Chapter 7). "Delivery" and its achievement should be in the minds of those needing supplies at the time these are first considered, and pre-urging planned.

(1) TARGETS FOR DELIVERY should be set and progress records consulted regarding the programme, how it can be carried out, and the performance of suggested suppliers (see also Chapter 12). Long delivery orders sometimes suffer due to the very length of the "horizon" obscuring the need for urgency and progressing at the early stages.

(2) "LETTERS OF INTENT" should be progressed on the appropriate date for cancellation, renewal or conversion into a firm order.

(3) ACKNOWLEDGMENTS should be routed via the progress section to keep them up to date and enable them to go into immediate action if necessary.

(4) CHECKING DELIVERIES OFFERED IN QUOTATIONS. The delivery quoted by suppliers is usually of more importance than price *alone*. Costs of idle production time and loss of future orders due to lack of a part, machine or materials often outweigh price savings on a lower bid. Sometimes it is found that the delivery date offered is as unreliable as the price quoted. The supplier may thus have gained an unfair advantage over his competitors who have stated deliveries they can maintain. (See Tables 12 and 25.) The purchasing officer in his official capacity as a representative of his company should personally acquaint the appropriate executives of the offending firm with the views of his own management. Reference back to progress records when studying quotations may radically affect negotiations or even the choice of supplier.

Progressing procedures

(*See also* Checklist 30.) The stages and type of communication used in progressing should be planned with knowledge of each supplier's performance and reactions. For example, what kind of communication does he take most notice of? Does he read, and sometimes even, "Can he read?"

The method of communication must be appropriate to the need: (*a*) a simple card for routine chasing; (*b*) a "word-processed" letter; (*c*) a special letter; (*d*) a personal visit (for an emergency). It should, however, be a rule that all verbal communications are confirmed in writing. There is always a possibility that the dishonest will deny and the diligent may forget or misunderstand a verbal message. (*See* later section—legal implications.)

It must be borne in mind that "the efficient progressor achieves delivery by a logical elimination of excuses or reasons for delay, wherever possible helping the supplier to overcome his difficulties". Progressing must be "progressive"; it must relentlessly follow up and build up pressure on the supplier. Behind a paperwork screen of progressing there is the activity of the manufacturer and the shipper. Versatility is vital to meet the many problems and delays which can hold up a job. Most situations are unique and a purely "red tape" progress system is useless.

Visits to suppliers

Visits to suppliers giving personal on-site contact can be highly rewarding, even if somewhat costly. A report of the visit (whoever makes it) with copies to those who need them should be normal practice. A copy of the report may also be sent to the supplier with special vetting of any confidential portions which are for internal use only. On the other hand, some may be deliberately left intact to inform the supplier, for example, that he is recommended for blacklisting! (*See also* Chapter 12.)

Pre-urging

Pre-urging and progress reports may be used for important requirements. Pre-urging involves the setting of a date for communicating with the supplier to establish that he will keep his promise. On stock materials this may be based on the bin level shown in Fig. 25 and called the "danger warning level".

Supplier's periodic progress reports

Progress reports may be requested from a supplier who is producing to a programme. Regular reporting constrains him to plan and to keep his customer's demands well in view. In some instances it is best for the purchaser to provide the form for completion so as to be in line with his own production procedures (*see* Fig. 67).

Lines of communication for progressing

Internally there should be no problem, but externally the line is often ill-defined and progress staff need to determine the best line for each supplier.

MONTHLY STATEMENT OF DELIVERY

Please return to:

THE PANEGYRIC CHEMICAL CO. LTD.,
5 DOCK GREEN, YATTON,
SOMERSET.

Date _____

Manufacturer's name   Manufacturer's reference

(1)	(2)	(3)	(4)	(5)	(6)	(7)
Order no.	Date of order	Req. no.	Branch	Description of goods	Date required	Delivery promised

Fig. 67. Supplier's monthly delivery statement

This form is sent each month (or other period) to the supplier. Column (3) is used where the information is circulated to branch depots who may wish to refer back to the original requisition. Column (4) shows the branch or depot for which each order is required. This does not apply in the case of a single perimeter firm.

(*a*) Local representatives are regarded by some suppliers as their "outposted headquarters" to deal with all customers' queries. A local man should be able to assess a problem and put pressure on his head office.

(*b*) Production managers act as the focal point in some suppliers, but where the planning and sequence of jobs is in the hands of a production manager he is likely to concentrate upon those larger jobs which show the maximum profit. Cries from a desperate purchaser for a small special order may go unheeded.

(*c*) Despatch departments in some firms act as the focal point for progressing. This can be useful where the lead times are short.

(*d*) Sales or contracts departments are the best contacts, provided their top management gives them support to ensure that the production department proceeds as they request—not, regrettably, a universal result!

(*e*) There is always the possibility of finding someone at the supplier's works who can make promises and see that they are kept. A visit to the supplier may be justified on this score alone.

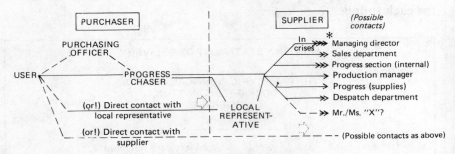

Fig. 68. *Lines of communications for progressing*
*Arrows suggest degree of success expected.

Figure 68 indicates a number of lines of communication for consideration when setting up and developing progressing section.

Planning and progress systems

There is no one system which fits all cases nor indeed will one system necessarily continue unmodified. For general purposes, however, the simplest method is usually the best.

Whatever method is adopted, charts, cards or other documents must be designed so that revised promise dates are followed up and the appropriate departments notified.

A fundamental need here is simplicity. Progress charts which require a team of clerks to operate them always fail. The grade of clerical labour needed to work the chart economically will be too low to take intelligent and vigorous selective action regarding individual jobs which need progressing. It is wasteful of manpower and should be replaced by "edp" releasing the manpower for "active" progressing.

Some simple arrangements for progressing are outlined below. In most cases these merely require an extra copy of each purchase order that is to be progressed.

(1) COMPOSITE ORDER/PROGRESS FORMS can eliminate the need for an extra progress copy of each order. Using the simply adapted form illustrated in Fig. 69, the single copy of each order is kept in "A–Z" sequence of suppliers in a multi-post visible edge binder until the final intake has been received. It can then be removed and filed or

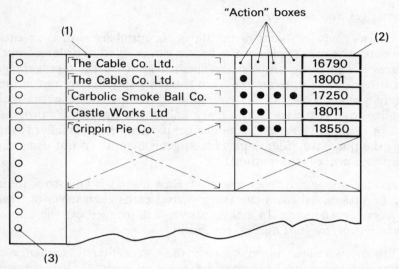

Fig. 69. Composite order/progress form for smaller companies
(1) Supplier's names on visible edge in "A–Z" sequence. (2) Order number in primary position, with heavy box to emphasise its importance, and the usual note to ensure it is quoted on all documents by both the supplier and the works. (3) Multiple punching to suit binder giving visible edge to display suppliers, "action" boxes and order numbers.

passed to the invoice section, according to the system of invoice clearance adopted. Heavy marks are made in the appropriate number of "action" boxes to signify the degree of progress action needed. (It is important to resist the temptation to use fancy colours, codes, heiroglyphs and especially loose signals.)

In Fig. 69 the following action was signalled thus (using heavy black, or red, dots to indicate special urgency):

(a) all blank means no progress action;

(b) one dot means check on first working day each month;

(c) two dots mean check on first working day each week;

(d) three dots mean check daily;

(e) four dots (or red) denote special urgency.

(2) PROGRESS COPY FILED IN "URGE-DATE" SEQUENCE. It should be noted that an urge date or action date is not the same as the delivery date, unless it is merely to check that the goods have been safely received.

Filing in urge-date sequence involves the continual movement of paper, a situation which should always be avoided. Where the volume of orders is large this method may become cumbersome and the individual orders difficult to locate. At this stage other alternatives may be tried.

(3) A DIARY may be kept with the order numbers shown at each urge date. The urge copies of the orders can be filed in order-number sequence. This is the simplest arrangement, but has the disadvantage that other orders outstanding from the same supplier are not immediately visible. This can be overcome by adding the name of each supplier to the entries in the diary and either keeping a "progress file" of orders in "A–Z" sequence or, particularly in smaller firms, using the purchase order copies filed in this manner (if not using the composite order form method).

(4) PROGRESSING FROM STOCK RECORDS. Raw materials and stock items may be progressed from the stock record cards themselves or from progress record cards. In either case signals trigger off the appropriate action, by staff and by computer.

(5) USE OF ASSEMBLY DRAWINGS AND PLANS, ETC. Where a sequence of operations is involved use may be made of a pictorial diagram or actual assembly drawing, shaded or coloured as deliveries occur. (Further advice can be found in Ministry of Works Advisory Leaflet No. 14, HMSO, 1972.)

(6) GANTT CHARTS (*see* Fig. 70) form the basis of most of the complex progress charts offered by "systems" manufacturers. Many of these are over-complicated and some involve coloured signals which, being loose, fall off, get misplaced or even lost, and, in any case, consume considerable man-hours.

The Gantt chart is popular for progressing construction schemes or production programmes where a number of parallel or sequential operations are involved.

(7) NETWORK ANALYSIS should be considered for major plant and construction schemes. Far from eliminating the progressing function, network analysis is likely to intensify progressing operations. The greater accuracy of planning will necessitate the arrival of supplies strictly to schedule.

When setting out programmes for production plans, civil works contracts, or the construction of a large unit of plant, each job is shown in its correct sequence and the allotted time for each operation carefully plotted. A very simple example is shown in Fig. 71 for part of the building of an office block. The "events" shown by numbers in circles must not be passed until all the preceding jobs have been completed. For example, painting cannot be started until joiners and glaziers have finished and plumbers have removed their blowlamps. The longer jobs indicated by heavy, continuous lines,

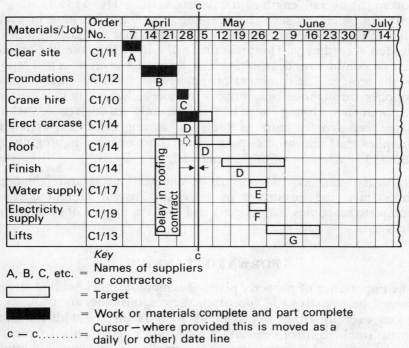

Fig. 70. Gantt chart: applied to planning and progressing

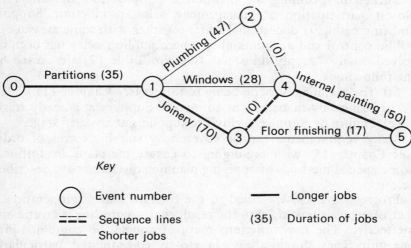

Fig. 71. Network analysis for planning and progressing
(*See* BS 6046.)

govern the overall length of the network. (BS 6046, 4335.)

It can be clearly seen that the necessary materials must be available at the time each event is reached and that progressing will be needed accordingly. The programme of a large and complex project can be computerised, resulting in a daily or weekly progress report of the project. The computer can, moreover, instantly reschedule all supplies throughout the network to meet changes in deliveries or requirements. Having "zero IQ" it can only make decisions which have been written into its program, leaving intelligent action to Supplies staff and others—particularly those engaged in progressing. (BS 4335 "Glossary of project network techniques.")

(8) VISUAL DISPLAY UNITS using on-line computers and telephone links have the advantage of providing instant communication, complete schedules, lists of parts and so on in respect of outstanding deliveries.

FORWARD PLANNING

The importance of properly planned achievable stockholding targets cannot be overstressed. Too often the responsibility for planning is taken over by other departments such as finance with no input from stock control, manufacturing, sales, etc. This frequently results in missed opportuntites for controlled improvement in stock-performance, for reducing stockholdings, for increasing service levels and for achieving profitable price breaks. (BS5729 Part 1 (7.1).)

Successful planning for manufacturing processes demands the closest participation of management, sales, production, Supplies and (increasingly) operational staff, together with some measure of public control and accountability where public money has been involved. Many "supply disasters" (see also Table 12) are caused by the following.

(a) The planning horizon being too short (see Chapter 11).

(b) Failure by management to involve Supplies at an early stage.

(c) Failure by Supplies to involve suppliers at an early stage.

Many requirements can be covered by suitable forms of order (see Chapter 15) with pre-urging to ensure the plans are fulfilled. Some special methods of applying planning disciplines are described below.

Progressing is closely allied to the forward planning operation, a fact often overlooked, with the result that progressing is erratic and ineffective. The two functions may, of course, be combined into one unit. They should always be closely co-ordinated, particularly on period contracts (see Chapter 11).

Considerable clerical labour is likely to be involved in planning, progressing and control, whether these are carried out by computer or manually.

Self-regulated forward planning

This technique should be examined by the reader whether or not he contemplates its use because it exemplifies the actual supply flow in most manufacturing plants. The technique is based upon the "Z" chart used for comparing sales and production achievements with pre-set targets. It is suitable for control of class "A" supplies particularly on medium to long-term horizons for budgetary control, stock levels or, as in this example, usage, i.e. supply flow.

METHOD. The following is an outline of the method (*see also* Fig. 72).

(*a*) Prepare forecast for the appropriate period ahead.

(*b*) Set targets for stages in period: line (1) in the table in Fig. 72.

(*c*) Tabulate these forecasts cumulatively at line (2).

(*d*) At line (3) enter the actual usage which occurred.

(*e*) At line (4) tabulate line (3) cumulatively.

(*f*) At line (5) enter the upper forecast limit (10 per cent above the target in this example).

(*g*) At line (6) enter the lower forecast limit (10 per cent below the target in this example).

(*h*) At line (7) enter the difference (+ or −) between lines (1) and (3).

(*i*) At line (8) calculate the results of line (7) cumulatively.

(*j*) At line (9) show the variances between lines (3), (5) and (6) indicating the amount above or below the limits set.

(*k*) At line (10) is entered the twelve month moving average. The figures shown are of course fictitious because data in the previous twelve months has not been shown. However, period (month in the example) 12 should be the same for lines (4) and (10).

INTERPRETATION OF THIS EXAMPLE.

(*a*) The smoothing effect of lengthy (twelve month) periods must not be overlooked at line (10).

(*b*) Whether the data is presented in the form of a computer printout or a manual tabulation it must be borne in mind that its interpretation and use requires objectivity and the application of the "exception principle".

(*c*) The need for graphical presentation depends upon the mathematical perception of the user. Most people find it beneficial.

(*d*) The "target line" showed an increased usage after month 5.

(*e*) It appears from mid-month 8 that a fall in usage has occurred

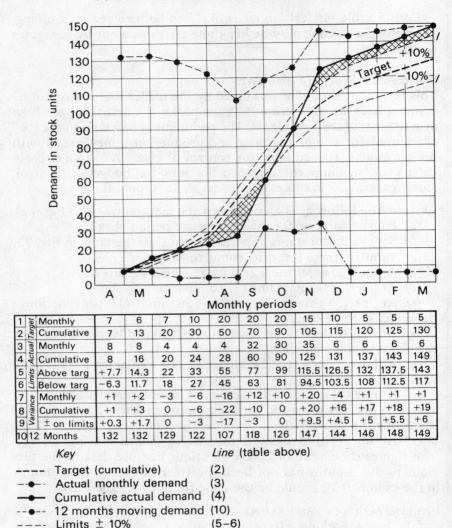

		A	M	J	J	A	S	O	N	D	J	F	M
1	Monthly	7	6	7	10	20	20	20	15	10	5	5	5
2	Cumulative	7	13	20	30	50	70	90	105	115	120	125	130
3	Monthly	8	8	4	4	4	32	30	35	6	6	6	6
4	Cumulative	8	16	20	24	28	60	90	125	131	137	143	149
5	Above targ	+7.7	14.3	22	33	55	77	99	115.5	126.5	132	137.5	143
6	Below targ	−6.3	11.7	18	27	45	63	81	94.5	103.5	108	112.5	117
7	Monthly	+1	+2	−3	−6	−16	+12	+10	+20	−4	+1	+1	+1
8	Cumulative	+1	+3	0	−6	−22	−10	0	+20	+16	+17	+18	+19
9	± on limits	+0.3	+1.7	0	−3	−17	−3	0	+9.5	+4.5	+5	+5.5	+6
10	12 Months	132	132	129	122	107	118	126	147	144	146	148	149

Key   Line (table above)

----   Target (cumulative)   (2)
--•--   Actual monthly demand   (3)
—•—   Cumulative actual demand   (4)
--•--   12 months moving demand   (10)
----   Limits ± 10%   (5−6)

Fig. 72. Self-regulating forward planning chart ("Z" chart)

and unless reporting has been improved stock surplus may result.

(*f*) Investigators should ascertain if usages at periods 6, 7 and 8 were seasonal and should therefore be predictable.

(*g*) Usages in periods 9-12 are still outside the target and stock must be re-scheduled.

(*h*) Slope of usage is a useful indicator of trends (*see* Fig. 25).

(*i*) Other questions to ask are as follows.

(i) Is the change in demand temporary?

(ii) Will the change be reversed, i.e. will a fall be followed by an increase?

(iii) Will any forecast change bring the curves to target?

(iv) Can suppliers cope with the changes?

(v) Are suppliers advised and monitored in relation to the data?

Materials Requirements Planning (MRP) (BS 5191 (2.2), 5729 Pt. 2 (5) Abb.)

BS 5729 suggests that where demands for various items of supply are interdependent that statistical forecasting from historical data is: "A poor way to control stock levels and a reorder level based upon such data may result in huge stocks or stock-outs." MRP is a "procedural" method of stock-control briefly outlined as follows (*see* BS 5729 for full details):

1. Prepare a master manufacturing schedule based on the production plan.

2. Take the master schedule as a forecast for supplies.

3. Break this down into demands for component parts, sub-assemblies etc.

4. Time-phase the schedule through to final product.

5. Take the schedule as "fixed"—i.e. no allowance for random fluctuations as in simulated forecasting.

6. Break down the schedule into components and sub-assemblies.

7. Break each of these down into raw materials or purchased parts etc.

8. Adjust these final results in the light of existing stocks, dues in, etc.

9. Insert latest time for each item in light of lead times, external and internal.

10. Program on computer, scheduling "to infinite or finite capacity" depending upon whether production capacity is unlimited or limited.

Dynamic balancing

(BS 5729 Part 3 (3.6).) This is an extension of the economic order quantity (*see* Chapter 10) and involves the calculation of acquisition costs and costs of holding enough stock for $1, 2, 3 \ldots n$ periods ahead. The basic price per item (or unit) is then added to the acquisition cost and also the holding cost per unit over the periods considered:

$$\begin{array}{l}\text{Successive total} \\ \text{costs for each} \\ \text{option}\end{array} = \begin{array}{l}\text{unit} \\ \text{price}\end{array} + \begin{array}{l}\dfrac{\text{acquisition costs}}{\text{total option in}} \\ \text{periods } 1, 2, 3 \ldots n\end{array} + \begin{array}{l}\text{Holding cost} \\ \text{per unit per} \\ \text{period}\end{array} \times \dfrac{\Sigma \text{total units} \times \text{periods held}}{\text{total units in option}}$$

Known future needs over the periods for which options are considered can be continuously substituted in the above formula until the lowest successive cost is discovered. Commitments are then made for this stock to cover the periods opted.

BS5729 suggests that the method requires computer aid if it is to be applied to more than a few items. However, the warnings on application of EOQ methods contained in BS5729 Part 3(3) and Chapter 10 of this volume should be studied before applying the method. Moreover, it entails close knowledge of future demands and where this is so stock may be reduced or even eliminated by contracts and controlled intakes phased with demand.

Advance production reservation: planning

In some industries (e.g. electricity supply) there is a continuing demand on suppliers for plant of more or less regular type for which technical or other details may vary slightly for each delivery. For example, a particular type of switchgear may be needed with a specific range of capacities in the same frame size but with differing protective equipment. The purchaser may know from forecast estimates, production plan or other means the overall needs for a considerable period ahead in broad terms, apart from the technical details. A forward supply arrangement or contract may then be arranged with the supplier (*see* Chapter 15). This manufacturer then becomes an extension of the planning and production arrangements and can thus plan his own production and supply supplementary to the FSA or FSC.

The purchasing officer can make arrangements for the manufacturer to reserve production capacity at a predetermined rate either in value or in units of output. For example, a planning arrangement may be entered into covered by a suitable contract for switchgear in one-month periods for twelve months in succession.

A provisional estimate may be given for numbers (or values) of basic units for, say, six months ahead. Three months in advance of each production month the purchasing officer states the final requirements for basic units in that month (three months being the lead time for these). One clear month prior to production, final details of quantity and specification including technical equipment are provided. The form illustrated at Fig. 67 may be adapted for this purpose.

For administrative reasons it may be opportune for the progress section to check off the amount taken or allocated during each advance period. This must agree with the supplier's records and programme or may be adjusted as the production periods approach. Usually suppliers set a deadline date ahead of each period related to lead time. After this date draw-off orders will no longer be accepted, but must go into the succeeding period.

LEGAL IMPLICATIONS OF PROGRESSING

Progress communications become "documents of record" supporting or amending the original order. As such they could, for example, be used in evidence as to the intentions of the parties to a contract including any intentions to modify a contract. An important instance could be the progressing forward of delivery to an earlier date than that originally proposed in the order. The company may well find themselves legally obliged to accept such earlier delivery, and such instructions should therefore only be given with management approval.

Staff should also bear in mind that verbal as well as written instructions are binding. It is best, therefore, always to confirm verbal communications in writing and to "fail safe" in this respect if in doubt.

AXIOM: A request to change delivery dates binds the buyer.

Penalty clauses, other sanctions and claims

The sanctions which can be imposed upon a bad or recalcitrant supplier must now be examined. A major requirement in this connection is usually that of "delivery on time" in accordance with the contract, and application of an appropriate discipline upon the supplier. In theory this could be achieved by the insertion of either of the following clauses on orders where appropriate:

(*a*) "that time of delivery is of the essence of the contract"; or

(*b*) "that late delivery shall carry a penalty of £xxx per day overdue".

The first clause would enable an aggrieved purchaser to cancel without compensation to the supplier if the latter were in default. The second clause might "terrorise" the supplier into keeping the agreement.

However, in practice such arrangements encounter the following problems.

(*a*) There is the difficulty of getting the supplier to accept the clauses, particularly the second.

(*b*) Cancellation is not much help if production will cease and there is no alternative supplier.

(*c*) The courts will not enforce any clause the objective of which is to inspire terror (referred to as "*in terrorem*").

The alternatives are liquidated or unliquidated damages, both of which are acceptable to the legal profession. A court must be satisfied that the sum for liquidated damages is a genuine evaluation of loss and not a guess or "penalty". The court will reject any claim if the sum stipulated greatly exceeds the likely loss, or if the same sum is claimed indiscriminately in the event of a number of things happening or not happening.

All this looks rather discouraging for the harassed purchasing officer. What remedies does he have?

(a) Progress staff must never threaten a supplier. However, when subjected to effective progressing the latter is likely to become sensitive to relationships with the purchaser and to the relationships within his Supplies department. Progress should let it be seen that they work in close liaison with the appropriate purchasing officers and are well aware of the disciplines (with the full support of management) that may apply to a bad supplier.

(b) While avoiding any threats, the mere mention of "damages", liquidated or otherwise, may have a salutary effect.

(c) The Sale of Goods Act gives some protection. This is greatly increased if the purchaser lets the supplier know that he relies upon the application of the Act as fundamental to his conditions of contract.

NOTE:

The Sale of Goods Act 1979, s. 10 states that: "If a seller in a commercial transaction promises to deliver goods on a certain date he must keep exactly to that date." The buyer can recover damages from the supplier if he can prove financial loss. If a condition of sale is accepted which states that: "time shall not be of the essence of the contract", the purchaser cannot then cancel a late delivery without giving reasonable notice to the supplier. It is common practice for conditions of sale to exclude liability for non-delivery or late delivery. If this clause is operative irrespective of cause of non-delivery or delay it should be strongly resisted by the purchasing officer at the very outset of the contract—particularly if the order has been placed with delivery in mind by a certain date or with urgency.

(d) The purchasing officer should make it clear at the outset what problems regarding the contract are significant.

(e) Instead of relying upon a mass of sometimes irrelevant and unenforceable terms and conditions of contract, the purchasing officer should make clear on the face of the order the items which are vital to the particular contract concerned.

(f) Always bear in mind that the court will look for the "intentions" of the parties to a contract.

Insurance against supply failure and product liability

Insurance against supply failure and product liability (*see* Chapter 16) can be arranged through specialist underwriters. Cover against supply failure can usually also be obtained in respect of consequential loss if the supplier should become insolvent, and as a result of this fail to honour his contract.

Underwriters usually expect the client to bear the first 10-15 per cent of any loss. This is intended to avoid diminution of initiative, diligence or acumen on the part of the purchaser.

When negotiating such cover the following points should be checked.

(a) How quickly will claims be met?

(b) Do insurers claim deductions for salvage value?

(c) Do they make any other restrictive conditions?

CHAPTER 19

The Packaging of Supplies

INTRODUCTION

Packaging is required for incoming supplies, and for the company's own end-product for shipment. Supplies staff will be involved in both aspects.

Importance of packaging

"Packaging"[142]-[145] has been defined as the "art, science and technology of preparing goods for transport and sale" and "the means of ensuring safe delivery to the ultimate consumer in sound condition at minimum overall cost" (the Industry Committee for Packaging and the Environment). (BS 3130.)

The above objectives are amplified in Checklist 31 in the three main sections under which this subject should be considered:

(a) materials management of the packaging itself;
(b) materials management of the contents;
(c) packaging in transit and "in use".

COSTS OF PACKAGING for many goods are a significant element in costs of supplies purchased. The estimated or quoted price for supplies usually conceals these costs. A glance through Checklist 31 will remind the purchasing officer of a number of points where there could be direct savings for his company, or savings for the supplier which his company should share in as a result of negotiations.

SAFE ARRIVAL OF GOODS is at least as important as their production. Damage during production may sometimes be rectified or the goods replaced without delay. Damage in transit may not be revealed until long after intake. By the time discovery is made a complete production stoppage may be inevitable. (BS 4826.)

It may be suggested that goods-inwards inspection should avoid this eventually. However, in low and medium technologies, at least,

368

goods-inwards inspection is often random, casual or lacking. The purchase order goods-inwards copy should make it clear if inspection is needed. Where a supplier uses transit labels provided by the purchaser this point can be covered by means of a signal or symbol on the label to alert the goods-inwards section when they receive the package. (*See* Table 1, note (7).)

Legal aspects
Whether obtaining supplies or selling them to customers the legal implications of any containers in which they are packed should be considered.

In the past it has been contended by suppliers that, provided the goods were of "merchantable quality" and "fit for purpose", they had discharged their duty regardless of the condition or suitability of the containers in which they were packed. Recent case law discredits this argument, whether the containers are sold with the goods, or hired or loaned and returnable. In principle, the containers (of whatever kind, from bottles to bags) must be such as will enable the purchaser to have full "enjoyment" of the contents. For example, the packaging should be adequate to give reasonable protection, and should be compatible with the contents (e.g. not reacting chemically).

Where the industrial purchaser intends to store the goods in their original container he would be wise to inform the supplier of this, and of the fact that he does not intend to use the goods for some time. Otherwise the court may decide what is "reasonable" and this may be a much shorter time than the purchaser had envisaged for storage of the goods.

The industrial purchaser may have decided that he will use the container for some other purpose after the contents have been used. Unless this is clear between the parties at the time of contract, the buyer will have no redress if the final containers turn out to be useless for the secondary purpose.

Inadequate or incorrect labelling may result in a successful claim for negligence as well as being a breach of s. 14 of the Sale of Goods Act, e.g. the omission of details of hazards resulting from storage of a chemical for example.

Finally, the Court of Appeal has ruled that a stipulation as to packaging in certain quantities per container is part of a contractual description.

On exports it is important to watch out for regulations at the countries of destination. For example, details should be obtained of any prohibitions at the port of intake, e.g. wooden cases or crates for Australia and New Zealand require special treatment and certifying documentation.

Packaging in design

Packaging should be studied at the product design and provisioning stages. For example, time can usefully be spent in "designing out" easily broken or projecting parts, and providing for attachments to packages for purposes of handling and transit. This may be achieved by combining these with other existing features of design. Such details not only reduce the risk of damage in transit, but can also speed up transit and sometimes reduce the cost of packaging.

Attention should be given to the facilities for mechanical handling if bulk or weight is considerable. Co-ordination of this with the supplier can effect savings at his works as well as at those of the purchaser. (BS 2837.)

In cases of sea transit the design of packages has a further significance in that the freight is based not only on weight but also on the volume occupied. In a shipment of goods to Australia, the removal of a small projection of 1 cm from the plain side of a large packing-case saved £400 freight.

The shape of containers should also be considered at the design and planning stage. For example, loss of pay-load results from circular packing stowed on a vehicle, thus increasing costs of dead carriage.

Integration

It should be clear that packaging impinges upon Supplies at many points and also upon almost the whole of a company's manufacturing activities. The involvement of other departments can be summarised as follows.

(a) Design: should include design *for* and *of* packaging.

(b) Production department: pack to suit production quantities.

(c) Sales: customer needs, costs, etc.

(d) Stores: shelf-life, storage modules, count, check, dispense.

(e) Despatch: loading on to vehicles, etc.

(f) Transport: handling and securing during transit—and intake.

(g) Purchasing: provision of materials for packaging.

(h) Legal department: statutory regulations, home/overseas markings, prohibitions, etc.

(i) Publicity: design of markings on packages.

(j) User: requirements of work-centre operatives.

(k) Cost and finance: allocation of packaging costs.

When placing orders Supplies should ensure that packaging methods are clear. Features which must be clearly defined are the methods of addressing and marking, including any necessary instructions such as indication of gross and tare weights and dimensions, lifting points and which side uppermost, fragility and stackability (*see Storehouse*). (BS 2770.)

Conservation of resources

Conservation of resources—materials and cash—and the avoidance of pollution demand that Supplies staff and designers study much more carefully in the future the materials used for packaging and also possibilities for recycling, disposal, re-use and so on.

CHOICE OF CONTAINERS AND PACKAGING

The choice of containers involves considerations and design features which are highly technical. However, the general guiding principles should be known by Supplies staff and these are summarised below. (*See* Tables 11 and 13.)

Characteristics of contents

Characteristics of contents are a major consideration. The first of these must be the physical properties of the item being packed (*see* Chapter 6, properties of materials), and the second is the effect of external conditions upon the contents, expansion of liquids due to changes in temperature. For hardware and machinery the factors to take into account will be those relating to the solid state, such as their nature, size, construction and weight, their value and the need for protection from damage by natural or human causes. For plant and machinery, special anchorages may be needed between the goods and the case or crate for handling and transportation.

Transit to destination

Consideration must be given to loading and unloading, load-factor of transport vehicles, loading gauge, roads, bridges (over and under), street widths, narrow corners, overhead services (particularly high-voltage power lines), hard standing, parking, cranage, warning signs, police escorts, notices to local authorities and authorities responsible for water, electricity, gas and fire, stacking and handling in and through stores, quantity per package—to suit batch or continuous production of customer and possibly of supplier—and finally and most important, the destination.

Kinds of transport

The kind of transport used can affect the type of container selected. The importance of the volume-weight ratio for air transit means a light and small packing is required. The short duration of air transit and the modern handling methods normally used at airports facilitate the use of such packing. The more conventional transport services such as road and rail using older methods need protection against shocks. Volume-weight ratio, while increasingly important in all forms of transport, is of less significance on land than on air transits. For sea shipments, whether inland, coastal or overseas, it will be a significant factor. A further consideration is that consignments for sea transit as deck cargo must be waterproofed to protect the contents from weather and sea spray. (*See Storehouse,* ISO containers.)

It must not be forgotten that in the case of exports, shipment may occasionally be made to countries where the pack-horse is the normal form of transit! Here the loads must be broken down to a convenient size and given protection against mountain cold or tropical heat, varying barometric pressure, snow, dew point, rain, dust, sea water, pests, etc.

Powered handling and its effect upon packaging
Powered handling has increasingly affected the design of packaging in recent times. Designers should look for new methods of packaging design to facilitate its increased use.

If packaging and handling are not planned together, circumstance will sooner or later compel this, as the following example shows. From time to time a purchasing department received requisitions for the same replacement items for units of plant which had been damaged. Investigation on site by the purchasing officer revealed that this was due to accidents when the units had been handled clumsily from the crane when unloading the delivery vehicles of the manufacturer. It was found that the supplier had:

   (a) provided no lifting points on the equipment;
   (b) failed to provide slinging instructions or lifting marks;
   (c) omitted to show gross/net weights, etc.

The slinger wound a rope sling under two 230 mm diameter X 50 mm projections on the units. The rope slipped and the load was lost. The purchasing officer called together colleagues from the transport and chief engineer's departments and the safety officer. The short (informal) meeting resulted in arrangements being made with the manufacturers (without extra cost) for standardised lifting attachments and suitable markings by them on all heavy plant in the future.

STANDARDS FOR PACKAGING

Standards for packaging, including labelling, are covered in great detail in British Standard BS1133[145] and ISO/R 210.211, etc.

(*See also* BS3130 "Glossary of packaging terms".) BS1133 should be included in every Supplies library. Provision must be made for updating *all* standards but particularly those for packaging where technological developments, introduction of new materials and feedback from customers, hauliers and users may generate changes. generate changes.

Once standards for packaging and handling have been agreed by technical staff, change should not be permitted without their further approval. Where a change of package is proposed by a supplier it may generally be assumed that he hopes to gain some financial benefit—again, the purchasing officer should obtain a share of the benefit for his company.

Packaging and load dimensions
The British Standards Institution is currently considering a standard for packaging and load dimensions. There is, however, an ISO standard 3676 which covers this subject.

Containers, pallets, units loads, etc.
Considerable space is devoted to the practical considerations of these in *Storehouse*. There is only space here to list the progression through the range available.

(*a*) Modular and preferred sizes of package should be examined, such as those proposed by the European Packaging Federation and EEC Directives.

(*b*) Pallets are now fairly closely standardised in size, and packaging modules should be made compatible.

(*c*) Tote pans and similar unit containers should also be planned with palletisation in mind.

(*d*) Unit containers such as roll pallets, etc. are an economical form of transit pack where used for distribution.

(*e*) Transit containers such as ISO units require that consideration be given right along the chain so that they may be effectively loaded conveniently, safely and fully. (*See also* Chapter 20, transport costs.)

Selection of containers
This is a matter for consultation between the shipper and supplier. Factors affecting the choice of a particular size and type of container include (BS 5073 (2.2 and 3.1):

(*a*) characteristics of the goods to be carried;

(*b*) the ways in which the goods will be loaded and unloaded;

(*c*) the nature of the route the container is likely to take;

(*d*) climatic conditions;

(*e*) availability of the preferred containers.

Pallet pools

Pallet pools are a form of hire service which warrant consideration, especially by smaller firms. Suppliers claim economies for clients hiring as few as fifteen or twenty pallets. Advantages to be expected from a pool are:

(a) costs of hire are usually less than cost of ownership *and* cost-in-use;

(b) dimensional consistency ensures correct clearances for handling and stowage;

(c) maintenance by the pool relieves the hirer of work for which he may not be equipped, such as test and repair—although he is still responsible for ensuring that damaged pallets are withdrawn from service.

The pool owner should, like a vehicle hire firm, be capable of meeting sudden changes in requirements.

Cage pallets, which are costly to own (*see* Fig. 75, G) are available for goods which are awkward to handle and those needing protection or stacking. These should be specified to fold flat for unladen transits, returns, etc.

Packaging for long hauls

Packing for long-haul overseas transit is covered in British Standard BS4672, "Guide to hazards in the transport and storage of packages" (the contents list of this publication supplements Checklist 31). Part 1 covers climatic hazards. Information is given on climatic conditions likely to be encountered by packages in every type of vehicle or ship, and in associated storage. The climatic problems affecting goods when static as well as when in transit are thus covered.

Part 2 provides maps and diagrams showing, for example:

(a) average, maximum and minimum air temperatures, shown seasonally;

(b) relative humidity diagrams;

(c) rainfall data;

(d) likelihood of storms or other hazards to goods at sea.

Whether buying packing, arranging imports of supplies or shipping end-products, the guide will be useful in alerting staff to the problems.

Life of packaging

An important consideration when ordering supplies is the life of packaging, which must obviously be not less than the shelf-life of the goods which are contained.

The final disposal of the packaging should also be considered. In the interests of conservation, the multi-trip, returnable package is desirable. Materials such as plastics pose a difficult problem for disposal. Bio-degradation or photo-degradation may assist the environmentalist but do nothing to solve the conservation problem. Where returnability is impracticable or uneconomic, use within the works should be considered.

Sources of advice and information

Bodies and institutions which are of relevance for packaging include:

The Institute of Packaging;

The British Standards Institution;

The British Productivity Council;

British Railways Board;

The Design Council;

PIRA (the Research Association for the Paper, Printing and Packaging Industries);

The Science Research Council;

Consultants in packaging (*see The Packaging Review, Directory and Buyers Guide,* published by IPC Business Press Ltd.).

CHAPTER 20

Transport and Handling
of Supplies

INTRODUCTION

Integration of transport and Supplies

Both Supplies and transport are service functions: they provide for the efficient movement of all materials. Co-ordination and co-operation are essential, particularly in such matters as:

(a) special loads;
(b) packaging;
(c) handling;
(d) routeings for collection, re-delivery and distribution;
(e) return of empties;
(f) pick-up and discharge points; equipment and access;
(g) vehicle availability;
(h) return loads, etc.;
(i) intake and despatch.

TRANSPORT: EFFICIENCY AND SUITABILITY

Aims of efficient transport

The aims of efficient transport are speed, safety, achievement of a good load factor, low running costs and regular loads. These aims must be subject to the freight being carried in suitable, well-maintained vehicles. Reliability is particularly important where a number of storehouses are served by a transport service. If deliveries are not reliable the stock levels in the storehouses served will inevitably become inflated to meet the risk of stock-out. This applies particularly where "concentration stores", sub-stores, etc. are used.

Suitability of transport

Unless other arrangements are made in the contract the onus under the Sale of Goods Act 1979 will be upon the supplier to select suitable transport for the efficient and safe delivery of goods. The result is that the supplier usually selects the type of transport to suit himself, and unless the purchasing officer intervenes the supplier is under no legal obligation to consider what happens at the purchaser's intake bay—that is a matter for the buyer. (*Caveat emptor!*)

Where the purchasing officer specifies the form of transport he must accept responsibility for its suitability for the traffic. He should therefore consider carefully the relevant items below.

(*a*) Speed of delivery required.
(*b*) Conditions at the supplier's loading point.
(*c*) Intake and off-loading facilities of purchaser.
(*d*) Specialised transport to reduce packing or handling costs.
(*e*) Types of materials to be transported and any hazards involved.
(*f*) Length of haul, speed, bulk and weight of load.
(*g*) Highway and route conditions, traffic.
(*i*) International boundaries.
(*j*) Self-loading/unloading equipment.

Sources of information

Information on transportation is available from the freight handlers themselves, and a number of other bodies, including the Freight Transport Association[173]-[174] and the International Cargo Handling Association.[176] The latter association has the objectives of promoting increased efficiency and economy in the handling and movement of goods from point to point in all modes and phases of the transport chain.

TRANSPORT COSTS

Freight is a significant element in acquisition costs of all supplies, whether shown in the offer or concealed in the price. Knowledge of the content of transport and packaging costs in total price is important to the purchasing officer.[138][146]-[155] Consideration of these factors may result in a change of transport method, packaging or even supplier. They are also of great importance when assessing suppliers' claims for price increases due to changes in haulage costs.

Similarly, arrangements negotiated for outwards transport of finished goods from a factory can have a significant effect upon final profit. Apart from the economics of the actual physical movement, there are other factors which may add to costs and thus reduce profits:

(*a*) complexity of transport administration;
(*b*) delays and errors in documentation;

377

(c) poor communications, e.g. unclear forwarding instructions or bad labelling.

These factors are particularly important in shipments abroad. A report issued by the International Freight Movement sector of the National Economic Development Council pointed out that "complexities are an 'invisible barrier' to improved export performance".

Elements of costs

Transport costs are related to tonne/kilometres hauled and to other factors such as:

(a) size of the consignment in relation to the payload capacity of the vehicle;

(b) suitability of vehicle for the goods being carried;

(c) efficient routeing and scheduling (*see Storehouse*);

(d) return loads;

(e) maintenance and standards of driving;

(f) ease of loading and unloading;

(g) insurance.

Checklist 32 suggests some ways of making savings in transport costs.

When considering suppliers' claims for price increases the purchasing officer may find it useful to note the following list of approximate running costs as percentages of total costs for a popular size of commercial vehicle: wages, 43 per cent; fuel, 11 per cent; tyres, 2 per cent; maintenance, 12 per cent. The remaining 32 per cent covers insurance, depreciation, licence, etc. Loading, unloading and transfer often incur large and unseen costs due to the use of unsuitable vehicles or to the lack of adequate or up-to-date handling equipment at the loading, unloading or transfer points or on the vehicle itself (*see Storehouse,* packing and packaging, and transport).

Size of loads

When negotiating for transport it will be found that many hauliers charge on a time basis. Where this is the case, loading and loading time and the use of unit loads become increasingly important. It must also be borne in mind that a truck containing unit loads may get preferential treatment at ports where rebates may also be given for unitised loads. Table 36 is based on figures presented at a conference held in 1975 by the Centre for Physical Distribution—later figures reveal similar ratios. Although they relate to retail distribution they can serve as guidelines when comparing options for intakes and shipments of supplies, or transport between stores or plants.

Size of load in relation to vehicle capacity usually has the greatest effect on the cost to the customer. "Dead carriage" is especially

TABLE 36. COMPARATIVE COSTS OF MOVING A 20-TONNE LOAD

Vehicle capacity (tonnes)	Relative cost per tonne	
	Long haul (150 km)	Short haul (15 km)
20, "articulated"	1.0	1.0
10, rigid	1.4	1.3
7, rigid	1.8	1.7
4, rigid	2.7	2.4

important on sole-user loads where the vehicle, vessel or plane is chartered to carry the goods as its only cargo. Here the batch size can, subject to demand, be increased if the saving in dead carriage exceeds the increase in storage charges due to the larger shipment.

Container capacity must be considered when making arrangements for shipment. A full container load (FCL) is clearly the most economical use of such equipment. Where this cannot be achieved a "groupage" or similar arrangement should be negotiated.

The costs of transport, like total storage and acquisition costs, carry fixed and variable charges. A break-even curve for optimum loads usually shows that costs per tonne/kilometre are high at the beginning of the curve—due to poor utilisation of vehicle capacity. At full load the curve levels out and beyond this may rise again as increased capacity is needed. Savings can then only be made by improving the turn-round of the vehicles, working them longer, and introducing specialised vehicles to suit the load.

"Delivered price"

Costs of transport which are concealed in a "delivered price" should be assessed in all significant orders and particularly on long-term contracts. Such costs are difficult to obtain and the obvious method is to ask the supplier to quote "loaded ex works" as well as "delivered". In many cases the supplier may reply that he delivers throughout the whole country and includes only a "notional cost" in his price, assuring the purchasing officer that he is getting the best of all worlds. Even so, a comparison from a local or national haulier or an estimate from the transport officer of the purchasing officer's own company may reveal the need for a harder line in bargaining for the delivered costs of the goods.

Small orders

Freight costs on small orders can build up to a significant loss of profitability. Particularly in a smaller firm, individual shipments may even exceed the price of the goods carried. If so, the supplier must recoup himself by inflating the price of the product—or he may go out of business. Those obtaining supplies particularly in smaller quantities, should consider the following possibilities.

(a) Arrange for regular intakes, stocking up for the period between each intake.

(b) Co-operate with other local firms for joint regular intakes.

(c) Make use of "in-plant" stock, etc. (the supplier makes his own economical deliveries; see Chapter 15).

(d) Collect from suppliers if this can form a return load.

(e) On larger transits utilise "groupage" or "freight forwarders".

(f) Review intake arrangements to speed vehicle turn-round.

(g) Use roll-pallets, etc. for mixed loads made up by supplier instead of separately packed small lots.

(h) Use ISO container as travelling mobile stores—swap for full container as required to replenish stock.

(i) Check and streamline procedures.

(j) Make up loads with other users (who are not competitors).

(k) Accept a "milk round" service to other firms en route.

Most of the above suggestions apply mainly to small orders which are short-haul and local. Some, however, such as (k) can apply with even greater force to long-haul deliveries with numerous drops.

When negotiating most of the above options, the haulier and the supplier should both enjoy economic benefits which they should share with their customer, e.g. as follows.

(a) Port and depot charges reduced for containerised shipments.

(b) Pallet weight excluded for freight charges.

(c) Discounts given.

(d) Handling facilities improved.

(e) Special attachments arranged to facilitate handling.

(f) Insurance charges reduced.

(g) Time saved by supplier and haulier in tallying, checking, counting, etc. (However, the supplier may claim that loading on to pallets and shrink wrapping or other covering consume time.)

Comparison ratios

Inter-firm comparison ratio (5) (see Appendix III) relates the costs of distribution and marketing to total sales. Although this gives some guide, a close analysis would be of benefit, and where firms manage and run their own transport further ratios are suggested for Supplies:

(a) transport costs per £1 of sales;

(b) transport costs per £1 of purchases.

TYPES OF TRANSPORT

Selection of the type of transport is governed by considerations somewhat similar to those which apply to powered handling within a plant. Frequent bulk movements between fixed points can best be handled by track-bound systems (similar in effect to a conveyor belt) such as rail, canal, etc. Those between variable points need fully mobile systems such as road.

Rail

Rail transport offers a network of fast goods services suited to bulk container loads. It is sometimes possible to share with others the use of ISO containers from areas of supply to their works with savings in time and cash. Methods of rapidly transferring loads from rail to road for terminal delivery, etc. are under continual investigation and experiment by the railways and private enterprise—participation by Supplies staff in such development could prove rewarding. Packaging for rail transit may need to take account of shock and vibration, but continuous vacuum brakes with close-coupled vehicles and improved methods of marshalling can be expected to improve matters in the future.

Road

Road transport provides flexibility for collection and delivery point to point usually without transhipment. Packing may often be less elaborate for road transport than for rail. The demurrage rates on road vehicles (particularly heavy goods vehicles) make it imperative to off-load quickly. This may mean that labour has to be taken off other work, possibly resulting in inexperienced lifting and handling (*see* below, materials handling).

Most firms of whatever size require some road transport vehicles of their own. The following are a few points which must be considered in the selection, purchase or hire of suitable units.

(*a*) Engine power and economy in operation must be weighed against capital outlay and availability of spares throughout the area of operations.

(*b*) Body size and shape must be looked at in the light of pallet size or other container modules.

(*c*) Access doors and translucent roofs for vans may be needed where frequent delivery or pick-up points are involved.

(*d*) Loading heights of bays and off-loading arrangements may decide if side or tailboard loading is essential.

(*e*) Flat-bed vehicles may be used for stable materials and pallets, but straight-sided or box vehicles for stacked goods.

Water

Water transport falls into four main categories: canal, estuarial, coastwise and sea-going.

(1) CANAL TRANSPORT is convenient where there are suitable terminal facilities for point-to-point regular bulk shipments. At first sight delivery may appear slow, but there are fewer delays than occur on either rail or road. Transit by canal is smooth and not liable to shocks. Special berths are required thus arrivals do not congest factory roads and sidings. The fact that special equipment is used for off-loading avoids switching labour and the risk of demurrage due to delays.

(2) ESTUARIAL TRANSPORT is used where vessels cannot berth alongside the quay. Barges which go alongside to collect the shipments may incur heavy charges for a minimum tonnage per barge. These charges must be set off against any savings achieved through avoiding harbour dues and other costs.

(3) COASTWISE SHIPPING is economical where lots of over 100 tonnes are transported over 250 km and access is suitable. There may be extra handling charges. Coastwise ships are usually of small size and delays due to weather or damage due to sea water may occur.

(4) SEA-GOING TRAFFIC is handled by three main groups of service: "tramp", "charter" and "liner". When negotiating incoming supplies or outgoing shipments, Supplies (or other staff) should ensure that the type of service is known. The tramp ship may reach its destination by a circuitous route since it travels where cargoes are available. Few readers will be likely to have sufficient cargo to charter their own ship but should they do so it is important to agree a timetable with the shipowner. Most goods will be transported through shipping agents who will select the line most suited for the traffic, etc.

Cost for ship transit is normally by volume (m^3) except where commodities have an average density exceeding 0.9 tonnes per m^3 in which case they will be charged by weight. Other points to which attention is needed are:

    (a) surcharges to cope with currency problems;
    (b) costs of bunkering;
    (c) delays due to congestion at port;
    (d) alternative routeings because of port closure;
    (e) special rates for containerisation;
    (f) surcharges for special and awkward loads.

Air

Air transport is particularly suited for delicate equipment, urgent spares, and valuable goods. Lighter packaging is possible than in other forms of transport, and insurance rates are low. On the other hand, freight and terminal costs are usually high. The gain in air speed may be lost on land journeys to and from the airport. There may also be delays due to weather. Restrictions in loading gauge affect the size and weight of shipment.

Package delivery by air can be attractive for urgent or regular shipments. Some contractors, for example, charge a flat rate for packages weighing up to a certain weight or volume, delivered to the main commercial centres of the world. As in the case of "groupage", some air services act as consolidators so that a number of shipments can be made under a single airline document and given a rate for a high weight level.

CONTRACT HIRE AND LEASING

Contract hire and leasing arrangements for transport (as well as other plant and machinery) require careful consideration by Supplies as well as by the financial advisers of the company.

The ownership of an impressive fleet of vehicles is an advertisement and a status symbol, but there are significant advantages in contract hire. Under this the ownership of the vehicles is transferred to contractors who are responsible for all except their operation and routeing. The following are some of the advantages claimed (*see also* Table 32).

(*a*) There is no capital outlay by the hirer.

(*b*) Administration is simplified and department costs reduced.

(*c*) Old vehicles are automatically replaced by new models.

(*d*) Vehicles can be painted and lettered to the hirer's requirements.

(*e*) In the event of breakdown or accident, the contractors replace the damaged vehicle from their reserve, and may handle all legal correspondence.

(*f*) Garaging can be provided or paid for by the contractors.

(*g*) Availability may be greater, thus eliminating the need for a reserve fleet to cope with exceptional demands.

(*h*) The contractor can buy vehicles cheaply in bulk.

(*i*) Financial services may be provided, such as leasing, buy and lease back, contract hire packages and fleet management.

FORWARDING AGENTS

Forwarding agents for outgoing transits can be particularly useful to smaller firms not having their own transport and distribution experts. The forwarding agents apply their expertise in the selection of vehicles, routes, loading, etc. and in the preparation of documentation and its clearance. Some agents progress consignments from production through packing, until, accompanied by all relevant paperwork, the goods are shipped through the agency's traffic department. Some provide a "comprehensive service" including land, sea, air, forwarding, shipping and collection and delivery as well as a transport service.

LEGAL IMPLICATIONS OF TRANSPORT

Duties and liabilities

It is important to gain a clear picture of the legal implications concerning a transit. At its start and unless other contractual arrangements have been made:

(a) the purchaser becomes the owner;
(b) the consignor becomes the purchaser's agent;
(c) the carrier becomes the bailee.

(See Sale of Goods Act, 1979 s. 32(1): "Where the seller is to send the goods, delivery to the carrier is deemed to be delivery of the goods to the buyer.")

During a transit damages may lie against a carrier for delay if he was aware of the urgency and if the delay was avoidable. This point emphasises the need for clear and precise communications throughout the supplies cycle, i.e. in this case from purchasing officer to supplier *and* from supplier to haulier. (Hadley *v* Baxendale (1854).)

Where goods are carried at owner's risk the trader must prove wilful misconduct before a claim can be sustained.

The transit ends when the goods are tendered to the purchaser. The act of tendering implies that the goods are held out to him and he must take them. That is to say in the absence of other arrangements in the contract the buyer is expected to provide off-loading facilities and to off-load—in most cases, however, the transport driver will assist. In any event the purchaser is responsible directly goods rise clear of the bed of the vehicle or pass over a ship's rail. At this stage the consignor is entitled to demand a clear signature for receipt. The remaining stages are examined in Chapter 21, goods inwards.

The legal aspects of transport in relation to supplies and materials management are continually changing and vigilance is essential. The following example indicates some of the problems which may be met in an apparently simple transaction. A firm wished to collect an urgent load of supplies which was beyond the rated capacity of the purchaser's own vehicle. They therefore hired a lorry and the haulier loaded it at the supplier's works. Unfortunately, the lorry overturned and the load was lost. The purchasing company lost its claim for damages when the following came to light.

(a) No one checked the adequacy of the vehicle selected.

(b) Whoever supervised the loading should have been aware that it was overloaded.

(c) If no one supervised the loading, the consignor was no less culpable—he should have supervised it!

(d) If the vehicle was loaded in the presence of the hirer, he could be presumed to have responsibility.

(e) The vehicle was inadequately "plated" as to capacity, etc.

Supplies staffs must be aware of the changes in legislation brought about by EEC Directives, etc. These impinge increasingly on almost every aspect of transport operations from hours worked by drivers to tyres and safety of vehicles. To repeat, ignorance of the law is no defence.

Conditions of carriage

When arranging transport it is essential to examine with great care the terms and conditions of the haulier. Checklist 33 indicates some of the areas likely to be covered. Any terms and conditions beyond these should be regarded with suspicion as relieving (or attempting to relieve) the contractor of his legal liabilities (*see also* Chapter 16). Special clauses may be composed or negotiated for special loads and transit conditions or circumstances. It has to be borne in mind that, as with all terms and conditions of contract (particularly those between businesses), each party will seek to transfer as many liabilities as possible on to the other party.

United Nations Convention on multimodal transport

When making, or studying, contracts for the importation of supplies or shipment of finished goods, the purchasing officer should be aware of the United Nations Convention on the legal obligations of International Multimodal Transport of Goods (1980). This imposes an agreed system of liability for the entire transit from the time the multimodal operator takes the goods in charge until delivery. Previously, each unimodal carrier was only responsible for his own stage of the journey. The Convention also sanctions the use of new documentation, and general provisions cover the following:

(a) regulation and control of multimodal transits;

(b) documentation for transit;

(c) liability of the operator and the consignor;

(d) claims and actions;

(e) supplementary provisions;

(f) Customs matters.

The Convention recognises the right of each state to regulate and control transit through its territory, including all steps taken in its national, economic and commercial interests. The Convention also sets limits to liability. It is mandatorily applicable to international multimodal contracts.

MATERIALS HANDLING

Materials handling is an important element in industrial engineering and its study is essential for good materials management.[156][157] Normally Supplies will only be responsible for movements under their direct control, but the principles involved should be known to the Supplies manager and his staff. He should seek to co-ordinate his methods of handling with those of the factory or other unit in which he is engaged. The practical aspects of handling are dealt with extensively in *Storehouse*, but the following brief notes provide a general introduction. (*See also* Checklist 34.)

Powered and manual handling

In one sense all handling is "mechanical handling" because mechanics is invariably involved regardless of whether a human or a power-driven machine is used. The term "powered" handling is used throughout to refer to the latter case. Below are summarised some significant similarities and differences between manual and powered handling.

(a) The human hand is capable of an almost infinite variety of grips and postures. When buying, planning or using handling equipment, it should be considered as a basic mechanical "hand".

(b) The human hand is helped or hindered by the existence—or absence—of suitable "handholds". So is the mechanical "hand". (*See* Chapter 19, powered handling and its effect upon packaging.)

(c) Both human and powered "machines" are limited by distance, height raised, weight, speed and duration of handling operations and the terrain over which they operate.

(d) However, whereas a "human machine" may complain to his foreman (or shop steward) if overloaded, his powered counterpart may break down without any warning, with costly and sometimes fatal results.

Health and safety

Under the Health and Safety at Work etc. Act the responsibility for the "safe and healthy" operation of all equipment is shared by management and workers, and the law must sooner or later catch up with the man who buys unsafe equipment.

Powered handling enables larger orders and their associated intakes and storage to be dealt with economically. However, although larger intakes at less frequent intervals may appear more economical on a basic-price basis, there may be harmful side-effects (*see* Chapter 21, large-volume intakes). Powered handling may also bring with it new hazards from two main causes, namely its ability to handle heavy loads and its ability to handle them more quickly than manual methods. In particular, hazards may arise from the following.

(*a*) Overloading of mobile equipment: haulage, lifting etc.

(*b*) Overloading of static equipment: racks, bins, etc.

(*c*) Damage to floors leading to failure of structure or floor surface.

(*d*) Accidents at corners, lintels, ramps, etc. due to height or width of large loads.

(*e*) Lack of training or retraining of operatives in handling.

Every firm, large and small, should, in addition to the Health and Safety at Work etc. Act, have available and study the following Health and Safety at Work Booklets: *Lifting and Carrying, Safety in Mechanical Handling* and *Safety in the Stacking of Materials.*[158] The local Health and Safety Inspectorate can provide a number of other technical data notes and advise on specialised booklets in the series.

Purchase of equipment

When buying handling equipment many of the guide-lines in Checklist 34 apply. (*See also* Chapter 6, materials and management, particularly cybernetics, terotechnology, tribology and ergonomics, and practical applications in *Storehouse.*

Training for powered handling and instructions for manual equipment must be adequate and need to be insisted upon when placing purchase orders. What a supplier describes as "training" may in the event prove to be two minutes spent with the operative following delivery of equipment. Inadequate training may lead to legal action under the Health and Safety at Work etc. Act.

Control of equipment

Storage, control and issue of handling and lifting tackle—chains, slings, attachments, etc.—is often unsatisfactory. This is particularly so in smaller firms where there is no maintenance department. In such cases a competent storekeeper may be the best person to look after the housing and administration of such equipment, its issue, test records, returns to store and storage.

Licensing of works trucks

The need to license works trucks is not always clearly defined. Usually such equipment is given a separate category of excise duty for goods vehicles designed for use in private premises and used on public roads only for conveying goods:

(a) between the premises and a vehicle in the road in the immediate vicinity;

(b) passing from one part of a premises to another across a road. Fork-lift trucks may sometimes be regarded as a "special case" in this regard. A discussion with the local police may save lawyer's fees and ensure that the law is not broken.

Sources of information

Those wishing to seek professional advice should contact:

(a) The National Materials Handling Centre which provides a wide range of advice and training in stores layout, distribution and handling;

(b) The Institute of Materials Handling;

(c) The Committee for Materials Handling Secretariat;

(d) The Institute of Purchasing and Supply.

CHAPTER 21

Goods Inwards ("Intake")

INTRODUCTION: PROCEDURES FOR INTAKE

Costs of delays

Goods inwards is almost the final stage in the supplies cycle and is a potential loss-centre to the extent that (apart from other factors) it adds to internal lead time. It should, however, be planned at the provisioning stage.

AXIOM: Each day supplies spend at intake adds a day of lead time.

Added lead time must raise the reorder level and thus inflate stockholding. Protracted delay may also result in a loss of validity for any claims on a supplier and cause hold-ups in production. This is of particular importance on urgent or overdue intakes.

Efficiency at goods intake

Although, like order picking, goods intake is never likely to be converted from a loss-centre to an area of profit, it can be greatly improved by work study and better administration. The following are some possible ways of improving efficiency.

(a) Cultivate sense of urgency.

(b) Ensure good liaison with progressing staff.

(c) Improve job satisfaction: competitions, suggestion schemes, etc.

(d) Streamline and simplify procedures.

(e) Prevent loss, misdirection and "stagnation" (goods not cleared promptly to their destination).

(f) Ensure all goods have identification numbers, codes, marks.

(g) Prevent staff "helping themselves" from goods-intake areas.

(h) Provide adequate goods intake space, and keep tidy and uncongested.

(i) Ensure suppliers show order number on all packages.

(*j*) Restrict access to authorised staff only—so far as practicable.

(*k*) Plan for intake (and storage) when orders are first placed.

(*l*) Improve form design (*see* Chapter 3 and *Storehouse*).

(*m*) Improve lighting and writing facilities.

(*n*) Give staff clerical training.

(*o*) Train in safety in handling, etc.

(*p*) Improve communications: regular messengers, pneumatic tube despatchers, etc.

(*q*) Package suitably for handling: orders to specify this.   er to

(*r*) Provide suitable handling equipment.

(*s*) Provide for knocking down, de-nailing, etc. of containers, and for salvage and storage.

(*t*) Accurate, suitable, automated measuring/counting equipment.

(*u*) Provide own labels with orders (*see* Table 1, note (7)).

(*v*) Provide adequate intake, sorting, quarantine areas.

However, streamlining must not impede the accurate control and flow of supplies. Administration must assist such flow without interruption or delay in the final transit stages. An important aspect is the procedure to adopt when extra urgency appears. This often provides a temptation to short-circuit the system—with results that are predictable! If such emergencies occur frequently then special streamlined procedures should be introduced.

Arrangements for different supplies

The nature of the incoming supplies has a bearing on the arrangements made for their reception. These vary with the kind of industry, but may include some or all of the following.

(1) FOR MAIN SUPPLIES a study of goods inwards should start at the planning and quotation stage before the purchase order is placed. The following points should be considered and included on the order form as appropriate.

(*a*) Packaging suitable for the handling equipment.

(*b*) Packaging for shelf-life required in stores.

(*c*) Quantity per package or container.

(*d*) Times for receiving and unloading.

(*e*) Precise location of goods-inwards point.

(*f*) Marking of cases: hazard signs, etc.

(*g*) Available storage space and reservation which may be needed.

(*h*) The type of binning or other storage required.

(*i*) Any special handling equipment.

Where batch production is in operation in conjunction with unit-loads it is important for these to be in phase. If not, there may be heavy movements of returns to store, with congestion there or at the production line. The latter often leads to wastage by operatives due to careless production through excessive quantities of material being available at the work-centre. (BS5729 Part 5 Table 1(5).)

(2) RECEIPTS FROM OUTSIDE SUPPLIERS obviously comprise the highest proportion of intakes. General supplies and supporting goods usually pass direct into store as quickly as possible without inspection.

(3) TRANSFERS between stores and stockyards within a works peri-meter (or between distant points in the same group) may involve special paperwork if warranted by the frequency and volume of movement. In smaller units the normal paperwork with suitable coding should suffice. At the very least, GRNs should be used.

(4) JIGS, FIXTURES, TOOLS, GAUGES, PATTERNS, ETC. usually pass direct to stores and may fail to go through goods inwards when returned from jobs in the factory. They can, however, arrive from outside sources such as subcontractors to whom they have been loaned. As with transfers from other storehouses, there may be no order copy or special paperwork to cover their receipt but at least a GRN should be raised. Difficulties of identification of the goods may result unless they have been carefully marked and the coding is correct. Most of these items will require inspection which is usually carried out by the tool-room inspectorate.

(5) WORK-IN-PROGRESS is unlikely to be physically moved through the goods-inwards bay unless it is received from a branch works. If so, and if it needs inspection before moving on to the next oper-ation, this should be covered by normal goods-inwards procedures.

(6) SUBCONTRACTED SUPPLIES present similar problems to work-in-progress so far as intake is concerned (see Chapter 15). Unless the volume of subcontracting involves special ordering methods the normal procedures will suffice. However, it is particularly important in the case of subcontracts that the order should emphasise the need for the order number to be clearly shown on all documents.

(7) FREE-ISSUE MATERIALS FROM CUSTOMERS require special care and attention. The company is bailee for these and special responsibility thus attaches to their safe custody. If free-issue orders have been issued to the customer and he quotes their number on his paperwork, considerable time may be saved at the receiving bay when identifying and moving the goods to quarantine for inspection, etc.

(8) RETURNS FROM CUSTOMERS fall into two broad groups; those under

"complaint" or "rejected" and those for servicing. These must be dealt with urgently, and the stores layout should include a "customer's" area into which they should be transferred immediately on arrival (*see* Fig. 2). The sales, service, inspection or production departments must be notified as appropriate. The administrative arrangements of many firms are poor in regard to this part of their organisation. It is an area where Supplies and sales collaboration is vital, and where Supplies may contribute to goodwill by prompt attention.

(9) REJECTED SUPPLIES also must have special priority. It is essential that rejects do not find their way into active stock. On incoming supplies they indicate an actual, or potential, hold-up in production. Supplies rejected by the goods-inwards or production inspectors must be returned to a quarantine area and remain there pending disposal or other action. (*See also* below, examination and inspection of goods inwards.) The planning, progress, production and accounts departments (in all instances) must be informed immediately as in the case of goods damaged in transit.

Negotiations with the supplier should be in the hands of the purchasing officer who may—on advice from the appropriate technical department—arrange for the rejects to be returned, corrected on site or scrapped. Replacement is a high priority and some purchasing officers issue a free-of-charge replacement order for this purpose. The practice is to be commended, since it brings the replacement into the normal administrative stream—including progressing and receipt.

(10) REJECTION OF THE END-PRODUCTS may occur following inspection at the work-centre. Such rejects can usually be passed to the scrap bins direct. In some cases—where patents or security are involved—there may be a company ruling that the parts are physically destroyed at the salvage bay.

(11) SURPLUS SUPPLIES FROM PRODUCTION, like work-in-progress, are unlikely to reach stores via goods inwards unless the plant is dispersed. However, its control is important and a storage area should be allocated for this. The following points should be noted.

(*a*) Surplus involves idle, non-productive movement of supplies.

(*b*) In high-technology plant a double inspection may be needed.

(*c*) It is necessary to investigate the causes, which may include:

(*i*) excessive rejection allowances;

(*ii*) inaccurate issues by stores;

(*iii*) excessively large purchase orders;

(*iv*) failure of operatives to use offcuts.

(*See also Storehouse,* surplus stocks.)

(12) SCRAP AND WASTE MATERIALS are usually in the custody of Supplies who provide for reception, handling, sorting, recycling or disposal. Cash benefits can accrue with correct identification and segregation of scrap. To cover the return of such materials, paperwork will be raised by the department sending it. Returns should only be accepted upon authorisation signified by the head of the department or work-centre. This prevents spoiled materials from being conveniently "lost" into the salvage bay, where they pass at nil or nominal value.

(13) MAJOR ITEMS OF PLANT, ETC. often require special treatment due to size or other features. All too often difficulties arise because management have taken such contracts out of the normal Supplies procedures—including those for intake. It is strongly recommended that management should use the Supplies organisation, amending and reinforcing procedures and disciplines to meet the special requirements.

Documentation of capital plant requires particular care in its completion. Apart from the high costs involved, other matters arise such as documentary evidence of "take-over dates", "progress payments", "running tests", "commissioning" and "confirmed delivery dates". These should be available through the normal centralised procedure.

(14) TRANSIT PACKAGING, e.g. cable drums, containers, gas cylinders and pallets: as in the case of jigs, fixtures, etc. (*see* (4) above) these are costly items and must be carefully accounted for if claims by suppliers are to be avoided. Stores must accurately record movements into and between stores as well as receipts and returns. Costs can be high and are a direct drain on cash flow needed for supplies.

Goods inwards in smaller companies
In most smaller firms the goods-inwards and despatch areas are combined, and sometimes even scrap and rejects have been found in the same area. Where physical separation cannot be achieved, barriers or screens should be erected, or use made of "air rights", i.e. a raised space, for one of these operations—preferably despatch. Further suggestions for smaller companies will be found in *Storehouse*.

Intake (reception) areas (BS 5729 Part 5 Table 1(3))
The physical arrangements for goods intake fall mainly within the province of stores and stockyard management and are therefore dealt with in some detail in *Storehouse*. However, they have con-

siderable implications for purchasing and supply management, and are outlined here briefly for that purpose. The arrangements made can significantly affect the total costs of supplies, and comprise four (at least) clearly identifiable areas, as follows.

(1) OFF-LOADING AREA to which the vehicle should be directed. In the case of large units this area may need to be clearly indicated on the purchase order. The delivery vehicle should never leave until a "simple quantitative inspection has been made" (*see* below, inspection of goods inwards).

(2) QUARANTINE HOLDING OR "BONDED" AREA (to avoid misunderstanding the word "quarantine" is used in these notes in place of "bonded" since the latter has other precise and legal connotations.) Goods must remain in this area to "await clearance by formal, qualitative and quantitative inspection".

(3) MARSHALLING AREA where goods are held awaiting:
(a) placement of goods into the correct stores location;
(b) direction to another stores, depot, site or plant;
(c) collection by the user, or despatch to him.

(4) REJECT/DESPATCH AREA. This must be a secure quarantine area in which goods which have failed inspection are held until:
(a) the supplier has examined them;
(b) they are returned to the supplier;
(c) they are removed for rectification by the purchaser in agreement with the supplier—and to his charge.

Goods which cannot be properly identified and returnable containers may also be held in this area.

Instructions to staff (BS 5729 Part 5 Table 1(5) and 5532 (4.7)) Instructions to goods-inwards staff should be included in any Supplies Manual (*see* Chapter 3) and must cover the following on incoming consignments:
(a) Receiving.
(b) Identification.
(c) Checking, counting, tallying.
(d) Preparation of goods received notes, signature of delivery notes and consignment notes.
(e) Action in event of non-arrival, shortages or damage.
(f) Arrangements for inspection and quarantine.
(g) Arrangements regarding materials for bonded stores.
(h) Action in relation to progress section when goods arrive.
(i) Weighbridge drill.
(j) Security: gate passes, etc.

(k) Disposal of packages and containers.

(l) Return of packages and containers.

(m) Disposal of hazardous packing materials: nailed battens, wire and plastic banding, etc.

Some of these points are discussed further below, and goods-inwards procedures are covered in more detail in *Storehouse.*

Identification of goods at intake (BS 5729 Part 5 Table 1 (1))
Identification of goods at intake is a stores function (*see Storehouse*). However, this process is helped or hindered according to whether or not the purchasing department uses vocabulary descriptions on all purchase documents and ensures that cross references are provided if the supplier's (or shop floor) vernacular produces alternatives from the company's own nomenclature.

Documents required for identification of intake include:

(a) copy of purchase order, giving identification details, quantity, etc.;

(b) supplier's advice note, giving details, date shipped, purchaser's order no. (BS 5191 (4.3));

(c) carrier's consignment note which "may be additional to but should never replace the supplier's advice note" (BS5729);

(d) supplier's packing note (usually within the package), giving details of contents of particular packages only (BS 5191 (4.3));

(e) supplier's contents note, usually on exterior of container, listing number of packages contained therein;

(f) supplier's delivery note, usually a copy of advice note and always accompanying the goods (BS 5191 (4.3));

(g) "receipt note" (BSI), referred to here as "goods received note" (GRN), prepared at goods inwards (intake) (BS 5191 (4.3)).

DOCUMENTATION

Logbooks (BS 5729 Part 5 Table 1 (4(1)))
A logbook (or "goods inwards book") may be kept to record the arrival of consignments. This is useful where there are a large number of small deliveries, and where immediate inspection is impracticable. Smaller companies which may not yet use a "goods received note" system would be wise to keep at least a logbook to record the arrival of consignments and names of hauliers, etc. (*See also Storehouse.*)

Goods received notes (BS 5729 Part 5 Table 1(4(2)). *See also Storehouse)*
A document of some kind is essential to record the goods delivered

on each intake. Usually this is a goods received note, known famili-
arly as a "GRN". This should show sufficient details of goods for
their correct identification and routeing, together with references to
the supplier's advice note, delivery note, etc. Use may also be made
of the GRN to record returnable containers, etc.

Other methods may be used in smaller firms, such as the following.

(a) Endorsement of the goods receiving copy of a purchase order.

(b) If part deliveries are involved, subsequent preparation of
GRNs for later intakes, or photocopies of the original order with
quantities adjusted to balance due are needed.

(c) Endorsement on suppliers' documents (advice notes, etc.),
by impressing with a rubber stamp the details to be completed.

Only very small firms can use these streamlined methods because
in most cases the following need to be notified of goods received.

(a) Purchasing department, to clear order.

(b) Progress section, to cease progressing completed supplies.

(c) Accounts department for evidence for clearing invoice.

(d) To advise the department which originated the demand.

(e) The department to which the goods are cleared from the
receiving department, for example, the stores or the quarantine
store to await inspection.

(f) Internal transport and distribution.

(g) Goods inwards department for record, etc.

(h) "Back orders", to make good any short deliveries.

Documentation for packages

Where traffic warrants its use, a package record must be arranged.
On this are registered packages, containers, pallets, etc. that fall into
the various groups discussed below.

(1) "RETURNABLE CHARGED AND CREDITED UPON RETURN" (*see also*
above, transit packaging). The supplier should be expected to credit
in full upon return of the items. However, this is not always so, and
is a point which the purchasing officer should watch. For example,
some firms demand payment for wear and tear, or impose a "penalty"
for overdue retention, etc. These are cases where checking the small
print of acknowledgments can be advantageous.

(2) "RETURNABLE, BUT ONLY CHARGED IF HELD BEYOND A STATED PERIOD"
is a similar category to (1) above. However, these usually comprise
items of lesser value upon which the supplier seeks to avoid the
costs of invoicing, claims, credits and recording. An economical
method which avoids clerical work should be arranged, such as the
return of the units on a "one-for-one" basis against new intakes.

(3) RENTED OR HIRED EQUIPMENT may include items which could be regarded as part of the production line of the supplier, e.g. cable drums or gas bottles. Hire charges, if they cannot be avoided, should be agreed during negotiations for the contracts. It is also important to fix the cost in the case of loss—this may be extremely high! Records, usually including the supplier's serial numbers, must be kept. Where possible these should be combined with stores records which they may partly duplicate. For example, cable paid off a drum may be recorded on a card attached to the drum and used as a bin card.

(4) HANDLING AND LIFTING EQUIPMENT may be provided by a supplier on extended loan for future shipments against a forward supply contract or as part of a major plant installation. In either case, inwards records must be kept and the equipment noted on the statutory register of lifting tackle, so that arrangements can be made for inspection, testing, marking, etc. Steps should be taken to avoid the absorption of this equipment into the company's maintenance store without proper segregation from company plant.

(5) PALLETS AND CONTAINERS are a special category, and their use has greatly expanded in recent years for international, inter-factory and internal transport. Co-ordination and control may add considerably to Supplies work in recording and controlling their movement. The following action may be required:
 (a) sorting according to ownership;
 (b) sorting for size and type;
 (c) segregating for inspection and repair;
 (d) marking and re-marking;
 (e) return to suppliers, pallet pool, etc.
Supplies staff should be made aware of special responsibilities for all handling equipment under Health and Safety at Work regulations. The Health and Safety Inspectorate may consider that while such equipment is in the possession of the factory it is part of the factory's own plant for purposes of the statutory register, inspection, marking, certification, etc.

NOTE:
 There is, of course, a further category, i.e. expendable pallets and other containers, usually considered as "non-returnables". However, in the present climate with its emphasis on conservation of resources, a purchasing officer may find it profitable, where large quantities are involved, to make special arrangements with the supplier for their collection and return in bulk, possibly as return

loads against deliveries from the supplier. Records, however, should be avoided for this category.

Signing for goods received

The importance of signing correctly for goods received must be emphasised. This applies particularly to any signatures on suppliers' documents which are a link in the chain of "documents of record" and which, in a legal dispute, could be taken in evidence. Signing should only be done by staff authorised for the task. The Sale of Goods Act 1979, s. 34(1) has a bearing on this and reads as follows:

> Where the goods are delivered to the buyer, which he has not previously examined, he is not deemed to have accepted them unless and until he has had a *reasonable* opportunity of examining them for the purpose of ascertaining that they are in conformity with the contract.

"If specific goods have been ordered and appear to have been accepted unambiguously against the signature of a duly authorised member of the firm then that will constitute heavy—though not unassailable—evidence that the goods have indeed been delivered and that payment is due." (*The Buyer,* Vol. 4 No. 2.)

A further aspect of importance in the signature for goods inwards concerns the provision of containers which are loaned or charged as part of a contract. The signature on the notes must indicate that the quantities have been checked. In one case a stores officer had insisted that he should personally sign *all* notes. He did this without leaving his desk after the storeman had unloaded the goods. He refused to delegate the job of signing to the storeman who unloaded them. Counting became slipshod and the company was committed to figures which bore no relation to the containers they actually had in their stores. The correct procedure would have been the delegation of signing to the storeman who handled the goods. This would have helped ensure an accurate count by inculcating a sense of responsibility and avoided a claim of £1500!

Internal distribution

The goods received note should bear clear instructions to indicate the routeing of the goods. The purchase order copy should have already informed the goods-received section whether inspection was needed and other details, such as urgency, precautions and hazards in handling.

Where a goods received note is not used, or where the supplier's advice note is used with a rubber stamp impressed on it, the stamp should show the route taken by the material.

After inspection the consignment may pass to the user or to the main storehouse as appropriate. The goods received note—or stamped imprint on the advice note—should make clear provision for this.

Release notes
Release notes are used in the larger and more specialised industries such as those in the high-technology category. Release from quarantine will only be permitted if this document is presented bearing the stamp of the company's own inspectorate or that of the visiting inspector of a customer.

INSPECTION OF GOODS INWARDS

Supplies inspection falls into the following two main categories as envisaged in BS 5729 Part 5 Table 4(2) and BS 5532 (4).

(a) Examination at intake by stores staff (as mentioned earlier) to check quantity (for shortage), obvious damage or loss. (BS5729 Part 5 Table 1(2(1)).)

(b) Quality control inspection to BS4891 (8.4), which comments as follows: "In determining the amount and nature of inspection at intake, consideration should be given to the controls at source and to objective evidence. If a supplier has effective quality control the purchaser may reduce his degree of goods inwards inspection. The purchaser's knowledge of a supplier's quality stems from proven performance, records and previous assessment. Inwards inspection should complement and supplement source quality control rather than ignore or duplicate it."

Where throughput is large, separate quarantine and other secure areas may be warranted for various categories such as the following (*see also* Fig. 2):

(a) materials awaiting inspection;

(b) returns from customers for service and repair;

(c) rejects from customers;

(d) production materials from suppliers;

(e) production materials surplus to requirements (if to be re-inspected).

Although such reserved space is costly this must be balanced against savings of materials lost, mislaid or going into production without inspection.

NATO unclassified document AQAP-4, entitled "Inspection of purchased materiel and services", is worth studying as a useful guide-line for inspection of industrial supplies. One important point emphasised in the document is that the purchase order shall contain a clear description of what is ordered and also details of "receiving inspection".

Rejections

(BS4891 (12) and BS5729 Part 5 Table 1(4).) Rejections can be classified into the following main categories (BS 5532 (4.20–4.61)).

(a) Outright rejection: goods cannot be rectified, modified or used.

(b) Qualified rejection: goods can be rectified, modified or used.

(c) Compatible defects: goods which would not be incompatible with the remainder of the assembly. They may not affect its final appearance so that if incorporated into the end-product their subsequent identification will be difficult. Even worse the defect might affect the functioning of the assembly and the flaw may not be revealed until the product is put into service. Under product liability legislation, which is likely to extend throughout EEC and other countries, customers who receive faulty goods may collect heavy damages.

(d) Less obvious defects which although missed by inspection would be found during assembly (i.e. the parts either do not fit or are an imperfect fit).

(e) Hidden defects which are not apprehended during inspection, production, assembly or examination by the customer. In this case they can involve a potential risk of failure in the short or long term. The final result may be very serious.

(f) Poor standards: defects may have no effect on assembly, production or use, but indicate a general deterioration of standards.

Weightings can be given to these various deficiencies and appropriate action should be taken. (*See also* Chapter 6, quality assurance and quality control.)

Action on reject notes must be given at least the same priority as shortage, damage and loss.

Action on shortage, damage or loss

Action must be prompt. If not taken in a "reasonable time", the buyer will be in a poor position to make a sustainable claim. If the goods or packages show evidence of suspected damage or shortage, it is best to "fail safe" and endorse the goods-inwards documents (particularly those of a supplier) with the words "unexamined", "damaged", "suspected damaged", or "suspected shortage" as appropriate. However, these are merely immediate warning signals. They must be followed up within the time stipulated by the supplier and haulier and shown in their contract documents.

Action must be firm, positive and immediate, and unless liquidated damages have been agreed, some clear idea of costs must be assessed. If not, the supplier, wishing to maximise his profit and to minimise his loss, may only offer a nominal sum in compensation in discharge of his obligations leaving his customer with no material and with the costs of stoppage. (*See also* Chapter 22, payment.)

If special forms are provided for notifying loss, damage or shortage, these should be given priority, and passed via the purchasing department to:

(*a*) the carrier;
(*b*) the supplier;
(*c*) invoice clearance office;
(*d*) stores.

In particular it must be borne in mind that the haulier as bailee of the goods is entitled to reasonable access to examine any goods claimed as damaged during transit.

In view of the urgency with which any shortage, damage or loss must be notified it may be worth considering the delegated procedure, together with appropriate letter/form, outlined in *Storehouse*.

Causes of damage

Investigation into causes of damage may be assisted by statistical analysis which may suggest areas for inquiry, such as those given as examples in Chapter 6 and the following:

(*a*) careless packing;
(*b*) inferior packaging;
(*c*) inefficient hauliers;
(*d*) unsuitable transport method;
(*e*) careless handling by supplier;
(*f*) careless handling at intake;
(*g*) poor (or lack) or supervision;
(*h*) cutting corners to gain bonus.

Under-deliveries

A distinction must be made here between inadvertent shortage due to spillage, loss or theft, and deliberate shortage by a supplier who cannot ship the order quantity. In the latter case, although much of the action is as already outlined, there are other implications. In earlier times a supplier would raise what was known as a "back order" to cover an under-delivery to his customer and notify him that the balance was to follow. In recent years this practice has been abandoned and many suppliers rely upon the purchasing officer of the customer to follow up for the balance or take such other action as may be necessary.

PHYSICAL ARRANGEMENTS FOR INTAKE

Layout and location of goods inwards

Lack of planning for intake of goods results in loss, delay and damage. Apart from the actual unloading, provision should be made for an unpacking area. For reasons of efficiency, security and safety, goods should not be unpacked in the immediate area at which they are received, but in designated unpacking areas.

Quarantine and unpacking areas may occupy up to 10 per cent of stores area and must be adequate to avoid congestion and encourage good industrial housekeeping. The following should be considered when laying out the stores:

(a) quarantine for goods awaiting inspection;
(b) supplies destined for other stores;
(c) returnable containers, etc.;
(d) ISO containers;
(e) bulk materials;
(f) returned materials from works;
(g) capital plant, etc. for projects;
(h) subcontract forwarding/receiving.

Strict security is essential for most areas, particularly (a), (b), (g) and (h). Return loads for delivery vehicles can prove profitable at (c) and (f) if the supplier accepts materials for reprocessing. ISO containers not only require space but also heavy lifting gear, special ramps or jacking equipment. As regards unloading containers, see BS 5073 (7) and also *Storehouse* for more detailed treatment. Bulk materials (loose lumps or particulates) require space reserved for conveyors, while liquids require the provision of pipe connections. Both involve bins, hoppers and silos and may incur hazards of fire and/or static electricity. Capital plant, etc. often requires special provisions due to size, weight and other features. Wherever possible the purchaser should arrange for delivery of plant direct to site without physically passing through the goods-receiving bay. (*See also* above, major items of plant.)

The goods-inwards bay should be located at the centre of gravity of the points served where this is practicable. The correct location will ensure that an orderly flow proceeds into the production lines or the stores complex. Cross- and counter-flow should be avoided. Location is particularly important where powered handling is not employed.

Whether the firm is large or small, it is essential that supplies should only be received at well-defined locations where proper recording arrangements have been established. The goods-inwards bay should be geographically distinct from stores and despatch, where this is practicable.

The provision of a suitable unloading area is vital. It should be designed with existing road (and rail) traffic in mind.

Large-volume intakes

Unnecessarily large consignments can prove costly. This may be particularly serious for a small firm which may need to withdraw labour from production to cope with the arrivals if demurrage is to be avoided. In larger companies, costs may be incurred if there is a permanent increase in stores handling equipment and personnel to deal with peak periods, leaving plant and operatives idle at other times. (*See Storehouse,* utilisation factors.)

If it is necessary to use personnel who have not been trained in handling, there may be further problems, as follows.

(*a*) Untrained staff are more accident prone. Over 30 per cent of all industrial accidents arise from lifting and handling—many of these in stores, goods intake and despatch.

(*b*) Pay differentials may lead to disputes.

(*c*) Lack of interest (in stores) may lead to carelessness.

(*d*) It is always more difficult to train, discipline and supervise people when outside their own work-place.

Where, however, powered handling is used efficiently the size of consignment is relatively unimportant. In fact, the larger the shipment the better the load factor on the handling plant—provided the load is within its capacity.

Intake measurements

The use of dip rods and weighbridges is discussed in *Storehouse*. However, it is important to note here that methods of measurement should be clearly covered on purchase orders. (*See* Chapter 10, units of measurement.)

CHAPTER 22

Invoicing and Payment for Supplies

INTRODUCTION

Receipt of invoices and their checking are the penultimate stages in the discharge of a contract. The final stage, payment, relies upon some form of check that the details on the invoice are correct. This in turn relies upon the accuracy of details on the purchase order, GRN, etc. Payment leads to the presumption that the supplier has satisfactorily completed his part of the contract. If payment is made with reservation (for example, if it is *ex gratia*, to assist a supplier with cash-flow problems or other contingency) these must be made clear to the supplier at the time of remittance.

AXIOM: Suppliers *tend* to overcharge.

There is no imputation of dishonesty in the above axiom. It is merely the result of many years of observing invoice queries. The facts are that the supplier's estimating and other costing staff, invoice clerks and checkers have a first duty to see that their company is not deprived of its due rewards as a result of any miscalculation or undercharge. Each therefore tends to err in one direction—"overcharge". Equally the purchaser's Supplies staff have a duty to ensure that an overcharge is not made—or paid.

Unpriced orders are an open invitation to a supplier to "adjust" his price when invoicing—"to meet increasing costs, inflation, etc.". Requests for price increases are dealt with later under contract price adjustment (*see also* Chapter 13).

CHECKING INVOICES

Methods
Invoices for large sums should be individually and fully checked. Normally such invoices are prepared from more sophisticated costing

data than are those for smaller jobs. The latter may be the result of merely costing on a materials content and value basis plus a percentage for oncost and profit (i.e. "value-added" basis). The cumulative effect of percentage price increases on a number of small invoices priced on an added-value basis may be considerable, and may include many previous errors resulting from the original data and formula and multiplied many times. The principal methods of checking are outlined below.

(a) 100 per cent check of all invoices against priced orders.

(b) 100 per cent check of all invoices with price lists and prices on orders: "belt and braces" method to check pricing of orders by purchasing department!

(c) 100 per cent check of all invoices using price lists where orders are unpriced. (In this case it is important to investigate why the orders were unpriced.)

(d) Check of invoices over a certain value only.

(e) Random sample check of a certain number each week.

(f) "Bad performers" to be subject to 100 per cent check for a reasonable period, or until they improve.

(g) Check by computer against order price or standard prices fed into the computer program.

(h) Invoices outside tolerance limits to be referred to purchasing department for them to query with suppliers.

Invoice checking: a mini-case study

Supplies costs can be saved by cutting out the tedious tasks of checking at the various stages of order processing. Not infrequently an investigation and report by an O and M team or by management consultants recommends elimination of what they regard as unprofitable cost-centres, namely the checking of requisitions, orders, acknowledgments and invoices. Although the mini-case study which follows is devoted to the checking of a simple invoice for a small sum, it calls attention to a number of side-issues which refute many of the arguments of the anti-checking theorists. For instance, the claim is sometimes made that suppliers do not overcharge habitually and that a supplier who knows he is trusted by his customer will be meticulous in his invoicing—but he may not!

The case study enumerates a number of queries which could be indicative of much larger costs and losses awaiting the opportunity to occur. Interesting results follow if the reader increases the quantity from 3 to 30 and again to 300 and 1,000 off as the requirement for "triconiums".

EXAMPLE:

(1) Draughtsman in firm "A" sends to the purchasing officer a purchase requisition for 3 "triconiums" which he priced at 3s. 5d. each less 2½ per cent for cash in seven days. He used one of the very old catalogues kept in the drawing office and greatly prized for the valuable "information" they contained. (*See also* Fig. 20). He ignored the fact that prices were by then decimalised and relied on the purchasing officer to make any correction.

(2) The purchasing officer, noting that the requisition was marked "urgent" and was a repeat of previous ones, immediately sent an unpriced order marked "price as before" to supplier "B".

(3) The cost office at "A" accepted the price on the requisition copy and allowed for 50p (i.e. 10s in pre-decimal terms) and a profit of 10 per cent (£1) on the sale—which had been quoted to customer "C" as £10 for the complete assembly.

(4) Supplier "B" sent a priced acknowledgment but this was not checked by the purchaser "A".

(5) No one asked, so no one was told, that the first assembly was a prototype and that an order from "C" for 1,000 units (3,000 "triconiums") depended upon its satisfactory performance.

(6) In the meantime firm "C", who had bought the prototype from "A" asked the latter to quote for 1,000 units which "A" did, including in their price the original figure. (Someone is going to lose £1,500!)

(7) Finally the invoice for the three triconiums arrived at "A", priced as in Fig. 73.

(8) The cost office of "A" checked up on the job and discovered that instead of £1 profit they had made a loss of £1.50 on this order.

(9) The purchasing officer, having failed to check requisition, order, acknowledgment or invoice, also failed to ascertain the job for which the "triconiums" were needed. Had he conferred with the sales department regarding future possible usage of triconiums this *might* have caused them to check future possibilities with customer "C".

(10) On the very day the purchasing officer received the "rogue invoice" under query with a caustic note from the managing director concerning the loss on the job a further requisition arrived for three more "triconiums". This was even more urgent than the previous one as the units were to replace the first three which had been damaged in stores. On this occasion the purchasing officer threw urgency to the winds and deferred action while he obtained a new catalogue. Upon its receipt he spent time studying the various options, as follows.

(a) Place an order for three "triconiums" and meet the surcharges

	INVOICE	Number 1001
	(duplicate)	

③

To:

Messrs. A. Mugg Ltd.,
Egg Street,
Eastwick.

From:

The Triconium Co. Ltd.,
222, Trinity Street,
Truro,
Cornwall.

Your order number AB 6002	Our ref: AM/TTT	Date 22nd February 19-5

Package marked AB 6002	Despatched by British Rail

Quantity	Description	Price each	Total price
3 only	Left-handed triconiums (1)		2.00
	Carriage charges (2)		.50
	Broken package charge (3)		.50
			————
	Net cash (4)		3.00

Please note:

(1) *Minimum order charge.* We regret that due to increasing costs of administration we are obliged to make a minimum charge of £2.00 for any order.

(2) *Delivery charge.* Our policy in the past has been to deliver free within 80 km of these works. Unfortunately we are now forced to charge carriage on consignments of less than £10 to one destination.

(3) *Broken packages.* Triconiums are now only packed in lots of ten. You will appreciate that broken packages incur costs for repacking and a charge of 50p is made where this occurs.

(4) *Settlement terms.* Our previous prompt cash discount of 2½ per cent from prompt cash (seven days) has been withdrawn. Terms are now strictly net. (This invoice is laid out in accordance with British Standard 1808.)

(5) Price will be that ruling at date of despatch, as indicated in our quotation and acknowledgment and standard terms and conditions.

(6) We reserve the right to invoice at the price ruling at date of invoice.

(7) Overdue accounts will be charged at the rate of 2 per cent per calendar month or part thereof following the date due for settlement.

(8) Duplicate copy of our invoice is for use as a debit advice.

Fig. 73. A "rogue" invoice

this time notifying the cost office accordingly.

(b) Order £10 worth (i.e. 20 triconiums) thus avoiding extra charges (see notes (1), (2) and (3) on Fig. 73) and leaving seventeen for stock.

(c) Order ten "triconiums" and avoid "broken package" surcharge (50p) but pay delivery costs.

(d) Calculate the economic order quantity.

(e) Send an enquiry for a firm-priced quotation thus avoiding the "price-ruling" charge which is examined later is this section.

Most of the options available involve the purchase of more "triconiums" than the three shown on the requisition. The purchasing officer must therefore assess probable annual usage before selecting which alternative to take. Assume however, that, again without collaboration with other departments, he bases his decision on the previous year's consumption which was five units. He can now calculate how many weeks any surplus "triconiums" may remain in stock unused before storage and holding costs break even with any savings in price on the initial transaction (See Fig. 51 but with time along O—X axis.)

Suppose storage and holding costs are 25 per cent of the mean stock value per year of 50 working weeks. This cost would be £0.5 per week per £100 of mean stock carried. With option (b) he would save £1.50 and be left with seventeen surplus "triconiums" (at 50p each) giving him about 3½ years' stock at current usage of five per annum. Cost per week (while *idle* in stores) would be:

$$\frac{£0.5}{£100} \times 50p \times 17 = £0.043 \text{ per week idle}$$

If the saving for option (b) was £1.50 the number of weeks the seventeen triconiums could remain idle and break even on the savings would be £1.50 ÷ £0.043 = 35 weeks (approx.). If, however, they remained in stock for 3½ years (175 working weeks) and were used at the steady rate of one every 10 weeks, the saving of £1.50 would be exceeded by the mean costs of storage and holding, i.e. £0.043 × 175 ÷ 2 = £3.76 (approx.).

He has of course saved acquisition costs and this must be taken into account separately unless he uses option (d) which in theory at least makes an allowance for this.

Other questions to ask are listed below.

(a) Why are only left-handed "triconiums" used? (Is there a large stock of right-hand units idle in the store?)

(b) Would the supplier give a better price if bought in pairs?

(c) If they are not standard stock items, should they be?

(d) Could "variety reduction" result?

(e) Could they replace another item in use?

(f) Could they be replaced by another stock item—or standard?

(g) Can they be eliminated entirely?

(h) As they are a small standard item, would an FSA be appropriate?

(i) Could an enquiry to sales have revealed that bulk quantities would be needed long before week 72?

(j) Is it worth checking invoices?

It should be clear that a dogmatic and doctrinaire approach based on invoice value alone may result in financial loss. This consideration may lead to the extension of the list of checkable invoices to include all those for direct materials and supplies used in the end-product.

Further comments on Fig. 73

CLAUSE (5). "Price at date of despatch" is not uncommon although it is unlikely that the supplier will add the explanatory note shown. It is, however, added here to alert the reader to the urgent need to watch out for this ruse at the enquiry stage, or at the latest at the acknowledgment stage. If inserted later it should be challenged as invalid under contract law—*see* (7) below.

CLAUSE (6). There is a subtle difference between this, "Price at date of invoice", and clause (5) and it is of course unlikely that both would actually appear on the same invoice. It is a device attempted by some suppliers to obtain a "windfall profit" (in one case, nearly £1,000) by merely delaying the invoice after delivery in order to take advantage of a price rise known to be pending or being negotiated with a central body. (*See also* Fig. 74, contract price adjustment.)

CLAUSE (7). "Overdue account surcharge" is of course the converse of a prompt cash discount and increasing numbers of suppliers seek to apply it. Such surcharges canot be legally supported unless they were stated at the contract (ordering) and acknowledgment stage, or subsequently communicated and agreed with the buyer.

CLAUSE (8). Duplicate invoices are sometimes submitted by suppliers without necessarily explaining their purpose. In one case a large multinational insisted upon sending duplicate copies—one to the chief accountant and the other to the purchasing officer of a large and complex multi-unit undertaking. It proved difficult, without costly checking procedures, to ensure that both copies of the invoice were never paid.

Who shall check invoices

This is sometimes a source of debate. There is no reason why the purchasing officer should see any invoices except those under query for price, discount or description.

Arguments for (+) and against (−) the purchasing officer checking invoices are listed below.

(a) Time is consumed on a non-Supplies task. (−)

(b) There is no check against collusion in dishonest practice with a dishonest member of the supplier's staff to rig prices and recover the difference. (−)

(c) Accountants are more expert in numeracy to check calculations, and therefore they should do it. (−)

(d) Invoice clearance is quicker and this improves supplier relationships. (±)

(e) Fewer invoices will get "lost" in the system, i.e. between offices. (±)

(f) Supply staff are kept alert on price and changes. (+)

(g) Valuable price information is accumulated. (+)

(h) Specialist Supply staff know and can check many invoices from memory with computer accuracy. (+)

(i) Checking can be combined with recording; annual rebate amounts, allocations on production schedules of suppliers, etc. (+)

Board intervention

In some undertakings the financial director or even the board makes a random or selective check on invoices after payment. The nature of the check can vary from verification of the actual need by the requisitioner to the price paid by the purchasing department. Such policing, though unpopular, can have important and not altogether unhelpful implications for the Supplies department. (*See* Chapter 4, terms of reference.)

Methods of raising queries with suppliers

A straightforward variance from the price shown on the purchase order may only need a request for a credit note, a corrected invoice or an explanation. However, in the case of invoices for large and complex contracts the methods of query are more complex. Some methods of notifying suppliers are as follows.

(a) Give full details of the alleged discrepancy. A miscalculation by the purchaser may result in an underestimate of the error! The supplier may accept this either deliberately (or in good faith) to his own advantage and against the purchaser. This procedure is therefore not always the best.

(b) Give no details. The supplier is merely asked to check his costings. Errors for large sums which have been only "half-suspected" have been found in this manner—and sometimes others than those which may have been suspected. This technique has the advantage that it is fair to the supplier and his staff in that it results in the error being checked back to the source. It also has a salutary effect upon careless suppliers.

(c) State the area of the suspected overcharge. This is a good compromise for the second method. It may speed up the settlement of the query but it may also result in other areas not being checked so that a partial overcharge may still take place.

CONTRACT PRICE ADJUSTMENT (CPA)

Contract price adjustment formulae have been developed for various product groups of industries. These seek to provide a fair and reasonable basis for changes in costs by relating them to materials and labour indices (*see* Fig. 74). The materials index is weighted in relation to the average contents of each constituent material in the end-product, and to its price. The labour cost is based on the nationally agreed rates for the industry concerned. The guiding principle is that the materials which have been ordered in the early stages of the contract will have been paid for by the time a datum line is reached. The supplier may have "contracted" to purchase his materials (possibly by "letter of intent"). He should certainly have included in his tender the prices of materials last published before its issue. Where a labour increase takes place before the datum line it will apply to the whole contract period. If, however, the wage award was after the datum line, it will only apply for the unexpired period of the contract, as in the example in Fig. 74.

All contract price adjustment claims should be checked, because of the many pitfalls which can occur and the large sums usually involved.

The establishment of correct dates is essential. For this purpose it may be necessary to challenge delayed deliveries—unless previously agreed. If this is not done, the datum may fall on a peak as shown in Fig. 74, greatly inflating the price. Calculation of the remainder of the agreed formula gives the adjustment to be applied to the contract for labour and materials.

Vigilance is no less essential in periods of inflation. At such times it is the *rate of change in increase* of price that may need checking. The date of invoice may be such that the operative datum misses a downturn in the rate of change.

Suppliers should always submit calculation sheets where CPA is applicable to the contract. Some have been known to omit sending

411

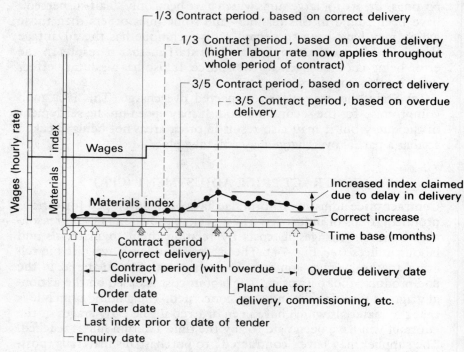

Fig. 74 Principles of contract price adjustment

(1) The enquiry has no effect on contract price adjustment and can be ignored for this purpose. (2) The tender should be based on the last indices published *prior* to its submission. (3) The order must be placed within the quotation validity period. (4) The contract period runs from the date of order to the date when due for shipment or a later agreed date. (5) Datum lines must be drawn at appropriate times during the contract in accordance with the regulations applying at the time of the contract.

calculation sheets, because, they explained, there had been no increase, when actually there had been a decrease!

Before entering into contracts which involve contract price adjustments the purchasing officer should make sure he has details of the formula appropriate to the product group from which he is buying, e.g. BEAMA, Civil Engineers and so on.

PAYMENT

Payment is the "moment of truth" for those who have ignored the control of commitments at the time of ordering supplies (*see* Chapter 2, commitment accounting). Money is commited at the moment of placing an order even though payment may not be made until

412

later. Actual payment is a financial and accountancy function which is normally outside the responsibility of Supplies. On the other hand, as with many other functions, Supplies have a considerable interest in payment and payment policy.

When negotiating a contract, extended settlement periods should be regarded as part of the price structure offered by the supplier. For example, an offer of 90 days payment compared with 30 days from another supplier should be assessed by calculating the saving in interest on borrowing or the "opportunity cost" on the different

TABLE 37. EFFECTS OF "MONTHLY CASH SETTLEMENT" PAYMENT POLICIES

Action and policy on payment	Cash effect	Effect on supplier relationships	Supplier reactions	Ethics and policy
(a) Pay when due, collect 2.5 per cent (i.e. pay in 7 days)	Gain approximately 36.1 per cent per annum	Good	May suppose the purchaser has unlimited cash	Good
(b) Pay when due but borrow cash to do so	Gain (or lose) difference between cost of loan and 2.5 per cent	Good	May suppose the purchaser has unlimited cash	OK
(c) Wait 30 days and pay in full	Gain 23 days free loan but lose 2.5 per cent cash discount	Not bad		OK
(d) Wait 60 days and take the 2.5 per cent	Gain 53 days free loan and steal 2.5 per cent from the supplier	Bad	A wise supplier will add 3 per cent to his next price	Bad
(e) Wait until supplier presses for payment	Gain free loan but lose 2.5 per cent, and more if supplier claims on overdue accounts (see Fig. 73. note (7))	Poor	May add "over-due clause" on future orders	Shaky

413

periods offered for the price involved in the transaction. For example:

$$\frac{(90 - 30)}{365} \times 10\% \text{ (say)} \times £50,000 \text{ (price of purchase)}$$

$$= £822 \text{ approx.}$$

Payment policies

Table 37 shows the effects of some payment policies when a 2.5 per cent discount on prompt cash settlement is offered.[159][160] It includes the unscrupulous practice of those who not only delay payment but then also (try to) take the prompt cash discount, perhaps from a firm smaller than themselves!

(1) DELAYING PAYMENT is a cheap method of borrowing money. However, the supplier may keep a record of "customer performance" similar to the purchaser's "vendor rating" scheme. He may then (if he is wise) on later orders seek to restore the position by inflating his price (see policy (d)), inserting a claim clause for "late payment" (see policy (e), or giving higher priority and better service to his more satisfactory customers.

(2) PROMPT SETTLEMENT is clearly a good method of building up satisfactory supplier relationships. The economics of taking "prompt cash discounts" are summarised in Table 37. Such discounts represent a very high rate of annual interest: in the example, 2.5 per cent for strictly monthly settlement yields 36.1 per cent per annum at compound interest. Most accountants can make arrangements for prompt clearance on a priority basis with a special reservation clause for the few smaller invoices which may be cleared without immediate checking, such as those against FSAs, etc.

Requests by suppliers for special or prompt payment should always be brought to the attention of the purchasing officer. Such requests may be the first distress signals of a supplier in trouble. Instant, firm and tactful action may be needed to ensure that free-issue materials, jigs, tools, gauges, or even fixtures loaned to the supplier are not impounded by a receiver.

(3) PROGRESS PAYMENTS must only be made against properly drafted progress certificates signed by duly authorised staff.

(4) MONTHLY (OR OTHER) PAYMENTS against consolidated invoices should be considered for use with forward supply arrangements and contracts, as part of the streamlined procedure resulting from these schemes.

(5) CREDIT TRANSFERS are used by some to settle invoices automatically through their bank. Advantages are speed of clearance, improved supplier relationships and simplicity (avoids numerous cheques, reduces postage, etc.). Disadvantages may be the amount of detail required by the bank and suppliers on transfer and difficulties in sorting out queries, complying with special discounts and rebates, etc.

(6) RETENTION MONEY is a proportion of the contract price (usually 5 per cent) which is withheld from payment until the end of the maintenance period agreed in the contract. The period (usually 12 months) is calculated from the actual date of commissioning and/ or of taking over. Its purpose is to ensure that the manufacturer or contractor shall carry out the terms of his contract in regard to the performance of the plant or construction works, etc.

(7) FACTORING of their invoices by suppliers may result in the purchasing firm being involved in payment of its supplier's accounts through their factor's invoicing and payment collection arrangements. The intervention of a factor may lead the purchaser to conclude that his supplier is weak financially and needs this action to bolster up his finances.

(8) PAPERLESS ELECTRONIC INVOICING as a method of payment was made legal by the Finance Act 1980. Although at the time of writing its application is chiefly restricted to large retail businesses, supplies managers should examine the possibilities of using it for invoicing and "on-line ordering".

Checking rebates

It is as important to check rebate statements as invoices—possibly even more so because it involves the actual recovery of money from suppliers. The latter may have in some instances overlooked the submission of rebate credits on the ground that they were "waiting for their customer to claim for rebate due".

An efficient accounts department with good Supplies liaison can be an effective method of applying the necessary discipline and procedure to ensure rebate payments are forthcoming when due.

Where the accountants cannot assist in this manner, or if an extra check is required, the following methods can be adopted.

(a) Use of commodity code plus supplier code and computer printout.

(b) File extra copies of orders with the rebated contract.

(c) Obtain extra copies of invoices on rebated contracts. (Not recommended practice but can be useful if great detail is needed.)

CHAPTER 23

Storage of Supplies

INTRODUCTION

This volume is chiefly concerned with supplies and materials themselves, and for that reason only a few leading principles on storage are given here. The physical aspects of handling and storage are dealt with in greater detail in *Storehouse.*

Storage of supplies involves the principle aspects of materials handling in supplies and materials management.[161][162] In order to maximise efficiency it must be fully integrated with the preceding and subsequent operations, i.e. goods inwards and goods issue operations (*see* Chapters 21 and 24). Instead of being considered as a loss-centre it should be studied, planned and managed as a profitability-centre, because, as in the case of other Supplies activities, savings made here can contribute directly to company profit—if not wasted elsewhere in the business!

Many of the points mentioned in the chapters on materials handling and transport are equally applicable to stores and should be read in conjunction with this chapter. For example, the training of operatives in all three fields has much in common and this again emphasises the need for integration of the whole Supplies operation.

SAFETY

Safety in stores should be a major consideration, for this is an area with an unexpectedly high accident rate. The costs of safety measures, including good training, must be weighed against the savings to be made from preventing damage to men, materials and plant as well as from improved job satisfaction.

Stores planning should be in the charge of a qualified executive such as a supplies manager, or his equivalent in a smaller firm. Workers employed in handling and stacking should be carefully selected and trained in basic safety rules for handling, lifting and stacking as well as in the elementary mechanics of safe loading, overturning, centre of gravity, and so on.

Storage is "static handling" with gravity and vibration as two of many enemies. Storage equipment such as bins, racks and hoppers must be marked clearly with the following:

(a) safe working load (mobile and static);
(b) warning and precaution notices (pedestrian and vehicular);
(c) loading and unloading points;
(d) lifting attachment points;
(e) floor bearing strengths, restrictions of moving loads;
(f) height and other loading gauge limitations;
(g) location of overhead pipes, cables and other services;
(h) aisle markings, corner guards, etc.

LOCATION AND LAYOUT

(BS5729 Part 5 Table 3(1(1)).)

Location
The location of the stores can affect work-flow and thus productivity and profitability—even in a small works. The siting of stores at the centre of gravity of demand appears an attractive solution. However, in a small, growing factory, this may lead to the stores being continuously compressed by the demands for more production space surrounding it, while at the same time having to carry increasing stocks to support the increasing production.

"A.B.C." analysis is a good starting point for location and layout. However, it must be noted that factors such as "frequency of demand" and "volume and weights" of supplies are often very different from the results of "A.B.C." analysis of variety against value. If statistics are to be used in this manner then a separate "A.B.C." analysis is needed for each set of data.

Layout
Layout of stores and stockyards should be on the "flow" principle. Reversal of flow wastes money and cross and counter-flow is likely to result in congestion and accident. When studying flow in stores the following points should be considered.

(a) Intake to stores.
(b) Setting in place in bins, racks, stacks, etc.
(c) Possible redeployment while in store.
(d) Selection and sorting for issue.
(e) Sequence of requirements.

417

(f) Frequency of movement.
(g) Distance moved, horizontally and vertically.
(h) Weight moved and stored, stacked, etc.
(i) Speed of movement.
(j) Whether track-bound or free-range movement.

COSTS OF STORAGE

This section examines only actual storage costs. The financial aspects of stock-holdings and their cash values are dealt with in Chapter 13.

The cost of storage should be a prime consideration, particularly in a small firm where liquid cash may be in short supply. Costs include insurance, the premiums for which are based on the value of the company's assets in plant, buildings and stock. (*See also* Checklist 35).

The costs of plant, buildings and equipment have an effect on the amounts available for expenditure on other activities such as sales promotion, production equipment, development and research and above all on supplies.

Storage volume

The storage volume allocated should be carefully related to the quantity to be held. Managements who look on every metre of storage space occupied as a metre lost to production tend to expand production space without a corresponding increase in storage capacity. The growing production is serviced by increasing stock flow through the same size of store intended for the previous smaller production. This may appear to improve the stores efficiency, but is usually a false economy. Often it results in congestion and chaos, with weakening efforts to maintain a good flow through the stores. Other losses arise from incorrect identification and bookings, duplications, deficiencies, stock-outs, and errors in issue.

Powered handling is one solution to the problems of increased production and overcrowded storage. It can improve flexibility of flow and make maximum use of "air rights".

Storage costs may be increased due to the over-application of economic order quantity formulae which do not, as a rule, take full account of storage volume occupied.

Storage capacity and the storage factor resulting from the levels carried should be continuously reviewed, as should the approximate cost per cubic metre of usable storage capacity available.

Intake quantities

Large intakes (based on EOQ) result in overloading of stores capacity. This in turn can lead to costly hire of additional storage capacity, or to the construction of new stores buildings and storehouse equipment which may not be fully used.

The cost of inspection and stock-taking may be increased if intake quantities are inflated. There may be congestion due to delay in completing the paperwork needed to cope with heavy shipments (*see also* Chapter 21, large-volume intakes).

Deterioration of stock will occur if the quantities are so large that the shelf-life is exceeded before consumption takes place. Shelf-life is essentially a technical condition of storage (*see* Table 13) but may to some extent be adjustable, e.g. the purchasing department may be able to get a specification giving longer shelf-life. It may be possible to achieve the same objective by improved storage conditions or packaging. Recommended storage conditions and shelf-life should be obtained by the purchasing department at the enquiry stage for all new supplies, particularly those of high technology. (Time may be needed to obtain special storage equipment.)

The position may also be improved by good store and stock control ensuring that issues of stock are on a FIFO basis. This avoids accumulations of old stock which will be doomed to pass their limit of shelf-life before issue. There is also possible loss of control where excessively large quantities are stocked so that less care and economy are exercised in their use. This may also lead to a drive to dispose of them and so avoid detection of overstocking.

Large intakes also increase the risk of obsolescence due to consumer choice, fashion, or technical development. Allied to the lack of control mentioned above there may arise increases in wastage, spillage, loss or theft. Safety may be involved, too. Many materials are hazardous when stored in bulk unless special, and sometimes costly, precautions are taken. (Hazards in stores are dealt with in detail in *Storehouse. See also* Chapter 6, Table 13, properties of materials.)

Suitability of storage equipment

The provision of bins and equipment which are not suited to the materials they are called upon to house can add greatly to the costs of handling and storage. Life of some equipment is relatively short and the method of depreciation should have careful study. Materials handling is a rapidly developing field and new, economical and efficient designs of equipment are continually appearing, rendering the old equipment obsolescent or even obsolete.

There is for all materials a "best method" of storing. New equipment may be needed for new materials and new lines of production. The considerations here will be whether the need is likely to be a continuing one, and also whether the supplier can be persuaded to provide packaging to obviate the provision of special equipment for storage and handling. Below are summarised some of the losses that can result from the use of unsuitable equipment and bad stores practices.

(1) WASTAGE (AND SPILLAGE). Losses due to wastage often arise in the handling of materials in liquid or powder form. Selection of suitable containers, stands and pouring arrangements improve the control of flow and accuracy of dispensing, and reduce wastage. The designs of chutes and pipes for fluid-flow are highly specialised and the services of a consultant may prove profitable. On simple schemes the provision of such elementary devices as a barrel tilt can prevent waste.

(2) SPOILAGE. This applies particularly to small components and particulates in congested store conditions where segregation is difficult and they become mixed. The resulting blend may produce a more or less useless mixture of waste. The provision of suitable unit containers, e.g. tote box types, may help. However, where the trouble is due to congestion, bad lighting or similar conditions, these must be rectified before any improvement can be made. Shelf-life, too, must always be taken into consideration under this heading.

(3) EVAPORATION. Loss of material due to evaporation may be unavoidable. It may also be due to bad storage conditions or equipment. The former should be recorded as percentage loss under normal conditions, so that the latter can be checked and watched.

(4) THEFT AND PILFERAGE. Such losses can also be added to storage costs. The chief causes are lack of proper discipline and supervision by (or of) stores personnel. Where free access to stores is permitted, thefts become more difficult to prevent or trace. Moreover, the vigilance of the stores personnel may be reduced because their authority is undermined.

SELECTION AND PURCHASE OF STORAGE EQUIPMENT

Selection and purchase of storage and handling equipment requires that attention be given to the following points:
    (a) first price and depreciation;
    (b) safety in use; stability, strength, accessibility;
    (c) suitability for use; for goods stored, containers etc.;
    (d) costs in use (life-cycle costs);
    (e) utilisation and storage factors, utilisation of building cube;

TABLE 38. STORAGE EQUIPMENT: ITS SELECTION AND USE

Type of equipment	Some applications
(1) Shelving: open-skeleton type	Boxed goods, tote pans, articles of regular shape
(2) Shelving: closed (bin) type	General stores
(3) Shelving: cantilever type	Larger assorted, awkward-sized goods and long lengths
(4) Cupboards: lockable	High-security and dangerous goods, etc.
(5) Cupboards: with small drawers	High-value small tools, gauges, etc.
(6) Tote pans in racks: fixed	Small but heavy items
(7) Tote pans on pallets or pallet frames	For transport to work-centre
(8) Tote pans on back-board	At open-access store points at work-centres
(9) As (8) but on trolley	Mobile stores to serve work-centres
(10) Pallets: flat, non-reversible, on floor or in racks	All general goods sufficiently regular in shape to stack on pallets
(11) Pallet converters	For conversion of flat non-reversible pallets to make them suitable for stacking
(12) Pallets: flat, reversible	Goods of sufficiently regular rectilinear shape and strength to support further pallet loads stacked on top of them
(13) Pallets: post for self-stacking (racks unnecessary but if used these will require bridges to accept feet)	Goods which although sufficiently regular and rectilinear in shape to stack on pallets are not strong enough to sustain further loads stacked upon them
(14) Pallets: box	Small items and those of irregular shape and/or those of a fragile nature
(15) Pallets: box with drop sides	As above at order-picking stations or for dispensing at work-centre
(16) Unit containers (closed and open top, hopper outlet, palletised base, etc.)	For powders, granular materials, etc.
(17) Tanks, hoppers, skips, etc. (palletised base, etc.)	For liquids, etc.
(18) Tree racks	Horizontal storage of bar, section tube, etc.
(19) Honeycomb racks	As (18)
(20) Vertical racks, single-sided (see Fig. 75), double-sided "A" type	Vertical storage of bar, section, tube, etc.
(21) As (18) but mobile	As (18) but giving much improved storage factor

TABLE 38 contd. STORAGE EQUIPMENT: ITS SELECTION AND USE

Type of equipment	Some applications
(22) Sheet racks: horizontal	Polished sheets can be interleaved, soft materials that will not stack on edge or deform
(23) Sheet racks: vertical	Better use of space than (22) and easier handling for friable materials such as glass
(24) Sheet racks: "A" frame	As (23)
(25) Drum racks	For bulk storage with FLT, etc.
(26) Drum pallets	For self-stacking with FLT, etc.
(27) Drum stands tilts	Oil stores, etc.
(28) Mobile bins: manual	Inexpensive method of making maximum use of space in small stores for slower moving goods
(29) Mobile bins: powered	For larger store units
(30) Pallet racks: fixed	If pallet loads are constant size there is no point in buying adjustable racking
(31) Pallet racks: adjustable	If sizes of goods vary rack spacing can be varied to improve storage factor
(32) Pallet racks: mobile	Where storage factor is important due to cost-in-use of building but selectability is less important
(33) Pallet racks: drive through	Improved storage factor but some loss of selectability

(f) integration of the storage and handling system.

Table 38 lists different types of storage equipment together with their applications.

Size and capacity of storage and handling equipment

These aspects need careful study before purchase and installation. Some authorities recommend that an over-capacity of 25 per cent be allowed above the expected current needs. However, while this may be a useful guide-line it is preferable to spend time and effort on a more realistic forecast. The "first cost" of extra capacity is not directly proportional to the increments in size (*see also Storehouse*) and too much unused capacity may prove very costly.

Costs

Costs of storage quipment together with its storage and utilisation factors are significant in the holding costs of stock. Figure 75 shows

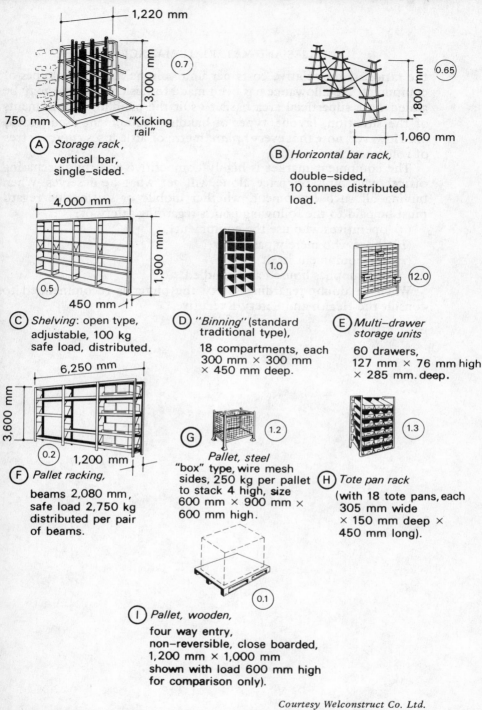

1,220 mm

3,000 mm

750 mm

"Kicking rail"

(0.7)

(A) *Storage rack*, vertical bar, single–sided.

1,800 mm

1,060 mm

(0.65)

(B) *Horizontal bar rack*, double–sided, 10 tonnes distributed load.

4,000 mm

1,900 mm

450 mm

(0.5)

(C) *Shelving*: open type, adjustable, 100 kg safe load, distributed.

(1.0)

(D) *"Binning"* (standard traditional type),

18 compartments, each 300 mm × 300 mm × 450 mm deep.

(12.0)

(E) *Multi–drawer storage units*

60 drawers, 127 mm × 76 mm high × 285 mm deep.

6,250 mm

3,600 mm

1,200 mm

(0.2)

(F) *Pallet racking*,

beams 2,080 mm, safe load 2,750 kg distributed per pair of beams.

(1.2)

(G) *Pallet, steel* "box" type, wire mesh sides, 250 kg per pallet to stack 4 high, size 600 mm × 900 mm × 600 mm high.

(1.3)

(H) *Tote pan rack*

(with 18 tote pans, each 305 mm wide × 150 mm deep × 450 mm long).

(0.1)

(I) *Pallet, wooden*,

four way entry, non–reversible, close boarded, 1,200 mm × 1,000 mm shown with load 600 mm high for comparison only).

Courtesy Welconstruct Co. Ltd.

Fig. 75. *Comparative costs per unit volume for various types of steel storage equipment*

Cost of standard binning (D) taken as base (1).

423

the ratios of the relative costs per unit volume for various types of equipment. No allowance has been made for aisles, etc. This may be added on a superficial area basis to suit the handling requirements of the situation, layout, types of handling equipment used and so on. However, note that every *square* metre of aisle loses *cubic* metres of volume of storage.)

The equipment market is highly competitive and the purchasing officer who buys on price alone will get what he deserves. When buying all such equipment, whether mobile or static, due regard must be paid to the following points regarding safety of:

(a) operatives who use the equipment;

(b) those who merely pass it by;

(c) the equipment itself;

(d) the supplies housed and handled.

When in doubt regarding safety the buyer is recommended to consult the Health and Safety Executive.

CHAPTER 24

Selection, Issue and Distribution of supplies

INTRODUCTION

Selection, issue and distribution form an interface between storage and production and require close integration to avoid production hold-ups and ensure smooth flow. In the modern concept, Supplies tasks are not complete until supplies reach their final destination in the works. Stores should therefore be responsible for internal distribution to work-centres. One result of this is that production staff leave their work-centre less frequently as goods and materials are fed to them, or provided in open-access bins at work-centres.

When placing orders the purchasing officer should have regard to ease of counting, dispensing, breaking and resealing packages, weighing, measuring and so on. Safety and ease of handling should also be studied, and above all use at work-centres themselves.

Good supply control, efficient service and security all demand that access to storehouses and stockyards should be restricted entirely to stores personnel who are the custodians of the goods. There are difficulties in keeping to this rule where drive-in trucks are used and where night shifts are worked with stores unmanned. In any case the whole stores issue procedure and the matter of access should be clearly laid down and enforced. Where this is not done stores discipline will be broken and careless and inefficient storekeeping result with breakdown of materials control

APPLICATION OF WORK STUDY TECHNIQUES

Selection and issue are the second phase in the inevitable double-handling of all stock, i.e. into and out of stores. "Work study" techniques can be usefully applied to stores issues, with particular reference to man-hours spent, distances travelled and loads carried. The provision of adequate marshalling areas affects not only materials management but also the original costs of stores layout and building. The amount of time and attention devoted to this important area is usually inadequate, resulting in very high costs due to congestion, loss, delay, damage, pilferage and many other losses. These will effectively prevent any other economies, such as those discussed below (*see* preparation in stores) and may also inhibit material conservation itself.

POLICIES FOR DISTRIBUTION OF SUPPLIES

Raw materials for production
Being mostly classification "A" requirements, these should have received special attention in regard to methods of packaging, handling and distribution to the work-centres or process, etc. Above all, their storage and inevitable double-handling "in" and "out", must be given special consideration.

General and miscellaneous supporting goods
These are classification "B", or sometimes "A". The problem here is to make them immediately available on demand and yet to avoid excessive issues beyond actual needs. Some suggestions are included later.

Embodiment goods and "direct" materials for production
The former fall into two categories: those required specially for specific jobs and those of a more general nature. The stock-control and purchasing arrangements for the first of these should make provision for tracing them to the actual job on which they are used if so required for costing purposes. Where not directly costed, consideration should be given to streamlined methods of issue such as open access and kit preparation. (See *Storehouse* for details.)

Free-issue and other customers' goods
Custody and issue of these goods are a special responsibility of the company and need close attention from the point of view of materials management, particularly handling and control of quantities issued, etc.

Transfers to other storehouses
Transfers to other storehouses may arise from demands by them for materials to replenish their bins, or from the need to reduce stock in the main store. The latter could be a warning sign of bad stock control, bad planning, or both. Transfer may take place due to work having been moved from one shop or work-centre to another

in a different part of the factory. In all cases the movements should be controlled and recorded in detail, not only for financial purposes but also to ensure that physical control is exercised. It is usual for special transfer vouchers to be used for this.

Where "concentration stores" are in operation the flow of materials is more difficult to record and control. It must be a matter for decision according to the merits of each case whether record and control shall be central or at each concentration store. The personnel in the latter know what they issue and to whom. Their records are likely to be immediately up to date. On the other hand, if the group of factories or depots is highly organised centrally the paperwork may flow to a central point for central control with computers and computer terminals and visual display units.

External distribution (and shipment overseas)
The practical, physical aspects are dealt with in *Storehouse*. Here we are more concerned with the administration, documentation and arrangements for distribution. Chapters 19 and 20 should be read in conjunction with what follows here.

The flow of materials to the despatch bay may fall into several groups. There may be spares and equipment for customers which, as extras to complete equipments, may not have passed through the production machinery. They may have been sent direct from the finished parts store to the despatch bay with the necessary paperwork for their release and shipment. In some industries, such as aircraft manufacture, inspection and special "release" documentation may be needed before despatch.

POSSIBLE SAVINGS AND CONTRIBUTIONS TO PROFITABILITY

Conservation in stores by good materials management
Economical issue from stores is an often neglected aspect of materials conservation. The issue of "smallest first" can prove highly profitable where demands arise sporadically for materials such as sheet, tube, bar, etc. Clearly this is a discipline which may prove unpopular with the operatives who naturally prefer full-size stock instead of short ends or offcuts! (*See* Chapter 25.)

Success in the application of the discipline will require a measure of integration and co-operation between Supplies and other functions, support from the production manager, and liaison with foremen and operatives on the shop floor. Those in the drawing office and works planning office can assist by suitable notes on drawings and work-sheets, etc.

It must of course be understood that there is a break-even point between the savings of using "smallest first" and any extra costs in setting-up, machining and other operations. If the result is negative it may pay to consider disposing of the "remnants" through the salvage bay. Alternatively the cost office may assist by making some adjustment in costs so as to produce a viable end-use for these items.

A valuable spin-off from "smallest first" is better housekeeping in stores due to the smaller accumulations of offcuts and other untidy and "difficult to store" goods.

Pre-preparation in stores

This may be considered part of the issuing and distribution process. A few suggestions are listed below (these are dealt with more thoroughly in *Storehouse*).

(a) Repackaging from bulk into smaller containers.

(b) Cutting heavy stock (e.g. 150 mm steel bar): avoids heavy transportation.

(c) Fettling, trimming and de-burring: avoids injuries to hands.

(d) Making up preliminary assembly kits (however, purchasing may buy ready made up).

(e) Making up sets of raw materials into stillages, pallets, etc.

In many of the foregoing the question of materials management and safety may be involved, for example, at (c) the avoidance of hand injuries. In cutting bar to length the transport of heavy stock to the works for cutting may be avoided. In some of the other suggestions the administrative savings by action at the purchasing and stock-control stages may be beneficial. There should also be a reduction in the risk of incorrect quantities being issued.

All of these considerations are, however, eclipsed by the economic one of reduction in period of stock commitment (*see* Fig. 49). Production time is often extremely short in relation to storage time. If preliminary work enables production to start later and still achieve the same completion date, clearly intake into stores can be later, too.

It must be granted that these concepts of store operations have several aspects which need careful attention from the point of view of the management and industrial relations.

Suitability for goods and materials stored

This aspect of materials management could fill a number of volumes. However, apart from specialist supplies required for specific industries, the range of common items is comparatively small and most do not need special storage. Nevertheless, in all cases the supplies manager and his staff should be aware of basic mechanical and chemical effects upon storage, handling and stock. (*See* Table 13 and *Storehouse*. Reference should also be made to BS5729 Part 5 Figure 2 "Examples of storage problems associated with certain materials".)

Delivery to work-centres
A less controversial activity than pre-preparation, and one which falls more legitimately within the province of Supplies, is delivery of materials to the work-centres (*see also* introduction to this chapter).

This is clearly a device for the larger industrial unit. Growing firms often lose the benefits they could gain by not introducing it at an early stage of their growth. Delivery to work-centres whether on demand or by regular time schedules, requires good advance planning. This is the point at which many production units show their inefficiency. While this aspect of production is beyond the terms of reference of this book, it emphasises still further the need for integration of the Supplies functions and consultation between Supplies and production. This is particularly true in regard to aspects of production related to materials handling.

Open-access bins at work-centres
The final phase mentioned here is a logical extension of those previously discussed (*see* Chapter 7). The pre-preparation work within the stores mentioned earlier could be looked upon as an intrusion of production into stores. Open-access bins (*see* Fig. 2) are an intrusion of stores into works. This method is in effect an extension of the issuing procedure. The most immediate economies result from savings in production time at the work-centre, in paperwork in the store and in the pre-planning stage.

Implications for stores staff
Many of the procedures outlined above put further responsibility on the storehouse operatives who must:

(*a*) be able to read correctly, parts schedules and possibly assembly drawings;

(*b*) have an eye to the articles they are handling as to their condition and suitability for use, noting if there has been any deterioration in store which could bring them below usable quality (i.e. practise good materials management);

(*c*) marshal and pack in an orderly manner to save the time of the operative using them.

CHAPTER 25

Recovery, Recycling, Salvage and Disposal

INTRODUCTION

Recovery, recycling, salvage and disposal (RRSD) are aspects of materials management which require integration into the total Supplies and materials concept upon which this book is based.[43][74][163][164] As in the case of stores, many firms regard this area as an inevitable loss-centre and in doing so throw away a significant amount of profit, or, in some cases, actually spend money in order to throw it away!

AXIOM: "Money saved is money earned " (Henry Ford).

TYPES OF SCRAP AND SURPLUS

"Arisings" take many forms which require different policies. Some forms are discussed below.

Returns

Returns, surplus from production, usually go into stores; if so, inspection may be needed, and/or the segregation of such "returns" from main stock may be essential.

Excessive returns may indicate prodigality of issue. This may possibly be due to inaccuracies at the works planning stage leading to careless use and wastage of materials. For these reasons, and where quantities are large, record should be made of such returns. The figures should be included in the periodic Supplies reports so that directives for corrective action may be given.

Offcuts and scrap

Other surplus materials (apart from raw materials) include offcuts, blanks from circles or from irregular stampings, short ends of rods, tubes and sections. Many industries produce large quantities of offcuts and tend to accumulate these as well as surplus materials from various jobs, many of which may never repeat. These tend to be hoarded "in case they are ever needed"! Arrival into stores of considerable quantities of offcuts should be investigated by Supplies. In production situations they may represent a serious and avoidable loss of profit. On the other hand, they may reflect bad buying or provisioning, or a failure in the works planning office or drawing office to define needs accurately.

RE-USE OF OFFCUTS, ETC. OFTEN REQUIRES SPECIAL EFFORT BY SUPPLIES STAFF. There may be resistance from operatives, who naturally prefer a single mass of material. This applies particularly where operatives are on piecework. (*See* Chapter 24, conservation in stores by good materials management.)

Where large volumes of materials are involved a careful balance must be drawn between contingent costs incurred in re-using material and the replacement cost of new material. It must be noted that from the latter must be deducted the salvage value of off-cuts if they were sold for scrap instead of being re-used.

In addition to offcuts most production departments produce quantities of waste such as swarf, turnings, drillings and millings. These are usually materials of one kind and grade per production run. They are of much greater value in this condition than if mixed by allowing them to accumulate with other jobs.

SEGREGATION OF SCRAP. With the foregoing in mind segregation should be done at the work-centre wherever practicable. Methods include conveyors from machines to scrap bays, the more usual types of simple equipment placed at the work-centres such as "skips" to be removed by fork-lift trucks (either tipping type or with a rotating head on the truck), tote pans with tote-pan trucks and paper sacks in sack stands.

Stores should collect and deposit the contents directly into the appropriate salvage bays without further sorting, and weighing can if necessary be carried out en route.

Labels may be needed for identification and/or record purposes and colour coding may be worth considering. Paper sacks are low in price, disposable and can be used without separate labels and are thus very suitable for smaller companies wishing to avoid unnecessary clerical labour.

Pollutants and by-products

Many pollutants are active chemicals, and many active chemicals are useful in industry as raw materials or catalysts. As such, recovery, salvage, recycling or disposal should always be investigated. For example, recovery of sulphur from gas streams can be profitable, besides improving the environment.

Materials management with enterprise and initiative may enable materials orginally categorised as waste to be sold as by-products. The intervention of the Health and Safety Executive to stop pollution by a factory process has also been known to lead to the pollutant being discovered to be a valuable by-product. Where this occurs it reveals a weakness in materials management. Like variety reduction, recovery, recycling and salvage are disciplines which must be continuously applied. They will not occur accidentally.

Oils

Cutting oils are a secondary "arising" from swarf (*see Storehouse*). A number of firms offer advice, service and equipment for the separation of such oils from swarf and other arisings. Most other oils (hydraulic, lubricating, transformer, etc.), besides many other fluids, can be profitably laundered. (*See* Checklist 37.)

Rejects

Production rejects are an important group of arisings which contribute to the tasks of RRSD. They fall into the following main categories.

(1) SUB-STANDARD PARTS, components or goods may be re-binned in some trades for sale at lower prices or they may be sent back for further treatment or machined to bring them up to standard. In both cases the physical and record controls must be strictly kept to prevent incorrect reissue—especially in times of short supply or when customers are pressing for delivery, and in high-technology areas.

(2) COMPLETELY SCRAP ITEMS may have some value as raw materials within the firm: for example, incorrectly machined castings in its own foundry. On the other hand, they may only be fit for sale as scrap to a scrap merchant, in which case it is important to decide whether they must be broken up before disposal to prevent their sale as "as new" or to make "gifts of designs" to competitors!

(3) PROTOTYPES may incorporate patent or secret features. Policy must, as a rule, be for such to be broken up beyond recognition. The list of approved purchasers should be closely vetted for this category of disposal.

Redundant plant

Redundant plant and vehicles may be advertised in trade publications or in the national press. Close attention needs to be paid to the increasing number of regulations relating to the sale of second-hand vehicles and also Health and Safety regulations relating to plant for which the vendor (in a direct sale for use) could be liable.

Surplus working stock

Surplus working stock (*see Storehouse*) must be given special attention. In the first place any significant surplus quantity of working stock must indicate a major error in planning, procurement, provisioning or production and as such should be investigated by management. Disposal also requires management policy, guidance and control so as to avoid the possibility of a competitor obtaining a low-price—or even free—sample of raw material. Direct sale through a local or national waste material exchange enables the vendor to exercise some control of the final destination of the material.

Building waste and scrap maintenance materials

(*See also* Chapter 5.) These are often a major cause of untidy scrap and salvage bays and sometimes prevent the proper segregation of waste from production to ensure good prices are paid on disposal. Suitable training of the company's own maintenance and building staff by courses such as those run by the Institute of Building (*see* Appendix VI) can lead to a more professional attitude to what may be a loss-centre at the salvage bays. The Institute also recommends closer attention to goods which, although not required for their original purpose, could be used elsewhere on site or at a different site.

POLICIES AND ACTIONS FOR SUPPLIES

Apart from other aspects, the purchasing department should be in touch with sources of supply and thus know where to "place" the surplus over wide markets. Moreover, ability to negotiate and knowledge of markets should enable them to get a good price. Company policy may include reservations as to the firms (such as competitors) to whom their scrap or surplus plant shall (or shall not) be sold. Circumstances may, in fact, demand that surplus is broken up before disposal.

Integration

Liaison by Supplies at all stages of materials management should be a corner-stone of policy in relation to RRSD. This should involve consideration by Supplies of the needs of design and development, the drawing office, production, packaging, stores, transport and so on. It should also involve their consideration of supplies. Once more it is important to emphasise the need for integration of whoever performs the various tasks mentioned.

Policy on salvage

Decisions on policy often call for vision and determination. The former is required to see what is likely to be needed and what is not. The latter is required to overcome the hoarding instinct. The decisions must be made jointly with all concerned and the economics of the situation carefully examined. The supplies manager who takes a unilateral decision on what to scrap invites trouble.

Whether the surplus or scrap is materials, goods or plant, three major factors in its re-use or disposal are as follows.

(a) *A good memory.* Good methods of recording. Otherwise scrap may get back into circulation.

(b) *Rapid communication.* Delay in decision-taking must not occur or the market for its disposal may be missed.

(c) *Good relations.* Production and design must make a suitable and concerted response to the approach for the use or disposal of surplus.

Security

Security becomes involved if effective RRSD policy results in the accumulation of a pool of valuable material. It is usually difficult to keep salvage bays as tidy as main stores, thus making the detection and prevention of theft more difficult. Records may be the only means of showing that the pile of valuable scrap is not building up as quickly as may be expected. (Thieves have been known to tunnel beneath scrap heaps of copper and to extract the lower layers without apparently disturbing the heap!)

Valuable and "attractive" materials should therefore be stored in locked compounds, regularly inspected and recorded. If scrap is disposed of to a scrap dealer on a contract basis, his co-operation should be sought in maintaining security. Where sales are on a casual basis, cash before collection should be insisted upon. It is important, however, to keep a balanced outlook and to avoid applying elaborate records and controls, the costs of which may exceed the value of the sales.

Salvage and sales

Salvage may be helpful in expediting delivery to customers. While one would not pretend that this could be a major factor in improving deliveries, there are some areas in which salvage can assist, particularly in the jobbing industry.

For instance, offcuts, if correctly identified, stored, and in some cases recorded, may enable an urgent job to be started in advance of the arrival of the main supply of materials. There is also the possibility of using salvage for "first-offs" or prototypes.

Similarly, a small surplus may arise from a number of jobs. Often the percentage allowed for scrap and reject components may be too pessimistic and the full quantity will pass inspection. The customer cannot, unless the contract is so worded, be compelled to accept these extra components. If they are carefully stored until the next time the same customer calls for an urgent shipment, they will be available to give a quick service.

Records
Records of waste and scrap (*see also* Chapter 3) must be kept to a minimum because they are a direct charge against any possible profit from salvage and recovery operations. Where quantities and value warrant, however, the following are useful ratios.

$$\text{Materials utilisation ratio} = \frac{\text{value of scrap and waste (at cost)}}{\text{total sales of product}}$$

$$\text{Recovery efficiency ratio} = \frac{\text{cash received for sales} + \text{value in re-use}}{\text{value of the same materials in product}}$$

Records may also be needed to enforce security. If so they must be geared to the Supplies communication system to ensure prompt reaction to apprehend whoever has breached the security.

Where flow is large and diverse an "A.B.C." analysis may show where areas of profitability can be concentrated upon to advantage.

Waste contractors
"Approved lists" of waste contractors on similar lines to those for suppliers may be needed if the output of scrap and waste is considerable and there are numerous outlets (*see also* Chapter 3).

Legal aspects
Legal aspects of RRSD must be carefully studied and covered suitably from contract for supply, through production to this latter stage, to ensure they comply with current enactments, national and inter-state, and with local bye-laws. New laws may be expected to cover not only the factory and its operatives but also the public, and to become increasingly stringent as regards pollution, transits and housing of dangerous materials.

The Control of Pollution Act 1974 brought together under one statute all previous legislation concerned with environmental pollution, including the Deposit of Poisonous Waste Act 1972. It should be studied by any who have significant quantities of hazardous materials and waste to dispose of.

AXIOM: Good materials management should eliminate much of this chapter!

The Institute of Purchasing and Supply

The Institute (the IPS) has about 16,000 Corporate Members, Associates and Students and is the second largest professional Purchasing and Supply organisation in the world.

IPS Members hold appointments in most sectors of industry, commerce and the public services and together they spend about £100 billion annually on goods and services. Their activities cover the whole range included in the chapter headings of this book and its companion volume *Storehouse and Stockyard Management.*

IPS Members exercise a central and significant influence on the management of enterprises great and small, in both the public and private sectors, and it is the Institute's principal objective to make as effective as possible the contribution to the economy of the Purchasing and Supply function.

The IPS is the central reference point in the United Kingdom for all matters affecting Purchasing and Supply. It sets, tests, and assesses professional standards and arranges appropriate supporting education and training facilities. It provides advice to government and national bodies and to the public on matters in which members' professional knowledge and experience can be helpful. Members, Associates and Students are required to adhere to the strict ethical code set out at the end of this appendix.

Education and training

The IPS attaches the greatest importance to its role in the educational field. The need for an increasing flow of men and women of high quality into the functions represented by the Institute is greater now than ever before and the IPS Professional Examinations Scheme is widely accepted as the best means of assessing the calibre of applicants for responsible posts. In addition the IPS offers courses at a supervisory level, leading to the ASPS Certificates in Purchasing and Stores (*see* below).

THE IPS PROFESSIONAL EXAMINATIONS SCHEME provides for a thorough grounding in business studies (including economics, statistics, finance and law) as well as studies of specialist Purchasing and Supply subjects. The examinations are in two parts—the Foundation and Professional stages—with appropriate entry points for holders of "A" level passes, BTEC and SCOTBEC awards, and degrees. Success in these examinations, together with three years' responsible experience, qualifies for admission to Corporate Membership and the use of the designatory letters MInstPS.

Over 120 educational establishments in the UK offer block release, part-and full-time courses leading to the IPS Professional Examinations Scheme and correspondence courses are available currently from two colleges.

The Institute has students in over thirty countries and holds its examinations twice a year almost anywhere in the world.

With the aim of increasing educational support for its students and to meet more fully their individual needs the Institute encourages employer-sponsored block release courses. It is currently developing linked private study courses (combining a correspondence course with the benefits of personal oral tuition), in-house courses to meet the specific needs of certain industrial, commercial and public service organisations, in the UK and overseas, and conversion courses for people transferring from other functions of management to Purchasing and Supply.

THE ASPS CERTIFICATES IN PURCHASING AND STORES offer an opportunity for those employed in purchasing departments, stores and warehouses (who do not have qualification required for IPS membership) to obtain a recognised qualification, leading to membership of the Association of Supervisors in Purchasing and Supply, which is sponsored by the IPS. The Association's members have the right to use the designatory letters ASPS and qualify to enter at the Foundation stage of the IPS Professional Examinations Scheme.

PRACTICAL TRAINING COURSES. The Institute's courses programme offers annually 170 courses of from one to five days duration. It is designed to cater for the full range of an organisation's training requirements in Purchasing and Supply, from courses providing a rapid introduction for the novice to tuition for senior managers with specialist requirements. Over twenty courses are provided to train buyers in the retail and distributive trades.

Specialist conferences and seminars

The IPS runs about fifty specialist conferences a year. These events differ from its courses in organisation, content and purpose. They aim to bring together buyers and suppliers and others with a common interest in an industry, activity or material to discuss current problems and longer-term questions of mutual concern. Specialist conference delegates are kept up to date with a commercial and technical environment which may be changing rapidly owing to such factors as market forces, legal decisions, EEC Directives, the introduction of new systems or product development.

"Specialist sections" are responsible for running these conferences and for maintaining liaison with members on matters of common interest, including over thirty specialist sections and subjects.

Technical Advisory Service

The Technical Advisory Service (TAS) answers members' enquiries on professional, technical, legal and contractual matters in the purchasing, supply, stores, materials management and distribution fields.

The TAS, through a system of subcommittees and working parties under the auspices of a national Technical Advisory Committee, is able to draw upon the experience and knowledge of IPS and ASPS members to deal with professional, technical, legal and contractual problems. One aspect of this work for which the IPS is particularly well known is the production of model conditions of contract for specific goods or services or for more general application. There is a standard work on the subject published by the IPS.

As a natural extension of TAS activities the Institute provides a *Technical Consultancy Service* for either large or small organisations.

External representation

Participation in public affairs, advice and comment upon public policy and specific legislative measures have become an increasingly large commitment for the IPS, demanding an allocation of resources commensurate with the growing recognition of the valuable contribution to economic well-being which can be made by the Purchasing and Supply function.

The *External Affairs Committee* deals with issues of public policy which affect Purchasing and Supply. It is also responsible for co-operative initiatives with other UK professional bodies and with the International Federation of Purchasing and Materials Management,* of which the IPS was a founder member. The *Technical Advisory Committee* with its wide coverage of technical and legal matters provided by its subcommittees and the Technical Advisory Service provides information and advice to members and also to non-members and other organisations, and conducts studies and surveys for government departments, NEDO and other public and professional bodies. The *Public Services Committee* and the *Construction Committee* have, respectively, the task of commenting and advising upon matters of particular concern to the public sector and the construction industry.

*Address: DILF, Charlotten lundvej 26, DK 2900 Hellerup, Copenhagen.

Personnel advisory services

IPS offers an Appointments Service for members and a Selection Advisory Service for employers.

Publications

The Institute publishes two journals. *Purchasing and Supply Management* is sent free to members monthly and provides a regular coverage of supply management problems, analyses of prices, supply trends, new products, legal matters affecting the buyer, information for students, feature articles covering the widest possible range of industries as well as in-depth interviews. *Procurement Weekly* is available by subscription and deals specifically with Purchasing and Supply. It provides national and international news, a weekly guide to prices of key materials with their annual movements and current trends, events in the commodity market, new products, wholesale price indices, and government initiatives and legislation.

BOOK SALES SERVICE. IPS supplies books to its students, members and non-members, as well as technical briefs and model conditions of contract.

Branches

IPS national activities are mirrored and reinforced by the activities of about fifty "geographic" branches and groups. There are also specialist branches for members in building and civil engineering. Their programmes and social events aim to cater for the varied interests of all grades of the membership and provide a forum for members to be kept up to date by expert speakers and for the friendly interchange of ideas. Branches are involved directly in the management of the Institute through the election of Branch representatives to the Council.

The management of the Institute

NATIONAL COUNCIL. The Institute's governing body is its Council which decides matters of policy and usually meets three or four times a year. The Council consists of approximately 100 members, the majority of them being elected via the Branches or by national ballot. A small number of members are co-opted to the Council for their specialist knowledge or experience.

BOARD OF MANAGEMENT. The Board which is chaired by the Chairman of Council, supervises and co-ordinates Institute policy on a monthly basis on behalf of the Council.

SECRETARIAT. The IPS has a Secretariat of over fifty people. Further information about the IPS and application forms for membership can be obtained from the Assistant Secretary (Membership) at Easton House, Easton on the Hill, Stamford, Lincs PE9 3NZ. Overseas readers in particular will be interested to know of the International Federation of Purchasing and Materials Management which at the time of writing has membership by association in some twenty-nine countries.

MEMBERSHIP

Corporate Membership

There are two methods of entry into Corporate Membership (MInstPS) of the Institute.

(a) *The Professional Examinations Scheme:* candidates have to pass the IPS Professional Examinations and gain three years' responsible experience in Purchasing and Supply.

(b) *The Assessment of Advanced Professional Competence (AAPC) Scheme* is designed for more mature candidates, particularly those whose early education, training and careers may have been spent in other business or professional disciplines before transferring to appointments in Purchasing and Supply, perhaps at a relatively senior level, or who may not have had the opportunity of participating in the Professional Examinations Scheme earlier in their careers. The level of knowledge and experience demanded is comparable to that which members of other leading professions are expected to reach some years after admission to their initial grade of Corporate Membership.

Fellowship (FInstPS) is the highest grade of Corporate Membership. A Fellow is required to have a depth of technical knowledge and a wide range of practical experience, at a suitable level of responsibility to ensure that he or she is equipped to assume an appointment as the principal Purchasing and Supply executive at or reporting to director level in a private or public sector enterprise.

Other categories

GRADUATE (GradInstPS). Those who have passed the IPS Professional Examinations but have not yet acquired the necessary practical experience for Corporate Membership.

IPS STUDENTS. Those who are registered for the IPS Professional Examinations.

ASSOCIATESHIP. Available to persons with an interest in the Purchasing and Supply function who do not either qualify for or wish to become Corporate Members.

Such persons have access to all the Institute's services to assist them in their professional duties and to encourage their participation in the Institute's activities. They must be over 25 years of age but need not necessarily be directly employed in Purchasing and Supply. Associates may subsequently become Corporate Members by completing successfully the Institute's Professional Examinations or meeting the AAPC requirements.

Membership of the Association of Supervisors in Purchasing and Supply
There are three principal grades of Membership of the ASPS.

CORPORATE MEMBERS. Those who have passed the First and Second Certificates in Purchasing and Stores and have gained the practical experience for Membership.

AFFILIATES. Those who have passed the two Certificate examinations but have not yet acquired the necessary practical experience for Corporate Membership of ASPS.

STUDENTS. Must have 4 "O" levels or equivalent, or be 21 years of age, or have two years' relevant experience to register for the ASPS examinations (an ASPS leaflet is available on request).

THE ETHICAL CODE OF THE INSTITUTE OF PURCHASING AND SUPPLY

Introduction
(1) In applying to join the Institute, members undertake to abide by "the Constitution, Memorandum and Articles of Association, Rules and By-Laws of the Institute." The Code set out below was approved by the Institute's Council on 26th February 1977 and is binding on members.
(2) The cases of members reported to have breached the Code shall be investigated by a Disciplinary Committee appointed by the Council; where a case is proven, a member may, depending on the circumstances and the gravity of the charge, be admonished, reprimanded, suspended from membership or removed from the list of members. Details of cases in which members are found in breach of the Code will be notified in the publications of the Institute.

Precepts

(3) Members shall never use their authority or office for personal gain and shall seek to uphold and enhance the standing of the Purchasing and Supply profession and the Institute by:

(*a*) maintaining an unimpeachable standard of integrity in all their business relationships both inside and outside the organisations in which they are employed;

(*b*) fostering the highest possible standards of professional competence amongst those for whom they are responsible;

(*c*) optimising the use of resources for which they are responsible to provide the maximum benefit to their employing organisation;

(*d*) complying both with the letter and the spirit of:

(*i*) the law of the country in which they practise;

(*ii*) such guidance on professional practice as may be issued by the Institute from time to time;

(*iii*) contractual obligations;

(*e*) rejecting any business practice which might reasonably be deemed improper.

Guidance

(4) In applying these precepts, members should follow the guidance set out below.

(*a*) *Declaration of interest.* Any personal interest which may impinge or might reasonably be deemed by others to impinge on a member's impartiality in any matter relevant to his or her duties should be declared.

(*b*) *Confidentiality and accuracy of information.* The confidentiality of information received in the course of duty should be respected and should never be used for personal gain; information given in the course of duty should be true and fair and never designed to mislead.

(*c*) *Competition.* While bearing in mind the advantages to the member's employing organisation of maintaining a continuing relationship with a supplier, any arrangement which might, in the long term, prevent the effective operation of fair competition, should be avoided.

(*d*) *Business gifts.* Business gifts other than items of very small intrinsic value such as business diaries or calendars should not be accepted.

(*e*) *Hospitality.* Modest hospitality is an accepted courtesy of a business relationship. However, the recipient should not allow him or herself to reach a position whereby he or she might be or might be deemed by others to have been influenced in making a business decision as a consequence of accepting such hospitality; the frequency and scale of hospitality accepted should not be significantly greater than the recipient's employer would be likely to provide in return.

(*f*) When it is not easy to decide between what is and what is not acceptable in terms of gifts or hospitality, the offer should be declined or advice sought from the member's superior.

(5) Advice on any aspect of the precepts and guidance set out above may be obtained on written request to the Institute.

The British Institute
of Management

Address: Management House, Parker Street, London WC2B 5PT.
Telephone 01 405 3456. Enquiries to be addressed to the Secretary.

Many executives responsible for Purchasing and Supplies will already be members of the British Institute of Management as well as of the Institute of Purchasing and Supply, whilst their companies in many cases will be Collective Subscribers to the BIM. The relevance of BIM membership to those engaged in supplies management is evidenced by the number of BIM publications referred to in the text which have a direct or indirect bearing on the subjects covered.

Individual membership of the BIM brings:
(a) recognition of training, experience and performance;
(b) provision of regular publications;
(c) information and library facilities;
(d) branch activities with other practising managers.

PUBLICATIONS listed in Appendix VII (and many others) are available from the Publications Sales Department at Management House. Applicants should state if they are members.

OVERSEAS FACILITIES, through close relations with overseas industrial and management bodies, give access to information on economic, political and social conditions in most countries.

THE LIBRARY contains over 56,000 books and other documents and 170 reading lists. The topics covered by the latter include budgetary control; classification and coding; freight transportation; leasing, hiring and purchasing; materials handling; purchasing; quality control; stock control; transport management; warehousing.

THE MANAGEMENT INFORMATION SERVICE provides direct answers to queries or refers members to the best sources elsewhere.

THE MANAGEMENT EDUCATION INFORMATION UNIT maintains up-to-date details of courses available, and provides advice as to the appropriate course for particular needs.

THE MANAGEMENT CONSULTING SERVICES INFORMATION BUREAU is concerned with the keeping of records on consultants and any feedback from users. It is intended for those interested in using consultants.

EXTRACTS FROM CODE OF BEST PRACTICE FOR THE PROFESSIONAL MANAGER IN THE UNITED KINGDOM

This was issued by the BIM in July 1974 and provides a guide to good management practice as regards:

(a) suppliers and customers;
(b) the environment.

As regards suppliers and customers

The professional manager should:

(a) Ensure that the terms of all contracts and terms of business be stated clearly and unambiguously, and honoured in full unless terminated or modified by mutual consent.

(b) Avoid "informal" price-fixing, market-sharing arrangements tending to falsify the process of tendering and open competition which are contrary to the law.

(c) Provide for the establishment with suppliers and customers of a satisfactory relationship which could be a continuing one, by accepting and delivering the products or service in the quantity, quality, time, price and procedure of payments agreed.

(d) When, for want of decision or other action which he is forbidden to take, and the interest of his client, customer or subordinate are, in his opinion, seriously at risk, inform them and his superior accordingly.

(e) In no circumstances supply inherently unsafe goods or services.

(f) Provide an after-sales service commensurate with the kind of product supplied and the price paid—in particular all terms of sale, conditions and warranties should be clearly and unambiguously stated and observed.

(g) Ensure that all mass media communications be informative, true and not misleading taking into account cultural and moral standards in the community and respecting the dignity of the individual; he should also be aware of other relevant Codes of Practice such as:

(i) The International Code of Advertising Practice;
(ii) The International Code of Sales Promotion Practice;

(iii) MRS/IMRA Code of Conduct;

(iv) Institute of Public Relations Code of Professional Conduct;

(v) Institute of Marketing Code of Practice.

(h) Operate an organisation's policy, or require one to be established, which excludes corrupt practices, with regard to the giving or receiving of gifts or benefits and not to tolerate any practice which could lead to commercial or other corruption.

As regards the environment

The professional manager should:

(a) Make the most effective use of all natural resources employed.

(b) Wherever economically possible, reprocess or recycle waste materials and remove harmful pollutants from industrial effluence.

(c) Conserve and wherever possible improve the quality of life in rural and urban societies.

(d) Conform to the national interest as expressed in government policy on environmental matters.

Centre for Interfirm Comparison Ltd.

The Centre for Interfirm Comparison is a non-profit-making organisation established in 1959 by the British Institute of Management in association with the British Productivity Council.

"PYRAMID" OF RATIOS FOR GENERAL MANAGEMENT

Figure 76 is an example of ratios used in comparisons for general management. The ratios are meant to show those used at director level to indicate:

(a) how the overall performance of the business, measured by return on capital, compares with other firms;

(b) why it differs, as indicated by carefully chosen subsidiary ratios.

In an actual comparison in any industry, the set of ratios used is modified and extended to suit the industry's particular needs, e.g. the division of costs may be different; and it is usual to give more detailed information on causes of differences in the ratios which appear at the bottom of the pyramid.

The key ratio which sums up the firm's success is its return on capital (operating profit/operating assets). This is selected as the primary ratio because it reflects the earning power of the operations of a business. A favourable ratio will indicate that a company is using its resources effectively, and will put it in a strong competitive position. A firm's operating profit/operating assets depends first of all on two other important relationships (ratios) namely that between its operating profit and its sales, and that between its sales and its operating assets.

Ratio (2) shows *what* profit margin has been earned on sales, whilst ratio (3) shows *how often* the margin has been earned on assets in the year. In fact, if you multiply ratio (2) by ratio (3) you will arrive at ratio (1).

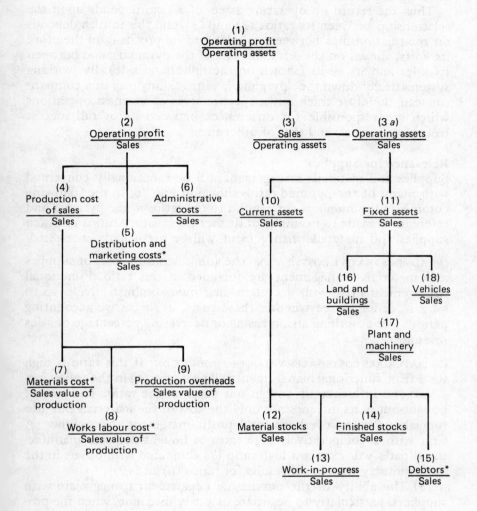

Fig. 76. Pyramid of ratios for inter-firm comparisons
*Explanatory ratios relating to possible reasons for inter-firm differences in
the ratios are used in an acutal comparison.

Ratio (3) shows how many times assets have been turned over in a year. Ratio (3a) expresses asset utilisation in an alternative form by showing the assets required per £1,000 of sales.

Thus the return on operating assets of a firm depends upon the relationship between its ratios (2) and (3), and this in turn depends on the relationships between its sales and its profits (and therefore its costs, shown on the left-hand side of the pyramid), and between its sales and its assets (shown on the right-hand side). By working systematically down the "pyramid", a firm taking part in a comparison can therefore track down specific areas of business operations which are responsible for differences between its overall success (return on capital) and that of other firms.

Relevance for Supplies

Supplies and materials management will be functionally concerned with many of the pyramid ratios shown in Fig. 76. In the following comments the numbers correspond to the ratios in the pyramid and reference is made to examples of further explanatory ratios in which supplies and materials management will be particularly interested.

(6) ADMINISTRATIVE COSTS/SALES. The administration costs of supplies and materials management are included in this ratio. Functional management may wish to relate their own administrative costs to sales in order to see whether these costs, in successive accounting periods, are absorbing an increasing or decreasing percentage of sales revenue.

(7) MATERIALS COSTS/SALES VALUE OF PRODUCTION. If this ratio is high for a firm, functional management will be interested in the following.

(a) The influence of bought-out parts on the ratio. The cost of bought-out parts includes not only the cost of the materials but also the labour costs, overheads and profit margin of the supplier. A firm with a comparatively high ratio of bought-out/own manufactured parts will expect a high ratio (7) compared with others in the same industry (and lower results for ratios (8) and (9)).

(b) The ability of the purchasing department to negotiate with suppliers, particularly to negotiate quantity discounts when the production demand for materials increases.

(c) Whether the ratio can be influenced favourably by changing the material specification without adversely affecting other ratios or sales.

(d) Whether a high ratio (7) may have been caused by poor materials utilisation. This will be influenced not only by production methods and skills, the suitability of plant and its maintenance, but also by unsuitable materials causing high scrap, waste and rectification work, and by the deterioration of materials in stores. Ratios can be selected to determine the factor responsible.

(9) PRODUCTION OVERHEAD/SALES VALUE OF PRODUCTION. These costs include direct production overheads, production plant maintenance, etc.—costs which tend to be fixed. Under-utilisation of capacity will cause this ratio to be high and supplies and materials management will be concerned to ensure that production is not lost because materials are unavailable. Functional management will, therefore, be interested in an analysis of the causes of unused capacity.

(12) MATERIAL STOCKS/SALES. This ratio may be high for a firm either because its materials content of sales is high (ratio (7)) or because it holds a higher number of days' worth of production in raw materials. If the latter is the case supplies and materials management will wish to question whether its buying, stock control and production scheduling are properly co-ordinated.

(13) WORK-IN-PROGRESS/SALES. Supplies and materials management will be interested in the level of investment in the stocks of parts to ensure that they facilitate production (for example, by allowing economic production runs) while keeping a close watch for increased investment in idle work-in-progress stocks.

(14) FINISHED STOCKS/SALES. Functional management are concerned to see that the overall level of investment in finished stocks is sufficient to sustain a satisfactory service level, and to ensure that the stock planning and control procedures result in a healthy balance between sales and production.

In conclusion it must be emphasised that the above are only a selection of the ratios that would be available either in an inter-firm comparison or in a company's internal management ratio system. It is important that no ratio should be considered in isolation but that management should aim to achieve such a balance between all factors that the primary ratio (the overall measure of operational management's success) is optimised.

Further information on inter-firm comparison and on management ratios is available from the Director, Centre for Interfirm Comparison Limited.

The British Standards Society

The British Standards Society is an association of individuals concerned with the application of standards and interested in the techniques and benefits of standardisation. Membership is open to any person interested in standards work, whether in the UK or overseas, on payment of an annual subscription. Members receive the annual *Members' Handbook*, quarterly *Bulletin* and monthly *BSI News*.

The Society assists management in the promotion and application of standards, contributes to training, and establishes contact with standards-users in other countries. The Society plays an important role in feeding back to the British Standards Institution information about the practical on-the-job requirements of industry.

Regular meetings are held at a number of centres on a wide range of standards-related topics. Meetings are open to non-members, and the Regional Committees welcome contact with local groups from institutions such as the Institute of Purchasing and Supply.

Enquiries will be welcomed by The Secretary, Miss G.M. Pierpoint, British Standards Society, BSI, 2 Park Street, London W1A 2BS (01-629 9000).

British Standards Institution (abb. BSI). Address as above. The recognised body in the UK for the preparation and promulgation of national standards: it represents the UK in the *International Organisation for Standardisation* (ISO), the *International Electrotechnical Commission* (IEC), and the West European organisations concerned with harmonisation of standards.

PERA (Production Engineering Research Association of Great Britain)

Address: Melton Mowbray, Leicestershire LE13 OPB.

PERA operates a "Technical Enquiry Service" which is free to members of the Association. Some of the subjects covered are listed below.

Commercial information	Mechanical design
Control engineering	Metal forming
Diecasting	Metrication
Effluent disposal	Office equipment
Electrical engineering	Packaging
Factory services	Plastics technology
Financial management	Product finishing
Foundry technology	Production equipment
Industrial chemistry	Quality control
Inspection	Safety engineering
Machining	Statistics
Management techniques	Subcontract capacity
Materials handling	Welding and joining
Materials technology	Work study

Advice is offered on location of suppliers, and best machines and materials including manufacturers for particular technical operations. In addition, amongst numerous technical services, PERA provides the following facilities.

(a) Consultation on materials selection and processing with qualified and experienced materials technologists and other specialists in manufacturing technologies.

(b) Immediate access to, and interpretation of, a data bank of world-wide materials references.

(c) Commercial information on manufacturers, stockists and suppliers.

(*d*) Selection of UK equivalents to foreign material and specifications.

(*e*) Identification of trade names.

(*f*) Immediate reference and appraisal of processing characteristics and properties of materials.

PERA also offers consultancy services to members and non-members in all areas of manufacturing industry, including management, public relations, marketing, industrial engineering, design, value engineering, production research and training.

The Institute of Building

The Institute of Building was formed in 1834 and is registered as an educational charity. Its 26,000 members are engaged in building, in administrative, commercial, educational and managerial posts, or are undergoing training.

Its objectives are the promotion of the science and practice of building, education and research, and maintenance of standards.

In all cases the person who signs purchase orders or contracts should satisfy himself that qualified personnel will be employed to carry out the work—members of the Institute of Building are so qualified. This comment applies no less if the orders are for building materials to be used by the company's own direct labour.

Publications of the Institute include *Maintenance Management—a guide to good practice, Building Management Note Book* and many others.

The Institute runs an Information Subscriber Service (ISS) which provides papers each year on building subjects.

Bibliography

The following list of books, articles and other sources of information is intended to enable the reader to study in further detail points referred to in this book. The numbers correspond to the numbers in superscript in the text. Those items marked* are on the IPS reading list, while those marked ** are recommended by the author for inclusion in the supplies manager's "library". For details about obtaining IPS (Institute of Purchasing and Supply) and BIM (British Institute of Management) publications, *see* Appendixes I and II respectively).

INTRODUCTION

1. Compton, H.K., *Storehouse and Stockyard Management* (Macdonald & Evans 1981 (Companion Volume)
2. *Planning in the Small Firm,* BIM Guide-lines for the Smaller Business No. 2
3. Gowers, Sir Ernest, *Complete Plain Words* (Penguin 1970)**

CHAPTER 1

4. Bailey, P. and Farmer, Dr D., *Purchasing Principles and Techniques* (IPS)*
5. *Britain's Commodity Markets and Shipping Exchange* (Central Office of Information)
6. *The London Commodity Exchange* (available free from LCE, Plantation House, Mincing Lane, London)
7. Lloyd, F.S., "Are commodity futures necessary?" *Procurement,* Nov. 1974 (IPS)
8. Watling, T.F. and Morley, J., *Successful Commodity Futures Trading* (Business Books 1978)*
9. Faraday, J.E., *The Management of Productivity* (BIM 1971)
10. Burbidge, J.L., *The Principles of Production Control* (Macdonald & Evans 1978)* **
11. *Cash Crisis: Longer Terms—Production Control,* BIM Checklist No. 40 (not specifically on Supplies but a valuable view of production problems interlinked with Supplies)
12. *Posting Managers Overseas,* BIM Checklist No. 36
13. *Foreign Languages,* BIM Checklist No. 18
14. *Exporting,* BIM Checklist No. 16

15. United Nations, *UN Commission on International Trade Law, Yearbook 1979* (HMSO)
16. United Nations, *Yearbook of International Trade Statistics* (HMSO)
17. *Contracts with Eastern Europe* (East European Trade Council 1980)
18. Lewis, D.E.S., *Britain and the European Community* (Heinemann Educational 1978)

CHAPTER 2

19. Kempner, T. (ed.), *A Handbook of Management* (Penguin 1975)**
20. Drucker, P.F., *The Practice of Management* (Pan Books 1968)* **
21. Koontz, H. and O'Donnell, C., *Principles of Management* (McGraw-Hill 1976)*
22. Humble, J.W., *Improving the Performance of the Experienced Manager* (McGraw-Hill 1973)*
23. Lee, L. and Dobler, D.W., *Purchasing and Materials Management* (McGraw-Hill 1977)* **
24. *Industrial Participation* (monthly), published by the Industrial Participation Association, address: 75 Buckingham Gate, London SW1E 6PQ
25. *Cash Crisis: Short Term—Stock-control Remedies,* BIM Checklist No. 59
26. Melrose-Woodman, J.E. and Kuerndal, I., *Towards Social Responsibility (Company Codes of Ethics and Practice)* BIM Management Survey Report MS28 (1976)
27. Giles, G.B., *Marketing* (Macdonald & Evans 1983)
28. Brand, G., *The Industrial Buying Decision* (Associated Business Programmes 1972)* **
29. Baker, M.J., *Marketing: Theory and Practice* (Macmillan 1976)
30. Stevens, J., and Grant, J., *The Purchasing/Marketing Interface* (Associated Business Programmes 1975)

CHAPTER 3

31. Baily, P.J.H. and Tavernier, G., *Design of Purchasing Systems and Records* (Teakfield/Gower Press 1970)
32. *Effective Communications,* BIM Checklist No. 76
33. *Simplification and Reduction of Paperwork,* BIM Information Note No. 56 (loan only)
34. Chappell, R.T. and Read, W.L., *Business Communications* (Macdonald & Evans 1984)
35. *Report Writing,* BIM Checklist No. 2
36. Melrose-Woodman, J.E., *Reporting Management Information,* BIM Survey Report No. 25 (1975)
37. Department of Industry, *Production Monitor PA1000 (Census of Production)* (HMSO)**
38. *Profit from Facts,* available free from Press and Information Services, Central Statistical Office, London WE1P 3AQ (gives information on sources and uses of statistics)
39. *Patents: a source of technical information* (available free from Sales Branch, The Patents Office, Orpington, Kent BR5 3RD)

40. *Technical Services for Industry,* available free from Department of Industry**

41. Book lists and publications lists available from the Design Centre, 28 Haymarket, London WE1Y 4SU (publications lists free)

42. Lists of publications related to economics, health, trade and development, science, etc., available from the United Nations Information Centre, 14-15 Stratford Place, London W1N 9AF

43. *The Environment—Sources of Information and Advice,* BIM Checklist No. 51

44. *Keeping Yourself Up To Date,* BIM Checklist No. 17

45. *Seeking Company Information Sources—United Kingdom Sources,* available from Small Firms Information Services (a valuable list of lists of sources)

46. Unesco, *World Guide to Technical Information and Documentation Services* (HMSO 1975)

47. *EEC Your Questions Answered,* available from EEC Information Unit, Department of Industry, 1 Victoria Street, London SW1H 0ET (a very useful publication covering trade, customs, procedures, reading lists, abbreviations, technical standards drafts, addresses and contacts in the UK and the rest of Europe)** (Note: Currently out of print)

48. Morrell, J.C., *Preparing an Organisation Manual* (BIM 1977)

CHAPTER 4

49. Farrington, B. and Woodmansey, M., *The Purchasing Function,* BIM Management Survey Report No. 50

50. *Managing Purchasing,* BIM Checklist No. 77

51. United Nations Industrial Development Organisation, *A Guide to Industrial Purchasing* (HMSO)

52. Department of Employment, *Training for Purchasing and Supply* (HMSO)**

CHAPTER 5

53. *Diversification,* Small Firms Information Centre Publication No. 11

54. *Managing Product Design and Development,* BIM Checklist No. 74

55. Department of Scientific and Industrial Research, *Engineering Design* (HMSO 1963)

56. International Research and Development, Fosseway, Newcastle upon Tyne: marketing brochures covering materials testing, chemical analysis, environmental technology, etc.

57. Reports on materials, design, manufacture, etc., details from Department of Industry, Technology Reports Centre, Orpington, Kent

58. Skinner, R.N., *Launching New Products in Competitive Markets* (Associated Business Programmes 1974)

59. Clifton, R.H., *Principles of Planned Maintenance* (Edward Arnold 1974)

60. Farmer, D.H. and Taylor, B. (ed.), *Corporate Planning and Procurement* (Heinemann 1975)*

61. Marsh, P.D.V., *Contracting for Engineering and Construction Projects* (Teakfield/Gower Press 1981)*

62. Johnston, K.F.A., *Electrical and Mechanical Engineering Contracts* (Teakfield/Gower Press 1971)

63. "Supplier analysis for capital equipment purchases", *Procurement*, Sept. 1974 (IPS)
64. *The Planning and Management of Building Contracts*, BIM Information Note No. 58
65. "Energy", *Purchasing and Supply Management*, Sept. 1978 (IPS)

CHAPTER 6

66. Ericsson, D., *Materials Administration* (McGraw-Hill 1974)* **
67. Rockley, L.E., *Finance for the Purchasing Executive* (Business Books 1978)
68. de Fremery, J.D.N., *General Guide to the Preparation of Specifications*, available from the European Organisation for Quality Control, PO Box 1976, Rotterdam 3
69. British Standards Institution, BS PD3542, "The operation of a company standards department"**
70. Brady, G.S., *Materials Handbook* (McGraw-Hill 1977)**
71. *Carriage of Dangerous Goods in Ships*, the "Blue Book" (HMSO) (a list of some thousands of materials, their safe storage, and regulations applicable to them)**
72. Port of London Authority, *Schedule of Dangerous Goods*, available from the Manager, Operations Secretariat, Port of London Authority, London E1
73. Wiener, N., *Cybernetics* (MIT Press 1965)
74. *The Environment—Management's Responsibility*, BIM Checklist No. 63
75. Murrell, K.F.H., *Ergonomics: Man in his Working Environment* (Chapman and Hall 1979)
76. Provins, K.A., *Ergonomics for Industry*, available from Department of Industry**
77. Johnson, L. Marvin, *Quality Assurance Program Evaluation*, available from the Institute of Quality Assurance**
78. Dane, A.A.J., "Quality assurance takes the air", *Procurement Weekly*, Aug. 1978 (IPS)
79. British Standards Institution, *British Standards Yearbook* (annually)**
80. Belbin, Dr R.M., *Quality Calamities and their Management Implications* (BIM 1970)
81. Juran, J.M., *Quality Control Handbook* (McGraw-Hill 1974)*
82. Caplen, R.H., *Practical Approach to Quality Control* (Business Books 1978)*
83. *Design Aspects of Terotechnology*, available from Department of Industry, Room 240, Abell House, John Islip Street, London SW1 4LN
84. Department of Industry, *Small Firms: Register of Research* (HMSO 1976)

CHAPTER 7

85. Oliver and Boyd, *Problems on Stocks and Storage*, Nomograph No. 4, ICI Ltd.
86. Battersby, A., *A Guide to Stock Control* (Pitman 1977)* **
87. "Commodity coding in the public sector", *Procurement*, Nov. 1974 (IPS)
88. *Classification and Coding*, BIM Management Guide MG1

89. *The Digital Computer,* BIM Information Note No. 44
90. Carter, L., "Simulation of stock control by computer", *Procurement,* Dec. 1974 (IPS)

CHAPTER 8

91. Harper, W.M., *Statistics* (Macdonald & Evans 1982)***
92. Moroney, M.J., *Facts from Figures* (Penguin 1969)*
93. Reichman, *Use and Abuse of Statistics* (Penguin 1970)
94. Anderson, R.G., *Data Processing and Management Information Systems* (Macdonald & Evans 1984)
95. *Pareto's Principle,* BIM Guide-lines for the Smaller Business No. 14
96. Sheridan, D., "What profit Pareto?" *Procurement Weekly,* Feb. 1974 (IPS)

CHAPTER 10

97. Lysons, Dr C.K., *Purchasing* (Macdonald & Evans 1981)
98. *Metrication—Questions for Management,* BIM Checklist No. 21

CHAPTER 12

99. *Patents and Trade Marks in the European Community* (Confederation of British Industry 1976)
100. Whiting, D.P., *Finance of International Trade* (Macdonald & Evans 1981)*
101. *Incoterms,* ICC publication No. 274 (available from the British National Committee of the International Chamber of Commerce, address: 6/14 Dean Farrar Street, London SW1H 0DT, and from other National Committees throughout the world, or from ICC Headquarters, address: 38 Cours Alber 1er, 75008, Paris, France)**
102. *Rules for Conciliation and Arbitration,* ICC publication No. 291 (for ICC address *see* 101)
103. *Uniform Customs and Practice for Documentary Credits,* ICC publication No. 290 (for ICC address *see* 121)
104. *Uniform Rules for Collections,* ICC publication No. 322 (for ICC address *see* 121)
105. *Standard Forms for Issuing Documentary Credits,* ICC publication No. 323 (for ICC address *see* 121)
106. *Importing into Britain,* available from British Importers Confederation, 69 Cannon Street, London EC4N 5AB

CHAPTER 13

107. Sizer, J., *Insight into Management Accounting* (Pitman 1979)
108. Goch, D., *Finance and Accounts for Management* (Pan 1977)
109. Harper, W.M., *Cost and Management Accounting, Vol. 2: Management Accounting,* (Macdonald & Evans 1982)* **
110. Eatwell, J., *Whatever Happened to Britain?* (Duckworth 1982)
111. Galbraith, J.K., *Money: Whence it came, Where it Went* (Penguin 1977)
112. *Price Index Numbers for Current Cost Accounting* (HMSO)**
113. Hague, D.C., *Pricing Checklist,* available from Centre for Business Research,

University of Manchester (although directed towards sales it has considerable interest for Supplies)

114. Hanson, J.L., *A Textbook of Economics,* (Macdonald & Evans 1977)* **
115. Hanson, J.L., *A Dictionary of Economics and Commerce* (Macdonald & Evans 1983)
116. Nicholson, J.F., *Modern British Economics* (Allen and Unwin 1973)*
117. Anderson, R.G., *Business Systems* (Macdonald & Evans 1977)
118. Rook, A., *Transfer Pricing,* BIM Management Survey Report No. 8 (1972)
119. Swallow, S., "Managing inflation and counter inflation", *Procurement,* Dec. 1974 (IPS)
120. *Added Value,* BIM Management Information Sheet No. 57
121. Woolf, E. and Allen, J., "Adding value to UK industry", *Management Today,* May 1978 (BIM)
122. HM Customs and Excise, *Added Value—General Guide-lines 700* (HMSO)
123. *Brainstorming and Creative Thinking,* BIM Occasional Paper No. 7
124. *Budgetary Control in the Smaller/Medium Size Company,* available on loan from BIM
125. *Budgetary Control for the Smaller Company,* BIM Management Guide No. 4
126. *Life Cycle Costing In Management of Physical Assets* (HMSO)
127. Wright, M.G., *Discounted Cash Flow* (McGraw-Hill 1973)
128. Wagner, Harold K., "The improvement curve concept", *Purchasing Journal,* 1970**

CHAPTER 14

129. Lewis, R., "Big business (the challenge of size to the buyer)", *Procurement,* July 1974 (IPS)

CHAPTER 15

130. Sykes, A., *The Lease-buy Decision,* BIM Management Survey Report MS29 (1975)

CHAPTER 16

131. Lowe, R., *Commercial Law* (Sweet and Maxwell 1976)
132. Major, W.T., *Sale of Goods* (Macdonald & Evans 1980)* **
133. Major, W.T., *The Law of Contract* (Macdonald & Evans 1983)* **
134. Benjamin, J.P., *Sale of Goods* (Sweet and Maxwell 1981)
135. Oliver and Allwright, *Terms and Conditions of Contract* (IPS 1978)* **
136. *Health and Safety at Work Act,* BIM Information Sheet No. 44
137. Roberts, D., *Conditions of Sale—Retention of Title* (Institute of Chartered Secretaries 1977
138. Gartside, L., *Commerce* (Macdonald & Evans 1977)
139. OECD, *Glossary of Terms Relating to Restrictive Business Practices* (HMSO)
140. *Performance Bonds and Guarantees* (CBI 1978)**
141. Tye, J. and Bowes, Egan, *Product Liability: The Complete Practical Guide* (New Commercial Publications 1978)**

CHAPTER 19

142. *Packing for Profit* (HMSO 1979) (covers break bulk, unit load techniques, and services available)**

143. Paine, F.A. (ed.), *Fundamentals of Packaging* (Institute of Packaging 1981)

144. Paine, F.A., *The Packaging Media* (Blackie 1977)

145. British Standards Institution, BS1133, "The packaging code"**

CHAPTER 20

146. *Vehicle Scheduling and Routeing*, BIM Checklist No. 48

147. *Understanding Freight Business*, available from Meadows & Co. Ltd., 36 Grosvenor Gardens, London SW1W 0ED

148. Wentworth, F. (ed.), *The Handbook of Physical Distribution Management* (Teakfield/Gower Press 1975)*

149. Freight Transport Association, *The Road Traffic Act 1974*, available from FTA, Hermes House, St John's Road, Tunbridge Wells TN4 9UZ

150. Freight Transport Association, *Drivers Handbook*, available from FTA (address as above)

151. *Carriage of Hazardous Goods—Conference, October 1977* (Oyez 1979)

152. International Cargo Handling Co-ordination Association. *(a) Cargo Security in Transport Systems, (b) Handling of Goods in Containers, (c) Stowing of Goods in Containers and on Flats, (d) Bulk Commodities in Small Loads, (e) Loss and Damage in Transport,* available from ICHCA, Abford House, 15 Wilton Road, London SW1V 1LX**

153. *Physical Distribution Management*, BIM Checklist No. 33

154. Benson, D. and Whitehead, G., *Transport and Distribution Made Simple* (W. H. Allen 1975)

155. *Costing your Transport Service*, BIM Checklist No. 47

156. *Materials Handling*, BIM Checklist No. 42

157. British Standards Institution, BS3810, "Glossary of terms used in materials handling"

158. Health and Safety at Work Booklets, No. 1, *Lifting and Carrying*, No. 43, *Safety in Mechanical Handling*, No. 47, *Safety in Stacking of Materials* (HMSO) (also available from local offices of the Health and Safety Executive)

CHAPTER 22

159. *Credit Control and Debt Collection*, BIM Management Guide No. 5

160. *Accepting Credit from Suppliers*, BIM Guide-lines for the Smaller Business No. 6

CHAPTER 23

161. Morrison, A., *Storage and Control of Stocks* (Pitman 1981)*

162. Burton, J.A., *Effective Warehousing* (Macdonald & Evans 1981)* **

CHAPTER 25

163. *War on Waste—a Policy for Reclamation*, Cmnd. 5727 (HMSO 1974)

164. Warren Spring Laboratory, *Annual Reviews*, available from the Laboratory at PO Box 20, Gunnels Wood Road, Stevenage, SG1 2BX

APPENDIX VIII

Checklists

The following checklists contain detailed checkpoints which are intended to help the reader apply the guidance contained in the text to his own situation.

NOTES:

(1) Many checkpoints are negotiable. (2) Check all checkpoints for change and content.

CHECKLIST 1. FIND YOUR PLACE AND THAT OF YOUR SUPPLIERS IN THE SUPPLIES CYCLE

(1) Industrial classifications of your firm and its suppliers.

(2) Supplies content of your own and suppliers' products.

(3) Supply problems of your suppliers—and their suppliers. ("Feedback" from progress staff may be of great value here.)

(4) Number of suppliers competing in each product group.

(4.1) Are numbers increasing or decreasing year on year? (Increase in numbers may indicate high-profit area ripe for new price negotiations—or new supply sources.)

(5) Ratio of staff to operatives in your firm and suppliers.

(6) Investment in new plant—your firm and suppliers.

(7) Ratio of research to sales—your firm and suppliers.

(8) Rate of technical change—your firm and suppliers.

(9) Increase or decrease in total sales by suppliers. (May suggest sensitive areas for profitable negotiations.)

(10) "Supply activities" of competitors. (Sales staff may have useful feedback on supplies used, new materials and sources, etc.)

(11) Suppliers' trade associations as information sources.

(12) Suppliers' supply horizons—they may welcome long-term contracts, or less formal arrangements.

(13) Own and suppliers' production problems. (There may be common ground for fruitful collaboration.)

(14) Labour relations in suppliers' product groups.

The following section should not be ignored by those who consider that importation does not concern them! Every trading nation is an importer and

461

almost every manufacturer a direct or indirect importer.

(15) World Trade and its effects upon: continuity of supply, stability of price, changes in specification.

(16) Check if any essential supplies are imported or influenced by conditions at (15) and those in Fig. 5. ("Essentiality" to the company may be more important than cash spent.)

(17) Are you clear on import regulations?

(18) Has direct importation been considered? BIM Checklist No. 16, *Exporting,* also applies to imports. (*See also* Checklist 24.)

(19) Could you communicate with overseas suppliers? *See* BIM Checklist No. 18, *Foreign Languages.*

(20) How would you cope with visits overseas? *See* BIM Checklist No. 37, *Business Travel.*

(21) Would you know where to contact overseas commercial attachés? (IPS can help, *see* Appendix I.)

(22) If your firm is small would you know where to go for information?

General notes

(1) Information on items (1) to (9) available from Business Statistics Office, Cardiff Road, Newport, Gwent: *Business Monitor PA1000, Census of Production,* published by the Department of Industry, available from HMSO Centre for Interfirm Comparison Ltd. *see* Appendix III.

(2) For checkpoint (22) contact Institute of Purchasing and Supply, Regional offices of Small Firms Information Centres, or Small Firms Division, Department of Industry, Abell House, John Islip Street, London SW1 4LN.

CHECKLIST 2. ETHICS IN SUPPLIES POLICIES AND PRACTICES

NOTE: No attempt has been made here to assess moral implications. Not all the checkpoints are unethical—some are merely ill-advised.

(1) Are drawings, specifications, prototypes, samples of one supplier sent to others? (Likely to be actionable under patent and copyright law: EEC conventions may also apply in due course.)

(2) Are prices of one supplier divulged to others? Or to "favourites"? (If one is told, all should be—and there must be *no* "favourites".)

(3) Are lower bids invented to force prices down? (May provoke a future "counter-attack" by rigged prices.)

(4) Are quantities exaggerated above known requirements? (May lead to a contract for unwanted supplies by "mistake".)

(5) Are unnecessarily short delivery times called for?

(6) Is "delivery" stated as "of the essence of the contract" unnecessarily?

(7) Are longer-term contracts promised or made than are warranted or practicable? (Checkpoints (5), (6) and (7) may result in unwanted commitment for the buyer.)

(8) Are some suppliers permitted to requote while others are denied this facility?

(9) Is deliberately false information given to stimulate competition?

(10) Is a dominant position used to take unfair advantage of a small supplier?

(11) Is personal bias or prejudice allowed to influence decisions?

(12) Is "prompt cash" or other discount taken when past the validity date?

(13) Are "small personal favours" solicited or accepted from suppliers? (This action transfers negotiating power to the supplier who will welcome it!)

(14) Are bribes, gifts of money or money's worth accepted from suppliers? (*See* Chapter 16 and Checklist 29. Pressure by suppliers.)

(15) Do personal relationships, e.g. with sales staff, affect decisions?

(16) Are negotiations conducted with courtesy or in a pompous and arrogant manner?

(17) Do Supplies staff hold undeclared financial interests in suppliers?

Reading: BIM Checklist No. 51, *Social Responsibility;* BIM *Code of best practice for the Professional Manager* (*see* extracts Appendix II); Association of Consulting Engineers, *Professional Rules and Practice:* IPS *The Ethical Code of the Institute of Purchasing and Supply* (*see* Appendix I).

CHECKLIST 3. CENTRALISATION AND DECENTRALISATION (CHECKPOINTS FOR MAKING AN "OBJECTIVE" DECISION WITH "SUBJECTIVE" SIDE-EFFECTS")

NOTES: (1) For location of stores, etc., *see Storehouse.* (2) This checklist does not attempt to evaluate benefits or disbenefits. The reader must apply his own value judgement and apply weightings where appropriate. (*See also* Table 4.)

(Stores) Buildings	*(Supply) Administration*	*Plant*
New buildings	*Communications*	*Physical aspects*
Economies of scale*	Shorter	Economies of scale*
Possible new layout	Quicker	Improved handling
Better housing for:	More accurate	Specialised handling
special equipment		New equipment
safety, security,	*Staff*	(*see also* Buildings
heating, lighting, air	More specialisation	column)
conditioning, humidity	Use local initiative	Bulk storage
control, fire risk,	Better workload	
access, environment,	Holiday cover	*Supplies, movement of*
job satisfaction, costs	Promotional ladder	Intake at single point
in use	Removal to/from	Intake at usage point
storage factors	central point	Intake at work-centre
	Local expertise	Intake at multiple
Use existing buildings	Job satisfaction	points
Costs of conversion	Supervision	Bulk intakes
and repair	Checking activities	Bulk packaging
Costs in use	Checking work done	Inwards inspection
Extensibility		Internal distribution

(Stores) Buildings	(Supply) Administration	Plant
Adaptability	*Supplies*	
Storage factors	Bulk buying	*Transport/handling*
	Local sources	Utilisation factor
	Control	Load factor
	Recording	Service factor
	Supplier relationships	Storage factor
	Reciprocal trading	Economics
	Service factor	

*"Economies of scale" should be examined in both "directions", e.g. smaller volume less heating, greater volume cheaper construction per cubic metre.

CHECKLIST 4. PROVISIONING OF RAW MATERIALS

(1) Full consultation with sales, production and top management.

(2) Check future estimated needs with past actual usage and estimates. (Examine magnitude and consistency of past errors in estimates.)

(3) Negotiate supply contracts to suit estimated agreed future needs. (Contract may need quantity variation clause.)

(4) Length of sales, production and supply "horizons".

(5) Type of contract required to maximise profitability. ("Bulk", "forward contract" or "forward supply arrangement", etc., *see* Chapter 15.)

(6) Scrap and waste: establish and maintain policies for the following.

(6.1) Allowance to be made—check if adequate.

(6.2) Recovery, recycling, salvage and disposal (*see* Checklist 36). (Collection at work-centres, segregation of materials, etc.)

(6.3) Pollution control—Health and Safety, etc.

(6.4) Waste avoidance and conservation of resources.

(7) Capacity (productive and financial) of supply sources.

(7.1) Multiple sources, such as primary and secondary, split 80:20.

(7.2) Can all sources match the specification equally?

(7.3) Are specifications identical?

(7.4) Do any extra prices/costs exceed losses avoided by assured supply?

(8) Is specification for the raw material clear, accurate and comprehensive?

(8.1) Can it be met by a number of suppliers?

(8.2) Do users (production, etc.) co-operate in exploring new sources?

(9) Has materials management been fully studied in regard to the following?

(9.1) Unit loads—integrated from supplier to work-centre?

(9.2) Containerisation in bulk? (Special hopper units, ISO type, etc.)

(9.3) Palletisation—returnable, "pool", expendable, special, etc.?

(9.4) Transport economies. (Special vehicles, return loads, shared transport, "groupage", regular schedules, supplier's own or public service vehicles.)

(9.5) Handling economies. (On-loading, at supplier's, off-loading at intake, in stores, to work-centre.)

CHECKLIST 5. PROVISIONING OF CLASSIFICATIONS "B" AND "C" SUPPLIES (MISCELLANEOUS AND GENERAL SUPPORTING GOODS)

(1) Costs of acquisition in relation to actual value of supplies bought. (Acquisition costs may exceed price of the supplies themselves!)

(2) Are orders fully processed through the purchasing department?

(3) Do Supplies insist on full procedure for every requirement?

(4) Do they alienate those who could (or should) use their services? (For example, by bureaucracy, dictating, interfering (unnecessarily).

(5) Can ordering be delegated by "SVOs", "LPOs", etc. (*see* Chapter 15)?

(6) Will those who do their own buying resist or resent any change? (Terms of reference given to Supplies can assist here.)

(7) Have those who do their own ordering built up an empire?

(8) Are large numbers of small orders placed by large numbers of staff?

(9) What are storage costs? (The air space in the bin may be worth more than the contents!)

(10) Need stock be carried? (Local stockists may give instant delivery at contract prices.)

(11) What is frequency of ordering? And frequency of usage? (*See* Chapters 10, order quantity, and 11, timing, frequency and duration.)

(12) Do varieties used reflect expensive prejudices of users?

(13) Has variety reduction and standardisation been attempted?

(14) Are "private stocks" built up in functional departments?

(15) If the answer to (14) is "yes", how much cash is tied up in this way?

(16) Are supplies obtained on petty cash?

(17) If so who is authorised, what are limits, and how is it controlled?

(18) Are those who buy independently of the Supplies department efficient in the following?

(18.1) Purchasing. (Prices paid, absence of "favouritism", supplier dependence, etc.)

(18.2) Storage. (Preservation of goods, shelf-life, etc.)

(18.3) Control. (Security, stock levels, issues, returns, etc.)

(18.4) Specification. (Company standard, British Standard, or do they take what the supplier dictates?)

(19) Are requirements duplicated—exactly or nearly so? (*See also* (13).)

CHECKLIST 6. PROVISIONING OF EMBODIMENT GOODS, PIECE PARTS, ETC.

(1) Identification and "A.B.C." classification, commodity catalogue. (Co-ordination of drawing, part and commodity catalogue numbers can be profitable.)

(2) Are any in sufficient usage to rank as "A" or "B" classification? (If so, examine Checklist 4 in parallel with this one.)

(3) Standardisation and variety reduction, elimination of non-standards.

(4) Simplification, substitution of other items, combination with other items.

(5) Are new items promptly identified, coded, catalogued?

(6) Do designers and draughtsmen use standards wherever possible?

(7) Do the above call for brand names regardless of alternatives?

(8) Is feedback from the shop floor encouraged regarding the following?

(8.1) Savings which could be made by suppliers in their product.

(8.2) Methods to improve assembly, etc., at work-centre.

(8.3) Modifications to improve assembly at work-centre.

(8.4) Material or design modified to increase feed and speed in machining.

(8.5) Methods for reduction of rejects during machining or assembly. (Suggestions for (8.1) to (8.5) could include methods of packaging, size of items, their shape, machining allowance and so on.)

(8.6) Improved transit, handling and dispensing at work-centres. (Use of special containers, tote pans, etc.)

(9) Are rejects only discovered *after* production has started? (Investigate faulty intake inspection, stores damage, etc.)

(10) Make or buy. (*See* Checklist 23.)

(11) Have the most economical types of contract been made? (Forward supply arrangements for classes "B" and "C", for example.)

(12) Which items need to be carried for customer spares, etc.? (Separate storage independent from production may be warranted.)

(13) Is liaison between Supplies and sales adequate on customer spares? (Service on spares may gain or lose customers!)

(14) Are customers encouraged to use commodity code numbers when ordering spares? (The numbers should also be used for spares storage—*see* (12).)

CHECKLIST 7. PROVISIONING OF MACHINE PLANT, TOOLS, JIGS AND FIXTURES, ETC.

(1) Output per machine hour per unit power consumed. (Expected, required, hoped for, guaranteed.)

(2) Cost per unit output.

(3) Useful working life.

(4) Operation and operatives.

(4.1) Loading and operating space needed.

(4.2) Prior consultation, job improvement, job satisfaction.

(4.3) Health and Safety at Work regulations—home/international/EEC.

(4.4) Skill and training needed—company training schemes and centres.

(4.5) Training given by supplier—adequate, some, nil?

(4.6) Feeds and speeds, adaptability, ease of setting up and adjustment.

(4.7) Provision for collection of swarf, offcuts, etc.

(4.8) Attachments for removal of dust and pollutants.

(4.9) Ease of loading, dispensing, etc. of raw materials.

(4.10) Operational acceptability—controls, comfort, safety. (*See* Checklists 15, Cybernetics, and 17, Ergonomics.)

(5) Maintenance (*see also* Checklist 8).

(5.1) Space needed for maintenance.

(5.2) Cranage or other handling needed.

(5.3) Servicing, interchangeability, etc.

(6) Tools, fixtures and spares.

(6.1) Indexing and cataloguing.

(6.2) Appraisal of, by operatives, planning, production engineers, etc.

(6.3) Use of plant numbers for identification, storage, purchase.

(6.4) Introduction of "tool club".

(6.5) Interchangeability of tools, fixtures and spares.

(6.6) Resharpening and similar services.

(7) Stores and storage of tools, fixtures and spares (*see also* Checklist 8).

(7.1) Use of proper tool cribs to preserve valuable tools, etc.

(7.2) Security from loss and theft by secure stores areas.

(7.3) Control of issue—"one for one", "open access", etc.

(7.4) Repeat orders, standard tools—streamlined ordering for.

(8) Is an efficient plant register maintained?

(8.1) Is it used for supplies (spares, etc.)?

(8.2) Are up-to-date parts lists, etc. kept for spares, breakdowns, etc.?

CHECKLIST 8. PROVISIONING OF MAINTENANCE MATERIALS, SPARES AND SERVICES FOR PLANT AND EQUIPMENT

(1) Did original enquiry ask for *full* maintenance details?

(2) Was a free maintenance period negotiated?

(3) Was "retention money" arranged for maintenance period?

(4) Servicing.

(4.1) Frequency, local availability for servicing, or ex works.

(4.2) Costs of servicing, replacements, spares, etc.

(4.3) Availability of service, replacements, spares, etc.

(4.4) Replace service-units, reconditioned, rebuilt, or new.

(4.5) Guarantees given with servicing, service-units, etc.

(5) Ease of maintenance, interchangeability of spares, space required for operatives carrying out maintenance.

(6) Health, safety and welfare in operation and during maintenance.

(7) Use of maker's spares only—with maker's conditional guarantee. (Purpose-made spares may be as good, better, cheaper, quicker.)

(8) Plant numbers, coding, stores catalogue, identification, etc.

(8.1) Are all items of plant numbered and recorded?

(8.2) Are such numbers always used methodically for maintenance, spares, etc.?

(8.3) Do Supplies staff use them—always, sometimes, never?

(9) Storage and physical control.

(9.1) Are special storage conditions maintained where necessary? (Sealed containers, shrink wrapped, anti-corrosive coatings, etc.)

(9.2) Are maintenance stocks examined regularly for condition, etc.?

(9.3) Are bin codes clear for rapid retrieval and issue of spares?

(9.4) Is stock control effective?

(9.5) Are fast moving spares given special attention?

(9.6) Are "difficult" items given special attention?

(10) Supplies and provisioning.

(10.1) Do Supplies ascertain requirements for spares when ordering plant? (*See* Checklist 7.)

(10.2) Is spares catalogue kept up to date? (Consider allocating task to purchasing analyst if there is no maintenance staff.)

(10.3) When plant is taken out of service are spares dealt with? (For disposal, transfer to another plant, etc.)

(10.4) Or is old plant cannibalised?

(10.5) Are awkward, unpredictable, strategic items given priority?

(10.6) Are fast moving items kept available in stock?

(10.7) Are Supplies records used to indicate plant spares performance?

CHECKLIST 9. PROVISIONING FOR BUILDING WORK, MAJOR PROJECTS, PLANT, ETC.

NOTE: *See also* Checklist 7.

(1) Adequate pre-contract preparation, cost-benefit analysis, etc.

(2) Departmental and other financial limits. (Clarity of instructions and methods of control, monitoring, etc.)

(3) Are "variation orders" issued? By whom, and how controlled?

(4) Do contractors make excessive claims on variation orders? (Some use them to recoup previous losses or inflate profits.)

(5) Who carries out the progressing and what methods are used? ("Variation orders" may be used to extend contract period.)

(6) Are surplus materials resulting from variation orders, etc. credited?

(7) Do contractors change specification without consultation? (May even claim the change is "an improvement"!)

(8) Are lowest tenders accepted regardless of standards?

(9) Subcontractors.

(9.1) Does someone make sure all subcontractors are known and approved?

(9.2) Is proper control of them monitored?

(9.3) Is a definite relationship established with them to ensure control?

(10) Advisers, consultants, architects, etc.

(10.1) Clarify areas of their responsibility and authority over the work.

(10.2) Is their remuneration geared to the amount they save?

(10.3) Is their remuneration geared to the amount they spend? (If so watch budgets and sanctions carefully!)

(10.4) Do they understand the technology of the plant? (A frequent source of disappointment or even disaster!)

(11) Have the appropriate authorities been consulted?

(11.1) Building surveyor, planning officer, Health and Safety Inspectorate.

(11.2) Fire Officer—fire precautions and access for fire brigade, etc.

(11.3) Police—access, exit, traffic flow, security, etc.

(11.4) Services—gas, water, electricity, sewers, culverts, telephones, etc.

(12) Finance, control, etc.

(12.1) Progress payments—who signs work certificates?

(12.2) Is accounts department clear regarding "progress payments" and "retention monies"?

(12.3) Do staff try to "beat the budget" by advance payments on contract instalments? (A ruse sometimes adopted to increase the next year's budget allowance by avoiding under-spending in the current year.)

CHECKLIST 10. PROVISIONING OF OFFICE SUPPLIES

(1) Stock.

(1.1) Is one person designated to look after stock?

(1.2) Are stock-control methods effective? How are issues controlled?

(1.3) Do staff help themselves to stock? Do they sign for it?

(1.4) Are storage areas kept clean and tidy?

(1.5) Are storage conditions satisfactory? (e.g. level surface for paper, correct temperature, humidity, light, etc.)

(2) Costs.

(2.1) Are staff alerted to high costs of stationery?

(2.2) Do some staff insist on "prestige" stationery and equipment?

(2.3) Does the printer hold type and lithos for future repeat orders?

(3) Purchasing.

(3.1) Are supplies tied to maker's designated sources (guarantee may so specify)? (Even so it may pay to investigate after guarantee ends.)

(3.2) Are simplified order methods used (especially for low cost items)?

(3.3) Is high pressure salesmanship guarded against?

(3.4) Is purchasing done by Supplies, departmental heads, or anybody?

(4) Standardisation, etc.

(4.1) Are British Standards, makers' standards, etc. used?

(4.2) Suitability of paper, ink, etc. for equipment? For computer, photo-printer, etc.?

(4.3) Are forms standardised and their proliferation controlled?

(4.4) Is their design standardised and a file of "masters" kept as "control" for modifications and reissues?

(4.5) Is variety reduction practised? Are multiple copies needed? Consider if there is an economic need for such copies.

(4.6) Horizontal and vertical alignments and spacings—particularly for computer software.

(4.7) Test ribbons ("printer" and typewriter) for life, quality of print and stability in operation (particularly for computers).

(4.8) Weight, calliper and quality for use in factory and outdoors.

(4.9) Inks, etc. "fast" for factory and outdoor use?

(5) Compare costs of microfilm and microfiche with other records.

CHECKLIST 11. PROVISIONING OF HEALTH, SAFETY AND WELFARE GOODS

(1) Liaison with the company's safety officer, safety committee, etc., or, if the firm is very small, with the "designated person".

(2) Consultation with the relevant public officials (Health and Safety Inspectorate, fire, ambulance, police, etc.).

(3) Storage.

(3.1) Regular inspection to ensure shelf-life: clothing, electrical gloves, etc.

(3.2) Clear marking of bins.

(3.3) Good industrial housekeeping to ensure clean state of goods.

(3.4) Security from pilferage—locked bins, secure areas, etc. (Many such goods are "attractive".)

(3.5) Clear notices regarding issue, etc.

(3.6) Issue control—to designated staff, etc.

(3.7) Method of issue control—"one for one", "staff clock number", etc.

(4) What part do Supplies play in provisioning for health, safety and welfare goods?

(4.1) Are Supplies represented on the safety committee, etc.?

(5) Fire and other health and safety equipment.

(5.1) Who makes the contract for the equipment?

(5.2) Are there service contracts—one year or longer duration?

(5.3) How are frequencies of replacement checked? (One supplier was found to replace more extinguishers than there were fire positions!)

(5.4) Are enquiries issued annually for all contracts, long or short? (Encourages "sitting contractor" to have good service and commercial outlook.)

(6) How are contracts for equipment arranged? (Some suppliers try to commit functional departments to their product.)

(7) General health and safety disciplines.

(7.1) Are these examined when buying normal factory needs?

(7.2) Are safety aspects (fire, toxicity, etc.) studied when new materials are introduced into the stores or process?

(7.3) Is suitable safety equipment purchased? (Viz. drip trays for oil stands, test arrangements for fork trucks, etc.)

CHECKLIST 12. PREPARATIONS OF SPECIFICATIONS AND STANDARDS FOR SUPPLIES

NOTE: Unless separately stated the checkpoints below apply to both specifications and standards as the latter must include the former.

(1) Are they always available from a technical department?

(2) If not who prepares them?

(3) If by non-technical staff who checks them? (Even in small firms someone should co-ordinate them.)

(4) Are they properly referenced, filed and circulated?

(4.1) Those who do not have copies may need a list of them.

(4.2) Procedure for updating must include circulation.

(5) Reasonableness and checkability of limits and tolerances.

(6) How rigidly must they be complied with?

(7) Present them in a manner to command respect and encourage use.

(8) Are they fixed for all time?

(9) Apply disciplines to ensure their full use.

(10) Do either specifications or standards proliferate unnecessarily?

(11) Are "variety reduction" and simplification continuously applied?

(12) Do specifiers understand the economic implications?

(13) Are other techniques examined in relation to specification? (Terotechnology, ergonomics, cybernetics and so on, *see* Chapter 6.)

(14) Do specifiers understtand and study manufacturing processes? (Those of their own factory *and* of suppliers.)

(15) Do specifications and standards conform and are they compatible with others? (Company's, national and international specifications and standards.)

(16) Do specifiers overspecify? (*See* Fig. 19.)

(17) Have features been introduced which:

(17.1) are non-standard;

(17.2) preclude the use of better or more up-to-date items;

(17.3) reflect the technical, aesthetic or other prejudice of specifier;

(17.4) do not contribute to function;

(17.5) fail to extend use of features to additional functions (viz. fixing down lugs used also to secure unit in transit);

(17.6) ignore economics of design—fabricate *v.* casting;

(17.7) conflict with health and safety regulations;

(17.8) are wasteful or costly in production man-hours?

(18) Are specifications and standards accurate, clear and complete?

(18.1) Do they cross refer to associated specifications and standards?

Comments

Checkpoints (6) and (7); a rigid, doctrinaire approach leads to frustration and loss of dynamic activity and technical and commercial initiative.

CHECKLIST 13. MONITORING SPECIFICATIONS AND STANDARDS FOR SUPPLIES

NOTES: (1) Use this checklist in association with Checklist 12. (2) It is intended for those who prepare specifications and standards for using or obtaining supplies. (3) *See also* the note at the head of Checklist 12.

(1) Text of specifications and standards.

(1.1) Ambiguity—more than one meaning can result in more than one supply.

(1.2) Incompleteness—can result in costly queries.

(1.3) Obscurity—can cause communication failure and incorrect supply.

(1.4) Inaccuracy—Supplies office may be the last chance to discover and correct this.

(2) Technical and other points.

(2.1) Do specifications "design out" waste of materials, etc.?

(2.2) Do they actively encourage conservation and recovery?

(2.3) Do they reflect indoctrination of the specifier by suppliers?

(2.4) Do they rely upon unproven claims by suppliers?

(2.5) Are non-essential clauses inserted? (Add to difficulties in supply, add to cost but not utility.)

(2.6) Are trade names used? (These tie the buyer to single source of supply.)

(2.7) Are they unmistakably clear to user, buyer and seller?

(3) Supplies staff activities.

(3.1) Are they encouraged to apply "diagnostic skill"?

(3.2) Do they possess, and apply, technical/commercial *ability*? (Ability rather than knowledge is emphasised here.)

(3.3) Do they understand the broad principles of specification and process?

(3.4) Are they expected to monitor aspects relevant to supply?

(3.5) Do they check that suppliers have understood requirements? (Particularly important with new suppliers and those in high technologies.)

(3.6) Is check made at enquiry stage? (Part of enquiry procedure.)

(3.7) Or when purchase order is placed? (Part of ordering procedure.)

(3.8) Or on receipt of acknowledgment? (Part of progressing procedure.) (Important to bear in mind the acknowledgment usually binds the purchaser.)

(3.9) Are commodity codes, stores catalogue, etc., fully integrated with specifications and standards?

(3.10) Do purchase orders state all the above (at (3.9)) clearly?

(3.11) Do they also specify inspection arrangements?

(3.12) Are health and safety aspects fully met and covered on orders, etc.?

CHECKLIST 14. BENEFITS OF STANDARDISATION WITH VARIETY REDUCTION

NOTES: (1) Few benefits are "automatic", most require continuing technical discipline applied for their achievement. (2) In many cases the supplier has similar benefits which the purchasing officer should seek for his firm to share. (3) Most of the checkpoints contribute to the "learning curve" (*see* Chapter 13).

(1) Larger quantities per order, benefits for production, etc.

(1.1) Longer production runs. (Improved and positive forward planning for supplier and buyer.)

(1.2) Better production scheduling—easier stock control and forward allocation of supplies.

(1.3) Fewer machine tool changes, lower setting up costs or changes.

(1.4) Fewer changes in process plant—less cleaning of pipes, pumps, vessels, etc.

(1.5) More efficient use of tools, equipment and power.

(1.6) Mechanisation of production and handling.

(1.7) Realignment of production or process flow.

(1.8) Inspection simplified, mechanised or even automated.

(1.9) More specialisation in production, inspection, handling, etc.

(1.10) Increased use of jigs, tools and fixtures.

(2) Administrative and other benefits.

(2.1) Fewer purchase orders and their standardisation.

(2.2) Fewer enquiries to send out and quotations to study.

(2.3) Supplier has fewer quotations to prepare.

(2.4) Savings in Supplies office administration. (Fewer records, less "filing and finding", goods inwards, etc.)

(2.5) Reduced work in production planning.

(2.6) Fewer "special" and other drawings, reduced design time.

(2.7) Fewer drawing and design queries to settle.

(2.8) Fewer tests, samples, prototypes, etc.

(2.9) Uniformity and emergence of "character" in designs.

(3) Practical benefits.

(3.1) Better interchangeability of plant, parts and spares.

(3.2) Better quality and reliability.

(3.3) Easier to apply "value engineering" and "value analysis".

(3.4) Greater uniformity in design may improve performance.

(3.5) Possibly fewer replacements in maintenance.

(4) Storage and inventory benefits.

(4.1) More effective use of stores vocabulary and commodity catalogue.

(4.2) Stock levels may be reduced for a given output. (Fewer items mean fewer bins and locations and better "flow".)

(4.3) Lower storage costs. (Greater throughput means fuller bins and better "storage factor".)

(4.4) Smaller range of spares need to be carried. (Saving to both customer and manufacturer.)

(4.5) More rapid location of spares in stores due to reduced locations.

(4.6) Total stock of spares for customers reduced but with improved "service factor".

(4.7) Sales can offer better after-sales service at lower cost.

CHECKLIST 15. CYBERNETICS IN SUPPLIES

DEFINITION: the study of the operation of controls and communication systems. It deals with both biological systems and man-made machinery. (*English Larousse*)

(1) Clarity of instructions and directions.

(1.1) Are controls arranged cybernetically?

(1.1.1) Are rows of identical control buttons zoned clearly and/or pictorially to indicate operations?

(1.1.2) Are type-faces, warning signs simple, clear and bold?

(1.1.3) Are knobs, levers, handwheels, push-buttons clearly labelled?

(1.1.4) Are indicating instruments digital or analogue (clock face)?

(1.1.5) Are traffic routes, storage areas, etc. clearly indicated?

(2) Response and feedback of controls, information, etc.

(2.1) Are emergency controls suitable: instantly operable, clearly visible— in times of lost power supply, in light and dark situations.

(2.2) Do automatic stops and "fail-safe" devices respond instantly? (e.g. limit stops on mobile bins, etc. *See Storehouse.*)

(2.3) Is response of ordinary controls acceptable in terms of speed, sensitivity and positive reaction to operation of controls?

(2.4) Do controls operate in logical sequence?

(2.5) Do controls operate in same sequence as other practices? (e.g. in one fork truck the brake and clutch were reverse of UK automotive practice, in another a control lever was pulled back to lower.)

(2.6) Sensitivity of feedback from Supplies—control and other systems.

(2.6.1) Changes in consumption, rates of delivery, lead times, prices, etc.

(2.6.2) Feedback from operatives using purchases supplies—materials, tools, etc.

(2.6.3) Do controls "feel good" to the operator?

CHECKLIST 16. CONSERVATION OF RESOURCES

NOTE: *See also* Chapter 25 and *Storehouse.*

(1) Is the quality specified the quality required? (*See* Fig. 19.)

(2) Do staff co-operate to select the most suitable quality?

(3) Raw materials—dimensions, etc.

(3.1) Are dimensions such as to minimise waste and offcuts?

(3.2) Do Supplies staff and others co-operate to this end?

(3.3) Do Supplies staff have a job specification clause to maximise profitability?

(3.4) Does production planning give guidance for supply dimensions?

(3.5) Do draughtsmen and designers consider the most economic design for economical machining to avoid waste?

(3.6) Have draughtsmen and designers had conservation in mind?

(3.7) Have Supplies staff shown enthusiasm in this?

(3.8) Is reject and scrap allowance adequate? Reordering costs money!

(3.9) Is the allowance inadequate? Prodigal supply invites waste!

(4) Could computer or wall charts optimise cutting economically? (also batching, cutting lengths, matching assemblies, etc.)

(5) Do Supplies, design, drawing office and production co-operate?

(5.1) Do designers and drawing office specify so as to maximise best use of materials and minimise waste and arisings?

(5.2) Is conservation a regular item on Supplies or works council agendas?

(5.3) Does it include conservation in purchase, stores and handling?

(5.4) Is feedback from the work-centres encouraged, heeded, acted upon?

(6) Records of resources consumed.

(6.1) Who, if anyone, keeps records?

(6.2) If so, what yardsticks are used? (*See* Appendix III.)

(6.2.1) Materials used per unit produced—cost each, or volume output.

(6.2.2) Scrap and waste as percentage of materials used. (*See* Checklist 36.)

(6.2.3) Prices obtained by purchasing officer for waste and scrap.

(6.2.4) Value or volume of materials, etc. recycled.

(6.2.5) Costs of separating and collecting "arisings".

(6.2.6) Costs of storing and actual disposal of "arisings".

(6.2.7) Cost of recycling.

(7) Energy flow and conservation (*see* Fig. 22).

CHECKLIST 17. ERGONOMICS AND SUPPLIES

DEFINITION: The study of the mental and physical capacities of persons in response to the demands made upon them by various kinds of work. (*English Larousse*)

NOTE: *See also* Checklist 15.

(1) Controls.
(1.1) Position of operator relative to controls.
(1.2) Can either, or both hands be used?
(1.3) Must operator reach, bend, stretch or strain?
(1.4) Are controls affected by heat, cold, damp, etc.?
(1.5) Can they be manipulated when cold, wet, damp, etc.?
(1.6) Position relative to direction of movement.
(1.7) Resistance to movement—stiff, jerky, loose, power-assisted.
(1.8) Lubrication—self-lubricated, non-lubricated, easy or difficult to lubricate.
(1.9) Grip on controls—diameter of handwheel, number of spokes, thickness of rim, length of lever, etc.
(1.10) Disposition and size of foot control pedals.
(1.11) How is maximum force for minimum effort achieved? (Length of lever, diameter of handwheel, etc.)
(2) Operator comfort, etc.
(2.1) Visibility—in direction of travel, all round (on vehicles), point of tool operation, etc. (on machine tools).
(2.2) Avoidance of fatigue—sitting, standing, reclining.
(2.3) Space for operative—driving, feeding a machine, setting up, etc.
(2.4) Size of operative catered for—normal, outsize, range of sizes.
(2.5) Provision for man or woman or either.
(2.6) Exceptions—disabled, blind, deaf, left-handed, short-sighted, colour-blind, dyslexic, language not indigenous.
(2.7) Protection needed from heat, cold, damp, wet, poisons, etc.
(3) Hand tools, manual handling, etc.
(3.1) Is leverage adequate for function? (Length of spanner, fluting on screwdriver handle, etc.)
(3.2) Mechanical advantage of lifting devices?
(3.3) Hand grips, height of handle, etc. for trucks.

CHECKLIST 18. STATISTICS AND DATA FOR SUPPLIES MANAGEMENT

NOTE: Not all items are direct data, some need objective and statistical correlation.

(1) Financial and economic statistics and controls.
(1.1) Supply commitments versus financial policy and stringency. (Group or individual company policies.)
(1.2) Market trends, conditions, prices.
(1.3) Own sales and production capacity, trends, conditions, etc.
(1.4) Hourly-machine, storage and other rates.
(1.5) Acceptable risks to the company for investment, etc.

(2) Supply statistics.

(2.1) Rate of replenishment and lead time of suppliers.

(2.2) Output capacity of suppliers, individual and total. (Maximum simultaneous or spread, for the same or diverse areas of supply.)

(2.3) Seasonal characteristics of supply (or demand)—shortage or glut.

(2.4) How many acceptable sources of supply are there?

(2.5) Are there restraints in supply—cartels, governmental controls, etc.?

(2.6) Do "customs of trade" affect quantities available or per unit of supply?

(3) Demand statistics.

(3.1) Probable usage in total period under consideration. (Usually the primary consideration for supply policy.)

(3.2) Maximum, minimum and mean rates of usage during period.

(3.3) Trends, cycles, seasonal fluctuations, peaks and troughs.

(3.4) Are conditions predictable, partially predictable or random?

(4) General check on data for analysis and producing statistics.

(4.1) If a trend appears, is it rising or falling?

(4.2) Are cycles regular in amplitude and length?

(4.3) Or is either of these changing regularly or with a trend?

(5) Diagnosis of "exceptions" — maxima, minima, cycles, etc.

(5.1) Are they very predictable? e.g. annual factory shut-down.

(5.2) Can their cause be changed/eliminated? By planning or policy?

(5.3) May they be partially predictable? Try statistical "models".

(5.4) Does such simulation show them unpredictable? If so apply frequent checks and control and monitoring of data.

(5.5) Study frequency and timing in the review period.

(5.6) Are direct causes known? Rejects of supplies, production, handling.

(5.7) Are there secondary causes? Bad control or provisioning.

(5.8) Are direct or secondary causes likely to recur?

CHECKLIST 19. ORDER QUANTITY DISCIPLINES

(1) Determination of quantity—internal major disciplines.

(1.1) Specified by user—control by departmental budget, etc.

(1.2) Sales plan—check past usage, "enthusiastic inflation" of quantity, etc.

(1.3) Production plan—close liaison with production management.

(1.4) Stock-control system—check accuracy of records, levels, forecasts.

(1.5) Economic order quantity—*always* check with actual needs.

(1.6) Production budget or other budgetary centre, "sanctions", etc.

(2) Determination of quantity—external (supplier) disciplines.

(2.1) Reliability of sources in the past—and for the future.

(2.2) Supplier's conditions—customs of trade, optimum order quantity, etc.

(2.3) Supplier's own EOQ for his supplies.

(2.4) Supplier's storage capacity, vehicle capacity, etc.

(2.5) Minimum shipment quantity closely allied to batch production quantity—or rigidly tied to it.

(2.6) Work-in-progress facilities may determine the size of batch and volume of goods he can clear from his stores and despatch bay to make room for further output.

(2.7) His handling equipment may also limit the weight or volume of the containers used.

(3) Supplies disciplines.

(3.1) Limits of storage capacity—bins, racks, tanks, compounds, etc.

(3.2) Limits of transport and handling capacity, intake facilities, etc.

(3.3) Stock policy—safety stock, reorder levels, maximum stock, etc.

(3.4) Is purchasing officer authorised to vary quantity bought?

(3.4.1) As precaution against prospective shortages.

(3.4.2) As speculation on changes in price.

(3.4.3) To take advantage of a "job lot" offer.

(3.4.4) Will metrication improve delivery, specification, price, etc.?

(3.4.5) To introduce EOQ.

(4) Miscellaneous contingencies, etc., which may affect quantity.

(4.1) Stock adjustments at stock audit.

(4.2) Damage in transit, handling, storage, dispensing or process.

(4.3) Evaporation, spillage, damage or loss in stores and elsewhere.

(4.4) Rejects—on intake, in process, etc.

(4.5) Setting-up allowance, offcut and scrap allowances.

(4.6) Scouring of pipes, tanks, containers, hoppers, etc. in stores/process.

CHECKLIST 20. TOTAL ACQUISITION COSTS AND SOME POSSIBLE SAVINGS

NOTES: (1) In acquisition costs are included all costs incurred up to and including actual intake and invoice clearance. (2) The checklist is divided into different cost areas.

Acquisition costs	Possible saving points
(1) REQUISITIONING.	
(1.1) Costs of requisitioning procedures.	Cut out "red tape", streamline and delegate as much as possible.
(2) ENQUIRIES.	
(2.1) Search for suitable suppliers.	Use "supplier/commodity" lists.
(2.2) Check specifications.	Use approved specification list.
(2.3) "Vet" suppliers.	Use "approved suppliers" list.
(2.4) Detailed queries—terms, etc.	Avoid having to repeat enquiries through inadequate preparation.
(3) RECEIVE AND HANDLE QUOTATIONS.	
(3.1) Collate offers.	Use simple summary form (see Fig. 62).
(3.2) Confer with requisitioner.	Encourage commercial outlook.
(3.3) Refer back *all* queries.	Obtain some working delegation.
(3.4) Refer back undelegated queries.	Indicate points of variance on copy order to requisitioner.

Acquisition costs	Possible saving points
(4) NEGOTIATION.	
(4.1) Visits to or from suppliers.	Make maximum use of visits by collaboration with colleagues.
(4.2) Meetings with suppliers.	Ensure collaboration of technical colleagues, etc.
(5) PLACE PURCHASE ORDER.	
(5.1) Process requisition for typing order.	Give typists clear, simple guidelines, for "repeats" use "model orders" or "pro-formas" (*see* Chapter 15).
(5.2) Typing order.	Give typist a copy-holder to speed and ease task.
(6) PROGRESSING.	
(6.1) Progress charts, systems, etc.	Avoid complex rigid systems.
(6.2) Correspondence, written and spoken.	Avoid useless or ineffectual methods —printed forms, etc.
(6.3) Records of performance.	Use simple and quickly located methods.
(7) PACKAGING.	
(7.1) Opening, denailing, disposal of packing materials, etc.	Confer with supplier to facilitate these tasks (*see* Checklist 31).
(8) TRANSPORTATION.	
(8.1) Supplier's, own or public.	Shared loads, "groupage", return loads, etc.
(8.2) Utilisation factor of transport.	Design packaging for good utilisation factor.
(9) HANDLING.	
(9.1) Loading at supplier's works.	Collaborate with supplier to minimise costs—including (8.1) and (8.2). *See also Storehouse.*
(9.2) Unloading at intake.	
(9.3) Recording returnable containers, etc.	
(10) INTAKE BY PURCHASER.	
(10.1) Complete logbook.	
(10.2) Check goods with description.	*See Storehouse.*
(10.3) Tally cases, etc. received.	
(10.4) Check for shortage, damage, etc.	
(11) COMPLAINTS PROCEDURE.	
(11.1) Clerical and communication costs.	Ensure use of rapid, effective simple routines.

(*contd.*)

Acquisition costs	Possible saving points
(12) INVOICE CLEARANCE.	
(12.1) Check all, some, no invoices?	Apply "exception principle" so that only what is incorrect consumes clerical staff time.

CHECKLIST 21. SUPPLIER SELECTION, PERFORMANCE, COMPLAINT APPRAISAL AND DIAGNOSIS

(1) Technical services.

(1.1) Specification: indaequate; unclear; incorrect; misleading?

(1.2) Personnel: incompetent?

(1.3) Design and development: lack of vigour, imagination, cash?

(1.4) Literature: inadequate; unclear; incorrect; misleading?

(1.5) General attitude to customer's problems?

(1.5.1) Not interested? Not understood? Will not understand?

(1.5.2) Refuse to meet special needs?

(1.5.3) Not available to discuss problems?

(1.6) Complaints: ignored; acknowledge but do not act; action very slow?

(1.7) Quality control: bad; poor; lacking.

(2) Product and production.

(2.1) Spares: unavailable; prices high; do not fit; fit badly; hard to fit?

(2.2) Product: dirty; dangerous; contaminating; inefficient; dimensions vary or unstable; limits vary; design obsolete; life short; fragile or weak; size range inadequate; pollutant?

(2.3) Production: capacity low; no reserve capacity; commitments made to other customers?

(2.4) Plant: old; obsolete; badly maintained; does not comply with Health and Safety at Work Act.

(3) Selling and service and management.

(3.1) Policies: dishonest; inconsistent; opportunist; poor long-term; none; seek to bribe?

(3.2) Management: "sleepers"; bad labour relations?

(3.2.1) Staff morale low; dispute procedure nil?

(3.2.2) Unionised: closed shop.

(3.2.3) Wages low; discontent high?

(3.2.4) Motivation: low?

(3.3) Representation: inefficient; ineffective; non-existent; poorly briefed; do not know product; call too often; call too seldom; behave unethically?

(3.4) Head office: too remote; too hierarchical; no personal contact; too many forms?

(3.5) Emergencies: fail to help; slow to help?

(3.6) After-sales service: poor; nil; do not support guarantees; no training for equipment?

(4) Delivery—progressing.

(4.1) Delivery information is:

(4.1.1) untrue—fradulent: accidental; careless?

(4.1.2) evasive?

(4.1.3) unco-operative? Salesmen ignored; HQ sales ignored; deliver too early; deliver too late?

(4.2) Promise made at different staff levels?

(4.3) Supplier plays one customer off against another?

(5) Delivery—physical.

(5.1) Shipment: delivered short; over-delivery; wrong goods to wrong destination; goods damaged, broken, lost; marks incorrect; pallets wrong size; containers wrong size; containers leak; goods contaminated, wet?

(5.2) Instructions ignored, e.g. "deliver between 8.00 and 16.00 hours"?

(5.3) Special instructions ignored, e.g. "send short wheelbase truck"?

(5.4) Transport staff: careless, insolent; unco-operative?

(5.5) Vehicles: too big; wrong kind; dilapidated?

(6) Communication.

(6.1) Correspondence: muddled; delay replies; do not reply; inaccurate—substance, specification, codes, omit references; wrong references; verbosity?

(6.2) Telecommunications: fail to ring back as promised; refuse to give identity; poor phone drill?

(6.3) Lines of communication: poorly defined; too multifarious?

(6.4) Documentation: delayed; inaccurate—quantities, specification, codes; omit references; omit instructions; wrong documents sent; acknowledgments late?

(7) Commercial and financial factors.

(7.1) Prices: uneconomic (supplier will later seek increase); unstable; subsidised?

(7.2) Price increase: unjustified, not agreed?

(7.3) Invoices: delay in submission; do not settle queries?

(7.4) Invoices incorrect?

(7.4.1) Differ from quantity ordered, delivered, accepted?

(7.4.2) Items were not ordered?

(7.4.3) Price: discount; unagreed price increases?

(7.4.4) Settlement terms?

(7.4.5) Carriage terms?

(7.4.6) VAT, import duty, etc.

(7.4.7) Bad credit control—unreasonable demands for prompt payment?

(7.5) Financial factors:

(7.5.1) financially unstable?

(7.5.2) lack of financial resources;

(7.5.3) owned, controlled or supported by a much larger competitor than you?

CHECKLIST 22. BUYING FROM MIDDLEMEN

NOTE: The term "middlemen" is used here collectively for all such supplier; *see* Chapter 12 for different classification.

(1) Delivery service, vehicles, etc.
(1.1) Is service regular, reliable, prompt?
(1.2) Is service daily, weekly, round-the-clock (for process plants)?
(1.3) Do vehicles suit purchaser's intake facilities?
(1.4) Are drivers helpful and co-operative—unloading, etc.?
(1.5) Are their handling and vehicles efficient? Sooner or later costs of inefficiency reach the purchaser.
(1.6) Are they strategically placed for economic speedy delivery?
(2) Their supply service — quality, advice to purchaser, etc.
(2.1) Is their test/inspection effective?
(2.2) Do they ship goods near (or after) expiry of shelf-life?
(2.3) Do their stores maintain supplies in prime condition?
(2.4) Do they deal expeditiously with small orders?
(2.5) Do they study local needs, and purchaser's needs?
(2.6) Do they provide technical and other advice on supplies?
(2.7) Is their stock control efficient?
(2.8) Are their sales staff experts in their supply areas?
(3) Financial and other matters.
(3.1) What is their pricing policy? Do they pass on increases at once and decreases sometimes?!
(3.2) Will they give rebate for an annual forward supply arrangement?
(3.3) What settlement terms do they give? Or credit?
(3.4) Are they members of a trading group?
(3.5) Are they members of a trade association?
(4) Physical aspects.
(4.1) What are their packaging methods? Do they provide containers?
(4.2) Will they make special arrangements to suit the purchaser?
(4.3) Are their handling methods adequate or are goods damaged?
(4.4) Are their stores automated? If so, have they means of handling supplies manually in the event of computer or plant failure?

CHECKLIST 23. "MAKE OR BUY", "HIRE OR BUY" DECISION-MAKING

NOTES: (1) *See* BIM Information Note No. 50, *The Break-even system.* (2) *See also* Checklist 24 and Chapter 15, Table 32.

(1) Points tending towards a "make" decision.
(1.1) Work needed to maintain plant and manpower utilisation.
(1.2) Newly installed plant needs this output.
(1.3) Security precludes use of outside suppliers.
(1.4) Traditional suppliers proved unsatisfactory, or lack capacity.
(1.5) Lay-offs likely if supplies bought outside. (Could lose valuable staff to a competitor.)

(1.6) If design changes are likely, problems with a supplier could be costly.

(2) Points tending towards a "buy" decision.

(2.1) Own production is overloaded.

(2.2) There is an actual or prospective plant failure.

(2.3) Increased business to suppliers could gain price reductions.

(2.4) Supplier already manufactures similar items very economically.

(2.5) Supplier has considerable expertise.

(2.6) Own labour problems, shortage, industrial relations, etc.

(2.7) Secondary source of vital supplies may be important.

(3) General points—affect either "make" or "buy" except where stated.

(3.1) Could supplier obtain better/cheaper supply of raw materials?

(3.2) Are there any taxation problems?

(3.3) What are marginal production costs with "make" option?

(3.4) Will drawings need modification on "buy" option?

(3.5) Who owns jigs, tools, gauges and (possibly) fixtures? (Ownership or part ownership is important in "buy" option.)

(3.6) What are statistics of demand? (*See* Checklist 18.)

(3.7) Are any special or secret manufacturing techniques needed?

(3.8) Is there a likely market elsewhere? (Supplier may be forbidden to exploit this to avoid competition or encouraged to do so to gain lower price.)

(3.9) Have quantities been optimised for purchase or production?

(3.10) Arrangements for inspection or sampling.

(3.11) Provision of "free-issue" materials, jigs, tools, gauges.

CHECKLIST 24. IMPORTATION

NOTE: Use this checklist in conjunction with Checklist 23.

(1) Why import?

(1.1) Goods not available on the home market.

(1.2) Goods available but delivery is long, seasonal, unreliable.

(1.3) Home-produced goods are at high or fluctuating prices.

(1.4) Home market is overloaded—temporarily or permanently.

(1.5) Home manufacturer cannot match specification or his is unreliable.

(2) Does purchasing, company or other policy call for importation?

(2.1) To establish or stimulate competition at home.

(2.2) Home customer calls for imported item to be used in product.

(2.3) To promote international trade.

(2.4) Purchaser is part of a multinational group.

(2.5) Overseas customer calls for his home-produced item to be used. (*See* Chapter 1.)

(3) Other general points.

(3.1) Goods imported for repair, treatment and re-export.

(3.2) Sample and prototypes for new supplies. (Note special arrangements with Customs regarding duties may be applicable.)

(3.3) Spares for plant already imported and in use. (May be exempt from VAT.)

(4) Points in negotiation, wording and placing of contract.

(4.1) Has adequate time been allowed for technical and translation work?

(4.2) Whose specification shall be used? And in whose language?

(4.3) Do goods comply with home regulations—safety, etc.?

(4.4) What financial arrangements, terms and currency rates? (Make sure seller accepts bank charges for transfer of currency.)

(4.5) Check for restrictions in imports—exchange control, legality, etc.

(4.6) Pollution and environmental regulations.

(4.7) Method of payment: cheques, "letter of credit", etc. (With a letter of credit some banks will arrange for certified inspection prior to payment.)

(4.8) Obtain "status report" on supplier—most good banks arrange this.

(4.9) Check on import duties, tariffs, deposits, drawback, bond, VAT, etc.

(4.10) Check insurance is adequate—if (as is usual) cover is by the supplier.

(4.11) Terms of contract—particularly trade customs or usages.

(4.12) Whose law and whose language shall prevail? (Make sure the interpreter is yours and any "asides" are translated.)

(4.13) Are "INCO" terms acceptable? Who shall arbitrate if there is a dispute? (*See also* (6.5) below.)

(5) Technical and practical points.

(5.1) Are spares held by the supplier in the importer's country?

(5.2) Are they interchangeable with home-produced items?

(5.3) Do they comply with British Standards or ISO, etc.?

(5.4) Can they be fitted using standard tools?

(5.5) Are power units suitable for importer's supply—gas, electricity, etc.?

(5.6) Is training given—does it cover use and maintenance?

(5.7) Are servicing facilities and service replacement units available?

(5.8) Arrangements for test, inspection, commissioning at works/on site, etc.

(5.9) Twelve-month guarantee period, output guarantees, etc.

(6) Materials and embodiment goods. (Items in (5) above could also have implications.)

(6.1) Overseas standards may not be compatible with production or process in-house.

(6.2) Costs of returning faulty materials or components for rectification could be high—should be negotiated in contract.

(6.3) Distances may cause delays in replacement and/or in inspection.

(6.4) Consumer liability for end-product could be affected.

(6.5) Ensure that ordering routines are adequate; e.g. form of contract, method of specifying, quality control, progressing, and throughout Supply cycle.

(7) Packing, transport and handling arrangements.

(7.1) Cargo space—amount required and advance booking.

(7.2) Packing for sea, rail, road or air.

(7.3) Handling—cranage, fork truck, straddle carrier, etc.

(7.4) Pilotage, lighterage, tugs, etc. at home port.

(7.5) Loading gauge, handling facilities at importer's works.

(7.6) Weights, markings, labels, hazard plates.

(7.7) Lifting lugs, fork clearance, etc.

(8) Buying from/selling to Eastern Europe or other centrally planned economies. (*See also* ss. (4), (5) and (6) above, and Chapter 1, counter-trading.)

(8.1) Will the transaction involve counter-trading?

(8.2) If so, gain best bargain by negotiating highest level of counter-trading to balance the transaction.

(8.3) Bear in mind that the trader's aim is usually to generate hard currency for his state.

(8.4) It is usually more satisfactory to negotiate for in-house use of counter-trading products than to sell them to a third party.

(8.5) When negotiating for in-house supplies treat as for "new product".

(8.6) Note that all negotiations must only be with official state negotiators.

(8.7) Systems vary from state to state; study each as necessary.

(8.8) Try to arrange counter-trading purchase and sale through the same Foreign Trade Organisation (FTO).

(8.9) Study and negotiate on standard terms and forms of the appropriate FTO.

(8.10) Arrange for FTO to open a separate bank account for each transaction.

(8.11) Ensure that written agreements are carefully drawn up and checked for each transaction.

(8.12) Select the best means of communication—telephone or telex may be more effective and quicker than mail.

(8.13) Consider advisability of a performance bond and guarantees.

(8.14) Avoid (if possible) giving breakdown price list of items—FTO may select some items from more favourable sources causing a loss on the transaction.

(8.15) Make sure all relevant bodies and other advisers are consulted, namely East European Trade Council, IPS Technical Advisory Service, bank, solicitor, BSI, etc.

CHECKLIST 25. VALUE ANALYSIS AND VALUE ENGINEERING

(Headings are intended as a rough guide only)   (p) = plant

Technical considerations	Physical properties	Operational qualities	Purchasing and financial
Specification	Machinability	Rating—continuous or intermittent (p)	Price, net contract price
Design service from supplier	Space occupied (p); operational/ maintenance	Capacity—normal and overload (p)	Price firm or subject to material and labour rates
Functions—multi or single purpose	Shelf-life		

(contd.)

Technical considerations	Physical properties	Operational qualities	Purchasing and financial
After-sales service, technical	Material content, weight, etc. (p)	Life—operational (p)	Prototypes, free or paid for
Training operatives	Surface finish	Raw materials, power/fuel consumed v. output (p)	Maintenance period free, length of
Properties: mechanical, electrical, chemical	Durability	Efficiency and losses (p)	Obsolescence (also a technical consideration)
	Limits and fits	After-sales service maintenance (p)	Delivery—availability
	Material utilised v. material wasted	Costs of setting up and tooling (p)	Delivery—reliability of promise
	Corrodibility		
	Friability	Amenities: noise; smell; dirt; smoke; vibration; fumes (p)	Stocks—at supplier's works
	Strength: mechanical, electrical		Stocks on consignment
		Health and safety (p)	Freight—delivered free, etc.
		Ease of assembly (p)	Development costs
			Ownership of tools, patterns, dies, etc.
			Service agreements
Does plant offered demand any special quality of raw materials, fuels, etc.?			Reciprocal or local trading

NOTE: Most of the features mentioned require consideration by more than one member of the team of technical, production and purchasing staffs.

CHECKLIST 26. DISCOUNT AND REBATE SCHEMES

(1) Does structure conceal hidden gains for the supplier?

(2) Are schemes simple to operate and easily understood by staff?

(3) Are they simple to evaluate and check?

(4) Does the purchaser have a system to monitor their payment?

(5) Are steps and targets realistic?

(6) Has supplier set targets which cannot be reached?

(7) Is there any restrictive or "loyalty" clause?

(8) Is there provision for revision due to price, demand or supply change?

(9) What happens if the supplier is taken over or involved in a merger?

(10) Has curve of net prices been plotted and examined for inconsistencies?

(11) Are invoices, rebate statements, credit notes checked for accuracy?

(12) If so, by whom and how are they checked? (*See* Chapter 22.)

(13) Were basic prices established *before* negotiating?

(14) Has supplier increased his profit by adding (say) 5 per cent before allowing a 5 per cent.

(15) Do steps have any provision for adjustment if a "near miss" to the target occurs?

(16) Check marginal units, i.e. would it pay to invest in stock to reach the next step?

CHECKLIST 27. SUPPLIER'S CLAIMS FOR PRICE INCREASES

(1) General basis—materials, labour, power, transport, packaging, statutory, etc.

(2) Does purchaser know the relative weightings of these factors in total product price? Will supplier divulge these?

(3) Internal general and historical factors.

(3.1) Increase said to be effect of previously unclaimed increases?

(3.2) If so, how did supplier absorb these increases in the past?

(3.3) Were his prices previously excessive?

(3.4) Is he trying to anticipate future expected costs?

(3.5) What was the date of previous increase?

(3.6) What is frequency/regularity of past increments?

(3.7) What profits does he show in his annual report?

(3.8) Does he claim increase due to increased production costs?

(3.9) Could a change in specification by the purchaser reduce these?

(3.10) Could a change in his own specification reduce them?

(3.11) Is increase due to labour costs? What is labour/price ratio?

(3.12) Increased packaging costs? Could a change of package help?

(4) External factors claimed by the supplier.

(4.1) Increased costs of supplies? Could change in specification help?

(4.2) Increased transport costs? Could change of transport help?

(4.3) Increase due to government guide-lines?

(4.4) If so, has he applied the maximum allowed?

(4.5) General market prices—compare with official figures.

(4.6) Is the claim in breach of any statutory ruling?

(5) Factors claimed to relate to action by the purchaser.

(5.1) Reduced demand by the purchaser?

(5.2) If so, how does this line up with supplier's discount structure?

(5.3) Increase due to changes in specification by purchaser?

(5.4) Were these properly costed and covered by amendment?

(5.5) Increases due to interference with contract by purchaser?

(5.6) If so, investigate liaison between Supplies and other staff.

(5.7) Does contract have an adjustment clause?

(5.8) Will supplier support claim with a breakdown of costs?

CHECKLIST 28. PURCHASING OFFICER'S INTERVIEW MINI-CHECKLIST

NOTE: *See also* Checklists 2 and 29, and Figs. 59 and 60.

(1) Interview arrangements by purchasing officer.

(1.1) Are representatives who call "on spec" seen or turned away promptly? (Many complain they are kept waiting indefinitely without explanation.)

(1.2) Are regular interview days/times arranged?

(1.3) Are representatives who have an appointment seen promptly? (*See* (1.1).)

(1.4) Does purchasing officer invite technical (or other) colleagues to attend? (Representatives complain that purchasing officers prevent them from seeing colleagues.)

(1.5) Representative's credentials—his authority to commit his firm, etc.

(1.6) Is the interview room conducive to frank discussion? (In open offices the representative may fear a competitor may overhear discussions.)

(2) Substance of interviews, negotiations, etc., with representatives.

(2.1) Are all parties fully briefed in advance of the interview?

(2.2) Is time wasted in irrelevant discussions, etc.?

(2.3) Does representative respond to probing? (His firm's size, delivery performance, their Supplies set-up, etc.)

(2.4) Does he provide information on his own products?

(2.5) Does he have information on competitive products? (His comments on his competitors may reveal new supply sources, his own deficiencies, etc.)

(2.6) What proportion of their product do they export?

(2.7) Do they give priority to exports? And delay home deliveries?

(2.8) Do they give priority to purchasers who export?

(2.9) How much do they spend on research and development?

(2.10) Is a list of personnel to contact available? For progressing, etc.

(2.11) Who shall the representative see in the firm apart from Supplies staff? (*See* (1.4).)

(3) Miscellaneous details.

(3.1) How long has product been on the market?

(3.2) Do they carry stocks locally or nationally? Or provide "consignment stock"?

(3.3) How do they distribute—direct, through stockists, wholesalers, etc.?

(3.4) Are samples, prototypes, drawings, etc. available—and are they free?

(3.5) Do they hold patents, copyrights, etc.?

(3.6) What are their spares, "service units" and servicing arrangements?

CHECKLIST 29. PRESSURE BY SUPPLIERS ON PURCHASING AND OTHER STAFF

NOTE: *See also* Checklist 2.

(1) Pressure and manipulation through bonuses (such as gifts, lunches, favours).

(2) Creation of an obligation to the supplier or his representative.

(3) Are the ethical codes and the various Acts on corruption known?

(4) If gifts, vouchers or other forms of credit are offered:

(4.1) can their precise worth be evaluated?—may affect value analysis;

(4.2) value may depreciate by redemption date:

(4.3) may prejudice recipients in favour of the donor (to the detriment of the profitability of the purchaser's firm);

(4.4) quality of gifts—many are bulk imports from low value sources;

(4.5) gifts may not comply with Health and Safety regulations;

(4.6) gifts may lead to personal or interdepartmental friction;

(4.7) vouchers may lead to administrative costs—sticking stamps in books.

(5) Other points in regard to the giving or acceptance of bonuses.

(5.1) May put some (smaller) suppliers at an unfair disadvantage.

(5.2) Not all suppliers offer the same bonus for the same purchase.

(5.3) There is sometimes a complication regarding VAT.

(5.4) Works Council, auditor or shareholders may wish to investigate.

(5.5) Pressure to inflate orders to achieve bonus.

(6) Surreptitious personal gifts. (One firm offered their gift "delivered home by monitored routeings"!)

(6.1) Whatever others may do the purchasing officer must resist "pressures".

(6.2) Learn to recognise "pressure manoeuvres"—"informal *lunch discussion*". (*See* Chapter 16 and comments on verbal commitments.)

(6.3) Do not fall for the opening gambit, "I wonder how we can help you?"!

(6.4) May lead ultimately to compulsive pressure by supplier as "gifts" escalate!

(7) Offers based on target purchases, e.g. a supplier may offer one extra machine for each six purchased.

(7.1) Does the firm need the extra unit?

(7.2) Where will it be allocated, or will it go for "home use"? ("Home use" implies larceny of company property.)

(7.3) May the extra unit result in excessive unauthorised consumption of expensive materials?

(8) Always protect junior staff from sales pressures.

CHECKLIST 30. DIAGNOSIS OF AND SOME REMEDIES FOR BAD DELIVERIES

(1) Statistical analysis of trends, exceptions, etc. (*see* Fig. 66).

(2) Examine causes.

(2.1) Has the purchaser "cried wolf" too often? (Supplier may find purchaser querying "urgent goods" long after delivery!)

(2.2) Is the purchaser demanding "specials" in design or materials used?

(2.3) Are unreasonable deliveries asked for? Invented to force delivery? (In the latter case the legal implications must be watched.)

(2.4) Did supplier offer an unreasonable delivery? Perhaps to secure the order?

(2.5) Was the forecasting of the purchaser poor or incorrect?

(2.6) Has shipper waited for full vehicle or container load?

(2.7) Has the shipper held delivery for later "shared load" to another customer?

(3) Examine procedures.

(3.1) Are regular contacts kept with the supplier? By purchasing or progress staff.

(3.2) Are regular contacts kept by the supplier with the purchaser? (It is no excuse for Supplies to allege supplier's failure in this.)

(3.3) Do orders call for regular reports or visits by representatives, etc.?

(3.4) Is the purchaser's progress system effective and regular?

(3.5) Does the order include a "liquidated damages" clause? (Can cover late delivery or other contractual failures.)

(3.6) Are delays administrative? Supplier's or buyer's fault?

(4) Examine possible remedies for poor delivery.

(4.1) Are the supplier's problems understood by the purchaser? (Has he even tried to understand?)

(4.2) Provision by the purchaser of free-issue materials to the supplier.

(4.3) Provision by the purchaser (on loan) of jigs, tools, gauges, etc.

(4.4) Or, as (4.2) and (4.3) but to the supplier of the supplier.

(4.5) Financial aid to the supplier—he may have cash flow problems.

(4.6) Would a delivery bonus assist?

CHECKLIST 31. PACKAGING

NOTES: (1) This checklist is intended for use by those who buy packaging for their own company's products or for use with incoming supplies. (2) The divisions in this checklist are not mutually exclusive.

(1) Conservation, economy and safety in use.

(1.1) Recycling, re-use at work-centres, in stores, etc.

(1.2) Returnable, knocked-down, folded, collapsible.

(1.3) Eliminate, e.g. bricks banded without pallets for fork-truck handling.

(1.4) Minimise overall size: can contents be nested?

(1.5) Minimise weight of package and contents: lighter packaging materials, etc.

(1.6) Reduce disposal costs: use degradable materials, etc.

(1.7) Design for nesting empty containers—for return or storage, etc.

(1.8) Avoid hazardous fasteners: nails, banding, etc. (Or provide facilities for their removal, denailers, etc.)

(1.9) Safety in stacking: crushing loads, stability, fork access, etc.

(1.10) Modular packs to suit standard pallets: metrication, etc.

(2) Protection of contents (in transit *and* storage).

(2.1) Study the contents to be shipped.

(2.2) Examine hazards: in transit, storage, at work-centre.

(2.3) Moisture or dryness: use of desiccants or moisturisers.

(2.4) Heat, cold or light sources, e.g. shaped wood often reverts to normal shape if subjected to bright sunlight.

(2.5) High or low barometric pressure: seals may be broken at high altitudes.

(2.6) Vibration, shocks, impact: cushioning materials may be needed.

(2.7) Fungi, insects, vermin, animals: seal or use fine wire mesh, etc.

(2.8) Security, attractability, vulnerability: provisions for inspection and resealing, by company staff, Customs, etc.

(2.9) Fumes, contamination of, or by, other goods: clear hazard notices.

(2.10) Radiation, electro-magnetic fields, etc.: metal screens, foils, etc.

(2.11) Shelf-life: examine storage conditions, observe supplier's recommendations.

(3) Packaging "in use" including in transit.

(3.1) Packs to suit supplier's, buyer's and standard pallets.

(3.2) Markings, advisory or mandatory: "flammable", "keep dry", "this way up", "fragile" and so on (*see* British Standard BS2770).

(3.3) May need opening and resealing in transit (see (2.8)).

(3.4) Locate and examine possible locations where impact may occur:

(3.4.1) supplier's loading bay—poor equipment, inexperienced staff, "panic" shipments;

(3.4.2) in transit—bad routeing, poor roads, badly laden vehicles, excessive speed, inexpert driving;

(3.4.3) at purchaser's inwards bay—as (3.4.1).

(3.5) Are suppliers given full transit labelling instructions?

(3.6) Are goods deck cargo? May require waterproof, shrink-wrap, sheeting, etc.

(3.7) Air freight: check airline regulations, overall size and weight.

(3.8) Rail transit: check and protect from impact *and* vibration.

(3.9) Will goods cross state boundaries? (*See* (2.8), (2.9), (3.2), (3.3).)

(3.10) Will transhipment be needed? Stowage charts may be required.

(3.11) Check methods and frequency of handling throughout transit.

(3.12) Provide for check on quantity/damage—provide "windows", use shrink-wrap, etc.

(3.13) If shipment for long-haul transit, *see* British Standard BS4672.

(4) General queries.

(4.1) Was packaging discussed at design/enquiry stage? Full practical consultation with designers, draughtsmen, production engineers, operatives, materials managers, safety officer, transport officer, fire and security officer, sales and Supplies departments.

(4.2) Has "feedback" from previous experience been sought *and used*? (Complaints and comments from customers, users, inspectors, transport, etc.)

(4.3) Are suppliers aware of the problems of the purchaser—or vice versa? (Did either communicate with the other?)

(5) Costs of packaging.

(5.1) First cost, life in years, total journeys, cost of repairs.

(5.2) Costs of carriage home empty—savings as return loads.

(5.3) Costs of reconditioning—inspection and testing—pallets and containers.

(5.4) Expense of administration for return, reconditioning, etc.

CHECKLIST 32. DISTRIBUTION COSTS AND POSSIBLE SAVINGS

(1) Have transport costs been analysed: product, customer, total, area?

(2) Have costs been allocated: Supplies, sales, inter-stores, etc.?

(3) Are fixed vehicle costs known? Can they be reduced?

(4) Driving time (actual) outbound: fully laden? If not, what utilisation factor?

(5) Driving time (actual) inbound: empty or return loads or shared loads?

(6) Standing time between loads? Do drivers have other work?

(7) Standing time at off-loading? Do drivers report bad customers?

(8) Standing time at on-loading? Do drivers report bad suppliers?

(9) Other major factors affecting costs.

(9.1) Distances of customers/suppliers: are permitted driving times exceeded? These are interdependent: can bigger

(9.2) Drop size/pick-up size. drops/pick-ups at less frequent inter-

(9.3) Frequency of drop/pick-up size. vals be accepted by customers and arranged with suppliers?

(9.4) Time taken to load: degree of mechanisation and powered handling.

(9.5) Time taken to arrive and locate customer's intake area? How well or badly are purchasers'/suppliers' facilities arranged?

(9.6) How are goods packed? Can purchasers/suppliers co-ordinate and co-operate?

(9.7) Load factor of vehicles? Are weights, loading gauge, etc, studied?

(9.8) Utilisation factor of vehicles? Can other neighbouring firms share loads?

(9.9) Is firm a multi-depot company? If so, can concentration store system assist?

CHECKLIST 33. CONDITIONS OF CARRIAGE

(1) Is carrier a "common carrier", i.e. does he accept any goods for any destination?

(2) Can conditions be changed by him? If so, is there provision for prior negotiation?

(3) Does he have special tariffs for "dangerous" goods? Are yours dangerous?

(4) Does haulier insist on right to subcontract?

(5) Are there any special conditions on the customer if the goods carried are not his property?

(6) What warranties and indemnities are agreed?

491

(7) Is the customer to warrant that any goods sent by him are packaged and fit to be carried and warehoused by the carrier?

(8) What clauses relieve the carrier of liability for loss, misdirection or damage?

(9) What limits are set to liability? And for indirect consequential loss?

(10) What are the time limits for claims?

(11) Does haulier claim the right to sell unclaimed/undelivered goods?

(12) Are times of delivery acceptable?

(13) Does haulier's driver assist unloading?

(14) What rights does the haulier claim for "lien" and "sale"?

(15) What arrangements are made in the event of breakdown or delay?

(16) Has the haulier been advised of any financial loss if delay occurs?

(17) Does he warrant that all regulations will be complied with?

CHECKLIST 34. GUIDE-LINES FOR MATERIALS HANDLING

(1) Volume and nature of supplies dictate the method of handling, storing, counting, recording, etc.

(2) Eliminate unnecessary storage by combining with assembly or process.

(3) Eliminate unnecessary transfer and handling. (Out-of-process handling adds to the cost of a product and risk of damage, but adds nothing to value.)

(4) Reduce the frequency and distance through which materials must be moved by arranging layout and locations to suit flow and output.

(5) For manual handling, bins with the fastest rate of turnover to be located nearest to the servery. Heavy materials should be in lower bins.

(6) For powered handling, heavy goods can be away from and above rapid flow (because of low cost of powered movement compared with manual).

(7) Integrate materials handling with actual storage.

(8) Analyse all stores-handling operations carefully and simplify where possible, e.g. gravity can ensure first-in first-out selection.

(9) Provide and organise systems of training.

(10) If any handling operation frequently requires two or more men, consider powered alternative.

(11) When planning stores layout, give priority to storage and handling methods.

(12) Utilise storage capacity to the full while maintaining immediate availability with minimum movement.

(13) Instruct architects on the following points.

(13.1) Doorways located and designed for ease of access for trucks and mechanical appliances.

(13.2) Treatments to floor surfaces, e.g. dustproofing, skidproofing, damp and oil resisting.

(13.3) Clear marking of aisles, passing points for vehicles, route directions.

(13.4) Floor loadings and aisle widths for both rolling and static loads.

(13.5) Flow to be considered part of the handling system: lift capacities, design of loading and unloading decks, despatch and receiving facilities, etc.

(14) Can transport vehicles be more efficiently integrated into the overall handling system?

(15) Arrange incoming materials to be supplied in unit loads from suppliers.

(16) Study range and size of containers; adopt standards.

(17) Select bins, pallets, racks, etc. to suit materials. And to suit transit inwards and issue to works or customer.

(18) Design shipping containers suitable for fork-lift handling direct without pallets, and loading into stores racking or stacking without racking.

(19) Collapsible containers require less storage space when empty and incur lower transport costs when returned.

(20) Obtain high load factor for materials handling equipment.

(21) Where utilisation factor permits, use specialised equipment.

(22) Test, safety and maintenance routines must be strictly observed in accordance with statutory regulations.

(23) Maintain planned system of handling. Do not allow unauthorised changes.

(24) Continually examine for improvements.

CHECKLIST 35. ESTIMATING STORAGE AND HOLDING COSTS

NOTE: As with acquisition costs (Checklist 20) no differentiation has been made here between fixed, semi-variable and variable costs.

(1) Interest on capital tied up in stock. (For great accuracy the continuous running mean should be taken.)

(2) "Cost in use" of buildings: check use on volumetric basis.

(3) "Cost in use" of plant: fixed, storage—plant, bins, tanks, racks, etc. (Check storage factor and suitability for materials stored.)

(4) "Cost in use" of plant: handling. (Check size, capacity, type, utilisation and load factors, power per tonne/km.)

(5) Costs of stores handling: number of movements "in" and "out", tonnage, distances, accidents and damage, etc. per tonne/km.

(6) Wastage in store and at issue: check causes—poor scheduling, pre-issue work, measuring equipment, staff training, communication.

(7) Spillage in store: lack of suitable dispensing equipment, etc.

(8) Loss in store: poor location systems, marking or lighting.

(9) Evaporation: uncovered tanks, lids left off kegs, etc.

(10) Pilferage: weak security, inadequate controls, unrestricted access.

(11) Obsolescence: lack of integration of Supplies with design, production, etc. (Stock-taking reports should highlight non-moving items.)

(12) Damage to goods: incorrect handling, housing, packing, stacking and destacking.

(13) Damage of goods by other goods: pollution, dilution, etc. (Bad location, inadequate segregation, etc.)

(14) Deterioration, ageing, etc.: stock levels set too high, order quantities exceed shelf-life at normal usage rate, etc.

(15) Damage and injuries to plant and staff: lack of training, poor equipment, lack of safety equipment, Health and Safety at Work Act ignored.

(16) Fire damage: bad siting or housing of stock, lack of fire drills or fire equipment.

(17) Excessive labour costs: lack of training, morale, "job satisfaction", remuneration or equipment—particularly in handling.

(18) Unrecovered losses: lack of insurance cover.

CHECKLIST 36. SALVAGE, RECOVERY, RECYCLING AND ENVIRONMENTAL CONTROL

Reproduced by kind permission of Bristol Polytechnic from a Symposium held at the Polytechnic in 1972.

(1) Management and salvage, recovery, recycling and environmental control.

(1.1) Are policies clear and disciplines well exercised?

(1.2) Is feedback from staff and operatives heeded?

(1.3) Is anyone trained and interested in this area?

(1.4) Continuous monitoring and examination by a designated person.

(1.5) Is local college engaged for training and research?

(1.6) Are waste, scrap and pollutants traced to actual source? (Sometimes the apparent source only is traced and side-effects ignored.)

(1.7) Does the company regard waste and scrap as potential assets?

(2) Supplies, purchasing action.

(2.1) Can supplies be obtained which produce less waste, scrap and pollutants?

(2.2) Is ordering controlled with shelf-life in mind?

(2.3) Are outlets explored for use in the firm (or group) or outside?

(2.4) Are adequate stocks of anti-pollutants held?

(2.5) Are new methods of recovery, recycling, etc. explored?

(2.6) Are national and international (e.g. EEC) regulations watched?

(2.7) Are profitable disposal arrangements made? (Sale back to suppliers, use of return loads, etc.)

(3) Production.

(3.1) Are production methods geared to reduce waste, scrap and pollution?

(3.2) Is every member of work-force encouraged to make suggestions?

(3.3) If so, are they studied and acted upon?

(3.4) Can production process be changed for improvement? And are they?

(3.5) Are arisings collected efficiently at source (i.e. work-centre)?

(3.6) If, so, are they sorted into kinds and grades? At work-centres?

(3.7) Are arisings left lying around work-centres, gangways, etc.?

(3.8) Are suitable containers provided at work-centres?

(3.9) Are these collected regularly, or directly material is changed?

(3.10) Are plant and machines bought with waste and pollution control in mind?

(4) Handling.

(4.1) Are arisings collected from source by those responsible for their custody, i.e. do production deliver it to the scrap bay or do stores staff collect it?

(4.2) Are they collected and housed in the most efficient manner?

(4.3) Is it worth considering special equipment for collection, handling, storage, transport to dealers, etc.? (Viz. sack stands, skips, stillages, pallets, unit containers, etc.)

(4.4) Are stores staff trained in the properties and care of these goods?

(4.5) Is security efficient?

(4.6) Do stock records throw up "exception reports" of obsolete, obsolescent, scrap, waste and surplus stocks?

(4.7) Do staff ensure arisings do not get back into live stock?

(4.8) Are off-peak times used to sort, segregate and tidy arisings?

(5) Disposal.

(5.1) Have disposal methods been studied effectively?

(5.2) Are oncosts regularly checked to maximise profit or at least to minimise loss?

(5.3) Is disposal prompt and regular? Necessary to maintain good industrial housekeeping, convert a loss into an asset as quickly as possible and feed money into the cash flow, to catch the market, avoid loss through missing the market.

(5.4) Are reliable dealers only employed? Is there an "approved list"?

(5.5) Is security maintained? And is weighbridge drill effective?

(5.6) Are access and loading of dealers' vehicles efficient?

(6) Finance.

(6.1) Are costs analysed, studied and acted upon?

(6.2) Have break-even points been established between revenue and costs of collection, storage, segregation, control, disposal?

(6.3) Have cost-benefits of social/environmental aspects been examined?

(6.4) Are ratios recorded of: scrap to total materials used; net value recovered (or recycled) to gross value of original arisings; net value sold to original gross value.

(7) General.

(7.1) Are salvage bays designed for ease of sorting, segregation, security, avoidance of offence to local amenities, intake and delivery, etc.?

(7.2) Is old equipment broken up, cannibalised, etc.?

(7.3) Are national advisory bodies used?

CHECKLIST 37. LAUNDERING OILS AND OTHER FLUIDS

(1) Does launderer collect and transport free to his works?

(2) Does he provide containers, on loan, or to rent?

(3) Does he redeliver free?

(4) Is reclaimed fluid treated to correct viscosity and other properties?

(5) Are additives available to improve performance, e.g. inhibitors?

(6) Can contractor add new fluid of correct specification to make up for loss in process?

(7) If so, at what price?

(8) Is laundered fluid fully compatible with existing (new) stock?

(9) If not compatible, are suitable storage facilities available?

(10) Is a quality control and test certificate available?

(11) If collection and delivery by bulk tanker check vehicle loading gauge; access to works; turning circle; whether pumping is required; size of hose; details of coupling.

(12) Precautions: earthing of tanker; fire extinguishing; protection against toxicity.

(13) Methods of measuring at collection and redelivery.

(14) Need for presence of authorised person during collection and intake.

Index